THE FIRST FORTY YEARS OF
WASHINGTON SOCIETY

Mrs. Samuel Harrison Smith (Margaret Bayard).

After the portrait by Charles Bird King, in the possession of her grandson,
J. Henley Smith, Washington.

THE
FIRST FORTY YEARS
OF
WASHINGTON SOCIETY

PORTRAYED BY THE FAMILY LETTERS OF

MRS. SAMUEL HARRISON SMITH

(MARGARET BAYARD)

FROM THE COLLECTION OF HER GRANDSON

J. HENLEY SMITH

EDITED BY

GAILLARD HUNT

ILLUSTRATED

CHARLES SCRIBNER'S SONS
NEW YORK :: :: :: 1906

PREFATORY NOTE

DURING the first forty years of its existence the city of Washington had a society, more definite and real than it has come to have in later days. The permanent residents, although appurtenant to the changing official element, nevertheless furnished the framework which the larger and more important social life used to build upon, and the result was a structure of society tolerably compact and pleasing and certainly interesting. It was emphatically official, but it did not include the lower class officials, who found their recreation for the most part at the street resorts, and its tone was dignified and wholesome. At any rate, it was genuine and national, even if it was crude, and the day of the all-powerful rich man and his dominance in social life had not yet arrived.

Samuel Harrison Smith, a writer and editor in Philadelphia, came to the city in the year 1800, soon after the government had moved there. He was the son of Jonathan Bayard Smith, a member of the Continental Congress, signer of the Articles of Confederation and Colonel of a Pennsylvania regiment during the Revolution; and although he was only 28 years old he established the first national newspaper printed in America, which he called *The National Intelligencer*. Just before his paper was started he returned to Philadelphia, and on September 29, 1800, married his second cousin, Margaret Bayard, and their wedding journey was from Philadelphia to Washington where they lived the rest of their lives; and for forty years their house was the resort of the most interesting characters in national public life. The first number of *The National Intelligencer* appeared October 31, 1800, and after conducting it successfully for a number of years Mr. Smith sold it to Joseph Gales, Jr., who afterwards associated with himself as editor, William W. Seaton. In 1813 President Madison appointed Mr. Smith the first Commissioner of the Revenue of the Treasury Department and on September 30, 1814, Secretary of the Treasury *ad interim*. From 1809 to 1819 he was President of the Bank of Washington and later President of the Washington branch Bank of the United States until the office was abolished ten years before his death. Undoubtedly, the success of his career was partly due to the assistance given him by his talented wife.

Margaret Bayard was born, February 29, 1778, in Philadelphia, the daughter of Colonel John Bayard, a famous revolutionary officer, Speaker of the Pennsylvania Assembly and member of the Continental Congress. Colonel Bayard's nephew and adopted son was James A. Bayard, a distinguished diplomat and Senator from Delaware, and James A. Bayard's son, having the same name, was also a Senator from Delaware, as was his grandson, the late Thomas Francis Bayard. Margaret Bayard was 22 years old when she married, and it was inevitable that one who wrote so readily should eventually print her pieces, and in due course she fell in with Godey, Mrs. Sarah Josepha Hale, Anthony Bleecker, J. Herrick and Miss Catherine Maria Sedgwick, and from 1823 up to a few years before her death she was an occasional contributor to the literature of the day. For Godey's *Lady's Book* she wrote "Domestic Sketches," an account of Presidential Inaugurations and a serial moral story printed in March, April and May,

1837, entitled "Who Is Happy?" She also wrote some Spanish tales, "Constantine" and several other Roman stories, "Lucy," "The Sister," and "Estelle Aubert," a translation from the French which Mrs. Hale printed in 1834. In 1835 she printed in *The National Intelligencer* a letter in verse anonymously to Harriet Martineau, and probably contributed to this paper on other occasions which cannot be identified. In 1837 she wrote for *The Southern Literary Messenger* and *Peter Parley* (Goodrich's) *Annual* "The Token," but anonymously. She contributed to Herrick & Longacre's "National Portrait Gallery," doubtless the articles on Mrs. Madison and probably one or two others. Her contributions were generally moral essays or stories, pitched high as the taste of the day required. The most ambitious product of her pen was a large novel in two volumes entitled "A Winter in Washington, or Memoirs of the Seymour Family," published in 1824 (New York: E. Bliss and E. White) anonymously. Her authorship was, however, not concealed and was generally known at the time, and the book after being a decided success has since become exceedingly rare. The characters were taken from real life, and it has historical value because of a number of anecdotes, chiefly of Thomas Jefferson, scattered through its pages. Another volume published by her was a story of 257 pages, printed in 1828 and sold at a fair held for the benefit of the Washington Orphan Asylum, bearing the title "What Is Gentility?" (Published by Pishey Thompson. DeKraft, Printer.) Undoubtedly Mrs. Smith's most interesting and valuable writings were those which she never intended for publication and which have hitherto never seen the light, being her private letters, in which she opens an intimate view of the famous political characters in Washington, whose acquaintance and friendship she

enjoyed. Those letters present a picture highly entertaining and valuable, and so do some of the reminiscences
which she wrote in her note-books.

She was the intimate friend of Jefferson—who was
her life's hero—and his family, and one of his most characteristic letters, that in which he discloses his views
on religion, was addressed to her; of the Madisons, the
Clays, the Calhouns; of William Wirt, the accomplished
Attorney-General for twelve years, and of William H.
Crawford, whose partisan in his candidacy for the Presidency she became, besides many others. She entertained Harriet Martineau when she came to Washington on her famous tour, held long conversations with the
Socialist, Owen of Lanark, and had as one of her intimate
friends Madame de Neuville, the wife of Hyde de Neuville, the most popular of the early ministers of France
to the United States. She was a remarkably truthful
letter writer, and never embellished her correspondence
with apocryphal gossip. She judged her fellow-man
charitably and believed in her country absolutely, and did
not herself participate in any of the party rancor which
raged around her. She was a Republican, to which party
her husband adhered, but she came of a Federalist family
and looked not unkindly upon her husband's opponents.
She died January 7, 1844, and her husband November 1,
1845.

In the valuable manuscript collection in my possession are several thousand of my grandmother's letters
and of letters to her from nearly all the prominent characters of her day. They were kept by her son, Jonathan
Bayard Harrison Smith, my father, under lock and
key during his life, and have only been seen since coming

under my control after my mother's death. From this mass of material Mr. Hunt has selected only those letters which give an intimate view of the social life of Washington nearly a hundred years ago. Most of the letters are addressed to Mrs. Smith's sisters, Jane, herself a woman of literary accomplishments, the wife of Chief Justice Andrew Kirkpatrick of New Jersey, and Anna, who married Mr. Samuel Boyd of New York; and her husband's sisters, Susan Bayard Smith and Mary Ann Smith; and her son, when he was a student at Princeton. Sidney, the country place from which she often wrote, was a farm of 200 acres, a portion of which the Catholic University now occupies; but the original house is still standing.

J. HENLEY SMITH.

ILLUSTRATIONS

THE FIRST FORTY YEARS OF
WASHINGTON SOCIETY

FORTY YEARS OF
WASHINGTON SOCIETY

TO MRS. KIRKPATRICK

Sunday evening, Nov. 16, 1800.

. . . . I thought I was coming into a land of
strangers; but with a husband so beloved, I hesitated
not to leave the kindest of fathers and the most indulgent
of friends. But, here in Mrs. Bell, have I met with a
mother, for sure no daughter could be treated with more
affection; in Miss Thornhill and Eliza, sisters, and in Mr.
English a most attentive brother. In Mr. and Mrs. Law,
Cap. and Mrs. Tingey,[1] Mr. and Mrs. Otis, Dr. and Mrs.
Thornton,[2] social and agreeable companions. In my last
letter I mentioned that Mrs. Bell was to drink tea with
me; the family all came and in my chamber, which I
assure you looked very smart, we passed an agreeable
afternoon and they were treated with my wedding cake.
Mrs. B. brought with her a large basket of sweet potatoes

[1] Thomas Tingey, born in London, September 11, 1750, an officer in
the British Navy, came to America before the Revolution, served in the
Continental Navy during the war, and in 1799 in the war with France.
He was not in the Navy at the time Mrs. Smith met him, but was living
in Washington as a private citizen. He was restored to the Navy in 1804
and was continuously in command of the Navy Yard until his death in
1829. He came to look upon the Yard as his property, and actually
included the commandant's house in the property which he disposed of
in his will. His first wife was Sarah Murdock, of Philadelphia.

[2] Dr. William Thornton was an Englishman born in the West Indies.
He made the first accepted designs for the Capitol. He invented a flutter-
wheel steamboat and accused Fulton of having wrongfully deprived him
of it. He was the first Superintendent of the Patent Office, and a man of
genius and rare social accomplishments. His wife was a Miss Bordeaux, who had come to America from France.

and some fine cabbages. Mr. St. Gêmme,[1] a French gentleman of reduced fortunes, accompanied her; he teaches Eliza french and drawing, and from a piece he painted, certainly possesses much taste and delicacy. I found him so agreeable that I asked him to repeat his visit. Tuesday was a most delightful day, and Mr. S. and myself sallied forth. Between Capt. Tingey and us, there extends a plain of near half a mile, the ground is elevated and commands a most beautiful view of the Eastern Branch. I will not say we walked along this, the elasticity of the air had given such elasticity to my spirits that I could not walk. On reaching the house, we were received in a very friendly way; altho' we had so long neglected returning the visits of this family. The Capt. was not at home; we sat more than an hour with the ladies; Mrs. T. is a good kind of a woman, and tho' not very agreeable, yet she appears very worthy; the girls seem good natured, but as yet I can say nothing more of them. Mrs. T. gave me some domestic information, bade me apply to her whenever I wanted advice, and to consider her as a mother. Said she was averse to form, and asked me to visit her in any way and at any hours. If I would ride, she would often call for me, as they always had a spare seat in the carriage. From there we walked to Mrs. Law's,[2] about a mile farther. She saw us from the windows and came to the door to

---

[1] Carré De V. Gêmme, afterwards chief of division in the préfecture, department of Charente.

[2] Thomas Law, a brother of Lord Ellenborough, came to Washington in 1795 with the idea of making an enormous fortune by speculating in real estate. In 1796 he married Eliza Parke Custis, a descendant of Lord Baltimore and granddaughter of Mrs. Washington. They lived unhappily, separated in 1804, and were divorced a few years later. There were rumors that she loved the world and its admiration too much; but Mr. Law was himself an oddity. One of the stories about him is that going to the post office for his letters one day he could not remember his name till an acquaintance addressed him.

meet us, took each by the hand and lead us in the parlour. We had sat only a few minutes when she said, "Lay down your hat Mr. Smith, we have a fine roast turkey, and you must stay and eat of it." Talking of conveniences in cooking, "Come," said she, "you are young housekeepers, come and look at my kitchen." She has a contrivance, more convenient than any I ever heard of and as you are in search of conveniences I will describe it. The chimney is six feet in width, in this is placed a thing called the Ranger, in the center is a grate, about two feet wide, on one side a place to boil in, which contains 6 or 8 gallons of water, on the other side a place of the same dimensions, for an oven, which opens in front, with a door, and has a shelf inside, so that two ranges of dishes can bake at the same time. Both the boiler and oven are heated by the pine in the grate; which at the same time can roast anything placed before it, and as many pots as you please can hang over it. The kitchen is well heated, and the oven and boiler are always of a uniform heat. Here, with a small quantity of coal, she has often cooked dinner for large companies. They are to be had at Baltimore. We left Mr. S. in the parlour, and she took me up stairs, where she was putting up curtains; I assisted her, went from room to room and we chatted like old acquaintance. Then while she dressed for dinner, I played with the little Eliza and her doll. The sweet little creature calls me aunt, and I am to call her my Mary Ann. When we went down to dinner, we found 4 or five gentlemen who had accidentally come in. Soon after Capt. Tingey's family joined us. Mr. Peter and Mr. Lewis her two brothers in law were of the party. Vivacity and good humour prevailed and our party was fifty times more agreeable than if we had all met by previous invitation. I have never met with any one so destitute of all form or ceremony as this sweet woman.

After dinner, the gentlemen all dispersed and I was about accompanying Mr. S., but Mrs. Tingey told me if I would stay to tea, she would take me home in the carriage. I agreed, Mrs. L. amused herself with a magazine, and left us to amuse ourselves as we chose. I cut out and fitted a muslin frock for my adopted niece à la mode Mary Ann, while she played by my side, and the Tingey ladies talked with me. About an hour after dinner, before the table was removed, a servant brought in a waiter of shusheng tea and a few biscuits. When we parted, I had two sweet kisses from Mrs. Law, with an invitation frequently to repeat my visit and a promise of soon seeing me. Of Mr. Law, I say nothing, it is impossible to describe this man; he is one of the strangest I ever met with; all good nature and benevolence; his ruling passion is to serve every one, which keeps him perpetually busy, about others. Scarcely a day passes without his calling, and at all hours; the other morning he was almost in the room before we were up. Cap. T. and Dr. May[1] subscribed to the paper, besides several of inferior note. Mr. S. received a letter from Lancaster, containing the names of 32 subscribers, out of the Pens. legislature. We find that an acquaintance with the gentlemen of this place, is advantageous to him, and that the best way of getting business, is by being generally known, and by being connected with the most respectable people. Induced by this, he has subscribed to the dancing Assembly.[2] The cards, he is to print, will amount really to the subscription. Mrs. Tingey called for me the other day, to accompany

[1] Frederick May came to Washington in 1795 and was the father of the medical profession in the city. His son John Frederick May was the first Washington physician whose reputation extended beyond the city.

[2] The Washington Dancing Assembly was started by Mr. Law, Captain Tingey, Dr. May and other gentlemen of the city, and was the first organized effort to give some form to its social amusements.

her to G. Town.   After shopping we drove to Mrs. Bells, where as usual I met a most affectionate welcome.   Bread, butter, ham and cakes were set before us, and when I came away my pockets were loaded with cake and apples; a bottle of milk, one of yeast, a bundle of hops, were put in the carriage for me, with an injunction of applying for more, when these were gone.   My good Betsy, continues to do well; always on coming home of an evening, I find the tea table set, the candles lighted and a good fire.   I wish you could peep on us at this period.   Mr. S. enjoys his tea so much, that it gives a double relish to mine.   Poor Bibby notwithstanding her stupidity makes a nice kind of biscuit, she is always delighted when I ask her to make them, and if I give any of them to the young men, she says "Au now Misses, why you give away wat I make for you sel."   Betsy too, desirous of trying her hand, made me this evening some very good short cakes. (What strange information to send 200 miles).

This morning Mrs. Otis sent her carriage for us and we went to church, where a good sermon was preached to a small but respectable congret.   After church Capt. T. Dr. May and Mrs. Foster came home with us, and I received them sans ceremonie in my chamber.   As I have but little more to say, I will not begin another sheet.   Mr. Paterson was here on Friday and was quite well.   Remember us to all our dear friends and bid them not to forget us.   Farewell my dear Sisters.

REMINISCENCES [1]

"And is this," said I, after my first interview with Mr. Jefferson, "the violent democrat, the vulgar demagogue,

[1] From Mrs. Smith's note book.   It was written in 1837, but relates to her first arrival in Washington.

the bold atheist and profligate man I have so often heard denounced by the federalists? Can this man so meek and mild, yet dignified in his manners, with a voice so soft and low, with a countenance so benignant and intelligent, can he be that daring leader of a faction, that disturber of the peace, that enemy of all rank and order?" Mr. Smith, indeed, (himself a democrat) had given me a very different description of this celebrated individual; but his favourable opinion I attributed in a great measure to his political feelings, which led him zealously to support and exalt the party to which he belonged, especially its popular and almost idolized leader. Thus the virulence of party-spirit was somewhat neutralized, nay, I even entertained towards him the most kindly dispositions, knowing him to be not only politically but personally friendly to my husband; yet I did believe that he was an ambitious and violent demagogue, coarse and vulgar in his manners, awkward and rude in his appearance, for such had the public journals and private conversations of the federal party represented him to be.[1]

In December, 1800, a few days after Congress had for the first time met in our new Metropolis, I was one morning sitting alone in the parlour, when the servant opened the door and showed in a gentleman who wished to see my husband. The usual frankness and care with which I met strangers, were somewhat checked by the dignified and reserved air of the present visitor; but the chilled feeling was only momentary, for after taking the chair I offered him in a free and easy manner, and carelessly throwing his arm on the table near which he sat, he turned towards me a countenance beaming with an expression of benevolence and with a manner and voice almost femininely soft and gentle, entered into conversation

[1] Col. John Bayard, Mrs. Smith's father, was a federalist.

Colonel John Bayard, father of Margaret Bayard.

A famous Revolutionary officer, Speaker of the Pennsylvania
Assembly, and Member of the Continental Congress.

on the commonplace topics of the day, from which, before I was conscious of it, he had drawn me into observations of a more personal and interesting nature. I know not how it was, but there was something in his manner, his countenance and voice that at once unlocked my heart, and in answer to his casual enquiries concerning our situation in our *new home*, as he called it, I found myself frankly telling him what I liked or disliked in our present circumstances and abode. I knew not who he was, but the interest with which he listened to my artless details, induced the idea he was some intimate acquaintance or friend of Mr. Smith's and put me perfectly at my ease; in truth so kind and conciliating were his looks and manners that I forgot he was not a friend of my own, until on the opening of the door, Mr. Smith entered and introduced the stranger to me as *Mr. Jefferson.*

I felt my cheeks burn and my heart throb, and not a word more could I speak while he remained. Nay, such was my embarrassment I could scarcely listen to the conversation carried on between him and my husband. For several years he had been to me an object of peculiar interest. In fact my destiny, for on his success in the pending presidential election, or rather the success of the democratic party, (their interests were identical) my condition in life, my union with the man I loved, depended. In addition to this personal interest, I had long participated in my husband's political sentiments and anxieties, and looked upon Mr. Jefferson as the corner stone on which the edifice of republican liberty was to rest, looked upon him as the champion of human rights, the reformer of abuses, the head of the republican party, which must rise or fall with him, and on the triumph of the republican party I devoutly believed the security and welfare of my country depended. Notwithstanding those exalted views of Mr. Jefferson as a political character; and ardently eager as I was for his success, I retained my previously conceived ideas of the coarseness and vulgarity of his appearance and manners and was therefore equally awed and surprised, on discovering the stranger whose deportment was so dignified and gentlemanly, whose language was so refined, whose voice was so gentle, whose countenance was so benignant, to be no other than Thomas Jefferson. How instantaneously were all these preconceived prejudices dissipated, and in proportion to their strength, was the reaction that took place in my opinions and sentiments. I felt that I had been the victim of prejudice, that I had been unjust. The revolution of feeling was complete and from that moment my heart warmed to him with the most affectionate interest and I implicitly believed all that his friends and my husband believed and which the after experience of many years confirmed. Yes, not only was he great, but a truly good man!

The occasion of his present visit, was to make arrangements with Mr. Smith for the publication of his *Manual* for *Congress,* now called *Jefferson's manual.* The original was in his own neat, plain, but elegant hand writing. The manuscript was as legible as printing and its unadorned simplicity was emblematical of his character. It is still preserved by Mr. Smith and valued as a precious relique.

After the affair of business was settled, the conversation became general and Mr. Jefferson several times addressed himself to me; but although his manner was unchanged, my feelings were, and I could not recover sufficient ease to join in the conversation. He shook hands cordially with us both when he departed, and in a manner which said as plain as words could do, "I am your friend."

During part of the time that Mr. Jefferson was President of the Philosophical Society (in Philadelphia) Mr. Smith was its secretary. A prize offered by the society for the best system of national education, was gained by Mr. Smith. The merit of this essay, first attracted the notice of Mr. J. to its author; the personal acquaintance which then took place, led to a friendly intercourse which influenced the future destiny of my husband, as it was by Mr. Jefferson's advice, that he removed to Washington and established the *National Intelligencer.* Esteem for the talents and character of the editor first won Mr. Jefferson's regard, a regard which lasted to the end of his life and was a thousand times evinced by acts of personal kindness and confidence.

At this time Mr. Jefferson was vice-President and in nomination for the Presidency. Our infant city afforded scant accommodations for the members of Congress. There were few good boarding-houses, but Mr. Jefferson was fortunate enough to obtain one of the best. Thomas Law one of the wealthiest citizens and largest proprietors of city property, had just finished for his own use a commodious and handsome house on Capitol hill; this, on discovering the insufficiency of accommodation, he gave up to Conrad for a boarding house, and removed to a very inconvenient dwelling on Greenleaf's point, almost two miles distant from the Capitol.[1] And here while I think of it, though somewhat out of place, I will mention an incident that occurred which might have changed the whole aspect of the political world and have disappointed the long and deep laid plans of politicians, so much do great events depend on trivial accidents. This out-of-the-way-house to which Mr. Law removed, was separated from the most inhabited part of the city by old fields and waste grounds broken up by deep gulleys or ravines over which there was occasionally a passable road. The election of President by Congress was then pending, one vote given or withheld would decide the question between Mr. Jefferson and Mr. Burr. Mr. Bayard from Delaware held that vote. He with other influential and leading members went to a ball given by Mr. Law. The night was dark and rainy, and on their attempt to return home, the coachman lost his way, and until daybreak was driving about this waste and broken ground and if not overturned into the deep gullies was momentarily in danger of being so, an accident which would most probably have cost some of the gentlemen their lives, and as it so happened that the company in the coach consisted of Mr. Bayard and three other members of Congress who had a leading and decisive influence in this difficult crisis of public affairs, the loss of either, might have turned the scales, then so nicely poised. Had it been so, and Mr. Burr been elected to the Presidency, what an awful conflict, what civil commotions would have ensued.

Conrad's boarding house was on the south side of Capitol hill and commanded an extensive and beautiful view. It was on the top of the hill, the precipitous sides of which were covered with grass, shrubs and trees in their wild uncultivated state. Between the foot of the hill and the broad Potomac extended a wide plain, through which the Tiber wound its way. The romantic beauty of this little stream was not then deformed by wharves or other works of art. Its banks were shaded with tall and umbrageous forest trees of every variety, among which the superb Tulep-Poplar rose conspicuous; the magnolia, the azalia, the hawthorn, the wild-rose and many other indigenous shrubs grew beneath their shade, while violets, anemonies and a thousand other sweet wood-flowers found shelter among their roots, from the winter's frost and greeted

with the earliest bloom the return of spring. The wild
grape-vine climbing from tree to tree hung in unpruned
luxuriance among the branches of the trees and formed
a fragrant and verdant canopy over the greensward, im-
pervious to the noon day-sun. Beautiful banks of Tiber!
delightful rambles! happy hours! How like a dream do
ye now appear. Those trees, those shrubs, those flowers
are gone. Man and his works have displaced the charms
of nature. The poet, the botanist, the sportsman and the
lover who once haunted those paths must seek far hence
the shades in which they delight. Not only the banks of
the Tiber, but those of the Potomack and Anacosta, were
at this period adorned with native trees and shrubs and
were distinguished by as romantic scenery as any rivers in
our country. Indeed the whole plain was diversified with
groves and clumps of forest trees which gave it the
appearance of a fine park. Such as grew on the public
grounds ought to have been preserved, but in a government such as ours, where the people are sovereign, this
could not be done. *The people,* the poorer inhabitants
cut down these noble and beautiful trees for fuel. In one
single night seventy tulip-Poplars were *girdled,* by which
process life is destroyed and afterwards cut up at their
leisure by the people. Nothing afflicted Mr. Jefferson
like this wanton destruction of the fine trees scattered over
the city-grounds. I remember on one occasion (it was
after he was President) his exclaiming "How I wish that
I possessed the power of a despot." The company at
table stared at a declaration so opposed to his disposition
and principles. "Yes," continued he, in reply to their
inquiring looks, "I wish I was a despot that I might save
the noble, the beautiful trees that are daily falling sacrifices to the cupidity of their owners, or the necessity of the
poor."

"And have you not authority to save those on the public grounds?" asked one of the company. "No," answered Mr. J., "only an armed guard could save them. The unnecessary felling of a tree, perhaps the growth of centuries seems to me a crime little short of murder, it pains me to an unspeakable degree." [1]

It was partly from this love of nature, that he selected Conrad's boarding house, being there able to enjoy the beautiful and extensive prospect described above. Here he had a separate drawing-room for the reception of his visitors; in all other respects he lived on a perfect equality with his fellow boarders, and eat at a common table. Even here, so far from taking precedence of the other members of Congress, he always placed himself at the lowest end of the table. Mrs. Brown, the wife of the senator from Kentucky, suggested that a seat should be offered him at the upper end, near the fire, if not on account of his rank as vice-President, at least as the oldest man in company. But the idea was rejected by his democratic friends, and he occupied during the whole winter the lowest and coldest seat at a long table at which a company of more than thirty sat down. Even on the day of his inauguration when he entered the dining-hall no other seat was offered him by the gentlemen. Mrs. Brown from an impulse which she said she could not resist, offered him her seat, but he smilingly declined it, and took his usual place at the bottom of the table. She said she felt indignant and for a moment almost hated the levelling principle of democracy, though her husband was a zealous democrat. Certainly this was carrying equality rather too far; there is no incompatibility between politeness and republicanism; grace cannot weaken and rudeness cannot strengthen a good cause, but democ-

[1] This anecdote is given in "A Winter in Washington," Vol. II, p. 40.

racy is more jealous of power and priviledge than even despotism.

At this time the only place for public worship in our new-city was a small, a very small frame building at the bottom of Capitol-hill. It had been a tobacco-house belonging to Daniel Carrol[1] and was purchased by a few Episcopalians for a mere trifle and fitted up as a church in the plainest and rudest manner. During the first winter, Mr. Jefferson regularly attended service on the sabbath-day in the humble church. The congregation seldom exceeded 50 or 60, but generally consisted of about a score of hearers. He could have had no motive for this regular attendance, but that of respect for public worship, choice of place or preacher he had not, as this, with the exception of a little Catholic chapel was the only church in the new city. The custom of preaching in the Hall of Representatives had not then been attempted, though after it was established Mr. Jefferson during his whole administration, was a most regular attendant. The seat he chose the first sabbath, and the adjoining one, which his private secretary occupied, were ever afterwards by the courtesy of the congregation, left for him and his secretary. I have called these Sunday assemblies in the capitol, a *congregation,* but the almost exclusive appropriation of that word to religious assemblies, prevents its being a descriptive term as applied in the present case, since the gay company who thronged the H. R. looked very little like a religious assembly. The occasion presented for display was not only a novel, but a favourable one for the youth, beauty and fashion of the city,

[1] This was Daniel Carroll, of Duddington Manor; not Daniel Carroll of Upper Marlborough, who signed the constitution, was a member of the first congress and a commissioner of the District. Historians usually confound the two. Mrs. Smith's spelling of proper names and her other spelling also has been preserved in the text.

Georgetown and environs. The members of Congress, gladly gave up their seats for such fair auditors, and either lounged in the lobbies, or round the fire places, or stood beside the ladies of their acquaintance. This sabbath-day-resort became so fashionable, that the floor of the house offered insufficient space, the platform behind the Speaker's chair, and every spot where a chair could be wedged in was crowded with ladies in their gayest costume and their attendant beaux and who led them to their seats with the same gallantry as is exhibited in a ball room. Smiles, nods, whispers, nay sometimes tittering marked their recognition of each other, and beguiled the tedium of the service. Often, when cold, a lady would leave her seat and led by her attending beau would make her way through the crowd to one of the fire-places where she could laugh and talk at her ease. One of the officers of the house, followed by his attendant with a great bag over his shoulder, precisely at 12 o'clock, would make his way through the hall to the depository of letters to put them in the mail-bag, which sometimes had a most ludicrous effect, and always diverted attention from the preacher. The musick was as little in union with devotional feelings, as the place. The marine-band, were the performers. Their scarlet uniform, their various instruments, made quite a dazzling appearance in the gallery. The marches they played were good and inspiring, but in their attempts to accompany the psalm-singing of the congregation, they completely failed and after a while, the practice was discontinued,—it was *too* ridiculous.

Not only the chaplains, but the most distinguished clergymen who visited the city, preached in the Capitol. I remember hearing Mr. E. Everet, afterwards a member of Congress, deliver an eloquent and flowery discourse, to a most thronged and admiring audience. But as a political orator he afterwards became far more eloquent and admired. Preachers of every sect and denomination of christians were there admitted—Catholics, Unitarians, Quakers with every intervening diversity of sect. Even women were allowed to display their pulpit eloquence, in this national Hall.

When Frederick the Great commenced his reign, in order to enforce universal tolleration in religion, he formed a plan which he believed would promote harmony between the different and numerous religious sects. This was to erect a spacious Edefice, or temple, in which at different hours the public service of all, and each of the christian denominations might be performed. He discussed this subject with Voltair, who with some difficulty convinced him of its impracticability, and that the religious prejudices which divided christians, were too strong to be conquered by either reason or despotic power. In the Capitol the idea of this philosophic monarch has been realized, without coercion; without combination. As Congress is composed of christians of every persuasion, each denomination in its turn has supplied chaplains to the two houses of Congress, who preach alternately in the Hall of Representatives. Some opposition was made both to a Roman Catholic and Unitarian, but did not succeed. Clergymen, who during the session of Congress visited the city, were invited by the chaplains to preach; those of distinguished reputation attracted crowded audiences and were evidently gratified by having such an opportunity for the exercise of their talents and their zeal. The admission of female preachers, has been justly reprobated: curiosity rather than piety attracted throngs on such occasions. The levity which characterized the sabbath-day assemblies in the capitol in former years, has long yielded to a more decorous and

reverent demeanor. The attendance of the marine-band
was soon discontinued, and various regulations made,
which have secured a serious and uninterrupted attention
to the religious services of the day.

For several years after the seat of government was
fixed at Washington, there were but two small churches.
The roman-catholic chapel in F. street, then a little frame
building, and the Episcopalian church at the foot of Capitol-hill; both, very small and mean frame buildings.
Now, in 1837 there are 22 churches of brick or stone.
Sunday used to be the universal day for visits and entertainments.   Only a few, very few of the gayest citizens
now, either pay or receive visits.   There was one sermon
delivered by Mr. Breckenridge at the commencement of
the war that was deemed quite prophetic—whether inspired or not, his predictions were certainly and accurately
fulfilled.   This pious and reverend preacher, made up in
zeal and fidelity, what he lacked in natural talents or
acquired knowledge, and in the plainest and boldest
language of reprehension addressed the members of Congress and officers of government present on that occasion.
The subject of his discourse was the observance of the
Sabbath. After enlarging on its prescribed duties, he
vehemently declaimed on the neglect of those duties, particularly by the higher classes and in this city, more especially by persons connected with the government. He
unshrinkingly taxed those then listening to him, with a
desecration of this holy day, by their devoting it to amusement—to visiting and parties, emphatically condemning
the dinner-parties given at the white-house, then addressing himself to the members of Congress, accused them
of violating the day, by laws they had made, particularly the carrying the mail on the sabbath; he en-
numerated the men and horses employed for this purpose

through the union and went into details striking and impressive.

"It is not the people who will suffer for these enormities," said he, "you, the law-givers, who are the cause of this crime, will in your public capacity suffer for it. Yes, it is the *government* that will be punished, and as, with Nineveh of old, it will not be the habitations of the people, but your temples and your palaces that will be burned to the ground; for it is by fire that this sin has usually been punished." He then gave many instances from scripture history in which destruction by fire of cities, dwellings and persons, had been the consequence of violating the Fourth commandment.

At the time this sermon was preached, the most remote apprehension did not exist of a British army ever reaching Washington, although war was impending. His predictions were verified. The Capitol, the President's House, and every building belonging to the government were destroyed and that by fire. Mrs. Madison told me that on her return to the city, after the British had left it, she was standing one day at her sister's door, for she had no house of her own, but until one was provided by the public, resided with her sister, and while there, looking on the devastation that spread around, saw Mr. Breckenridge passing along, she called to him and said, "I little thought, Sir, when I heard that threatening sermon of yours, that its denunciation would so soon be realized." "Oh, Madam," he replied, "I trust this chastening of the Lord, may not be in vain."

I am afraid the good man's hopes were never realized, for as far as I recollect, there was not for many, many years afterwards any change in the observance of the Sabbath.

TO MISS SUSAN B. SMITH[1]

January 1, 1801.

. . . The other evening, Mrs., Miss Tingey and the Capt., Dr. May, (our Physician, an amiable handsome young man) Genl. Van Courtland[2] and Mr. Holmes,[3] *sans ceremonie* passed the evening with us, and were very merry over the successive dishes of fine oysters. Capt. T. sings a good song, his wife and daughters accompany him. As not one of these folks were either scientific or sentimental, these songs very agreeably supplied the place of conversation. Our company all appeared to enjoy themselves, and therefore I was quite content. Mrs. Tingey and the girls are most truly friendly, they are constantly urging our visiting them in a social way, and they set us a good example by often visiting us. . . . Mrs. Law has been absent for some time and I have only seen her once, within 6 weeks; excepting the evening I passed with her at the last assembly. Mrs. Law, Mrs. Tingey, Mrs. Otis, Brown, and Bailey,[4] from N. Y. and myself sat together the whole evening; seated between Mrs. Brown and Law, and occasionally talking to different gentlemen, my time passed more agreeably, than if I had danced. I could not help wishing for you, my dear Susan, to accompany me; I should have derived much pleasure from seeing you in the dance; especially with such a partner, as the beautiful, graceful and all accomplished Genl. Van Courtland, who with his powdered wig, made a most conspicuous figure in the room. The first time I observed him was from Mrs. Law's pinching me and asking in a

---

[1] Mr. Smith's younger sister.
[2] Philip Van Cortlandt, of Cortlandt Manor, N. Y., a Representative.
[3] David Holmes, a Representative from Virginia; afterwards Senator from Mississippi.
[4] Wife of Theodorus Bailey, of Dutchess Co., a Representative.

low voice "If that gentleman was a relation of mine."
"A relation of mine!" repeated I with astonishment, "why
I hope you do not think so from any likeness that exists?"
"No," said she, smiling, "I only wanted the liberty of
laughing at him." And to be sure, his erect attitudes,
and studied motions made us think he had taken lessons of
some antique dancing Gentleman, of the yr. one. There
was a lady, too, who afforded us great diversion, I titled
her, Madam Eve, and called her dress the *fig leaf*. Next
Winter my dear Sister I trust I shall enjoy the satisfaction, of dressing your flaxen locks, (let Sister Mary
say what she will, they certainly must be curled) and
ornament your person. Whenever our plains are adorned
by Spring, and our woods have regained their leafy honors, I shall expect you and Sister Mary here to participate
in the pleasures of that delightful season. If such a
thing is *possible,* I am determined you shall both like
Washington, as well as you do Abington. If warm affection and sincere friendship, can render an abode comfortable and happy, then my dear sisters will you be both
comfortable and happy in the house of your affectionate Brother. Mr. St. Gêmmes, passed most of this evening with us. To me, his society is more interesting and
pleasing than any I have met with in this place. He has
no striking or prominent traits of character and differs
from other Frenchmen by more solidity and sobriety of
manner. Mary will like him and will, I predict, have
many long and interesting confabulations. He, Mr.
Foster, Mr. and Mrs. Brown, are our weekly visitors.
The other afternoon, these, together with Mr. and Mrs.
Bailey and Mr. Nicholas,[1] drank tea here. They were a
sober set, and we discussed sober and interesting subjects.

[1] Wilson Cary Nicholas, Senator from Virginia, probably the ablest man
in Congress.

I do not think, Susan, you would have been highly delighted, and as for Mr. Nicholas (I mean the Senator) he may be a man of fine talents, but that of conversation is not among the number. His manners were so benumbing, that I could scarcely make my tongue move. Many other gentlemen of congress occasionally visit us, but as one of our *rich, great men* here, observed, they are just like other men, and so they are not worth individual notice. This old gentleman, this great, rich man, has passed his life within this territory, and when the Members of Congress arrived, he went to *look at them* and told Mr. Law he saw no difference between them and other men, they were made alike, had the same kind of faces and talked as they did!

We were this evening informd that the apples and butter had arrived, and I promise you they shall receive a sincere welcome, and be treated with the greatest distinction. I am every day more and more pleased with Betsy. She is one of the smartest and most attentive servants I have ever met with. She never waits for me to tell her to do her work; but takes pride in doing it well. She has a great deal of *pride,* but if I can but make it an instrument of industry and order, I shall begin to think the better of it. My old man and woman, are equally faithful and industrious. In fact I have no *kind of trouble.* Dear Susan I wish you were as happy.

I believe I have more than answered all your questions, and I have only now to beg of you, not to let our friends forget us, and to assure them that they are remembered by us. I am determined you shall not pay postage for nothing. It is now past 11 o'clock; your brother half asleep is chewing a biscuit and I, half awake, bid you a good night and pleasant dreams.

Aaron Burr.

From a portrait by John Vanderlyn, in the possession of
Pierrepont Edwards, Elizabeth, N. J.

MR. JEFFERSON'S ELECTION [1]

February, 1801.

It was a day, "big with our country's fate"—a fate not suspended on the triumph or defeat of two contending armies, drawn forth in battle array—but on two contending political Parties, who after years of conflict, were new brought to issue. The power, which had been originally vested in the Federal party, had been gradually diminished by the force of public opinion, and transferred to the Democratic Party. For a while equality of power was maintained—but the equipoise did not last long,—a great and preponderating majority in the Presidential election, decided the relative strength of parties, the Democrats prevailed and brought into office, on the full-tide of popularity, the man who had been long recognized as the head of their Party.

According to the constitutional form, two men were to be run, the one for President, the other for vice President, and he who had the greatest number of votes was to be President. Such was the form of the law of election, but in the execution of that law, the people knowingly designated the vice-President, and voted for him concurrently with the President; this produced an unlooked for result and a constitutional difficulty. In the minds or inclinations of the people, there had been no misapprehensions, no dubiousness of choice. They as manifestly gave their votes for Mr. Jefferson as President and Mr. Burr as vice-President, as if each vote had been accompanied with such a designation. With this understanding the votes for one were as unanimous as the votes for the other, and the result, of course, an equality. In this unlooked for emer-

[1] From the note book.

gency what was to be done? The constitution decided. The choice of President was to be made by Congress.

There was not a shadow of doubt or uncertainty as to the object of the people's choice. It had been proclaimed too widely and too loudly for any individual to remain ignorant of the fact.

But this accidental and uncalculated result, gave the Federal party a chance of preventing the election of a man they politically abhorred—a man whose weight of influence had turned the scale in favour of the opposing Party. No means were left unattempted (perhaps I ought to say no *honest* means) to effect this measure.

It was an aweful crises. The People who with such an overwhelming majority had declared their will would never peaceably have allowed the man of their choice to be set aside, and the individual they had chosen as vice-President, to be put in his place. A civil war must have taken place, to be terminated in all human probability by a rupture of the Union. Such consequences were at least calculated on, and excited a deep and inflammatory interest. Crowds of anxious spirits from the adjacent county and cities thronged to the seat of government and hung like a thunder cloud over the Capitol, their indignation ready to burst on any individual who might be designated as President in opposition to the people's known choice. The citizens of Baltimore who from their proximity, were the first apprised of this daring design, were with difficulty restrained from rushing on with an armed force, to prevent,—or if they could not prevent, to avenge this violation of the People's will and in their own vehement language, to hurl the usurper from his seat. Mr. Jefferson, then President of the Senate, sitting in the midst of these *conspirators,* as they were then called, unavoidably hearing their loudly whispered designs, witnessing their

gloomy and restless machinations, aware of the dreadful
consequences, which must follow their meditated designs,
preserved through this trying period the most unclouded
serenity, the most perfect equanimity. A spectator who
watched his countenance, would never have surmised, that
he had any personal interest in the impending event.
Calm and self possessed, he retained his seat in the midst
of the angry and stormy, though half smothered passions
that were struggling around him, and by this dignified
tranquility repressed any open violence—tho' insufficient
to prevent whispered menaces and insults, to these however he turned a deaf ear, and resolutely maintained a
placidity which baffled the designs of his enemies.

The crisis was at hand. The two bodies of Congress
met, the Senators as witnesses the Representatives as
electors. The question on which hung peace or war, nay,
the Union of the States was to be decided. What an
awful responsibility was attached to every vote given on
that occasion. The sitting was held with closed doors.
It lasted the whole day, the whole night. Not an individual left that solemn assembly, the necessary refreshment they required was taken in rooms adjoining the
Hall. They were not like the Roman conclave legally
and forcibly confined, the restriction was self-imposed
from the deep-felt necessity of avoiding any extrinsic or
external influence. Beds, as well as food were sent, for
the accommodation of those whom age or debility disabled from enduring such a long protracted sitting—the
ballotting took place every hour—in the interval men ate,
drank, slept or pondered over the result of the last
ballot, compared ideas and persuasions to change votes,
or gloomily anticipated the consequences, let the result
be what it would.

With what an intense interest did every individual

watch each successive examination of the Ballot-box, how
breathlessly did they listen to the counting of the votes!
Every hour a messenger brought to the Editor of the N. I.[1]
the result of the Ballot. That night I never lay down
or closed my eyes. As the hour drew near its close, my
heart would almost audibly beat and I was seized with a
tremour that almost disabled me from opening the door
for the expected messenger.

What then must have been the feelings of that Heroic
woman, who had assented to her almost dying husband
being carried in this cold inclement season, the distance
of nearly two miles, from his lodgings to the capitol?

In a room adjacent to the Hall of R, he lay on a bed
beside which she knelt supporting his head on her arm,
while with her hand she guided his, in writing the name
of the man of his choice. At the return of each hour the
invalid was roused from his disturbed slumber, much to
the injury of his health, to perform this important duty.
What anxiety must this fond wife have endured, what a
dread responsibility did she take on herself, knowing as
she did and having been appealed to by his physicians, to
resist his wish to go, that her husband's life was risked, by
his removal from his chamber and the following scene.[2]
But it was for her country! And the American equalled
in courage and patriotism the Roman matron.

For more than thirty hours the struggle was maintained, but finding the republican phalanx impenetrable,
not to be shaken in their purpose, every effort proving un-
availing, the Senator from Delaware [James A. Bayard][3]
the withdrawal of whose vote would determine the issue,
took his part, gave up his party, for his country, and

[1] National Intelligencer.
[2] Joseph Hopper Nicholson of Maryland was the member. He was
carried to the House through a snow storm.
[3] Mrs. Smith's first cousin and adopted brother. He was a Representative.

James A. Bayard, Senator from Delaware.

From an engraving of the original painting by Wertmuller.

threw into the box a blank ballot, thus leaving to the republicans a majority. Mr. Jefferson was declared duly elected. The assembled crowds, without the Capitol, rent the air with their acclamations and gratulations, and the Conspirators as they were called, hurried to their lodgings under strong apprehensions of suffering from the just indignation of their fellow citizens.

The dark and threatening cloud which had hung over the political horrison, rolled harmlessly away, and the sunshine of prosperity and gladness broke forth and ever since, with the exception of a few passing clouds has continued to shine on our happy country.

TO MISS SUSAN B. SMITH

March 4, 1801.

Let me write to you my dear Susan, e'er that glow of enthusiasm has fled, which now animates my feelings; let me congratulate not only you, but all my fellow citizens, on an event which will have so auspicious an influence on their political welfare. I have this morning witnessed one of the most interesting scenes, a free people can ever witness. The changes of administration, which in every government and in every age have most generally been epochs of confusion, villainy and bloodshed, in this our happy country take place without any species of distraction, or disorder. This day, has one of the most amiable and worthy men taken that seat to which he was called by the voice of his country. I cannot describe the agitation I felt, while I looked around on the various multitude and while I listened to an address, containing principles the most correct, sentiments the most liberal, and wishes the most benevolent, conveyed in the most

appropriate and elegant language and in a manner mild
as it was firm. If doubts of the integrity and talents
of Mr. Jefferson ever existed in the minds of any one,
methinks this address must forever eradicate them.   The
Senate chamber was so crowded that I believe not another
creature could enter.   On one side of the house the Senate sat, the other was resigned by the representatives to
the ladies.   The roof is arched, the room half circle, every
inch of ground was occupied.   It has been conjectured by
several gentlemen whom I've asked, that there were near
a thousand persons within the walls.   The speech was
delivered in so low a tone that few heard it. Mr. Jefferson
had given your Brother a copy early in the morning,[1] so
that on coming out of the house, the paper was distributed
immediately.   Since then there has been a constant succession of persons coming for the papers.   I have been
interrupted several times in this letter by the gentlemen
of Congress, who have been to bid us their adieus; since
three o'clock there has been a constant succession.   Mr.
Claibourn,[2] a most amiable and agreeable man, called the
moment before his departure and there is no one whose
society I shall more regret the loss of.   You will smile
when I tell you that Gouveneur Morris, Mr. Dayton and
Bayard[3] drank tea here; they have just gone after sitting
near two hours.

Mr. Foster will be the bearer of this letter; he is a
widower, looking out for a wife; he is a man of respectable talents, and most amiable disposition and comfortable

---

[1] The original in Jefferson's handwriting is among the papers of Mr. J.
Henley Smith; also his second inaugural address in his handwriting and
signed.
[2] William Charles Cole Claiborn, Representative from Virginia, had just
been appointed Governor of Mississippi.
[3] All three being strong Federalists and the *National Intelligencer* a
Republican paper. Jonathan Dayton was then a Senator from New
Jersey, and James A. Bayard Representative from Delaware.

fortune. What think you my good sister Mary of setting your cap for him? As for you, Susan, you are rather too young, and I have another in my eye for you. One recommendation Mr. F. will have in your eyes, that he has been this winter on the most social and friendly terms with us, seen us very often and can tell you a great deal about us.

I trust my dear sisters we shall see you soon after you receive this letter. I have been so often interrupted while writing it, that I have felt inclined to throw it aside, but as I have a great many more letters to write by Mr. Foster, I must let you take it as it is. How is Mrs. Higginson? I wish to hear particularly something about her. If I had not so many correspondents already, I should ask communications from herself. I have written this in a hasty and desultory manner. Adieu.

TO MISS SUSAN B. SMITH

May 26, 1801.

. . . Our City, is now as gay as in the winter; the arrival of all the secretaries, seems to give new animation to business, and the settlements of their families, affords employment to some of our tradesmen. Mrs. Gallatin[1] is in our neighborhood at present, she is extremely friendly and seems to consider me as her most intimate friend. I see her often and have spent two or three mornings visiting and shopping with her. The house Mr. G. has taken is next door to the Madisons' and three miles distant from us.[2] I regret this circumstance, as it will prevent that intimate intercourse which

[1] She was Hannah Nicholson, of New York, daughter of Commodore Nicholson.

[2] The house is still standing on the north side of M. St., near 32d.

I wished to enjoy, with her and Maria N.[1] Mrs. Madison is at the President's at present; I have become acquainted with and am highly pleased with her; she has good humour and sprightliness, united to the most affable and agreeable manners. I admire the simplicity and mildness of Mr. M.'s manners, and his smile has so much benevolence in it, that it cannot fail of inspiring good will and esteem. Genl. Dearborn,[2] we have also for our neighbour, he some times visits us and his conversation is so intelligent, and filled with so many useful observations, that he is a most agreeable companion. These I believe are all the additions we have had to our society, since my last letter; I was prevented calling on the ladies at Mr. Meredith's[3] until yesterday, when I found no one at home. During the last week I was quite a prisoner for the want of a carriage, as we could procure none; I regretted this more on Brother John's account than on my own. He and sister Margaret left me this morning, after a visit of 2 days. Mr. Meyers, tho' lodging at a tavern, has passed all his time with us. He takes a book and goes out among the trees, where he sits most of the day. On Saturday last we dined at the President's. The company was small, and on that account the more agreeable; he has company *every* day, and seldom more than twelve at table. I happen'd to be seated next to him and had the pleasure of his conversation on several subjects.

Your Brother waits for this, I must therefore abruptly bid you good-night.

[1] Maria Nicholson, Mrs. Gallatin's sister.
[2] Henry Dearborn, Secretary of War.
[3] Samuel Meredith, Treasurer.

TO MISS MARIA BAYARD[1]

May 28, Thursday, 1801.

. . . . Since I last wrote I have formed quite a
social acquaintance with Mrs. Madison and her sister;[2]
indeed it is impossible for an acquaintance with them to
be different. Mr. Smith and I dined at the President's,—
he has company every day, but his table is seldom laid
for more than twelve. This prevents all form and makes
the conversation general and unreserved. I happened
to sit next to Mr. Jefferson and was confirmed in my
prepossessions in his favour, by his easy, candid and gentle manners. Before and after dinner Mrs. Cranch[3] and
myself sat in the drawing-room with Mrs. M. and her
sister, whose social dispositions soon made us well acquainted with each other. About six o'clock the gentlemen joined us, but Mr. Jefferson's and Madison's
manners were so easy and familiar that they produced
no restraint. Never were there a plainer set of men, and
I think I may add a more virtuous and enlightened one,
than at present forms our administration. Genl. Dearborn and Gallatin being in our neighbourhood, visit us
as neighbours. Mrs. Carrol, the neighbour I last mentioned, has grown quite attentive, within the last week,
she has spent an afternoon and morning with me, and
has at several times sent me salad and asparagus, and
what I still more highly value, large bunches of fine roses
and magnolias.

[1] Mrs. Smith's younger sister.
[2] Anna Payne, who married Richard D. Cutts in 1804.
[3] Wife of Judge William Cranch, then Junior Assistant Judge of the
Circuit Court of the District of Columbia.

TO MISS MARY ANN SMITH[1]

Washington City, July 5, 1801.

My Dear Sister.

Mr. Craven, a neighbour and acquaintance of ours, departing for Phila. to-morrow, I cannot deny myself the pleasure of passing a few minutes with you, chiefly to draw a picture, which I know will give your patriotic heart delight, a picture of Mr. Jefferson in which he was exhibited to the best advantage. About 12 o'clock yesterday, the citizens of Washington and Geo. Town waited upon the President to make their devoirs. I accompanied Mr. Sumpter (?). We found about 20 persons present in a room where sat Mr. J. surrounded by the five Cherokee chiefs. After a conversation of a few minutes, he invited his company into the usual dining room, whose four large sideboards were covered with refreshments, such as cakes of various kinds, wine, punch, &c. Every citizen was invited to partake, as his taste dictated, of them, and the invitation was most cheerfully accepted, and the consequent duties discharged with alacrity. The company soon increased to near a hundred, including all the public officers and most of the respectable citizens, and strangers of distinction. Martial music soon announced the approach of the marine corps of Capt. Burrows, who in due military form saluted the President, accompanied by the President's March played by an excellent band attached to the corps. After undergoing various military evolutions, the company returned to the dining room, and the band from an adjacent room played a succession of fine patriotic airs. All appeared to be cheerful, all happy. Mr. Jefferson mingled promiscuously with the citizens,

[1] From Mr. Smith to his sister.

Thomas Jefferson, by Gilbert Stuart.
The property of T. Jefferson Coolidge.

and far from designating any particular friends for consultation, conversed for a short time with every one that
came in his way. It was certainly a proud day for him,
the honours of which he discharged with more than his
usual care. At 2 o'clock, after passing 2 hours in this
very agreeable way, the company separated. At 4 a
dinner was given at McMunn and Conrad's,[1] where
all the civil and military officers attended, and a number of citizens, which, including the former, amounted
to about 50. Everything here was conducted with great
propriety, and it was not unamusing to see Mr. Gallatin,
Madison and Dearborn on one side directly opposite to
Mr. Meredith, Harrison, Steele, &c., on the other. It
was my good fortune to find myself next to Mr. Miller,
who was very polite and conversable. About dark I left
the company and joined a small party at Mrs. Law's,
who had assembled there to hear the music. Among
them we met Mrs. Clay, a charming little woman from
Richmond. Thus you see that we are here at least all
Republicans and all Federalists. I hope the same spirit
has animated you. At any rate I think our example will
be of some use in recommending General Lamory.

Yours affectionately,

S. H. S.

TO MRS. KIRKPATRICK

Washington, July 21, 1801.

I never write with so much ease as when I answer a
letter immediately after its receipt. We then feel our
sentiments of affection enlivened, and all we write flows
from the heart. For 3 weeks or a month past, the
weather has been oppressively warm, and has had a

---

[1] Boarding house near the Capitol.

greater effect on my mind than on my body. I have felt indisposed to read or write, or converse, but from necessity I have been very busy. At one time I was entirely without help, and at all times with such bad help that the comfort of the family depended on my activity. One woman I dismissed on account of her excessive intemperance, and the old woman I took in her place is such a scold that she is hated by all the family; but her neatness and honesty reconciled me to her, and I was congratulating myself on her good conduct, when last night, on my return home, I found her, too, in a state of intoxication. But I am not so badly off as Mrs. Gallatin; she has still more wicked and profligate wretches about her.

I am uncommonly fortunate in having such a woman as Mrs. Smith[1] at my command. During the time I was without a servant, there was nothing that unasked she did not do. I one morning found her on her knees scrubbing the parlour. "This is what I would not do for any other person living," said she. "And I do not believe," answered I, "you would like to have done it, had I asked you." "Indeed, you are mistaken, there is nothing you could ask which I would not do." My plan in regard to her is, for her to come about October and assist in cleaning house, and in the necessary preparations for an approaching event. I shall prepare a large room for her, in which she will sleep and sit, and in which the two boys will eat and sit of an evening. They are now so rude and troublesome at their meals, and in their manners, that I promise myself they will be much benefited by being with her. She is to make and mend their clothes. She can make all Mr. S.'s except his coats, and is likewise a good mantua-maker and seamstress. She is to iron and clear starch, and when I am prevented

---

[1] Her housekeeper for some years.

by other duties from discharging the delightful cares of a nurse, she is to take my place. In general, I shall always choose to be nurse and house-keeper myself, and to let her do the sewing of the family; for even if she did not sew as well as I did, yet I have always been of opinion that mistakes or negligence in this department of household business was less disadvantageous to domestic order and comfort, than in either the care of children, or in economical arrangements. We are so much the creatures of habit, that if possible I shall always, if Providence blesses me with children, devote my time chiefly to them, and as far as I can consistently with the comfort of those around me, have them constantly in my presence.

TO MISS SUSAN BAYARD SMITH

December 26, 1802.

. . . . Since my last letter to you, I have unexpectedly been in a good deal of company and have seen much more than I designed. We have dined twice at the President's, three times at Mr. Pichons, and they have dined twice here, four times at Mrs. Tingeys and once at Genl. Mason's (the Island Mason). I have drank tea out three or four times and declined several invitations to balls. I have often gone out with the ague, sometimes with fever on me, so much has habit done in reconciling me to this enemy. I know that nothing will keep off the fit, and may as well have it in one place as another. I very seldom now go to bed, but sit up, or lie down on the sopha, have a bowl of tea and a basin by me, and then give no one further trouble, but take my fit with the greatest *sang froid*.

Madm. Pichon[1] and myself are now on the most intimate footing, every interview seems to have endeared us
to each other and I believe we mutually feel the affection
and confidence of old friends. The similarity of our
present situation, even as to the time, calls forth the same
hopes, the same anxieties. We have sat whole days
together and talked of nothing but the care of infants
and the education of children. She often comes and sits
the morning with me, and when we go there she sends
the carriage for us and sends us home again. Last Sunday, this day week, they dined here. Madm. P. came
between eleven and twelve and they staid till 9 in the
evening.—I ought to tell you a great deal about Mrs.
Randolph and Mrs. Eppes,[2] who have both been with
their father for this month past. Mrs. Eppes is beautiful, simplicity and timidity personified when in company,
but when alone with you of communicative and winning
manners. Mrs. R. is rather homely, a delicate likeness
of her father, but still more interesting than Mrs. E.
She is really one of the most lovely women I have ever
met with, her countenance beaming with intelligence,
benevolence and sensibility, and her conversation fulfils
all her countenance promises. Her manners, so frank
and affectionate, that you know her at once, and feel
perfectly at your ease with her. I have called twice of a
morning on them, they have been here three mornings
and they have promised to come and sit part of a morning with me, as I told them this was my only chance of
seeing them, as I did not give entertainments of which
they assured me they were heartily tired. I dined at the

---

[1] Wife of Louis André Pichon, French Chargé d'Affaires at Washington
from 1801 to 1805.

[2] Jefferson's daughter, Martha, married Thomas Mann Randolph; another,
Maria, married John Wayles Eppes. Both sons-in-law were able men and
represented Virginia in Congress.

P.'s since they have been there and really passed a most delightful day.   Before dinner he conversed with me, and after dinner for two hours I had an interesting conversation with Mrs. R.   She gave me an account of all her children, of the character of her husband and many family anecdotes.   She has that rare but charming egotism which can interest the listener in all one's concerns. I could have listened to her for two hours longer, but coffee and the gentlemen entered and we were interrupted.   But I became almost as agreeably engaged with the lovely Ellen, her daughter, without exception one of the finest and most intelligent children I have ever met with.   She is singularly and extravagantly fond of poetry; I repeated to her Goldsmith's Hermit, which she listened to with the most expressive countenance, her eyes fixed on mine and her arms clasped close around me. We became mutually attached to each other and I begged Mrs. R. to let her spend a day with me.   Her Mama brought her the other morning and sent for her about seven in the evening.   She really was most charming society for me.   .   .   .   *1221658*

FROM SAMUEL HARRISON SMITH[1]

Washington, April 26, 1803.   Saturday Evening.

Have just returned, my dearest Margaret, from a dining party at Genl. Dearborn's, where I met with Mrs. Madison and Mrs. Duval who, together with the ladies of the house, enquired in a very friendly manner respecting you and Julia.   I have rarely spent more agreeable hours at a dinner table.   Mr. Granger,[2] who was present

---

[1] Mrs. Smith was on a brief visit to her relatives at Brunswick.
[2] Gideon Granger, of Connecticut, Postmaster General for thirteen years, and an active politician all his life.

and who is a very agreeable man, after a few bottles of champagne were emptied, on the observation of Mr. Madison that it was the most delightful wine when drank in moderation, but that more than a few glasses always produced a headache the next day, remarked with point that this was the very time to try the experiment, as the next day being Sunday would allow time for a recovery from its effects. The point was not lost upon the host and bottle after bottle came in, without however I assure you the least invasion of sobriety. Its only effects were animated good humour and uninterrupted conversation.

Yesterday a most furious storm, attended with rain, arose, and the temperature of the air from summer heat, the mercury was at 83, was exchanged for that of a piercing cold. You know how the rain beats and the wind roars here. Recollecting the enthusiasm you feel in such scenes I could not help wishing for your presence, and when the awful rolling of thunder enhanced the sublimity of the scene, that wish was increased. The same storm however may have extended to Brunswick, and while I was indulging these feelings, you may have been thinking of me. Thus it is, my dearest friend, that affection associates with those recollections it most delights to cherish, every extraordinary incident. The painful idea of separation and distance is overcome by the illusion produced by a community of thought with the beloved object. It is thus that I often enjoy the purest and the most complete satisfaction, that I inspire you to be present, and thus congratulate myself on my delusion.

TO MR. SAMUEL H. SMITH

[Brunswick] Tuesday, May 17, 1803.

. . . . I trust your interposition with Mr. Grainger will prove equally effectual, or rather I am in hopes that Col. Morgan's [1] assertion is not true. I have seldom known anything provoke such indignation as the threatened removal of the postmaster here. He is so good, orderly and respectable a citizen, has performed the duties of his office so punctually, is so obliging to the citizens and so exact in his accounts, at the same time he is so inoffensive in his manner and so moderate in his political opinions, that it is impossible to believe he is discharged for any fault of his, but only to provide for another man; that man is a stranger in Brunswick, is idle, contemptible and intemperate, he has been for a long time dependent on Col. Morgan, and has been a cause of much domestic disquiet to his wife and family. I have all the feelings of a republican about me and dread anything unjust and offensive being done by a party I feel so much attached to. The appointments already made in this place have been very unfortunate, and I am sure if Mr. J. had not been greatly deceived they never would have been made. It is supposed that Mr. Grainger is now putting in as many of his own party as he can, in order to influence the elections; if he makes many changes without sufficient reasons, will not he give too much ground for such a suspicion? I cannot help feeling a deep interest in a cause which you have embraced, and nothing but this attachment would have induced me to say a word about

[1] Probably Col. James Morgan, an officer of the Revolution and a prominent Federalist. Jefferson's administration was on the spoils system. He removed nearly all the Federalists from office and appointed none but Republicans.

such matters in my letters to you. Tell me, I beg of you, in your next letter, how my amiable friend, Madm. Pichon, is.   .   .   .

FROM SAMUEL HARRISON SMITH[1]

July 5, 1803, Washington.

.   .   .   .   By the by, what do you think of my going to such an extent as to win 2 Doll. at Loo the first time I ever played the game, and being the most successful at the table?   I confess I felt some mortification at putting the money of Mrs. Madison and Mrs. Duval into my pocket.[2]

Yesterday was a day of joy to our citizens and of pride to our President. It is a day which you know he always enjoys. How much more must he have enjoyed it on this occasion from the great event that occasioned it. The news of the cession of Louisiana only arrived about 8 o'clock of the night preceding, just in time to be officially announced on this auspicious day. Next to the liberty of his country, peace is certainly the dearest to his heart. How glad then must that heart be which with loving participancy in obtaining and securing the one, has placed the other on an impregnable basis. This mighty event forms an era in our history, and of itself must render the administration of Jefferson immortal. At an early hour the city was alive,—a discharge of 18 guns saluted the dawn, the military assembled exhibiting a martial appearance, at 11 o'clock an oration was deld. by Capt. Sprig (?) (well written but poorly pronounced), at 12

[1] Mrs. Smith was in New York, visiting the family of Rev. Dr. John Rodgers, whose daughter her eldest brother had married.

[2] It will be discomforting to fashionable ladies of the present day who play "bridge" for money to know that Mrs. Madison subsequently gave up playing cards for stakes and was sorry she had ever indulged in the practice.

company began to assemble at the President's; it was, more numerous than I have before marked it, enlivened too by the presence of between 40 and 50 ladies clothed in their best attire, cakes, punch, wine &c in profusion. After partaking of these mingled pleasures the company separated about 2, and at 3, the greater part assembled at Stille's to the number of near 100. Before dinner I had the honor of reading the declaration of independence; pleased as I was with the distinction I confess I was not sorry when it was over, not having been perfectly well for a few days I was not without some apprehension of being unable to perform the duty with decency, and tho' I did not have the ambition to be eloquent, yet I felt anxious to escape the implication of inability. As it happened, however, the reading went off very well, and I was complimented for the precision and spirit with which it was deld. and I was pleased with learning that not a word was missed in the utmost parts of the room. Margaret, there is no person on earth but yourself to whom I cd. speak so frankly. Receive this very openness as a coincidence of my unbounded confidence, confidence which nothing but love and esteem strong as my heart entertains for its best heaven, could inspire. At dinner our toasts were politics, our songs convivial. At nine I left the company, part of which remained, I believe, till day light. Mr. Granger spoke to me of having seen you, without knowing you as Mrs. S. tho' he was sure he had before seen you. I often dwell on the happiness I shall derive from Julia on your return, the novelty of which will render it irresistibly captivating. A few months must have given her a new existence, and widened the budding powers of her heart and mind a thousand times more interesting. When we do meet again, my dearest wife, we shall indeed be happy.

Farewell.

TO SAML. HARRISON SMITH

Friday, July 8, [1803] New York.[1]

Perhaps this letter may reach you, if it does it will assure you of my participation in your satisfaction on the interesting event which has occurred. Your letter this morning induces me to believe that the whole of Louisiana is ceded, whereas my federal friends here will have it, that only the Island of New Orleans is given up. I have been sending about for the *National Intelligencer,* but could not find it. I long to see your enunciation of this matter and to ascertain what is true. Every one seems to rely on what you assert as the truth; but charge you with being silent on Mr. Livingston's merit in this affair, and your wishing to give the glory to Mr. Munroe, while on the contrary it is believed here that the latter had nothing to do with it.[2] Even Mr. Jefferson is supposed to have had little or no agency and this act on the part of the French is supposed to result from their war with Britain. It is said that when Mr. King expressed his uneasiness at the conduct of the Spanish intendant, the english ministry assured him he need be in no ways anxious, because war would soon take place, in which case the British would immediately take possession of Lous'na, and as they would be our neighbours and friends, we need have no apprehensions about the French. On this information, Mr. King wrote the same to Livingston who urged this to the French administration, as a motive for giving up that territory to us, thereby preventing their enemy from gaining such a valuable territory and such

[1] Mrs. Smith was visiting her sister, Mrs. Samuel Boyd.
[2] Monroe had nothing to do with it. The negotiations were entirely completed before he arrived in France.

Samuel Harrison Smith, founder of *The National Intelligencer*.
After the portrait by Charles Bird King.

an accession of strength; this proved effectual and the whole transaction was settled before Munroe arrived. The first news of this event gave me great joy, as I had heard Mr. J's. conduct in preferring negotiation to invasion, brought as a new proof of timidity and when I had ventured to say it arose from love of peace, they quite laughed me to scorn, and said it was cowardice alone. I did not know the interest I felt in political concerns, until lately, and this event has given me such real satisfaction that were you to hear me, you would not again tax me with indifference. I have reserved all my political thoughts and observations for conversation. Your letter was quite interesting. I thought of you all day on the fourth of July and wished most heartily to be with you at the Presidents. I believe I feel more highly gratified by any mark of respect shown to you, than you can yourself. I felt very anxious to hear how you delivered the piece you speak of, and thought I should have trembled with anxiety had I been near you. Dear husband it is your modesty only, that could induce you to think it such a mark of confidence, to tell me that you were approved of. But let the motive be what it will, I entreat you ever to repose this kind of confidence in your wife, who feels far more gratified by every testimony of regard towards you, than those paid to herself. Never then, my best friend, conceal from me, what will give me more pleasure than anything else. Tomorrow week, I expect dearest husband to be again in your arms! Yes indeed we shall be happy. I pray you let nothing interfere to disappoint us. I feel a kind of dread about me, and your mentioning that you were not very well, makes me fear that illness may detain you. I yesterday purchased a *certain* cure for the ague for you. I shall come home with two or three infallable medicines and hope if I

am with you, to prevent your suffering from this depress-
ing disease.   I did not half like the idea of your [*illegible*] but I will scold you when I see you, and my chiding
will not be very severe.   I have for more than a week
past sung Julia to sleep with these words, "Papa is coming to bring Julia some cakes."   .   .   .   .

TO MISS MARY ANN SMITH

Washington, Monday night. [1803.]

Here I am my dear sisters, once more safely and happily seated at *home*.   I have no time to write tomorrow,
so that this letter must serve for my Philadelphia and my
Brunswick Julia and sisters.   I was so completely fatigued this morning that I could not write, and now steal
an hour that should be devoted to repose.   Tomorrow I
shall be wholy engaged in making provision for my country residence, to which I shall repair on Wednesday
morning.   Our ride from Phila. to Lancaster was horri-
bly fatiguing, I never experienced anything like it, and if
crying could have done any good, I should have followed
Julia's example and have cried all the way.   At Lancaster
we had a miserable dinner which altho' hungry we could
scarcely eat; it was the same case at supper; we supped at
the Susquehanah.   Julia slept profoundly, and we nearly
as well; rose at three next morning, travelled all day over
good roads thro' a beautiful country, Julia playful and
good, excellent provision, a ravenous appetite, and fine
spirits.   At 6 we arrived at Frederick town, but little
tired, after riding 75 miles.   At supper we met several
very agreeable people, among the rest Mr. Randolph[1]
(of Congress) Mr. Taylor, an acquaintance of your

[1] John Randolph, of Roanoke.

Brothers, a man of some talent, polite manners, but desultory habits of life.

Mr. Randolph conversed most agreeably until 10 o'clock, when I withdrew from his agreeable society and soon lost ourselves in sweet and refreshing slumbers. After breakfast next morning we had a call from Mr. and Mrs. Beckly, who are on their way to Bath. At nine we left F. in a private carriage in which Mr. B. had come the day before. Mr. Taylor who resides in this place, came with us. He was a most entertaining companion, a perfect poetical miscellany; there was no subject on which he could not quote fine lines of poetry. Homer, Virgil, Tasso, Ariosto, Milton, Goldsmith, Pope, Waller, and twenty others, contributed to our entertainment. The sun was shaded with clouds, the breeze cool and refreshing. The scenery romantic and wild beyond any we had seen. We arrived at Montgomery court house at three o'clock, when it began to rain, and continued to rain until evening. This did not much impede our journey and we arrived safely at home at 10 oclock. Mrs. Smith was a bed, but Milly was looking out of the window. On perceiving us, she screamed out "There's Mistress; there's Mistress," and flew half wild with joy to receive us; she danced, capered and followd in most extravagant manner; Mrs. Smith soon run down and demonstrated much more joy than I imagined she could feel. We got tea, with which Julia was delighted. You never saw a little creature so frolicsome as she has been ever since we left Lancaster. She slept almost half the time, laughd and danced the other half. All this day I have been resting. I found the house in perfect order, the parlour set off with oak boughs, curtains white as snow; and all neat as wax work. At five this afternoon we got a hack, and visited our retreat. I shall not pretend now

to describe it. All I will say is that I am *delighted* with
it. A good house on the top of a high hill, with high
hills all around it, embower'd in woods, thro' an opening
of which the Potomack, its shores and Mason's Island
are distinctly seen. I have never been more charmingly
surprised than on seeing this retreat, but enough of it by
and by. We go there on Wednesday. On my way
home I called on Madam Pechon. On seeing her, I believe, I have seen one of the happiest of human beings.
She had her little son in her arms, which however did not
impede her hastening to embrace me. I was affected to
tears. I folded her to my bosom, with sensations of
almost equal pleasure with which I embraced my dearest
sisters. She is perfectly well, so is her son, so is her
spouse. My friend expressed what I must believe to be
true pleasure on seeing me. I have already promised to
be almost a daily visitor. But I must stop. When I get
among my little mountains and towering woods, I shall
write you wonderful letters. My kindest love to Papa
and all my other excellent friends.

TO MRS. KIRKPATRICK

Monday, January 23, 1804.

. . . . My family affairs go on pretty well; I have
an old woman in the kitchen as a drudge, for she cannot
cook; I have a miserably idle dirty girl as a waiter, whom
I shall get rid of as soon as possible. Milly is my stand
bye, she cleans the house, makes beds, irons, clear
starches, and attends Julia while I am in the kitchen,
which is two or three hours every day, as I cook every
dinner that is eat by the family and have even to assist
in dishing up dinner. I have had a fine little girl of 5

yrs old bound to me by Dr. Willis. While I work, she plays with Julia and keeps her quiet, she is gay, good temper'd and well behaved, Julia is extremely fond of her, and she of Julia; and I hope to have some comfort in her. Since Mrs. S. left me I have totally neglected musick, reading and writing, and altho' I sew all the morning and evening, yet the interruptions from company, from family calls, from Julia &c are so frequent, that I found my work go behind hand, and Mr. Smith who is always urging me to resume my old employments, has induced me to get a woman to work whenever it was necessary. I had to get over my pique to Mrs. Jones and she is now working for me. I give her 12s. 6d. pr week and shall get her to do all my large work in the course of a week or two and shall then have leisure for my little things. It is so entirely the custom to visit of a morning here, that if we keep up any intercourse with society, our mornings are most of them sacrificed. Of an evening some one or more of the gentlemen of congress are always here. This, my dear sister, is an unprofitable way of life; but there is no alternative in this place, between gay company and parties and perfect solitude. Since my last letters, we have been at a large and splendid ball at Mr. Robt. Smith's,[1] a dining party at Md'm Pichon's, a card party at Mrs. Gallatins, at Mr. Beckley's,[2] and at Mr. Van Ness's[3] and at the city assembly. Mrs. R. Smith's was by far the most agreeable. Mrs. Merry[4] was there

[1] Secretary of the Navy, a man of wealth and fashion.
[2] John Beckley, of Virginia, Clerk of the House of Representatives, an active political agent for the Southern Republicans.
[3] John Peter Van Ness, of Kinderhook, N. Y., member of Congress in 1801, lost his seat in 1803 by accepting the post of Major in the Militia of the District of Columbia. He married Marcia Burns in 1802, and from her acquired a large fortune. Latrobe built him a splendid house and he and his beautiful wife entertained lavishly for many years.
[4] Wife of Anthony Merry, British Minister. She made an international question of her right to go in to dinner at the White House on the President's arm.

and her dress attracted great attention; it was brilliant and fantastic, white satin with a long train, dark blue crape of the same length over it and white crape drapery down to her knees and open at one side, so thickly cover'd with silver spangles that it appear'd to be a brilliant silver tissue; a breadth of blue crape, about four yards long, and in other words a long shawl, put over her head, instead of over her shoulders and hanging down to the floor, her hair bound tight to her head with a band like her drapery, with a diamond crescent before and a diamond comb behind, diamond ear-rings and necklace, displayed on a bare bosom. She is a large, tall well-made woman, rather masculine, very free and affable in her manners, but easy without being graceful. She is said to be a woman of fine understanding and she is so entirely the talker and actor in all companies, that her good husband passes quite unnoticed; he is plain in his appearance and called rather inferior in understanding. I am half tempted to enter into details of our city affairs and personages, but really I shall have to be so scandalous, that I am affraid of amusing you at such a risk. But certainly there is no place in the United States where one hears and sees so many strange things, or where so many odd characters are to be met with. But of Mad'm [1]————I think it no harm to speak the truth. She has made a great noise here, and mobs of boys have crowded round her splendid equipage to see what I hope will not often be seen in this country, an almost naked woman. An elegant and select party was given to her by Mrs. Robt. Smith; her appearance was such that it threw all the company into confusion, and no one dar'd to look at her but by stealth; the window shutters being left open, a crowd assembled round the windows to get a look at this beautiful little creature,

[1] A well-known American woman, the wife of a foreigner.

for every one allows she is extremely beautiful. Her
dress was the thinnest sarcenet and white crepe without
the least stiffening in it, made without a single plait in the
skirt, the width at the bottom being made of gores; there
was scarcely any waist to it and no sleeves; her back, her
bosom, part of her waist and her arms were uncover'd
and the rest of her form visible. She was engaged the
next evening at Madm P's, Mrs. R. Smith and several
other ladies sent her word, if she wished to meet them
there, she must promise to have more clothes on. I was
highly pleased with this becoming spirit in our ladies.
Mrs. Moreton, of whom you have heard me speak, received the visit of —— and his lady in *bed*. No one
however follow'd the fashion they wished to set. I
could write many more such anecdotes, but this is enough
for one letter. .   .   .

FROM THOMAS JEFFERSON

Th: Jefferson presents his respectful compliments to
Mrs. Smith, and being charged with those of a distant
friend of hers, he cannot give better evidence of them
than her own letter, which he incloses with his salutations.
July 10, 05.

TO MRS. KIRKPATRICK

Washington, December 6th, 1805 Thursday.

.   .   .   . Friday morning. Maria is seated at *her*
writing table in my room, and I have the stand placed
beside the fire in the parlour and the children playing
round me. I shall accustom myself to write and read
with them in the room and I shall soon find it easy, tho'
at present, it somewhat disturbs me   I tell Maria she may

remain at her writing table until 12, the rest of the day we
will pass together. Mrs. Potts does extremely well at
present, my man John is neither one of the best nor one
of the worst of waiters, and is so good natured there is
no scolding him, and my kitchen work goes on sure and
slow. I have never since I lived in Washington been so
comfortably and agreeably fixed. Mrs. P. is very attentive to the children and does a great deal of sewing.
When I rise I always find the parlour in neat order, a
good fire, breakfast ready. I have made a few reforms
in house-keeping,—one is rising a little after 7, and having breakfast precisely at 8, the other baking my own
bread. I have had a close stove put up in the kitchen,
which saves one half of the wood that used to be consumed; we cook entirely on it. Our standing dinner is
one dish of meat, two of vegetables, and soup, and the
stove exactly holds these. We have hot rolls for breakfast and biscuit or other little cakes for tea. Our wood
yard is filled from our farm, our garden has afforded a
sufficient supply of vegetables, and occasionally butter; I
go to market myself once or twice a week, in fine, everything is as it should be and my only wish is that no change
may occur. Maria I suppose mentioned that my good
Mrs. Doyne kept a boarding house. I have interested
myself very much for her and recommend her to Mr. Barlow,[1] he has taken a parlour and bed room which are very
neatly furnished, and the stable,—he pays her 40 dollars
a week for himself, wife and 2 servants, besides them she
has 10 gentlemen at 10 dollars a week only for board and
lodging, as they find fuel, candles, etc. and so I think she
will do very well. We have all the surrounding houses
filled, but I have not yet become acquainted with many of

---

[1] Joel Barlow, poet, literary man and diplomatist, moved soon after this
to Kalorama, a handsome estate north of the city.

my new neighbours.   Dr. Mitchell[1] lives directly opposite
and we have several ladies next door.   We passed a very
agreeable evening at Mrs. Gallatin's.   The Turks amused
our eyes.   I have had so much running about this morning, salting away beef, &c, that I am not in much of a
letter-writing mood, but delays are dangerous.   While
we were at breakfast this morning, a large parcel was
brought in, with a note from Mr. Law.[2]   The roll, when
untied, proved to be his poem—*Agitation,* submitted to
my ladyship's judgement.   Maria was delighted, as she
had been quite anxious to see it, having heard Mr. N's
account of it; if worth copying, you shall have it.   I expect we shall be favoured with occasional visits from the
muses this winter as we have two or three voluntarys
in our vicinity, Dr. B. and Dr. M.   Dr. Barlow is so
thoughtful and absent in company, that I cannot yet say
what I think of him.   My pen drags so heavily along, and
my thoughts are so drawn off by my little Sue, who is begging to be taken up, that I must lay this sheet aside for
another occasion, tho' I am sensible what I have said,
is not satisfactory.   I intended my dear sister to have
answer'd your letter more fully, but am disappointed.
Adieu.

TO MRS. KIRKPATRICK

Sydney,[3] May 4, 1806, Sunday.

.   .   .   .   On Sunday morning Mrs. Randolph and
Madison called and I promised to take tea with Mrs. R.
in the evening.   We found no company, and all the fam-

[1] Samuel L. Mitchill, the scientist, then a Senator from New York.
[2] Mr. Law wrote a great deal of *vers de société,* which was much admired
by his friends.   Fortunately little of it has been preserved.
[3] Their country place which they bought in 1804.   It occupied the tract
a part of which is now the Catholic University of America, adjoining the
grounds of the Soldiers' Home.   Its name when Mr. Smith bought it was
Turkey Thicket.   He sold it in 1835 for $12,000.

ily were out, but Mr. J. and Mrs. R. She was seated
by him on a sopha and all her lovely children playing
around them. With what delight did I contemplate this
good parent, and while I sat looking at him playing with
these infants, one standing on the sopha with its arms
round his neck, the other two youngest on his knees, playing with him, I could scarcely realise that he was one of
the most celebrated men now living, both as a Politician
and Philosopher. He was in one of his most communicative and social moods, and after tea, when the children
went to bed, the conversation turned on agriculture, gardening, the differences of both in different countries and
of the produce of different climates. This is one of the
most favorite pursuits and indeed the conversation the
whole evening turned on his favorite subjects. I was
seated on the sopha which he and Mrs. R. occupied and
Mr. Smith close by me, and almost fronting him. You
know the effect of such a disposition of places on the free
flow of conversation, and I am certain that had he been
on the other side of the chimney we should not have
heard half as much. There are five *cons* necessary to
make a good fire, and there are at least two, to kindle
the warmth and animation of social intercourse, contigu-
ity and congruity. The evening passed delightfully and
rapidly away, and I felt quite ashamed to find it almost
ten when we rose to depart. Mr. J. gave me some winter melon-seed from Malta, he doubts whether it will
come to perfection here, on account of the early frosts,
so it will not do for Brunswick. .   .   .

TO MISS SUSAN B. SMITH

Washington, July 31, 1806 Thursday Evening.

. . . . Last Sunday[1] while I had my little flock around me, the noise of carriages drew us to the door and Mr. and Mrs. Madison, Dr. and Mrs. Thornton and Mrs. B.[2] came to spend the evening. Mrs. M. was all that was tender, affectionate and attractive as usual; Mr. M. was in one of his most sportive moods, the Dr. in his philosophical and the ladies disposed to be pleased. The afternoon was passed sans ceremonie, they sat on the benches beneath the trees, swung in the hammoch, walked about and Mrs. T. led the way through the kitchen to look at my milk house; she was so pleased that she called the Dr., and he so pleased he called all the rest, and so my milk house underwent the inspection of the secretary, the phylosopher and the good ladies. It was in nice order with about a dozen or fifteen large pans of milk ranged around; Sukey, who was sitting on the steps cutting smoked beef, was quite proud of their praise. I, as a country woman ought to do, set out my large table, with nice white cloth, plates, knives, home made bread, &c. &c. My butter which was as hard as in the middle of winter, was highly praised and when Mrs. Thornton observed my woman made excellent butter, I realy felt a sensation of pride, which I do not often feel, in telling her it was my own making and that since the first of May, I had never missed churning but once. You can not think what a right down farmer's wife I am, but next winter will I hope convince you, that at least I am a good dairy maid, as you will eat of the fine butter I pack away. I have made

[1] At Sidney.
[2] Mrs. Bordeaux, Mrs. Thornton's mother.

about 60 lbs. this summer and have packed near 30 away.
I tell you these little nothings, dear Susan, to bring you
amongst us in fancy at least; ah, how I wish you were
here in reality! Surely the country is as favorable to
the health of the soul as to that of the body, for never
do I feel the power of my mind so active, or the affections
of my heart so warm as when surrounded by the works of
nature. . . .

TO MRS. KIRKPATRICK

Washington, Feb. 9, 1808.

. . . . Well, I shall never grow any older, I really
think, and it appears to me both a moral and physical impossibility that 30 years have passed since I was born. I
wish I had you at Washington a little while and you
would not think Aunt Margaret the only strange personage in the world. The other evening Susan and I
were very much diverted by two most venerable senators,
who came to drink tea with us. I perceived Judge R.
minutely surveying the forte pianno, and supposed he
might be fond of musick, so asked Susan to play for
them. When she took her seat, they both drew nigh
and what I supposed to be attention marked on their
countenances, I afterwards found out to be astonishment,
for I believe it was the first time they had seen or heard
such a thing. They looked and looked, felt all over the
outside, peeped in where it was open, and seemed so curious to know how the sound was produced, or whence it
came, that I beged Susan to open the lid and to display the
internal machinery. Never did I see children more delighted. "Dear me," said the judge, "how pretty those

---

[1] It appears to be "Judge R" in the MS., but there was no Senator who
fills the description. Perhaps Mrs. Smith meant Senator Buckner Thurston, of Kentucky, as one of the backwoodsmen.

white and red things jump up and down, dear me what a parcel of wires, strange that a harp with a thousand strings should keep in tune so long." "Pray," said the other senator, "have you any rule to play musick?" We tried to explain how the keys were the representatives of the notes, they did not seem to comprehend, supposing all Susan's sweet melody was drawn by chance or random from this strange thing. When the examination was over, they both said it was a very pretty thing. The same good judge, the other day went up to General Turreau in the senate, surveyed him from head to foot, lifted up the flaps of his coat all covered with gold embroidery, asked him the use of the gold tassels on his boots, what was such a thing and such a thing and how much it all might cost, all which the general very good humourdly answered. Do not think now these good men are fools, far from it, they are very sensible men and useful citizens, but they have lived in the back woods, thats all. If you have read my letters, you will have seen Capt. Pike [1] mentioned as one of the most agreeable young men who visited here. Well, here we were teasing Susan about him, (and in fact it would not have been a surprising thing if an impression had been made on her heart) when lo and behold he the other day told us he was a married man and had a daughter as big as Julia. For his sport, he had been masquerading here all winter, and was a favorite beau among all the belles. Poor Susan can hardly get over it, but her forte-pianno will make her forget every thing else I believe, for she does little else but play. I am in such a scribbling mood dear Mary, that I could have filled a folio sheet for you, had I not been affraid of frightening you from our pro-

[1] Zebulon Montgomery Pike, the explorer, had made his expedition into the Louisiana Territory the year before.

posed correspondence. But you must take me for better or worse, folios and quarto's, prose or verse, nonsense or much sense, gaiety or dullness, but always warmly and unchangeably,

Affectionately and sincerely your friend

Love to all our friends.

TO MISS SUSAN BAYARD SMITH

Saturday, 26 February [1809].

Mr. Hauto was a very welcome visitor to us all. He left his packages first and called an hour or two afterwards, wisely conjecturing that they would pave the way to a welcome. He came about 1 oclock, between two and three he arose to take his leave, but I begged he would sit still and take his dinner with us. At four, Mr. Smith came home and brought Caleb Lowndes with him. "I have come to take my dinner with you without your knowing anything about it," said he, "You will be the only sufferer by that," I replied : "but I never make appologies to Philosophers, and I mean to treat you, Mr. Hauto, as well as Mr. Lowndes as a philosopher. I always take it for granted they are such intellectual beings, that they care but little for the gross articles of food and drink, and that you prefer the feast of reason and the flow of soul, to all the ragouts and champagne a prince could give, and then," continued I, shaking the hand Mr. Lowndes still held, "I will give you what is a rarity even in Palaces, a cordial welcome." "And that," said Mr. L. "is a sauce which will give a relish to the plainest food." After this preface, which seemed as the first course for the feast of reason, we sat down to our roast beef, cold veal, peas, porridge, &c with good appetites and

had a desert of indian pudding season'd with some wit
and a great deal of mirth and good humour.   Mr. Hauto
to our great entertainment, had some difficulty in making
way with his indian pudding and molasses, but when I
assured him that this dish was immortalized by the greatest poet of our country, he made out to mortalize it.[1]   I
like Mr. Hauto very well and shall say more of him in my
letter to Maria, if it does not go all out of my head.   I
like this Caleb Lowndes[2] very much Susan, and I am
sure Mary would like him prodigiously.   I mean to give
him a packet to you and desire him to call and see you
all.

Yes, Susan, I do indeed feel sorry when I think that
we are soon to lose our dear good President.   You
know mine is not a common regard, that I not only ven-
erate and admire his character, but am personally attached to him,—his long visit last autumn in the country,
in which I had a tete-a-tete of more than two hours; and
in which the conversation was free and various and I
might say confidential, has made me more intimately acquainted than ever.   The notes which on several occasions I have received from him I treasure up among my
most precious relics.   When he has gone, Washington
will not be Washington to me.   I cannot think of his departure without tears.   I do love him, with all my heart
I love him, but this letter is to lay by me for the weeks
journal and here I am filling it already.   We have been
very gay lately,—last night made the 7th or 8th ball this
winter, besides a great many card parties.   We had a
large and agreeable one at Mrs. Thornton's last week.   I
have been tired of them for some time, but the girls do
not seem inclined to miss one.   To them they have still

[1] "Hasty Pudding" was the title of the poem, and the "greatest poet"
was Joel Barlow!
[2] A Philadelphian; not of the South Carolina family.

the charm of novelty.   Well, I will stop now and write
a little every day this week.

Sunday morning.   I left off about four o'clock yesterday, soon afterwards we dined, the table was just cleared
away and I seated with Mordaunt in hand, when Caleb
Lowndes came in, as he often does to take his dinner with
us.   I set the little table out for him and soon mustered
up a comfortable dinner, and afterwards we sat and conversed by firelight until Mr. Pederson[1] came, lights were
then brought in, Mr. Smith soon after came home with
the two Mr. Brent's.[2]   The girls had both gone up to
the house, as Congress was still in session.   About 9
oclock Mrs. Bayard came in, and Mr. P. and she alternately had several games of chess.   This morning Mr. P.
came to go with us to church, and we had nearly reached
the Capitol when we met Mr. Coles[3] who told us there
was no church.   So we turned back and Mr. P. has been
sitting these two hours with me and for want of conversation, I made him read to me.   All this has so deranged
my ideas and so I will write no more at present.

Thursday.   Monday, tuesday, wednesday, is it possible three days already gone?   And all in company, in a
desultory way.   On Monday morning, Mr. de Calve, Mr.
Pederson, and 7 or 8 ladies, took up all the time until
dinner.   In the evening it rained, but that did not hinder
our going to Mrs. Gallatin's, where we had a squeeze, of
all our grandees.   I procured a seat next Mrs. Wharton,
which always ensures me a pleasant evening; Genl. Turreau,[4] was there in all the splendor of gold and diamonds;

---

[1] Peter Pederson, Consul and Chargé d'Affaires of Denmark.   He married
in 1820 Ann Caroline Smith, of Charleston, daughter of William Laughton
Smith, Representative in Congress.
[2] The Mayor of Washington was then Robert Bent, but there were several
of the family, a large one, who would have been likely to visit Mrs. Smith.
[3] Jefferson's Private Secretary.
[4] The French minister, a marshal of France.

he took a chair next to me and had a long talk ; he said he
had been often wishing this winter to visit me of an evening but we had so many politics at our house, he was
afraid a Frenchman might be a restraint. The next
morning, after school was over, I went to Mrs. Bayard's [1]
and passed the morning with her. A stormy evening
prevented every one but Mr. Pederson from coming.
We passed the evening soberly at chess. On wednesday
morning the weather was delicious. I went with the
girls and Mr. and Mrs. Jenkinson to the barracks, the
fineness of the weather, the gay appearance of the soldiers and the delightful musick, animated every one, but
particularly the children. We then went to the Navy
Yard, through the vessels, and then to the new-Bridge,
over the Potomack. It was near four oclock when we
reached home. This spring day awakened all my rural
feelings and makes me impatient for the country. In
the evening we went to Capt. Tingey's where we had a
charming dance. I am wearied, positively wearied with
company and shall enjoy the solitude of the country as
much as any one ever did rest after fatigue. The city is
thronged with strangers. Yesterday we saw 4 or 5 car-
riages-and-four come in and already two have passed
this morning. The Miss Carrols, Miss Chases, Miss
Cooks, and I dont know how many more misses have
come from Baltimore. There are parties every night,
and the galleries are crowded in the morning. Ah, my
dear Susan, a stormy day in the country, with you to read
to me while I worked, I should prefer to any scene however gay. Had we a house that would admit it, I should
this week have a great deal of company; as it is, I can
see them only of an evening. This sheet is full. I must
go to Mrs. [*illegible*]. Adieu.

[1] Mrs. James A. Bayard presumably.

TO MISS SUSAN B. SMITH

Saturday, March, 1809.

I have just returned from the solemn and affecting
scenes of this day,—to many they were scenes of greatness, gaiety, and exultation.   To me they were melancholy.   My heart is oppressed, my dearest Susan with a
weight of sadness, and my eyes are so blinded with tears
that I can scarcely trace these lines.   It is some pleasure
to me to write to you who participate in my sentiments
of affectionate veneration for this best of men.   For the
last time I have seen him in his own house.   He is
happy, he has enjoyed all his country can bestow of greatness and honor, he could enjoy no more were he to remain in office his whole life time.   He only lays down an
irksome burden, but carries with him an increase of popularity, of esteem and love.   He goes to be *happy* without ceasing to be *great*.   I ought to rejoice, too, but when
I think of what *we* are to *lose,* I forget what *he* is to *gain*.
To-day after the inauguration, we all went to Mrs. Madison's.   The street was full of carriages and people, and
we had to wait near half an hour, before we could get in,
—the house was completely filled, parlours, entry, drawing
room and bed room.   Near the door of the drawing room
Mr. and Mrs. Madison stood to receive their company.
She looked extremely beautiful, was drest in a plain cam-
brick dress with a very long train, plain round the neck
without any handkerchief, and beautiful bonnet of purple
velvet, and white satin with white plumes.   She was all
dignity, grace and affability.   Mr. Madison shook my
hand with all the cordiality of old acquaintance but it was
when I saw our dear and venerable Mr. Jefferson that my
heart beat.   When he saw me, he advanced from the

crowd, took my hand affectionately and held it five or six
minutes; one of the first things he said was, "Remember
the promise you have made me, to come to see us next
summer, do not forget it," said he, pressing my hand, "for
we shall certainly expect you." I assured him I would
not, and told him I could now wish him joy with much
more sincerity than this day 8 years ago. "You have
now resigned a heavy burden," said I. "Yes indeed" he
replied "and am much happier at this moment than my
friend." The crowd was immense both at the Capitol
and here, thousands and thousands of people thronged the
avenue. The Capitol presented a gay scene. Every inch
of space was crowded and there being as many ladies as
gentlemen, all in full dress, it gave it rather a gay than
a solemn appearance,—there was an attempt made to
appropriate particular seats for the ladies of public characters, but it was found impossible to carry it into effect,
for the sovereign people would not resign their privileges
and the high and low were promiscuously blended on the
floor and in the galleries.

Mr. Madison was extremely pale and trembled excessively when he first began to speak, but soon gained
confidence and spoke audibly. From the Capitol we
went to Mrs. M's., and from there to Mr. Jefferson's. I
there again conversed a few minutes; Mr. Smith told him
the ladies *would* follow him, "That is right," said he,
"since I am too old to follow them. I remember in
France when his friends were taking leave of Dr. Franklin, the ladies smothered him with embraces and on his
introducing me to them as his successor, I told him I
wished he would transfer these privileges to me, but
he answered 'You are too young a man.' " Did not this
imply, Susan, that now this objection was removed? I
had a great inclination to tell him so.

Sunday morning. Well, my dear Susan, the chapter draws to a close. Last night concluded the important day, on which our country received a new magistrate. To a philosopher, who while he contemplated the scene, revolved past ages in his mind, it must have been a pleasing sight. A citizen, chosen from among his equals, and quietly and unanimously elevated to a power, which in other countries and in all ages of the world has cost so much blood to attain! Would the size of a letter allow of it, I would allow my pen to follow the current of thought, but to a reflecting mind, which can withdraw itself from the interests and desires of life, which can ascend for a little while to another life, and look down upon this, the differences of rank, grandeur, power, are inequalities of condition, as imperceptible as those the traveller discerns in the valley, when he looks down upon it from the summit of the Alps. The tallest tree of the valley, does not then appear higher than the little shrubs it shelters. The storms roll harmless beneath his feet, clouds which darken those below, obstruct not his view of the sun, and while the inhabitants of the valley are distressed and terrified by the strife of the elements, he enjoys perpetual sunshine.

Thus have I endeavored to raise my own mind, and to contemplate the scenes that are acted before me. Sometimes I can gain this abstraction, but oftener, all the weaknesses, the vanities, the hopes and fears of this vain show, level me with the lowest of earthly minds.

Last evening, I endeavored calmly to look on, and amidst the noise, bustle and crowd,[1] to spend an hour or two in sober reflection, but my eye was always fixed on our venerable friend, when he approached my ear listened

---

[1] This was the first Inauguration Ball. See for an account of it *The Century* for March, 1905.

Mr. Madison.

Mrs. Madison.

Silhouettes from life.

Mr. Jefferson.

to catch every word and when he spoke to me my heart
beat with pleasure. Personal attachment produces this
emotion, and I did not blame it. But I have not this
regard for Mr. Madison, and I was displeased at feeling
no emotion when he came up and conversed with me.
He made some of his old kind of mischievous allusions,
and I told him I found him still unchanged.[1] I tried in
vain to feel merely as a spectator, the little vanities of my
nature often conquered my better reason. The room
was so terribly crowded that we had to stand on the
benches; from this situation we had a view of the moving
mass; for it was nothing else. It was scarcely possible to
elbow your way from one side to another, and poor Mrs.
Madison was almost pressed to death, for every one
crowded round her, those behind pressing on those before, and peeping over their shoulders to have a peep of
her, and those who were so fortunate as to get near
enough to speak to her were happy indeed. As the
upper sashes of the windows could not let down, the
glass was broken, to ventilate the room, the air of which
had become oppressive, but here I begin again at the
end of the story. Well, to make up for it I will begin at
the beginning. When we went there were not above 50
persons in the room, we were led to benches at the upper
fire place. Not long afterwards, the musick struck up
Jefferson's March, and he and Mr. Coles entered. He
spoke to all whom he knew, and was quite the plain, unassuming citizen. Madison's March was then played and
Mrs. Madison led in by one of the managers and Mrs.
Cutts and Mr. Madison, she was led to the part of the
room where we happened to be, so that I accidently was

---

[1] In public life and as a writer, James Madison was the most solemn of
men. In private life he was an incessant humorist, and at home at Montpelier used to set his table guests daily into roars of laughter over his stories
and whimsical way of telling them.

placed next her. She looked a queen. She had on a
pale buff colored velvet, made plain, with a very long
train, but not the least trimming, and beautiful pearl
necklace, earrings and bracelets. Her head dress was a
turban of the same coloured velvet and white satin (from
Paris) with two superb plumes, the bird of paradise
feathers. It would be *absolutely impossible* for any one
to behave with more perfect propriety than she did. Unassuming dignity, sweetness, grace. It seems to me that
such manners would disarm envy itself, and conciliate
even enemies. The managers presented her with the
first number,—"But what shall I do with it," said she, "I
do not dance." "Give it to your neighbor," said Capt.
Tingey. "Oh no," said she, "that would look like par-
tiality." "Then I will," said the Capt. and he presented
it to Mrs. Cutts. I really admired this in Mrs. M. Ah,
why does she not in all things act with the same propriety? She would be too much beloved if she added all
the virtues to all the graces. She was led to supper by
the French Minister,[1] Mrs. Cutts by the English Minister,[2] she sat at the centre of the table, which was a cres-
sent, the French and English ministers on each hand, Mrs.
Cutts the next on the right hand, Mrs. Smith[3] the next
on the left and Mr. Madison on the other side of the table
opposite Mrs. M. I chose a place where I could see Mrs.
M. to advantage. She really in manners and appearance,
answered all my ideas of royalty. She was so equally
gracious to both French and English, and so affable to all.
I suspect Mrs. Smith could not like the superiority of
Mrs. Cutts, and if I am not mistaken, Mrs. Madison's
———[4] causes her some heart burnings. Mr. Jefferson did

---

[1] General Turreau de Garambonville.   [2] Honorable M. Erskine.
[3] Wife of Robert Smith, then Secretary of the Navy, but soon to be Secretary of State
[4] The blank is in the original.

not stay above two hours; he seemed in high spirits and
his countenance beamed with a benevolent joy. I do
believe father never loved son more than he loves Mr.
Madison, and I believe too that every demonstration of
respect to Mr. M. gave Mr. J. more pleasure than if paid
to himself. Oh he is a good man! And the day will
come when all party spirit shall expire, that every citizen
of the United States will join in saying "He is a good
man." Mr. Madison, on the contrary, seemed spiritless
and exhausted. While he was standing by me I said,
"I wish with all my heart I had a little bit of seat to
offer you." "I wish so too," said he, with a most woe
begone face, and looking as if he could scarcely stand,—
the managers came up to ask him to stay to supper, he
assented, and turning to me, "but I would much rather
be in bed" said he. Immediately after supper Mr. and
Mrs. M. withdrew, the rest of the company danced until
12, the moment the clock struck that hour, the musick
stopped, and we all came home tired and sick. "And
such," said I as I threw myself on the bed, "such are the
gaiety and pleasures of the world! Oh give me the solitude of our cottage, where after a day well spent, I lay
down so tranquil and cheerful." Never do I recollect
one night, retiring with such a vacuum, such a dissatisfied
craving, such a restlessness of spirit, such undefined,
vague desires, as I now do. No, the world is not the
abode of happiness, for while we have the weakness of
humanity about us, vanity, pride, ambition, in some form
or other will invade and disturb the breast of the humblest
individual. But when far away from such excitements,
all within is peace in the performance of known duties; in
the enjoyment of intellectual and social pleasures, the best
part of our nature is satisfied, the ambition of having the
first blown rose, or the sweetest strawberry, lead only to

pleasing anxiety and activity, the object of our ambition being attainable, we are not tormented by unsatisfied desires. After enjoying all the pomp and grandeur of the greatest empire in the world, after conquering nations, and the most splendid triumphs, Diocletian, this proud master of the world, voluntarily forsook these delusive pleasures, and often said while tilling his own garden, I take more pleasure in cultivating my garden with my own hands, and in eating the cabbages I have planted and rear'd than in all, that Rome could ever give me. Like him, our good and great Jefferson will taste the sweets of seclusion. But far happier is our president than the Roman Emperor. His retirement is a home endeared by the truest friendship; the most ardent and devoted affection, where his children, his grand children and great grandchildren, will lavish on him all the peculiar joys of the heart. How I have rambled in this long letter, but I am sure all these details will be pleasing to you, so I make no appology. To you they will not appear extravagant, to Maria B. perhaps they will.

And now for a little of humbler themes. We propose this week removing to the country, I never felt more impatient to go, as I propose a number of little improvements,—such as having a little poultry yard enclosed with boards, where I intend raising a great many chickens. The well-diggers are to go out very soon, and we shall try to get water. Mr. Madison last night enquired among other things about this matter. "Truth is at the bottom of a well, is the old saying, and I expect when you get to the bottom of yours, you will discover most important truths. But I hope you will at least find *water,*" continued he, smiling. Indeed I hope we will, and I am sure you join in this wish, knowing how much we suffer from the want of it. . . .

VISIT TO MONTICELLO AND MONTPELIER

Monticello, August 1st, 1809.[1]

In a visit Mr. J. made our little cottage last autumn, we were speaking of all the various charms of nature, storms of winter, "But," said he, "you can here form no idea of a snow storm, No, to see it in all its grandeur you should stand at my back door; there we see its progress— rising over the distant Allegany, come sweeping and roaring on, mountain after mountain, till it reaches us, and then when its blast is felt, to turn to our fire side, and while we hear it pelting against the window to enjoy the cheering blaze, and the comforts of a beloved family." Well, I have seen those distant mountains over which the winter storm has swept, now rearing their blue and misty heads to the clouds, and forming a sublime and beautiful horrison round one of the finest and most extended scenes the eye ever rested on.—I have seen that beloved family, whose virtues and affections are the best reward and the best treasure of their parent and their country's parent—I have seen, I have listened to, one of the greatest and best of men. He has passed through the tempestuous sea of political life, has been enveloped in clouds of calumny, the storms of faction, assailed by foreign and domestic foes, and often threatened with a wreck, of happiness and fame. But these things are now all passed away, and like the mountain on which he stands, fogs and mists and storms, gather and rage below, while he enjoys unclouded sunshine. How simple and majestic is his character, my affection for him is weighed with much veneration, that, meek, humble, gentle and kind, as he is in his manners,

[1] From Mrs. Smith's note book.

I cannot converse with him, with ease. My mind is busied in thinking of what he is, rather than listening to what he says. After a very delightful journey of three days, we reached Monticello on the morning of the fourth. When I crossed the Ravanna, a wild and romantic little river, which flows at the foot of the mountain, my heart beat,—I thought I had entered, as it were the threshhold of his dwelling, and I looked around everywhere expecting to meet with some trace of his superintending care. In this I was disappointed, for no vestige of the labour of man appeared; nature seemed to hold an undisturbed dominion. We began to ascend this mountain, still as we rose I cast my eyes around, but could discern nothing but untamed woodland, after a mile's winding upwards, we saw a field of corn, but the road was still wild and uncultivated. I every moment expected to reach the summit, and felt as if it was an endless road; my impatience lengthened it, for it is not two miles from the outer gate on the river to the house. At last we reached the summit, and I shall never forget the emotion the first view of this sublime scenery excited. Below me extended for above 60 miles round, a country covered with woods, plantations and houses; beyond, arose the blue mountains, in all their grandeur. Monticello rising 500 feet above the river, of a conical form and standing by itself, commands on all sides an unobstructed and I suppose one of the most extensive views any spot the globe affords. The sides of the mountain covered with wood, with scarcely a speck of cultivation, present a fine contrast to its summit, crowned with a noble pile of buildings, surounded by an immense lawn, and shaded here and there with some fine trees. Before we reached the house, we met Mr. J. on horseback, he had just returned from his morning ride, and when, on approaching, he

Monticello—North front.

recognized us, he received us with one of those benignant smiles, and cordial tones of voice that convey an undoubted welcome to the heart. He dismounted and assisted me from the carriage, led us to the hall thro' a noble portico, where he again bade us welcome. I was so struck with the appearance of this Hall, that I lingered to look around, but he led me forward, smiling as he said, "You shall look bye and bye, but you must now rest." Leading me to a sopha in a drawing room as singular and beautiful as the Hall, he rang and sent word to Mrs. Randolph that we were there, and then ordered some refreshments. "We have quite a sick family," said he; "My daughter has been confined to the sick bed of her little son; my grand-daughter has lost her's and still keeps to her room and several of the younger children are indisposed. For a fortnight Mr. and Mrs. Randolph have sat up every night, until they are almost worn out." This information clouded my satisfaction and cast a gloom over our visit,—but Mrs. R. soon entered, and with a smiling face, most affectionately welcomed us. Her kind and cheerful manners soon dispersed my gloom and after a little chat, I begged her not to let me detain her from her nursery, but to allow me to follow her to it; she assented and I sat with her until dinner time. Anne,[1] (Mrs. Bankhead) who had been confined 3 weeks before and had lost her child looked delicate and interesting; Ellen, my old favorite, I found improved as well as grown. At five o'clock the bell summoned us to dinner. Mr. Randolph, Mr. Bankhead, and Jefferson R. were there. They are 12 in family, and as Mr. J. sat in the midst of his children and grand-children, I looked on him with emotions of tenderness and respect. The table was plainly, but genteely and plentifully spread, and his im-

---

[1] Jefferson's eldest daughter.

mense and costly variety of French and Italian wines,
gave place to Madeira and a sweet ladies' wine. We sat
till near sun down at the table, where the desert was succeeded by agreeable and instructive conversation in which
every one seemed to wish and expect Mr. J. to take the
chief part. As it is his custom after breakfast to withdraw to his own apartments and pursuits and not to join
the family again until dinner, he prolongs that meal, or
rather the time after that meal, and seems to relish his
wine the better for being accompanied with conversation,
and during the 4 days I spent there these were the most
social hours. When we rose from table, a walk was proposed and he accompanied us. He took us first to the
garden he has commenced since his retirement. It is on
the south side of the mountain and commands a most
noble view. Little is as yet done. A terrace of 70 or 80
feet long and about 40 wide is already made and in cultivation. A broad grass walk leads along the outer edge;
the inner part is laid off in beds for vegetables. This terrace is to be extended in length and another to be made
below it. The view it commands, is at present its greatest beauty. We afterwards walked round the first circuit.
There are 4 roads about 15 or 20 feet wide, cut round the
mountain from 100 to 200 feet apart. These circuits are
connected by a great many roads and paths and when
completed will afford a beautiful shady ride or walk of
seven miles. The first circuit is not quite a mile round,
as it is very near the top. It is in general shady, with
openings through the trees for distant views. We passed
the outhouses for the slaves and workmen. They are all
much better than I have seen on any other plantation, but
to an eye unaccustomed to such sights, they appear poor
and their cabins form a most unpleasant contrast with the
palace that rises so near them. Mr. J. has carpenters,

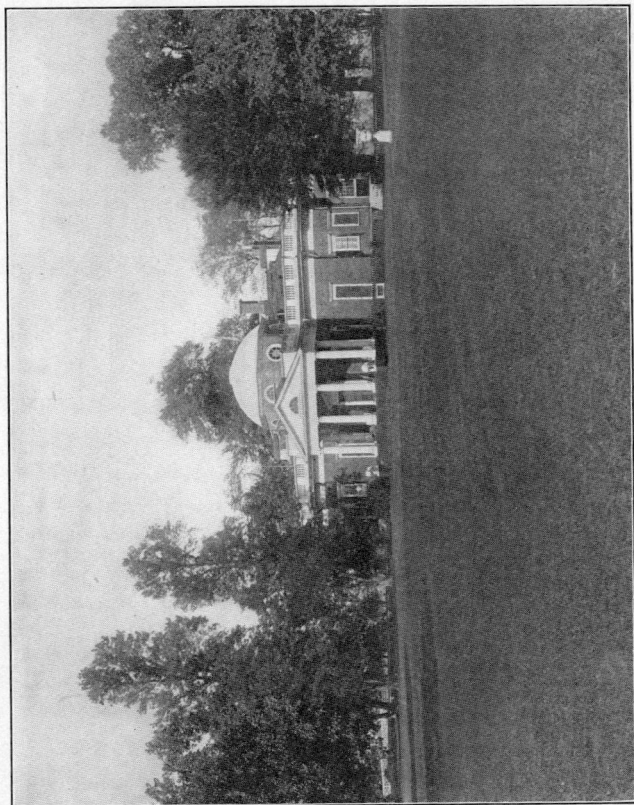

Monticello—South front.

cabinet-makers, painters, and blacksmiths and several other trades all within himself, and finds these slaves excellent workmen. As we walked, he explained his future designs. "My long absence from this place, has left a wilderness around me." "But you have returned," said I, "and the wilderness shall blossom like the rose and you, I hope, will long sit beneath your own vine and your own fig-tree." It was near dark when we reached the house; he led us into a little tea room which opened on the terrace and as Mrs. R. was still in her nursery he sat with us and conversed till tea time. We never drank tea until near nine, afterwards there was fruit, which he seldom staid to partake of, as he always retired immediately after tea. I never sat above an hour afterwards, as I supposed Mrs. R. must wish to be in her nursery. I rose the morning after my arrival very early and went out on the terrace, to contemplate scenery, which to me was so novel. The space between Monticello and the Allegany, from sixty to eighty miles, was covered with a thick fog, which had the appearance of the ocean and was unbroken except when wood covered hills rose above the plain and looked like islands. As the sun rose, the fog was broken and exhibited the most various and fantastic forms, lakes, rivers, bays, and as it ascended, it hung in white fleecy clouds on the sides of the mountains; an hour afterwards you would scarcely believe it was the same scene you looked on. In spite of the cold air from the mountains, I staid here until the first breakfast bell rang. Our breakfast table was as large as our dinner table; instead of a cloth, a folded napkin lay under each plate; we had tea, coffee, excellent muffins, hot wheat and corn bread, cold ham and butter. It was not exactly the Virginian breakfast I expected. Here indeed was the mode of living in general that of a Virginian planter.

At breakfast the family all assembled, all Mrs. R's. children eat at the family table, but are in such excellent order, that you would not know, if you did not see them, that a child was present.   After breakfast, I soon learned that it was the habit of the family each separately to pursue their occupations.   Mr. J. went to his apartments, the door of which is never opened but by himself and his retirement seems so sacred that I told him it was his sanctum sanctorum.   Mr. Randolph rides over to his farm and seldom returns until night; Mr. Bankhead who is reading law to his study; a small building at the end of the east terrace, opposite to Mr. Randolph's which terminates the west terrace; these buildings are called pavilions.   Jefferson R. went to survey a tract of woodland, afterwards make his report to his grand father.   Mrs. Randolph withdrew to her nursery and excepting the hours housekeeping requires she devotes the rest to her children, whom she instructs.   As for them, they seem never to leave her for an instant, but are always beside her or on her lap.

Visitors generally retire to their own rooms, or walk about the place; those who are fond of reading can never be at a loss, those who are not will some times feel wearied in the long interval between breakfast and dinner.   The dinner bell rings twice, the first collects the family in time to enter the room by the time the second announces dinner to be on table, which while I was there was between 4 and 5 oclock.   In summer the interval between rising from table and tea (9 oclock) may be agreeably passed in walking.   But to return to my journal.   After breakfast on Sunday morning, I asked Ellen to go with me on the top of the house; Mr. J. heard me and went along with us and pointed out those spots in the landscape most remarkable.   The morning was show'ry,

the clouds had a fine effect, throwing large masses of
shade on the mountain sides, which finely contrasted with
the sunshine of other spots.   He afterwards took us to
the drawing room, 26 or 7 feet diameter, in the dome.
It is a noble and beautiful apartment, with 8 circular windows and a sky-light.   It was not furnished and being
in the attic story is not used, which I thought a great pity,
as it might be made the most beautiful room in the house.
The attic chambers are comfortable and neatly finished
but no elegance.   When we descended to the hall, he
asked us to pass into the Library, or as I called it his
sanctum sanctorum, where any other feet than his own
seldom intrude.   This suit of apartments opens from the
Hall to the south.   It consists of 3 rooms for the library,
one for his cabinet, one for his chamber, and a green
house divided from the other by glass compartments and
doors; so that the view of the plants it contains, is unobstructed.   He has not yet made his collection, having but
just finished the room, which opens on one of the terraces.
He showed us everything he thought would please or interest us.   His most valuable and curious books—those
which contained fine prints etc.—among these I thought
the most curious were the original letters of Cortez to the
King of Spain, a vol of fine views of ancient villas around
Rome, with maps of the grounds, and minute descriptions
of the buildings and grounds, an old poem written by
Piers Plowman and printed 250 years ago; he read near
a page, which was almost as unintelligible as if it was
Hebrew; and some Greek romances.   He took pains to
find one that was translated into French, as most of them
were translated in Latin and Italian.   More than two
hours passed most charmingly away.   The library consists of books in all languages, and contains about twenty
thousand vols, but so disposed that they do not give the

idea of a great library. I own I was much disappointed
in its appearance, and I do not think with its numerous
divisions and arches it is as impressive as one large room
would have been. His cabinet and chamber contained
every convenience and comfort, but were plain. His bed
is built in the wall which divides his chamber and cabinet.
He opened a little closet which contains all his garden
seeds. They are all in little phials, labled and hung on
little hooks. Seeds such as peas, beans, etc. were in tin
cannisters, but everything labeled and in the neatest order.
He bade us take whatever books we wished, which we
did, and then retired to our own room. Here we amused
ourselves until dinner time excepting an hour I sat with
Mrs. R. by her sick baby, but as she was reading I did
not sit long. After dinner Ellen and Mr. Bankhead accompanied us in a long ramble in the mountain walks.
At dark when we returned, the tea room was still vacant;
I called Virgina and Mary (the age of my Julia and
Susan) amused myself with them until their grand papa
entered, with whom I had a long and interesting conversation; in which he described with enthusiasm his retirement from public life and the pleasures he found in
domestic.

Monday morning. I again rose early in order to ob-
serve the scenes around me and was again repaid for the
loss of sleep, by the various appearances the landscape
assumed as the fog was rising. But the blue and misty
mountains, now lighted up with sunshine, now thrown
into deep shadow, presented objects on which I gaze each
morning with new pleasure. After breakfast Mr. J.
sent E. to ask me if I would take a ride with him round
the mountain; I willing assented and in a little while I
was summoned; the carriage was a kind of chair, which
his own workmen had made under his direction, and it

Monticello—Entrance hall.

was with difficulty that he, Ellen and I found room in it, and might well be called the sociable. The first circuit, the road was good, and I enjoyed the views it afforded and the familiar and easy conversation, which our sociable gave rise to; but when we descended to the second and third circuit, fear took from me the power of listening to him, or observing the scene, nor could I forbear expressing my alarm, as we went along a rough road which had only been laid out, and on driving over fallen trees, and great rocks, which threatened an overset to our sociable and a roll down the mountains to us. "My dear madam," said Mr. J., "you are not to be afraid, or if you are you are not to show it; trust yourself implicitly to me, I will answer for your safety; I came every foot of this road yesterday, on purpose to see if a carriage could come safely; I know every step I take, so banish all fear." This I tried to do, but in vain, till coming to a road over which one wheel must pass I jumped out, while the servant who attended on horseback rode forward and held up the carriage as Mr. J. passed. Poor Ellen did not dare to get out. Notwithstanding the terror I suffered I would not have lost this ride; as Mr. J. explained to me all his plans for improvement, where the roads, the walks, the seats, the little temples were to be placed. There are two springs gushing from the mountain side; he took me to one which might be made very picturesque. As we passed the graveyard, which is about half way down the mountain, in a sequestered spot, he told me he there meant to place a small gothic building,—higher up, where a beautiful little mound was covered with a grove of trees, he meant to place a monument to his friend Wythe. We returned home by a road which did not wind round the mountain but carried us to the summit by a gentle ascent. It was a good road, and my terror vanished and I enjoyed conversation. I found Mrs. R. deeply engaged in the Wild Irish Boy sitting by the side of her little patient; I did not stay long to interrupt her, but finding Mrs. Bankhead likewise engaged with a book, I withdrew to my own room to read my Grecian romance. At dinner Mrs. Randolph sent an apology, she hurt her eye so badly, that it produced excessive inflamation and pain, which obliged her to go to bed. After dinner I went up to sit by her, Mr. J. came up soon after and I was delighted by his tender attentions to their dear daughter. As he sat by her and held her hand, for above an hour, we had a long social conversation in which Mrs. R. joined occasionally. After he had gone, finding her disposed to sleep, I went down. It was now quite dark and too late to walk, so I took my seat in the tea room with my little girls and told them stories till the tea bell again collected the family.

Tuesday. After breakfast I went up and sat all the morning by Mrs. Randolph; she was too unwell to rise; part of the time I read, but when we were alone, conversed. Our conversation turned chiefly on her father, and on her mentioning their correspondence, I begged her to show me some of his letters. This she willingly assented to and it was a rich repast to mind and heart. Some of them were written when he was minister in France and she in a convent. These are filled with the best advice in the best language. His letters come down to the last days of his political life; in every one he expresses his longings after retirement. She was so good as to give me one of these precious letters. When I went down stairs I found Mr. J. in the hall and Mr. S., and we had a long conversation on a variety of topics. He took us a charming walk round the edge of the lawn and showed us the spots from which the house appeared to most advantage. I looked upon him as he walked, the top of this mountain, as a being elevated above the mass of mankind, as much in character as he was in local situation. I reflected on the long career of public duties and stations through which he had passed, and that after forty years spent on the tempestuous sea of political life, he had now reached the haven of domestic life. Here while the storm roared at a distance, he could hear its roaring and be at peace. He had been a faithful labourer in the harvest field of life, his labours were crowned with success, and he had reaped a rich harvest of fame and wealth and honor. All that in this, his winter of life he may enjoy the harvest he has reaped. In him I perceive no decay of mind or debility of frame and to all the wisdom and experience of age, he adds the enthusiasm and ardour of youth. I looked on him with wonder as I heard him describe the improvements he designed in his grounds, they seemed to require a whole life to carry into effect, and a young man might doubt of ever completing or enjoying them. But he seems to have transposed his hopes and anticipations into the existence of his children. It is in them he lives, and I believe he finds as much delight in the idea that they will enjoy the fruit of his present labours, as if he hoped it for himself. If full occupation of mind, heart and hands, is happiness, surely he is happy. The sun never sees him in bed, and his mind designs more than the day can fulfil, even his long day. The conversation of the morning, the letters I had read, and the idea that this was the last day I was to spend in his society, the last time I was ever to see him, filled my heart with sadness. I could scarcely look at or speak to him without tears. After dinner he went to the carpenter's shop, to give directions for a walking seat he had ordered made for us, and I did not see him

again until after sun-set.   I spent the interval in walking
with Mr. Smith round the lawn and grave, and had just
parted from him to join the children to whom I had
promised another story, when as I passed the terrace, Mr.
J. came out and joined us. The children ran to him and
immediately proposed a race; we seated ourselves on the
steps of the Portico, and he after placing the children
according to their size one before the other, gave the
word for starting and away they flew; the course round
this back lawn was a qr. of a mile, the little girls were
much tired by the time they returned to the spot from
which they started and came panting and out of breath
to throw themselves into their grandfather's arms, which
were opened to receive them; he pressed them to his
bosom and rewarded them with a kiss; he was sitting on
the grass and they sat down by him, untill they were
rested; then they again wished to set off; he thought it too
long a course for little Mary and proposed running on the
terrace. Thither we went, and seating ourselves at one
end, they ran from us to the pavillion and back again;
"What an amusement," said I, "do these little creatures
afford us." "Yes," replied he, "it is only with them that a
grave man can play the fool." They now called on him
to run with them, he did not long resist and seemed delighted in delighting them. Oh ye whose envenomed
calumny has painted him as the slave of the vilest passions, come here and contemplate this scene! The simplicity, the gaiety, the modesty and gentleness of a child,
united to all that is great and venerable in the human
character. His life is the best refutation of the calumnies
that have been heaped upon him and it seems to me impossible, for any one personally to know him and remain
his enemy. It was dark by the time we entered the tea-
room. I was glad to close the windows and shut out the

Monticello—Salon.

keen air from the mountains. The mornings and evenings are here always cool and indeed Mrs. Randolph says it is never hot. As it was the last evening we were to pass here, Mr. J. sat longer than usual after tea. All the family except Mrs. Randolph were at tea. I gazed upon Mr. J. in the midst of this interesting circle and thought of the following lines, which I copied from one of his letters.

"When I look to the ineffable pleasures of my family society, I become more and more disgusted with the jealousies, the hatred, the rancourous and malignant passions of this scene, and lament my having ever again been drawn into public view. Tranquility is now my object; I have seen enough of political honors, to know they are but splendid torments; and however one might be disposed to render services on which many of their fellow citizens might set a value, yet when as many would deprecate them as a public calamity, one may well entertain a modest doubt of their real importance and feel the impulse of duty to be very weak," and again, in another of a later date, 1797 he says,

"Worn down here with pursuits in which I take no delight, surrounded by enemies and spies, catching and perverting every word which falls from my lips, or flows from my pen, and inventing where facts fail them, I pant for that society, where all is peace and harmony, where we love and are beloved by every object we see. And to have that intercourse of soft affections, hushed and suppressed by the eternal presence of strangers, goes very hard indeed, and the harder when we see that the candle of life is burning out and the pleasures we lose are lost forever. I long to see the time approach when I can be returning to you, tho' it be for a short time only—these are the only times existence is of any value to me, continue then to love me my ever dear daughter, and to be assured, that to yourself, your sister and those dear to you every thing in my life is directed, ambition has no hold upon me but through you, my personal affections would fix me forever with you. Kiss the dear little objects of our mutual love," etc. etc.

By these dear objects, I saw him now surounded. I saw him in the scenes for which his heart had panted, at the time when others looked upon his elevated station with envy, and did not know that these honors which his country lavished on him and which they envied, were splendid torments, to his unambitious spirit and affectionate heart. But why then it will be asked, did he not withdraw from public life? A satisfactory answer is often found in his letters; in one he says (it was while secretary) that he had made up his mind to retire, that he had arranged his affairs for it, but contrary to all his wishes he was persuaded by his friends of the necessity of remaining, that a retreat at that time would be attributed to timidity or fear of the attacks made by the papers and might ruin the party of which he was the head. In one of his letters he says—"The real difficulty is that once being delivered into the hands of others, where feelings are friendly to the individual and warm to the public cause; how to withdraw from them, without leaving a dissatisfaction in their minds and impressions of pusilanimity with the public." From many other passages of his letters, it is evident that his own wishes were subordinated to the remonstrances of his friends and to the wish of supporting the republican cause,—on which he sincerely and honestly believed the happiness of his country to depend.

After tea, fruit as usual was brought, of which he staid to partake; the figs were very fine and I eat them with greater pleasure from their having been planted rear'd and attended by him with peculiar care, which this year was rewarded with an abundant crop, and of which we every day enjoyed the produce.

Wednesday morning.   Mrs. Randolph was not able to come down to breakfast, and I felt too sad to join in the conversation.   I looked on every object around me, all was examined with that attention a last look inspires; the breakfast ended, our carriage was at the door, and I rose to bid farewell to this interesting family.   Mrs. R. came down to spend the last minutes with us, As I stood for a moment in the Hall, Mr. J. approached and in the most cordial manner urged me to make another visit the ensuing summer, I told him with a voice almost choked with tears, "that I had no hope of such a pleasure—this," said I, raising my eyes to him, "is the last time I fear in this world at least, that I shall ever see you—But there is another world."   I felt so affected by the idea of this last sight of this good and great man, that I turned away and hastily repeating my farewell to the family, gave him my hand, he pressed it affectionately as he put me in the carriage saying, "God bless you, dear madam.   God bless you."   "And God bless you," said I, from the very bottom of my heart.

Mr. Smith got in, the door shut and we drove from the habitation of philosophy and virtue.   How rapidly did we seem to descend that mountain which had seemed so tedious in its ascent, and the quick pulsations I then felt were now changed to a heavy oppression.

Yes, he is truly a philosopher, and truly a good man, and eminently a great one.   Then there is a tranquility about him, which an inward peace could alone bestow. As a ship long tossed by the storms of the ocean, casts anchor and lies at rest in a peaceful harbour, he is retired from an active and restless scene to this tranquil spot. Voluntarily and gladly has he resigned honors which he never sought, and unwillingly accepted. His actions, not his words, preach the emptiness and dissatisfaction attendant on a great office. His tall and slender figure is not impaired by age, tho' bent by care and labour. His white locks announce an age his activity, strength, health, enthusiasm, ardour and gaiety contradict. His face owes all its charm to its expression and intelligence; his features are not good and his complexion bad, but his countenance is so full of soul and beams with such benignity, that when the eye rests on his face, it is too busy in perusing its expression, to think of its features or complexion. His low and mild voice, harmonizes with his countenance rather than his figure. But his manners,—how gentle, how humble, how kind. His meanest slave must feel as if it were a father instead of a master who addressed him, when he speaks. To a disposition ardent, affectionate and communicative, he joins manners timid, even to bashfulness and reserved even to coldness. If his life had not proved to the contrary I should have pronounced him rather a man of imagination and taste, than a man of judgement, a literary rather than a scientific man, and least of all a politician, A character for which nature never seemed to have intended him, and for which the natural turn of mind, and his disposition, taste, and feeling equally unfit him. I should have been sure that this was the case, even had he not told me so. In an interesting conversation I had one evening—speaking of his past public and present domestic life—"The whole of my life," said he, "has been a war with my natural taste, feelings and wishes. Domestic life and literary pursuits, were my first and my latest inclinations, circumstances and not my desires lead me to the path I have trod. And like

a bow tho long bent, which when unstrung flies back to
its natural state, I resume with delight the character and
pursuits for which nature designed me.

"The circumstances of our country," continued he, "at
my entrance into life, were such that every honest man
felt himself compelled to take a part, and to act up to the
best of his abilities."

August 4th, Montpelier, Wendnesd even.

The sadness which all day hung on my spirits was
instantly dispelled by the cheering smile of Mrs. Madison
and the friendly greeting of our good President. It was
near five oclock when we arrived, we were met at the
door by Mr. M. who led us in to the dining room where
some gentlemen were still smoking segars and drinking
wine. Mrs. M. enter'd the moment afterwards, and after
embracing me, took my hand, saying with a smile, I will
take you out of this smoke to a pleasanter room. She
took me thro' the tea room to her chamber which opens
from it. Everything bespoke comfort, I was going to
take my seat on the sopha, but she said I must lay down
by her on her bed, and rest myself, she loosened my riding
habit, took off my bonnet, and we threw ourselves on
her bed. Wine, ice, punch and delightful pine-apples
were immediately brought. No restraint, no ceremony.
Hospitality is the presiding genius of this house, and
Mrs. M. is kindness personified. She enquired why I
had not brought the little girls; I told her the fear of
incomoding my friends. "Oh," said she laughing, "I
should not have known they were here, among all the
rest, for at this moment we have only three and twenty
in the house." "Three and twenty," exclaimed I! "Why
where do you store them?" "Oh we have house room in
plenty." This I could easily believe, for the house seemed

immense. It is a large two story house of 80 or 90 feet
in length, and above 40 deep. Mrs. Cutts soon came in
with her sweet children, and afterwards Mr. Madison,
Cutts, and Mr. Smith. The door opening into the tea
room being open, they without ceremony joined their
wives. They only peeked in on us; we then shut the
door and after adjusting our dress, went out on the
Piazza—(it is 60 feet long). Here we walked and talked
until called to tea, or rather supper, for tho' tea hour, it
was supper fare. The long dining table was spread, and
besides tea and coffee, we had a variety of warm cakes,
bread, cold meats and pastry. At table I was introduced
to Mr. William Madison,[1] brother to the President, and
his wife, and three or four other ladies and gentlemen all
near relatives, all plain country people, but frank, kind,
warm-hearted Virginians. At this house I realized being
in Virginia, Mr. Madison, plain, friendly, communicative,
and unceremonious as any Virginia Planter could be—
Mrs. Madison, uniting to all the elegance and polish of
fashion, the unadulterated simplicity, frankness, warmth,
and friendliness of her native character and native state.
Their mode of living, too, if it had more elegance than
is found among the planters, was characterized by that
abundance, that hospitality, and that freedom, we are
taught to look for on a Virginian plantation. We did not
sit long at this meal—the evening was warm and we were
glad to leave the table. The gentlemen went to the
piazza, the ladies, who all had children, to their chambers,
and I sat with Mrs. M. till bed time talking of Washington. When the servant appeared with candles to show
me my room, she insisted on going up stairs with me,
assisted me to undress and chatted till I got into bed.
How unassuming, how kind is this woman. How can

---

[1] Of Woodbury Forest, about six miles from Montpelier.

Montpelier.

Madison's home near Richmond, Virginia.

any human being be her enemy. Truly, in her there is
to be found no gall, but the pure milk of human kindness.
If I may say so, the maid was like the mistress; she was
very attentive all the time I was there, seeming as if she
could not do enough, and was very talkative. As her
mistress left the room, "You have a good mistress Nany,"
said I, "Yes," answered the affectionate creature with
warmth, "the best I believe in the world,—I am sure I
would not change her for any mistress in the whole
country." The next morning Nany called me to a late
breakfast, brought me ice and water, (this is universal
here, even in taverns) and assisted me to dress. We sat
down between 15 and 20 persons to breakfast—and to a
most excellent Virginian breakfast—tea, coffee, hot wheat
bread, light cakes, a pone, or corn loaf—cold ham, nice
hashes, chickens, etc.

TO MRS. KIRKPATRICK

[Washington.]   Sunday 6th, 1810.

. . . . Since we came, we have seen a great deal
of company; I went to the drawing room one evening,
and spent a few hours most charmingly seeing and talking to at least 50 people I had not seen for a year, but the
salutations of no one pleased me half so well as those of
Mr. Quinsey,[1] the moment he saw me, he approached with
so smiling and friendly a countenance that I involun-
tarily stretched out my hand which he cordially shook;
we conversed a long while but the subject of Miss Lowels
death affected him so much that he abruptly left me,
twas not long after, I saw him approach Mr. Smith, shake
hands and then stand and converse with him. I cannot

[1] Josiah Quincy, of Massachusetts, a bitter Federalist, the first man to
suggest secession in Congress.

describe to you my dear Maria the sensation of pleasure
this sight afforded me, but you who knew my anxiety on
the subject, may judge of it.   He told Mr. Smith that
he wished to ride out with him to Sidney to collect petri-
faction; in fine having once broken the ice, no shadow of
reserve remained.   The next day Mr Smith called on
him and the day after he came here Mr. S. was not at
home but he came up to our parlour; it was at the moment
my alarm for Bayard was first excited.   Mrs. Clay was
sitting with me preparing some wine-drops, while her
woman was heating water to bathe him.   He would not
sit long and I have not seen him since; but if he does not
again call, I mean to send and ask him to tea—I relate
this first, as the most pleasant circumstance that has occurred since my arrival.   At the drawing-room Fanny
Clifton sat most of the time by me, she enquired particularly after you.

.   .   .   .   .

After the drawing room evening I did not again leave
the house and scarcely the room, until new-years day,
when Mrs. Clay persuaded me to go to the levee, and
as on the drawing room evening, made her nurse attend
to Bayard.   As for the poor girls, the regular lessons I
planned to give them are out of the question, for as I
said before Bayard[1] and company break through all reg-
ularity, and they have had but one or two lessons; if
Mr. S. would let me I should immediately send them to
school, for under present circumstances joined to the
prospect before me, I do not see how I can possibly teach
them.

We have a large company in this house—Mr. and Mrs.
Mumford,[2] Mr. and Mrs. Clay, (Henry Clay the admired

[1] Mrs. Smith's son, who was then an infant a few months old.
[2] Gurdon S. Mumford, Representative from New York.

orator,) and a number of gentlemen the Vice-President, and John Law [1] you know. I have formed habits of sociability with Mr. and Mrs. Clay only—Mrs. Clay is a woman of strong natural sense, very kind and friendly. She often brings work of an evening into our room and in the morning I go to hers—we help each other dress and she always offers us seats in her carriage when we visit together,—or go a shopping, and her woman who has been the nurse of all her children, attends to mine whenever I wish it. With the rest I have little intercourse except at breakfast and dinner. Our parlour is as retired as if in our own house. We have our tea table set as regularly and as comfortably as at home, and Mrs. Wilson endeavors in every way to make us comfortable. She always sends up a snack for the children and myself between dinner and breakfast, and whenever I want it for supper. After the children go to bed I generally sew and if I want company I have only to go down stairs, where there is generally a large circle. I have only passed one evening down below and that was to play chess. We have a great chess player here, Mr. Marke from New York—he is invincible. He is a most amiable young [man] and I like him the better for being the intimate acquaintance of our friends in New York. I yesterday morning visited Miss Lansdale, now Mrs. Sprigg, her wedding will give rise to a great many parties. We are asked to two for the ensuing week, but I feel no inclination to go.

Mrs. Craven is a near neighbor and has been already very neighborly. Poor Margaret Wingate is still pursued by new misfortunes. Her husband has broken through all arrangements made for him here and gone to New England without any ones knowing when, or if ever

[1] Son of Thomas Law by his first wife.

he will return.   We yesterday dined with a large party at
Mr. Galatin's, it was a very pleasant party and it would
do your heart good to see Mrs. Montgomery so fat, and
rosy, and cheerful and good humour'd.   I never admired
or liked her half as well.

I wish I could do more justice to your letters my dear
sisters, for this time excuse me and I will try and do better
hereafter.   But I make no promises, I have ever given up
resolutions, for I find myself so irresistibly carried down
the current of circumstance and not piloted by reason.   I
feel every way better since our removal to town and
never was more sensible to the beneficial effects of society.
I had grown dull and out of humour with myself, in a
solitude where I had nothing to divert the irksome-
ness of indisposition.   Adieu my dearest sisters, in every
mutation, in every vicissitude I am without change, yours
most affectionately

TO MRS. KIRKPATRICK

[Sidney, Summer of 1811]

.   .   .   .   Monday.   For the last 10 days I have resumed my ordinary occupations and feel as descending
from an ideal existence to the realities of life.   We have
had many more visitors than usual, my acquaintance have
been very kind and attentive, but above all the rest Mrs.
Clay.   She is what you call a good woman, but has no
qualities of mind to attract,—none of the heart to en-
dear.   She is a most devoted mother, and to sew for her
children her chief, almost exclusive occupation.   She
has no taste for fashionable company or amusements, and
is a thousand times better pleased, sitting in the room
with all her children round her, and a pile of work by
her side, than in the most brilliant drawing room.   She
has shown more affection and kindness of disposition,

since my sickness, than I believed her capable of. She is always showing me and mine some attention, takes me out in her carriage whenever I will go, wishes me to be often with her. Ann and Julia have just return'd after passing a week with her. She trim'd their bonnets for them from her own store of ribands, and bought Susan a handsome present on her birth-day. This was on Thursday last and was without exception the most agreeable celebration we ever had. Mr. Cutting intended to have given us a fète champètre, at the old Cottage in the afternoon, and I was to have given the dinner, but a showery morning disappointed him. But that the abundant preparations he had made, might still be as much his party as possible, I had a table with benches round it in the front Piazza, to which we removed after dinner to eat our desert, and which we called going to Mrs. Cutting's party. Pine apples, oranges, cakes, sugar plumbs nuts figs &c &c adorn'd with the gayest flowers and lilies in abundance; to which elegant repast (for such it really was) I added nothing but ice-creams. Mrs. Clay and her six children, two sons of Mr. Lowndes, whom he has left here at school, and Mr. and Mrs. Cutting making 20 including our family, were all the company. They came out early and amused themselves rifling my flower borders, and making wreaths. Mrs. Clay was as much engaged as any of the children and as much delighted and she and I were as gaily deck'd as the girls. The boys too had their wreaths, some of oak and some of myrtle. My dear Lytleton,[1] I must call him so, for he feels like my own son, quite charm'd every one, he was the very spirit of the frolic and we were all so familiar, Mrs. Clay calling him Lytleton and treating him with the same familiarity as I did. Ann Clay is half in

George Littleton Kirkpatrick, her nephew.

love with him. I wish in all soberness time would ripen this inclination, what a charming match it would be. She is not too young for him. Now Mary[1] will laugh at this and at me. When Mr. Tracy, (who was an important personage on the occasion) brought the cart to the door Lytleton and all the boys jump'd in it and went to the woods for boughs. L. drove furiously along to the no small delight of the boys and soon return'd like the moving wood in Macbeth. The Piazza was soon transform'd into a bower,—every hand was busy,—Mrs. Clay, Mr. Smith and all. When the sun was completely excluded, the Pianno was placed at one end of the large piazza and the sopha at the other, and a table on which the big bowl (which is used only on grand occasions) the birth day cake crown'd with lilies and roses and fruit was placed, and we drank punch, and eat cake, till they all felt in a good humour for dancing. Mrs. Clay was the musician and the company with their gay wreaths in this bower appear'd very pretty and romp'd rather than danced till a late dinner. The day clos'd without finding any one weary and the little company dispersed, feeling what in this world is so uncommon, that their expectations of pleasure had been realized. Ann and Susan go into the city tonight with Mrs. Cutting to pass a week. I spend tomorrow with Mrs. Clay, in riding about and visiting. I feel very sensibly the want of a carriage and would as Mary used to say rather have our old one than none. This latter part of my letter is for her. So altho' you will pay double postage, it will be no more than if the sheets had been separately directed. I wish my dear sister if our carriage has not left Newark, Brother John[2] would put his horses in and bring you here.

[1] Mrs. Kirkpatrick's eldest daughter.
[2] John Murray Bayard, the elder brother, who lived eight miles from New Brunswick.

TO MRS. KIRKPATRICK

[Sidney] Tuesday, July 20, 1813.

. . . . I every day from the time I received Maria's, intended writing to press you to come on and pass a few weeks or more with us and to bring Fanny and Elizabeth. I believed such a jaunt might be highly serviceable to you all. But it is now out of the question and will be so while the British are such near neighbours and continue to menace us. Until the late alarm I have never been able to realize our being in a state of war; but now when such active preparations are made, when so many of our citizens and particular acquaintance have marched to meet the enemy, I not only believe but feel the unhappy state of our country. Mr. Seaton and Mr. Gales[1] are both with our troops at Warburton, and Mrs. Seaton and Miss Gales anxiety naturally excites ours. It is generally believed impossible for the English to reach the city, not so much from our force at Warburton, tho' that is very large, as from the natural impediments; the river being very difficult of navigation. Every precaution has been taken to ensure the safety of the city. Fort Warburton is in a state of perfect defence and our troops are each day augmented by hundreds and thousands from the adjoining country who come pouring in. The presence of Genl. Armstrong and Col. Monroe animates and invigorates our soldiers. And our little army is full of ardour and enthusiasm. Mr. Gales and Seaton have each been up to look after the paper and give a most interesting and animating picture of the scene. There is so little apprehension of danger in the city, that not a

[1] They were brothers-in-law and edited *The National Intelligencer* from 1812 to 1860, when Gales died. Gales acquired the paper from Mr. Smith in 1810.

single removal of person or goods has taken place,—a
number of our friends have desired leave to send their
trunks here and a number have determined to come themselves, should the British effect a passage by the fort, so
you see we are esteemed quite out of danger.   As for our
enemy *at home* I have no doubt that they will if possible
join the British; here we are, I believe firmly in no danger, as the aim of those in the country would be as
quickly as possible to join those in the city and the few
scatter'd s———s about our neighbourhood, could not
muster force enough to venture on an attack.[1]   We have
however counted on the possibility of danger and Mr. S.
has procured pistols &c &c sufficient for our defence, and
we make use of every precaution which we should use
were we certain of what we now only reckon a possibility.
In the city and George town the gentlemen who by their
age or other circumstances are exempted from service,
have formed volunteer companies both of horse and foot,
who nightly patrol the streets.   The members of congress have determined to join the citizens, in case of an
attack and there are many old experienced officers
amongst them.   The affair of Hampton,[2] which I dis-
believed until the publication in the Intelligencer, inspires us with a terror we should not otherwise have felt.
There were 300 French men at that attack and it was
chiefly these wretches who perpetrated these horrors.
Their intention was to desert to our side and they
march'd near to our militia with a view to surrender, but
were fired on and so obliged to fight in their own defence,
—20 did desert and are now at the fort.   The French
prisoners taken from the English jails, will it is supposed, and the Irish likewise all desert the moment they

[1] Wherever there were slaves there was terror of their insurrection.
[2] The village of Hampton, Va., was sacked June 25, 1813, by the British
and given over to pillage and rapine by Cockburn's orders.

are landed. Mrs. Seaton behaves with admirable self
command, I quite admire her composure and serenity, as
I am certain loving as she loves her amiable husband,
it must require great effort. We one and all resist the
intrusion of useless anxiety and alarm. We go on regularly with our every day occupations. I spend the
morning in my family affairs and school. Ann sits with
our guests and after dinner we all assemble and while
the rest sew, Miss Gales reads some amusing book. If
we did not resolutely adhere to this plan of occupation our
fancy would augment our fears and we should be sad
enough. As it is we are quite animated, each strength-
ens the resolution of the other and since we have been so
well provided with fire arms, my apprehensions have
quite ceased. *For those whom I fear'd are easily intimidated.* Mr. Smith has this morning gone in to the Bank,
and Mrs. Seaton and Miss Gales, to see Mr. Seaton who
has come up to arrange the paper. If Susan is with you,
read or show her this letter as you think proper, or if at
Princeton and you think it may allay her anxiety, please
to send it. Ann is quite a Heroine. She makes no protes-
tations but her cheerfulness and freedom from unnecessary alarm shows that she is not easily intimidated.
She is a dear good girl. I love her every day more and
more. And if danger comes, I shall not think of or
risque more for my children than her. We expect Mrs.
Clay, her sister Mrs. Brown, Mrs. Cutting and many
others to come to us in case of a serious alarm. At
present all the members and citizens say it is impossible
for the enemy to ascend the river, and our home enemy
will not assail us, if they do not arrive. . . .

TO MRS. KIRKPATRICK

[Sidney,] August 2d, 1813.

. . . . An agreeable change in our affairs, has produced a delightful change in my feelings. Mr. S. has received an appointment[1] to a new and most respectable office, which will enable us to pass our winters in the city. I cannot describe what a revolution it has produced in my feelings. I now feel no dread of the winter. . . . . New scenes, new objects, new characters, will carry our thoughts and feelings abroad; we shall have something to think of and feel for besides ourselves. . . . . I expect in many ways this change will be highly beneficial to our sisters and children. For Mr. Smith and myself we were quite contented and happy, tho' both of us still retain a sufficient relish for society, to be pleased with prospects of passing a few months of the year in the city.

It was a most unlooked for affair, and offer'd by Mr. Madison in the most flattering and obliging manner. It was quite as much of a surprise to Mr. S. as to myself. We had laid all our plans in the country for the next 3 or 4 years, and some serious regret mingles with the pleasure Mr. Smith feels. He took very great delight in his rural occupations and was healthier and happier than I have ever known him. But the interests of the family conquered every selfish feeling. . . .

[1] Commissioner of the Revenue. He held the office till it was abolished by law.

TO MRS. KIRKPATRICK

[Washington] Feb. 13th, 1814.

. . . . Yesterday Mrs. Clay passed the day with us. She brought her children,—in the evening some gentlemen dropped in and we were unusually gay, the children danced, Mrs. Clay and Mr. Taylor[1] sang for them while they danced, then Mr. Smith and Mr. Fisk[2] played checkers, Ann and Mrs. Stevens chess, Susan and I sewed,—this easy, social, gay manner of passing the evening is better than a ball. After the children were tired of dancing, Mr. Taylor (of New York) took up Marmion which lay beside him, and read the first introduction, with all the enthusiasm of a poet, which I am told he is. You will occasionally see his speeches in the paper and will judge whether the talents ascribed him, are justly so or not. He is by far the most agreeable new acquaintance we have made. All our new appointments have been surprises. 8 years ago G. W. Campbell[3] addressed Eliza Bell, who rejected him. She was very ambitious and he then an obscure member of Congress. Mr. S. then said, If it is greatness she desires, she will repent her refusal, for I predict that G. W. C. will attain great eminence, and may one day be our President. This he said from an intimate knowledge of his talents. He has ever since silently but surely been adding to his influence and usefulness and has for some time been looked up to as the head of the republican party in the senate.

Mr. Bacon is an old acquaintance of ours, he is a man of great financial talents and always very respectable on

---

[1] John W. Taylor, a Representative, subsequently Speaker of the House.
[2] Jonathan Fisk, of Newburgh, N. Y., a Representative.
[3] Of Tennessee. He had just resigned from the Senate to be Secretary of the Treasury.

the floor of congress.[1]   Mr. Rush[2] has risen early and unexpectedly, but I am mistaken if he does not aspire to still
higher dignities.   His manners are extremely concilia-
tory and popular, his father's over again.   The dear
children are all well.   Susan and Julia I fear make little
progress at school, dancing excepted.   We have no good
schools here.   .   .   .

TO MRS. KIRKPATRICK

Washington.   March 13, 1814.

.   .   .   .   When I first came to the city, I found myself almost as much a stranger as I did 12 yrs ago, and
when I recalled to mind that society which had so often
circled round our fireside and beheld them scatter'd over
the world, separated by the waves of the Atlantic, some
by the ocean of eternity, sadness and sorrow mingled with
the pleasure of recollection.   Altho' destitute of those
strong and tender ties with which affection and friendship bind me to other places, Washington possesses a
peculiar interest and to an active, reflective, and ambitious mind, has more attractions than any other place
in America.   This interest is daily increasing, and with
the importance and expansion of our nation, this is the
theatre on which its most interesting interests are discuss'd, by its ablest sons, in which its greatest characters
are called to act, it is every year, more and more the
resort of strangers from every part of the union, and all
foreigners of distinction who visit these states, likewise
visit this city.   There are here peculiar facilities for
forming acquaintances, for a stranger cannot be long
here, before it is generally known.   The house of repre-

[1] Ezekiel Bacon, of Massachusetts, Comptroller of the Treasury.
[2] Richard Rush, the Attorney General, son of Benjamin Rush, the Signer.

View of the east front of the President's house, with the addition of the north and south porticos.

From a drawing made in 1807 by B. H. Latrobe, surveyor of the public buildings, Washington.

sentatives is the lounging place of both sexes, where acquaintance is as easily made as at public amusements. And the drawing-room,—that centre of attraction,—affords opportunity of seeing all these whom fashion, fame, beauty, wealth or talents, have render'd celebrated. It has this winter been generally very much crowded, seldom has the company been less than 2 or 300, and generally more. I cannot tell you what an interest is imparted to this assembly by the entrance of some celebrated personage. I was there the evening of Perry's first appearance and had some interesting conversation. The last evening we were there, the room was empty, there were not above 50 or 60 persons,—after tea we adjourned to the music room, which is comparatively small, 3 or 4 sophas surrounded the fire and we form'd quite a social circle. I have not this winter passed a more agreeable evening. Ann, who has been long kept at home, was very much admired and really looked very beautiful. Mr. Ogilvie, who is quite the Ton here and Mr. Forsythe,[1] the universal favorite of the wise men, and fashionable women, were quite devoted to her. For myself, seated in one corner of a sopha, conversation with 4 or 5 agreeable and intelligent men pass'd the time most pleasantly away. Mr. Forsythe promises to be one of our most distinguished men, he is now allowed to be the greatest orator on the floor of congress. You may perhaps recollect him and his brother at Princeton. I knew him there and we have lately renewed our acquaintance. He is a young man of genius, fine taste, a most animated, engaging, prepossessing countenance; most attractive manners, Ann says *winning*. I am afraid he will be spoiled,—he is so much carress'd and admired, particularly by the girls,

---

[1] John Forsyth was then a Representative from Georgia, later a Senator, Minister to Spain and Secretary of State under General Jackson.

who think because he is a married man, they need not
conceal the pleasure his charming conversation affords.
The debates in congress have this winter been very attractive to the ladies. Mr. Ingersol,[1] is among the number of orators most admired. But Mr. Pinckney[2] carries the palm from all the congressional orators, Forsythe
excepted. His resignation of his office, seems to have
added to his popularity, and animated him in his pro-
fessional pursuits. Never have his talents been displayed
with such power and brilliancy. Curiosity led me
against my judgement, to join the female crowd who
throng the [Supreme] court room. A place in which I
think women have no business. The effect of female
admiration and attention has been very obvious, but it
is a doubt to me whether it has been beneficial, indeed I
believe otherwise. A member told me he doubted not,
there had been much more speaking on this account, and
another gentleman told me, that one day Mr. Pinckney
had finished his argument and was just about seating himself when Mrs. Madison and a train of ladies enter'd,—he
recommenced, went over the same ground, using fewer
arguments, but scattering more flowers. And the day
I was there I am certain he thought more of the female
part of his audience than of the court, and on concluding,
he recognized their presence, when he said, "He would
not weary the court, by going thro a long list of cases to
prove his argument, as it would not only be fatiguing to
them, but inimical to the laws of good taste, which *on
the present occasion,* (bowing low) he wished to obey."
The court was crowded while he spoke; the moment he sat
down, the whole audience arose, and broke up, as if the

---

[1] Charles I. Ingersoll, of Philadelphia, a Representative.
[2] William Pinkney, of Maryland (Mrs. Smith spells the name wrong; the
Pinckneys being the South Carolina family), had just resigned the Attorney
Generalship.

court had adjourn'd.   The women here are taking a station in society which is not known elsewhere.   On every public occasion, a launch, an oration, an inauguration, in the court, in the representative hall, as well as the drawing room, they are treated with mark'd distinction.   Last night Mr. Ogilvie while he censured the frivolous, elevated the rest of our sex, not only to an equality but I think to a superiority to the other sex.   I think the manners here different from those in other places.   At the drawing room, at our parties, few ladies ever sit.   Our rooms are always so crowded, that few more could find a place in the rooms, the consequence is, the ladies and gentlemen stand and walk about the rooms, in mingled groups, which certainly produces more ease, freedom and equality than in these rooms where the ladies sit and wait for gentlemen to approach to converse.

Tuesday morning.   I resume my pen, and as Mr. Stevens who was here last evening inform'd me he was going in a few days, I will scribble on, hoping to amuse, even at the risque of wearying you.   Mr. Ogilvie has this moment left us, he found Susan, Ann, Mrs. Cutting and myself busied with our needles; he brought a new work of Lord Byron's the "Bride of Abydos,"—he would not read it to us, but presented it to Ann who in return is hemming him some cravats.   I think you would have agreed with him in his criticisms, which tho' it approved the harmony and fancy of the poet, condemn'd the principles, sentiments, misanthrophy and morbid sensibility of the man.   In speaking of true sensibility, (that which feels for others as for ourselves) he said it was like the bee, which tho' it cull'd sweets from everything in creation, carried a sting with it.   Last evening after dining *en famille* at the Presidents he came here with Mr. Jones,[1]

[1] Probably Charles Jones.

one of our most respectable citizens, in wealth, talents
and station. John G. Jackson,[1] Mr. Stevens and other
gentlemen were here. The conversation took a charming turn and it was half past twelve, e'er we thought it
ten. Mr. O. never recites in private, as he used to, but
his witicisms are instructive and amusing. I know not
whether he can be called a man of original genius, but
he is certanly one of highly cultivated taste, a man of
great research, not only in classical learning, but in natural history, philosophy and morals. Whatever his own
opinions are, respecting religion I know not, but I have
never heard him in public or private, utter a sentiment
that could wound or offend the most pious. We are
going this evening to hear his recitations. How much
more rational these amusements than our balls or parties.
He receives the most flattering attentions and is not a
day disengaged. . . .

TO MRS. KIRKPATRICK

Brookville. [Md.,]   August, [1814.]

On Sunday we received information that the British
nad debark'd at Benedict. They seem'd in no haste to
approach the city, but gave us time to collect our troops.
The alarm was such that on Monday a general removal
from the city and George Town took place. Very few
women or children remain'd in the city on Tuesday evening, altho' the accounts then received were that the
enemy were retreating. Our troops were eager for an
attack and such was the cheerful alacrity they display'd,
that a universal confidence reign'd among the citizens and
people. Few doubted our conquering. On Tuesday we
sent off to a private farm house all our linen, clothing and

[1] Representative from Virginia.

other movable property, in the afternoon Dr. Bradley's family came from the city and took tea with us,—the Dr. said several citizens from the camp brought information of the enemy's remaining quiet at N. Marlborough, but that 3 of the volunteer companies, ———,[1] Davidsons and Peters were order'd to attack the Pickets and draw the B—— on to a general engagement.   This was the last news; until we were roused on Tuesday night by a loud knocking,—on the opening of the door, Willie Bradley called to us, "The enemy are advancing, our own troops are giving way on all sides and are retreating to the city.   Go, for Gods sake go."[2]   He spoke in a voice of agony, and then flew to his horse and was out of sight in a moment.   We immediately rose, the carriage and horses were soon ready, we loaded a wagon with what goods remained and about 3 oclock left our house with all our servants, the women we sent to some private farm houses at a safe distance, while we pursued our course. I felt no alarm or agitation, as I knew the danger was not near.   I even felt no distress at the idea of forsaking our home.   I could not realize the possibility of the B. gaining possession of the city, or of our army being defeated. We travel'd very slowly and as it was dark I walk'd part of the way.   Ann was equally composed.   At sunrise we stop'd to breakfast at Miss Carrol's and then pursued our journey.   The girls were quite delighted with our flight, novelty has such charms at their age, that even the exchange of comfort and peace, for suffering and distress, has its charms.   Even for myself, I felt animated, invigorated, willing to encounter any hardship, calmly to meet any danger, patiently to bear any difficulty.   I suffer'd considerable pain during the ride, and fear'd every moment being taken ill, but happily I was not, and we

[1] Illegible.   [2] The battle took place August 24.

all reach'd this place at one oclock in perfect health. We received a most kind reception from Mrs. Bently, and excellent accommodations. The appearance of this village is romantic and beautiful, it is situated in a little valley totally embosom'd in woody hills, with a stream flowing at the bottom on which are mills. In this secluded spot one might hope the noise, or rumour of war would never reach. Here all seems security and peace! Happy people may you never be obliged to fly from this peaceful spot, which now affords so hospitable a shelter to our poor citizens!

Thursday morning. This morning on awakening we were greeted with the sad news, that our city was taken, the bridges and public buildings burnt, our troops flying in every direction. Our little army totally dispersed. Good God, what will be the event! This moment a troop of horse have enter'd, they were on the field of battle, but not engag'd. Major Ridgely[1] their commander, disapproving Genl. Winder's order, refused to obey, left the army and is taking his troops home. E. Riggs, who was likewise there has given us a sad detail. He was in Loughbourough's, who with ten men form'd a reconnoitering party, and Riggs was employed in carrying messages from Winder. His account was that the first skirmish was near Marlborough, where Peters, Davidson's and Strul's (?) companies were ordered to attack the enemies picquets, but on finding how inefficient their force were, order'd to retreat, which they did in great disorder. Winder finding the enemy marching on the Bladensburg turnpike, forsook the posts he had taken and march'd towards the city, where they station'd themselves on the hills near Bladensburg bridge. The enemy march'd on in solid column and attack'd with coolness,

[1] One of the Maryland militia officers.

and order.   The 5th regiment from Baltimore commenced the attack and stood their ground firmly, but for
a short time only, they were almost destroy'd and our
whole troops gave way and began a disor'd retreat.   The
President who was on the ground, escap'd and has gone
into Virginia.   *Winder* with all the men he can collect
are at the court house.   He has directed our poor broken
militia to make the best of their way to Baltimore.   Every
hour the poor wearied and terrified creatures are passing
by the door.   Mrs. Bently kindly invites them in to rest
and refresh.   Major Ridgely's troop of horse all break-
fasted in town, that not a man was left to breakfast in the
tavern.   Ann and I hasten'd to assist Mrs. B. in getting
their breakfast,—and Julia and Susan wanted to do
something, help'd to set the table, &c.

Noon.   We were much alarm'd by Mr. Milligan, who
called and told Mr. Smith, Genl. Winder had ordered him
to come here for an express, that Montgomery C. H.
was burnt by the British, who were then on their march
for Frederick.   But a person who knew him assured us
he was crazy, his account afterwards proved untrue, as
a great many have passed since.   Our men look pale
and feeble but more with affright than fatigue,—they
had thrown away their muskets and blankets.

Just as we were going to dinner, a tremendous gust
arose, it has broken the trees very much, in the midst of
it, a wagon came to the door with a family going they
knew not whither.   Poor wanderers.   Oh how changed
are my feelings, my confidence in our troops is gone, they
may again be rallied, but it will require a long apprentice-
ship to make them good soldiers.   Oh my sister how
gloomy is the scene.   I do not suppose Government will
ever return to Washington.   All those whose property
was invested in that place, will be reduced to poverty.

Mr. Smith had invested a large portion of his in bridge stock,—both the bridges are destroy'd,—it serves to beguile the time to write, so my dear sister I will write a kind of journal to you, and send it when I can. I wish you to keep it. If better times come, it will serve to remind me of these.

Thursday evening. Our anxiety has been kept alive the whole day. Our poor men are coming in some two or three, sometimes a dozen at a time, just now another troop of horse have come in, they have not been in the engagement, as they did not arrive until a retreat had been order'd. Mr. Carr one of the clerks of the Bank was here just now and has given us the most correct account we have yet had. Our position was a bad one, so placed that neither the artillery or cavalry could act. Barney[1] took a position on a hill, the enemy had to pass and as they ascended rak'd them prodigiously but they never halted one moment, but marched on in solid mass, disregarding the dead bodies that fell before them. Barney and his men did not leave their cannons until they were within 5 yrds, then spik'd them and retreated,— Barney badly wounded. They [the enemy] never left the turnpike but enter'd the city after our retreating army. They first march'd to the navy yard which is wholly consumed; then to Capitol Hill. They had great difficulty in firing the capitol, several houses on the hill were burnt by cinders from the Capitol, but none by design, the President's house, the Potomac bridge, and all the other public buildings. Mr. Lee went to their camp at Marlborough (as a citizen unmolested) conversed with the officers, several of whom he had known in London. They told him that resistance would be vain; that in-

[1] Captain Joshua Barney, U. S. N., was the only man who reaped glory in this, the greatest disgrace to American arms.

The President's house, Washington, after the conflagration of August 24, 1814.

stead of 7000, they wished we had 40,000 militia, as it would make the greater confusion. They bade Mr. Lee tell the citizens that private property would not be injured, if the houses were not deserted, or private persons molested, that they intended to destroy the public buildings and shipping, and then to march to Baltimore on one side while Lord Hill with his fleet would attack it by water. I left our house with reluctance, but when I urged Mr. Smith to let me remain to protect the house, he would not hear of it, his duty called him away, and my situation being so critical, he said no consideration would induce him to leave me, for altho' the troops when under their officers might behave well, yet small parties or drunken soldiers might alarm or injure me in my present situation. And Ann declared she would not leave me if she were to die by my side. I had therefore to yield. I am afraid the consequence of leaving the house empty will be its destruction. Our house in the city too is unprotected and contains our most valuable furniture. In a week more and we may be penniless! for I count little on the continuance of Mr. S.'s salary. God only knows when the executive government will again be organized. But I can say with truth, the individual loss of property, has not given me a moment's uneasiness. But the state of our country, has wrung tears of anguish from me. I trust it will only be momentary. We are naturally a brave people and it was not so much fear, as prudence which caused our retreat. Too late they discovered the dispreparation of our troops. The enemy were 3 to 1. Their army composed of conquering veterans, ours of young mechanics and farmers, many of whom had never before carried a musket. But we shall learn the dreadful, horrid trade of war. And they will make us a martial people, for never, never will

Americans give up their liberty. But before that time comes, what sufferings, what reverses, what distress must be suffer'd. Already, in one night, have hundreds of our citizens been reduced from affluence to poverty, for it is not to be expected W—— will ever again be the seat of Govt. Last night the woods round the city and G. T—— were filled with women and children and old men and (r flying troops. One poor woman, after wandering all night, found at day light she wander'd 10 miles, —a lady in our neighbourhood, the wife of one of Mr. S.'s clerks, went out of her senses, her son was in the army. Mrs. Genl. Mason,[1] that lovely woman whom you knew, is likewise laying dangerously ill. Her husband was in the engagement and her anxiety has render'd a common fever dangerous. I am going tomorrow to see her.

Night, 10 oclock. The street of this quiet village, which never before witnessed confusion, is now fill'd with carriages bringing out citizens, and Baggage waggons and troops. Mrs. Bently's house is now crowded, she has been the whole evening sitting at the supper table, giving refreshment to soldiers and travellers. I suppose every house in the village is equally full. I never saw more benevolent people. "It is against our principles," said she this morning, "to have anything to do with war, but we receive and relieve all who come to us." The whole settlement are quakers. The table is just spread for the 4th or 5th time, more wanderers having just enter'd.

I know not when you will get this letter. I suppose the mail will be impeded. How is Maria,—is N. Y. menaced. My health is improved, thank a kind Provi-

---

[1] Wife of Armistead Thomson Mason then Colonel of a cavalry regiment. He was killed in a duel by his brother-in-law John M. McCarty. They fought with muskets at six paces on the famous Bladensburg duelling ground.

dence, the event so dreaded has not taken place and I now begin to think I shall continue well. I have not yet read this letter. I know not what I have written. I thought you would be anxious for intelligence, for tho' you were no friend to Washington, yet the recent event is interesting to the nation. The enemy are in the centre of union!

I will now bid you good night,—let Maria and Susan Smith know we are safe. Susan particularly,—she will be miserable.

Farewell, dearest sister, God grant this letter may contain more news, than I may ever have occasion to write again. Farewell,

TO MRS. KIRKPATRICK

Brookville, August. [1814].

Saturday morning. On Thursday evening I closed my letter to you. The next morning soon after breakfast I went to see Mrs. Mason. She had found refuge in a farm house, with a poor but respectable family, about 4 miles from this place. She had her 3 eldest daughters with her and 2 servant maids. She was very ill, of a highly inflamatory billious fever. When I enter'd her chamber her spirits were much affected. She was too ill to talk, but when I offered to stay, gladly accepted the offer. She felt cheerless and desponding, had no confidence in her young physician or servants, who indeed seem'd very ignorant. She thought herself in danger, if not of her life, yet of derangement of mind, so continued and violent was the pain in her head. I immediately took on the functions of a nurse and being much accustomed to her disease, I soon succeeded in procuring her entire relief from the pain of her head, and other

alarming symptoms. I did not leave her a moment during the day and sat up part of the night. Dr. Worthing-
ton, her physician arrived. He distress'd me excessively
by his conversation. He exulted in the defeat of our
army in the capture of our city. "Did I not tell this,"
said he, "I suppose, Mrs. Smith, your wise men will now
believe a standing army a necessary thing and a navy in
the bargain." "If they do" (I answer'd) "they will certainly aim at establishing them, for however mistaken
in judgement, be assured sir, in all their measures, the
administration have honestly and sincerely endeavour'd
to promote the welfare of their country. It was believed, and all history has proved it to be so, that a standing army is an instrument of despotism; but if our liberties cannot be preserved without; the lesser evil will be
chosen,—the risk run." "I do not allow," said he, "a
standing army to be the instrument of despotism, but I
allow it to be inseparable from a monarchy." "I am not
competent to discuss such questions, Sir, but I beg at such
a moment as this, you will not thus seem to rejoice at
what every friend of his country must mourn over."
The tears started in my eyes, and seeing my distress
silenced him at the time, tho' every now and then his
evident satisfaction broke forth. Surely it is not possible that such is the disposition of all the federal party, no,
no, few I hope could speak as he did. On Saturday
morning Genl. Mason arrived, this was joyful tidings for
his poor wife. I left them together and did not see the
Genl. until breakfast. He appeared excessively har-
rass'd. He and Mr. Rush had never left the President
since our disgraceful retreat. He had crossed over with
him into Virginia, where he had collected troops and
2000 brave fellows then following his steps to our poor
city, commanded by Genl. Hungerford a revolutionary

officer. Wherever they pass'd, they as well as our flying forces were received with the most affectionate kindness, not only at large houses but at every hovel; the women came out with milk, bread, spirits, or something to offer the weary soldiers and to press them to rest and refresh. Everywhere he met indignation at the invading force and an alacrity to march against them, but the most prominent sentiment was mortification at the precipitate retreat of our army. The President and himself had arrived the night before and staid at Mrs. Bently's where we were. Mrs. Mason begged him not to stay one moment on her account, but urged him to depart that he might to the utmost serve his country. After breakfast he return'd to Brookville, soon after Mr. Smith sent for me and I was obliged to leave this amiable woman. She parted with me with reluctance as I was the only one near her who had any experience in her disease. When I arrived to-day at Brookville, the President and his suite had gone. The girls were very sorry I had been absent, as the scene in B. had been novel and interesting. Just at bed time the Presd. had arrived and all hands went to work to prepare supper and lodgings for him, his companions and guards,—beds were spread in the parlour, the house was filled and guards placed round the house during the night. A large troop of horse likewise arrived and encamp'd for the night, beside the mill-wall in a beautiful little plain, so embosom'd in woods and hills. The tents were scatter'd along the riverlet and the fires they kindled on the ground and the lights within the tents had a beautiful appearance. All the villagers, gentlemen and ladies, young and old, throng'd to see the President. He was tranquil as usual, and tho' much distressed by the dreadful event, which had taken place not dispirited. He advised Mr. Smith to return to the city, whither he was himself going. Mr. Monroe and some other gentlemen join'd him and about noon he set off for our suffering city. The rest of the day we pass'd tranquilly. It is now night, all around is quiet. All the inhabitants of this peaceful village sleep in peace. How silent! How serene! the moonlight gilds the romantic landscape that spreads around me. Oh my God, what a contrast is this repose of nature, to the turbulence of society. How much more dreadful is the war of man with man, than the strife of elements. On Thursday the hurricane which blew down houses, tore up trees and spread terror around, pass'd in a few minutes and nature recovered her tranquility. But oh my country, when will the destroying tempest which is now ravaging and destroying thy property and happiness, when will that be hushed to peace! At this moment, escaped from danger, I, and my family, all I hold most dear, are safe. But when I think of my good fellow citizens, when I think of our poor soldiers, flying on every part, sinking under fatigue and pain and hunger, dying alone and unknown, scattered in woods and fields—when I think of these horrors, I can hardly enjoy my own security.

Tuesday 30. Here we are, once more restored to our home. How shall I be sufficiently thankful for the mercies I have experienced. Once more the precious objects of my affection are gathered round me under our own roof. But how long shall I enjoy this blessing! The blast has pass'd by, without devastating this spot. But the storm is not yet over, dark, gloomy, lowering is the prospect, and far more dreadful scenes may be impending. Never did I feel so affected, so hopeless and sunk, as I did yesterday in the city. Oh my sister, what a sight! But to resume my journal. On Sunday morning we left Brookeville. Our ride was pleasant. All the way we

were conjecturing how we should find our dwelling.
We saw no vestige of the late scene, till we approach'd
the gate that open'd in to our farm, then in the woods
we saw a cannon whose carriage was broken, near the
ruins of our cottage.   On descending the hill, at the foot
of a tree we saw a soldier sleeping on his arms,—leaving
the woods we saw four or 5 others crossing the field and
picking apples.   When we reach'd the yard, a soldier
with his musket was standing by the gate and asked permission to get a drink.   These men were only passing
over the farm.   We found the house just as we had left
it, and the vestige of no enemy, but the hurricane of
Thursday which had blown down fences and trees.   Julia
and Ann cook'd us up a little dinner and in the afternoon
we rode to the city.   We pass'd several dead horses.
The poor capitol! nothing but its blacken'd walls remained! 4 or 5 houses in the neighbourhood were likewise in ruins.   Some men had got within these houses
and fired on the English as they were quietly marching
into the city, they killed 4 men and Genl. Rosse's horse.
I imagine Genl. R. thought that his life was particularly
aim'd at, for while his troops remained in the city he
never made his appearance, altho' Cochburn and the
other officers often rode through the avenue.   It was on
account of this outrage that these houses were burnt.
We afterwards look'd at the other public buildings, but
none were so thoroughly destroy'd as the House of Representatives and the President's House.   Those beautiful pillars in that Representatives Hall were crack'd and
broken, the roof, that noble dome, painted and carved
with such beauty and skill, lay in ashes in the cellars beneath the smouldering ruins, were yet smoking.   In the
P. H. not an inch, but its crack'd and blacken'd walls remain'd.   That scene, which when I last visited it, was so

splendid, throng'd with the great, the gay, the ambitious
placemen, and patriotic Heros was now nothing but ashes,
and was it these ashes, now trodden under foot by the
rabble, which once possess'd the power to inflate pride, to
gratify vanity. Did we ever honour the inhabitants of
this ruin the more for their splendid habitation,—was this
an object of desire, ambition, envy? Alas, yes and this is
human grandeur! How fragile, how transitory! Who
would have thought that this mass so solid, so magnificent, so grand, which seem'd built for generations to
come, should by the hands of a few men and in the space
of a few hours, be thus irreparably destroy'd. Oh vanity of human hopes! After this melancholy survey, Mr.
Smith went to see the President, who was at Mr. Cutts'
(his brother in law) where we found Mrs. Madison and
her sister Mrs. Cutts. Mrs. M. seem'd much depress'd,
she could scarcely speak without tears. She told me she
had remained in the city till a few hours before the English enter'd. She was so confident of Victory that she
was calmly listening to the roar of cannon, and watching
the rockets in the air, when she perceived our troops rushing into the city, with the haste and dismay of a routed
force. The friends with her then hurried her away, (her
carriage being previously ready) and she with many
other families, among whom was Mrs. Thornton and
Mrs. Cutting with her, retreated with the flying army.
In George town they perceived some men before them
carrying off the picture of Genl. Washington (the large
one by Stewart) which with the plate, was all that was
saved out of the President's house. Mrs. M. lost all her
own property. The wine, of which there was a great
quantity, was consumed by our own soldiers. Mrs. M.
slept that night in the encampment, a guard being placed
round her tent, the next day she cross'd into Virginia

The Capitol after the conflagration of August 24, 1814.

where she remained until Sunday, when she return'd to meet her husband. Men, soldiers, expresses were round the house, the President was in a room with his cabinet, from whence he issued his orders. The English frigates were laying before Alexandria and as it was supposed only waiting for a wind to come up to the city. The belief was that about 700 or more sailors were to be let loose in the city for plunder, dreadful idea. A universal despondency seem'd to pervade the people,—we every where met them in scatter'd groups, relating or listening to their fears. We drank tea at Mrs. Thornton's, who described to us the manner in which they conflagrated the President's H. and other buildings,—50 men, sailors and marines, were marched by an officer, silently thro' the avenue, each carrying a long pole to which was fixed a ball about the circumference of a large plate,—when arrived at the building, each man was station'd at a window, with his pole and machine of wild-fire against it, at the word of command, at the same instant the windows were broken and this wild-fire thrown in, so that an instantaneous conflagration took place and the whole building was wrapt in flames and smoke. The spectators stood in awful silence, the city was light and the heavens redden'd with the blaze! The day before Cockburn paid this house a visit and forced a young gentleman of our acquaintance to go with him,—on entering the dining room they found the table spread for dinner, left precipitally by Mrs. M,—he insisted on young Weightman's sitting down and drinking Jemmy's health, which was the only epithet he used whenever he spoke of the President. After looking round, he told Mr. W. to take something to remember this day. Mr. W. wished for some valuable article. No, no said he, *that* I must give to the flames, but here, handing him some ornaments off the mantle-piece, these will answer as a memento. I must take something too, and looking round, he seized an old hat a *chapeau de bras* of the President's, and a cushion off Mrs. M.'s chair, declaring these should be his trophies, adding pleasantries too vulgar for me to repeat. When he went to burn Mr. Gale's office, whom he called his "dear Josey"; Mrs. Brush, Mrs. Stelle and a few citizens remonstrated with him, assuring him that it would occasion the loss of all the buildings in the row. "Well," said he, "good people I do not wish to injure you, but I am really afraid my friend Josey will be affronted with me, if after burning Jemmy's palace, I do not pay him the same compliment,—so my lads, take your axes, pull down the house, and burn the papers in the street." This was accordingly done. He told Mrs. Brush and several others, that no houses should be injur'd but such as were shut and deserted. Mr. Cutting and Mrs. B. saved ours, by opening the windows. Cockburn often rode down the avenue, on an old white mare with a long main and tail and followed by its fold to the dismay of the spectators. He, and all his officers and soldiers were perfectly polite to the citizens. He bade them complain of any soldier that committed the least disorder and had several severly punished, for very slight offenses. All provisions were paid for. He stop'd at a door, at which a young lady was standing and enter'd into familiar conversation. "Now did you expect to see me such a clever fellow," said he, "were you not prepared to see a savage, a ferocious creature, such as Josey represented me? But you see I am quite harmless, don't be afraid, I will take better care of you than Jemmy did!" Such was his manner,—that of a common sailor, not of a dignified commander. He however deserves praise and commendation for his own good conduct and the discipline of his sailors and Marines, for these were the destroying agents. The land troops and officers were scarcely seen while in the city, but kept close qrs at the navy yard. Cockburn had ordered Col. Wharton's and Capt. Tingey's (?) houses (both public property) and the barracks and arsenal to be burnt, but on a remonstrance from the citizens, and an assurance the fire would destroy private property he desisted, "I want to injure no citizen," said he, "and so your Barracks may stand." I must praise his moderation, indeed his conduct was such as to disarm the prejudices that existed. During the stay of their troops in the city, it was so still you might have heard a pin drop on the pavement. The negroes all hid themselves and instead of a mutinous spirit, have never evinced so much attachment to the whites and such dread of the enemy. I could fill sheets with similar anecdotes, but the above will give you an idea of Cockburn. They left the city precipitately, from the idea that Winder was collecting his forces and would by going round them, cut off their retreat to their ships. And this could have been done, and our poor soldiers were willing and able for any enterprise, but their commanders,—Ah their commanders, Armstrong and Winder on their shoulders lies the blame of our disastrous flight and defeat. Our men were all eager to fight and were marching on with a certainty of victory, more than 2000 had not fired their muskets, when Armstrong and Winder gave the order for a retreat, and to enforce that order added terror to authority! The English officers have told some of our citizens that they could not have stood more than 10 minutes longer that they had march'd that day 13 miles, and were exhausted with thirst, heat and fatigue. It is said 2 Irish regiments wish'd to be taken and were on the point of joining us when the retreat commenced. I have con-

versed with many of our officers and men. All agree in
this statement, that the troops wish'd to fight, and were
full of spirit and courage. The English expected great
resistance. Yesterday when in the city I conversed with
a great many citizens, they were all disponding, dishearten'd. The President is determined on making a
resistance in case the enemy return. But our citizens
sent a deputation begging him not to attempt it, as it
would be ineffectual, and would only be making them and
the roofs that shelter'd them a sacrifice. "They now,"
they said, "had neither their honor or property to loose.
All they valued was gone." The President's orders
however, were enforced and all day yesterday while I
was in the city I saw them collecting. Troops are order'd from all around, and 3000 are expected tonight.
Alexandria has surrender'd its town with all their flour
and merchandize and the frigates are now laying before
that town, loading the Alexandria shipping with the
goods of the citizens. What will be our fate I know not.
The citizens who remain'd are now moving out, and all
seem more alarm'd than before. I brought Eliza Doyne
(that was) out with me. Mrs. Brush is coming out this
evening and has sent out all her furniture. I prefer offering our house as an asylum to the poor than the rich.
There is dreadful individual suffering,—one of Mr. S.'s
clerk's was here this morning, his house and furniture
were all burnt, even his clothing and he and his family are
reduced to penury. Hundreds, I may say thousands of
our flying troops pass'd thro our farm after the engagement. The English got within half a mile of us and
have plunder'd our neighbours on the adjoining farms,—
the intervening wood hid us from them. On their retreat through Bladensburg they have done a great deal
of injury, destroying furniture, carrying off cattle &c.

The consternation around us is general. The despondency still greater. But *I* look forward with hope, our troops are again collecting and altho' the poor citizens are dishearten'd by the fate of their city, the rest of the army are still willing to fight. Universal execration follows Armstrong, who it is believed never wished to defend the city and I was assured that had he pass'd thro' the city the day after the engagement, he would have been torn to pieces. The district certainly was not in a state of preparation, whether from want of ability or want of inclination on the part of the administration we can not know. The city was capable of defence and ought to have been defended. But we will retrieve, yes I trust we will retrieve our character and restore our capital. Oh that I a feeble woman could do something! This is not the first capital of a great empire, that has been invaded and conflagrated; Rome was reduced still lower by the Goths of old, than we are, and when its senate proposed removing the seat of government, they were answered, Romans would never be driven from their homes, Rome should never be destroy'd. May a Roman spirit animate our people, and the Roman example be followed by the Americans. Meanwhile, you will ask for some domestic details. We are in that state of confusion, which with our clothes and furniture all removed you may imagine. Mrs. Brush and Mrs. Grammar (E. Doyne) are added to our family. Every hour brings a different rumour; we know not what to believe and scarcely what to hope. We are determined however not again to quit the house, but to run all risques here, as we find our enemy not so ferocious as we expected and that property is much endanger'd by quitting it. I shall persuade Ann to go to Brookville and take the children, if more alarming intelligence arrives. I am

now so harden'd to fatigue and alarm, that I do not fear
my health will suffer.   The same external symtoms continue and I am astonished I am not much weakened by
so long a continuation.   But I am not [*torn out*] no
depression, but feel wound up to be [*torn out.*]   I trust
when the hour of alarm or trial comes I shall be enabled
to support it.   Ann is as composed and easy as if all was
peace.   She is all that is kind and attentive to me and
the children, and in the absence of our servants, she and
Julia do everything.   Do not be so anxious about us my
dearest sister.   The back is fitted to the burden.   As yet,
my strength has not been tryed.   I trust not in myself,—
the firm, the innate, the deep felt conviction that every
thing is over ruled by a great and a good God, reconciles
me to every event.   The late astonishing events in Europe, and the dreadful ones here, seem to have so sunk all
human grandeur, all human concerns in my estimation,
and human life appears so short, so very short, that
instead of anxiety, I feel almost indifference.   All will
soon be past, whether life is spent in suffering or enjoyment, is of little moment, so that it is well spent,—we
cannot suffer long.   External circumstances are of little
consequence, so that in all we do our duty.   Such are my
reflections; and my whole effort now, is not to escape
from suffering and danger, but to be active in the performance of the duties they bring with them.   Please to
send my letter to Maria.   I cannot write over,—dear,
dear sister adieu.   Do not be anxious about me,—I am
not uneasy myself.

TO MRS. KIRKPATRICK

Sidney Sept 11. [1814]

. . . . The affairs of our country grow more and more gloomy; last night the perusal of the papers made me quite melancholy, at Plattsburgh, N. London, N. Haven, all was consternation and alarm, families removing their property, and many, I suppose, as in this place wandering from their homes, without knowing where to find a shelter. All around our neighborhood was fill'd; those who could not get into houses encamp'd in the woods. In our old church there were 9 families. At Mrs. Fries 5 families with 18 children with scarcely anything to eat. Every day we are hearing of new instances of the cruelty of the soldiery and individual suffering. It has been the poor who have been the principle sufferers. At Bladensburgh which was inhabited chiefly by poor persons, the gentlemen having large houses and farms around the houses are much damaged by cannon ball &c—many of them occupied by the British wounded and our wounded men. (The army left all of their wounded for us to take care of)—The poor owners thus excluded, their gardens, corn fields and enclosures laid waste; their horses all taken. In the army's march from Benedict they made tents and beds of all the green corn, for which purpose they cut down whole fields. I am told this country (from Benedict to Washington) is totally laid waste; you can scarcely get anything for man or horse to eat. They strip'd the people of their clothing, taking women's and even children's clothes. All this was done by the straggling parties of soldiers who robb'd only the poor. At Bladensburg, Marlboro' and Wood Yard, the officers had guards placed around the

houses of many considerable and wealthy persons and
obtruded no further than to go to lodge, breakfast or
dine with the gentlemen, except where they found houses
empty and deserted, in which case they generally destroyed them.   We ran a great risque in deserting ours.
We are again establish'd and I now think nothing (excepting an army of Cossacks) shall induce me again to
leave it.   The battle was very near to us.   In the next
farm, there was skirmishing, and 10 dead bodies were
found (of the enemy) some only 4 or 5 days ago.   A
poor old lady, one of our nearest neighbors, heard the
bullets rattling around her house and has found a good
many in the yard.   I say I will remain, tho' all who did,
say nothing would induce them to again go through such
scenes.   I have heard of two persons I knew, who have
lost their senses, and several I have seen are very much
alter'd in their looks.   Mrs. Bradley is the only one who
would go thro' the same scenes again—she is generally
timid, but she says when the hour of trial came, courage
came with it.   Several hundred of our flying troups
were at her house, she dress'd their wounds and gave
them meat and drink.   I am persuaded the enemy lost
many more than was at first supposed, as bodies are daily
found, unburied, under bushes, in gulleys.   Alas poor
wretches, how many anxious hearts in England may be
looking for your return!   The wounded and prisoners
who remain, all express themselves delighted with this
country, many who have been in France and Spain, say
they never saw so beautiful or so rich a country and wonder how so happy a people could go to war.   It is supposed between 4 or 500 blacks have either [*obliterated*]
taken.   They have behaved well, been quiet, and [*obliterated*] in general appear to dread the enemy as much as
we do.   Thus we are spared one evil and the one I had

most dread of. Muskets, cartridge boxes, were found
by 100's and in possession of the blacks, who have all
cheerfully given them up, to the persons sent to look for
and collect them. Our black men found 3 on our farm,
which they immediately gave up. Citizens have returned and are slowly and despondently resuming business, but society and individuals have received a shock it
will require a long time to recover from. I now begin
to feel a little composed and able to resume my ordinary
employments. Mr. Smith has lost considerably by the
destruction of the Bridges, in both of which he had invested a large sum. We shall make some change in our
living, so as to reduce our expenditures. We have given
up our house in the city, as it was much wanted and we
shall not go there next winter. Excuse me for writing
on one subject only. It is the only one of which we talk
or think. But our country, our poor country. It seems
surrounded. No place seems safe. I will not begin on
another sheet, but conclude this with begging you my
dear sister to write as soon as you can. All our family
are perfectly well. Matty as well as ever she was in her
life, she was quite safe during the alarm, in an obscure
farm I had sent her to.

TO SAML. HARRISON SMITH[1]

Lone house—by the way side. [1815]

What a novel letter I could write you if I but had the
time and if the passing stage will not take me up, I shall
have time enough, for here I must stay till they do, if
its all day and night too. A few miles this side of Ches-
ter, our stage broke, but the mud was so deep, the gen-

[1] Mrs. Smith was on her way to Philadelphia to visit her brother Andrew
Bayard, President of the Commercial Bank of Philadelphia. She finished
the letter in Philadelphia.

tlemen would not let me get out, we all sat on the upper
side, (one of the braces was broke and the carriage
rested on the axel) and were drag'd thro' the mud to
this house, about two miles off.   It was ten o'clock and
the people all abed and it was a long time before we
could waken them.   At last the door was open'd by a
nice good looking old quaker lady, with fear and trembling however.   There were no men and no assistance
of any kind—the moon was just down and the night so
foggy that the driver said it would be very dark.   I
therefore begged the old lady to keep me all night.   The
gentlemen said they could get on the horses or walk and
as they were anxious to get on, they bade me farewell
and commended me to the lady's care.   It was eleven
o'clock before they got off, the stage supported by an old
rail.   I then begged my good quaker, to take me to the
kitchen fire, as I was very cold and wet.   My feet had
been wet all day, and getting in and out of the stages in
the rain, for it had rain'd hard all day, had wet my
clothes.   Two sweet looking young women got up and
soon made a fine fire.   I got in to the chimney corner,
for the chimney was like old Mrs. Tracy's, undress'd and
dried and warm'd myself.   I ask'd them if it would not
be too much trouble, if they could give me something for
supper.   They said they really had nothing at all in the
house they didnt often accommodate people, it being a
house just for the market folks to stop at.   I told them a
bowl of tea, with brown sugar would do, for I felt chilly
and weary.   They put on the tea kettle, and on my asking
for an egg, found *one*.   They seem'd curious about me,
and when I told them that I came from *Washington*, I
became an object of curiosity to them and they asked
me a hundred questions,—particularly about its being
taken by the British, and about slaves.   While my kettle

was boiling, I sat in one corner and the old lady in the
other corner of the chimney.   She was a pale, delicate
looking woman, with an uncommonly sweet face.   She
regretted much having no better accomodation, but I told
her truly it was more agreeable than a public house, that
I could feel as if she was my mother, at least take as good
care of me and that her daughters were just the age of
mine.   Here I must say, a few tears would in spite of me
break from my full heart, at the thought of *home* dear
home—dangers being now over my courage was over
too.   The dear old lady was so kind.   In a few moments I went on with my history of the taking and burning of Washington, which all listen'd eagerly to, while
we sat cowering over the fire.   I related all the little
anecdotes I could remember, our fears at Sidney, and
when they heard that I could fire a pistol and had slept
with a loaded pistol under my head, and Ann with a pen-
knife in her bosom, they were lost in astonishment and
look'd on me as something wonderful.   The simplicity
of the good folks amused me and their extreme interest
excited me to tell them all about Ross Cockburn &c &c
I could recollect and like the old soldier I sat by the "fire
and show'd how fields were won"—lost I mean.   Whenever I was about to pause, they begg'd me to go on.
My little table was put in the corner by me, my bowl
of tea and *one* egg and two crackers I was wrapped in
my flannel gown, and my clothes hung round the stove
to dry.   The sheets for my bed were hung on a chair
before the blaze, and if I had indeed been her daughter
she could not have been more careful of me, but there
was a sick child upstairs whom they had to watch by.
I therefore summon'd up courage to go to bed alone
(the only thing I dreaded) they took me thro' five or
six doors, into another house which had been built in

addition to this. I requested the candle might be left.
In vain I tried to sleep. It was raining and blowing, the
windows and doors rattling. I became every moment
more nervous, something in the room, threw a shadow
on the wall exactly like a coffin—that night week dear
Elizabeth had died—her image, almost herself was by
me, the candle was almost out, I trembled so the bedstead
shook under me. I felt almost sure if left in the dark
I should fall into some kind of fit, at last I jump'd up
and without waiting to put on my flannel gown, I took
my almost expiring candle, determined to find my way
to the kitchen, and if I could not find another candle, to
sit in the chimney corner all night. I open'd the door of
a chamber next me, hoping some one of the family might
be there, but I saw a bedstead, the idea that some one
might have just died there struck me. I dared not look
farther, but found my way down stairs into a large empty
room, with four doors, I opened the one nearest to me,
the wind rushed in and blew out my candle. I then
groped all round the room. Two doors were bolted, at
last I found one that yielded to my hand, I open'd it, but
knew not where I was and was afraid of falling down
steps. I thought it best to return to my chamber, tho'
with a horror I cannot describe—then I thought I would
sit down in the empty room on the floor. The windows
shook with the storm, as if they would have fallen in—the
wind blew most violently and some open door was creak-
ing and slaming. I shook, so I could scarcely stand and
was quite unable to find the door at the foot of the stairs.
At last, some one called out—Who's there? I answer'd
and the old woman came to me with a light, and look'd
quite frightened to see me there. She took me in the
kitchen,—the fire was still burning, and they had been
making up bread, &c. I told them I felt unwell and had

come down for another candle—they mixed me a glass
of toddy, as they saw me shaking as if I had an ague.
After I got warm'd I began one of the stories that had
interested them so much and was very eloquent indeed,
in hopes of beguiling them to sit up an hour or two with
me, but they were too sleepy, for even my most wonderful
stories to keep them awake. At last finding neither
Cochburn's murders, nor negro conspiracies, nor Georgia
negro buyers could keep their eyes open, I again ask'd
for a bed fellow and said I felt so lonely I could not sleep.
But the daughter could not be spared, and I again returned with a whole candle and crept into bed, where the
kind girl tucked me in. But it was in vain, I repeated
poetry and exerted my reason. I whose courage had that
morning been so admired and extoll'd by my fellow travellers, when in danger of losing my life was now ill with
imaginary terrors. After about an hour, I heard doors
opening and shutting then foot steps ascending the stairs
—then some one at my door, who whispered, "Are you
awake?" To which I gladly answered "Yes," for even
the entrance of robbers would have been welcome. But
it was my good old lady, who feeling uneasy, had made
her youngest daughter, a little girl the size of Anna Maria
get up and brought her to me as a bed fellow. The
moment I felt *warm* flesh and blood near me and her little
arm round me my trembling and shiverings ceased and
soon I drop't into a sweet sleep, from which I was
awaken'd by a bright sun, shining in my windows. My
pretty bed fellow assisted to dress me and when I went
down in the sitting room, I found a fine looking grey-
headed old man that put me in mind of Mr. K. He
was the father of the family, and I had again in answer
to his questions to relate my dangers and hair breadth
escapes. A little breakfast table was set for me, and

when done they cut this sheet of paper out of a book for
me and with an old stub of a pen, I am sitting by the stove
to write.   No stage has yet pass'd.   I think it probable
the roads were so dangerous near the Susquehanah and
so deep elsewhere, something may have happen'd and
that they will not be along till in the evening or night,
like us.   I can find no book in the house, so for my own
amusement as well as yours will write on, if it be all day
and by way of making it answer for a chapter in the
great work, will go into details in the novel style—this
will be killing two birds with one stone.

Now to begin my journal.   Like all other times of
war and peace, it affords little to say.   My ride to Baltimore was as pleasant as on a summer's day, my companion a very agreeable man who knew everybody I knew in
New York, and we talked of all the old acquaintance of
twenty and 30 years back—he told me who he was, his
business and family.   I told him who I was, my husband's
business and our family and before we reached Baltimore
felt like old acquaintance.   When the stage stopp'd we
were taken into the stage office and found on enquiry,
not a single passenger was going on to Philad.   Mr.
Dey, said if I would wait he would go to the other stage
office and enquire.   There were a parcel of men standing
round, but no one offer'd me a chair.   I asked one of
them to carry my letter into Mr. Williamson.   Soon after
the bar keeper came and asked me to walk into a parlour,
where a very genteel young man, came and in the most
respectful way, enquir'd what he could do for my accomodation, stating his father was very ill, but he would
execute any commands I might give him.   When he
understood my wishes, he begg'd me to walk in a better
parlour up stairs, while he would go to the other stage
office and learn what passengers there were, begging

me to feel quite at home and order what I pleased. He soon return'd, likewise Mr. Dey, with information there were two gentlemen going on to Philad. I then ordered a slight dinner, while Mr. D. went to take my seat and speak to the gentlemen and Mr. ———— The stage stopp'd and I left off. In the stage were very clever people, but you may judge of the state of the roads, when I was four hours coming 15 miles. At four o'clock I got safely here, but alas not to find all as happy as I had hoped, the whole family were in the greatest anxiety as Sally was very ill. I did not see sister or Elizabeth untill this morning, her life was in danger I believe for some hours, at one, the child was born—it was six months, it is still alive but no probability of its living. I hope Sally is out of danger, but poor sister and brother are very, very anxious. In this state of the family I feel in the way, tho' all are kind enough to persuade me to stay longer, I think it best to go tomorrow. Brother would have gone with me, had not this event occur'd. Oh how frail is the tenure of human felicity. This happy family may soon be plunged into the greatest grief. Mrs. Bayard, Caroline, Susan and Mrs. Hodge[1] and several other friends came in to see me and have been again this morning. I can scarcely steal time for a few lines, and am writing with them all around me. All are unsettled, going and coming from Sally's. I feel anxious but shall go tomorrow. I am perfectly well, all the better for the exposure and adventures I have met with. I meant to give you an account of the passage of the Susquehannah, and the rest of my journey, but now I feel in no spirits to write it. All our friends and connections of all the different families are in deep mourn-

---

[1] Mrs. Smith's mother, Col. Bayard's first wife (he was married three times), was Margaret Hodge. Her visitors were all members of her family.

ing. I do not want the girls to get any, but it might be as well to lay aside their gay ribbons. Things seem very different here and at Sidney—they have just come in to say Sally is much better and has fallen asleep. This is very favorable. I wrote those few lines from Elketon under the impression the mail to Washington would be missing, but it was the northern mail which was deranged. I cannot write more now, for every moment some one is coming in. Heaven bless you all.

I cannot even read over what I have written.

FROM THOMAS JEFFERSON[1]

Monticello, August 6—16

I have received, dear Madam, your very friendly letter of July 21, and assure you that I feel with deep sensibility its kind expression towards myself, and the more as from a person than whom no others could be more in sympathy with my own affections. I often call to mind the occasion of knowing your worth which the societies of Washington furnished; and none more than those derived from your much valued visit to Monticello. I recognize the same motives of goodness in the solicitude you express on the rumor supposed to proceed from a letter of mine to Charles Thomson, on the subject of the Christian religion. it is true that, in writing to the translater of the Bible and Testament, that subject was mentioned; but equally so that no adherence to any particular mode of Christianity was there expressed; nor any change of opinions suggested, a change from what? The priests indeed have heretofore thought proper to

[1] Mr. J. Henley Smith read this letter before the Historical Society of the District of Columbia, and it was printed in *The Evening Star*, Feb. 6, 1900, and in the proceedings of the Society for that year.

ascribe to me religious, or rather anti-religious, sentiments of their own fabric, but such as soothed their
resentments against the Act of Virginia for establishing
religious freedom. They wish him to be thought atheist,
deeist, or devil, who could advocate freedom from their
religious dictations, but I have ever thought religion a
concern purely between our God and our consciences for
which we were accountable to him, and not to the priests.
I never told my own religion nor scrutinized that of
another. I never attempted to make a convert, nor wish
to change another's creed. I have ever judged of the
religion of others by their lives; and by this test, my dear
Madam, I have been satisfied yours must be an excellent
one, to have produced a life of such exemplary virtue and
correctness, for it is in our lives and not from our words,
that our religion must be read. By the same test, the
world must judge me.

But this does not satisfy the priesthood, they must
have a positive, a declared assent to all their interested ab-
surdities. My opinion is that there would never have
been an infidel, if there had never been a priest. The
artificial structure they have built on the purest of all
moral systems for the purpose of deriving from it pence
and power revolts those who think for themselves and
who read in that system only what is really there. These
therefore they brand with such nicknames as their enmity
chooses gratuitously to impute. I have left the world in
silence, to judge of causes from their effects; and I am
consoled in this course, my dear friend, when I perceive
the candor with which I am judged by your justice and
discernment; and that, notwithstanding the slanders of the
Saints, my fellow citizens have thought me worthy of
trust. The imputations of irreligion having spent their
force, they think an imputation of change might now be

turned to account as a bolster for their duperies.   I shall
leave them as heretofore to grope on in the dark.

Our family, at Monticello is all in good health.   Ellen
speaking of you with affection, and Mrs. Randolph always regretting the accident which so far deprived her
of the happiness of your former visit.   She still cherishes
the hope of some future renewal of that kindness; in
which we all join her, as an assurance of affectionate
attachment and respect.   TH. JEFFERSON.

TO MRS. KIRKPATRICK

[Washington,] Wednesday morning.   [1816]

Good Heavens! my dear sister, what a picture have
you drawn of my good, my old friend Col. Johnson.   The
most tender hearted, mild, affectionate and benevolent of
men.   *He* a man of blood!   He delight more in the
sword than the Pen!   He, whose countenance beams
with good will to *all*, whose soul seems to feed on the milk
of human kindness!   No indeed, never did he draw his
sword, but to defend his invaded country.   War is not his
trade, and when he fought, it was not for *hire*.   At the
time when the western states were attack'd, he by his own
personal influence rais'd a volunteer corps of young men
of family and education, who follow'd him thro' every
danger, hardship and suffering to our frontier, and with
a deep river on one side, an impassable marsh on the
other, he attack'd a large body of indians, with a cool
and determined bravery, which none but great souls can
[*torn out*].   During his march thro' the enemy's country,
the women and children of the English came to him for
protection, and never came in vain.   He would not allow
his men to pick even an apple from a tree, tho' often

almost fainting from want. After vanquishing the enemy he return'd home, covered with glory and wounds, and more than ever beloved by his countrymen, and is now without any comparison the most popular and respected member from Kentucky. Mr. Clay would stand no chance if opposed to him. He is a man of domestic habits and disposition, and his mild and amiable disposition was not alter'd by a short campaign. Last winter when he defended the widow and the orphan's cause (in the case of Mrs. Hamilton)[1] as pathetically as eloquently, there was scarcely a dry eye in the house. His eloquence is not that of imagination, but of the heart. His mind is not highly cultivated, or rather I should say his taste. He has always been too much a man of business to have much time for reading. He is one of the leading men in Congress, and therefore on a number of committees. He might have been quite a fashionable man, as he is always invited to parties. But he preferr'd home and is plain in dress and manners. I should not so warmly have vindicated a favorite, but that I shrewdly suspect he is a great admirer of your daughter. And I most sincerely believe, if she wished it, she might convert him into your son. He was here all last evening and hung or if you please sat enamour'd by her while she play'd and sung. But Mary does not much fancy him. She thinks him *too* much *too* old (he is about 40), then he wants grace, polish and a fashionable [*torn out*] and above all he lives in Kentucky. Now I think the last is the only objection, in all other respects, (as far as I *now* know) for my own part I should like him for a son. But Mary only laughs at all I can say, and like other young girls thinks she has the world before her to choose

---

[1] Johnson advocated the bills for relief of widows of Revolutionary soldiers in several impassioned speeches.

and will not have one who to solid worth does not join
the graces and everything which is requisite to a perfect
character. I shall make close inquiries of Mrs. Clay
about his family &c before he visits much oftener, in case
of consequences. I have passed the last 4 days and nights
almost exclusively with Mrs. Clay, who has lost a lovely
infant of three months old with the whooping cough.[1]
Mrs. Brown (her sister) Mrs. Lowndes and myself divided the task of attending it, and on Monday night it
died in my arms. I shall pass this evening with her instead of the drawing room, to which otherwise we should
have gone, as Mrs. Madison, who was here the other
morning, press'd us, particularly the young folks, to come
every evening, and this is to be a full evening. But they
seem quite contented to stay at home. . . .

TO MRS. KIRKPATRICK

[Washington,] Decr. 5th 1816. Thursday morning.

. . . . We were at the drawing room last night,
there were not above 200 people, and it was too thin to
feel at one's ease. A crowd is certainly animating.

Just as I was dressed and just putting the finishing
touches by the parlour glass, the door opened, without
a knock and in come Mrs. Caldwell and Mr. Finley,[2]
ushered in by Lytleton. I had een to put on my handkerchief and tie on my ribands before them. Mrs. C.
had forgotten it was drawing room evening. I told Mr.
F. he had better go along,—meaning it quite for a joke,
but he took it quite in earnest, and said, Why really he

---

[1] This was their ninth child. They had eleven, six daughters and five
sons.
[2] Rev. Robert Finley, of New Jersey, a Presbyterian divine, who founded
at this time the American Colonization Society.

should like it very much. "But," said I, "what are you to do with your boots?" "Why, certainly, a clergyman may go in boots." "I don't know," said I, "but I should be afraid a clergyman's boots would tear the ladies' dresses as much as any other." "Well," said Mrs. Caldwell, "there is a shoe store near, and he can get a pair of shoes." "Agreed," said Mr. F., "if Lytleton will show me the way." Accordingly they went, and when he came back, he assured us everything favoured his going for the very first pr. of shoes that he took hold of fitted him. His toilet was finished before the parlour looking glass, and off we set, leaving Lytleton who would not go, (not being yet equip'd) and Mrs. Caldwell with the girls. I wanted Mary or Ann to ride with the dominie, but he insisted on my enjoying a tête-à-tête ride with him; this was the first frolic he said he had had since he accompanied me 20 years ago to the fourth of July party. I of course was led in by the parson, and had to show him how to take my hand and lead me in &c. Mr. Smith led Mary, Mr. Todd Ann. I anticipated a crowded room and own I felt somewhat awkward on being led across a large room to the place where sat Mrs. Madison, Mrs. Monroe, Mrs. Decatur and a dozen other ladies in a formidable row. There was not a single chair, and had not some of the ladies rose to talk with us, we should have been somewhat at a loss.

The President asked Mr. S. who it was led me in, and on Mr. F.'s being introduced to him, conversed a good deal with him. Mr. Smith introduced him to Mr. Monroe and several other gentlemen and our good Parson went home, to use his own expression, perfectly satisfied and gratified. Mary looked uncommonly well. I think she is very much improved in her looks since she came here, which is to be ascribed to her improved health.

She had a fine colour, her eyes sparkled and she was perfectly at her ease and conversed with great vivacity with the gentlemen. Mrs. Madison expressed a wish that she would play and sing, as she had heard that she played *most elegantly.* But Mary declined. Had it been a *squeeze,* I should have urged her playing, but in so thin a room, I knew she would be too conspicuous. I will not deprive Mary of an opportunity of displaying her descriptive powers and therefore will say nothing of the appearance of the French Legation, which was superb, but not so genteel as the plain clothes of the English. The circle, last evening, was not so imposing, as the first drawing room the girls went to last winter and even if it had been I do not think Mary would have been in such ecstatics. Mary is much more quiet in the expression of her feelings and on that account a much greater favorite with my good husband. I never knew Mr. Smith to be so much pleased with any young person, he frequently when alone commends her in the highest terms. I could spend my whole life happily with Mary, I never before have met with a disposition which so perfectly accords with mine.

I now begin to feel settled. My domestic arrangements are all made and my servants so good that I have nothing to do. I scarcely realize I am keeping house. The change from our country establishment is very agreeable. There I had such a variety of things and persons to attend to without, as well as within doors, and a kitchen so crowded with farm servants and children, that I had little pleasure in performing my household duties. But here I have a most excellent woman in the kitchen, who keeps the key of the store room and goes thro' her work without requiring any direction from me. A very good girl does the chamber work and washing, an un-

commonly good boy waits in the house and Mr. Tracy
who drives the carriage, supplies all the deficiencies in the
others. He markets, and shops, and goes of errands,
puts up curtains, bedsteads &c—in fact is my *maitre
d'hôtel* as well as coachman. So that I am a lady at large
with nothing in the world to do, but sit up for company,
and make visits. I go in the kitchen for 5 or 6 minutes
before breakfast, give my orders for dinner, then give
the girls their breakfast, send them to school. I arrange
my side-board and closet in the dining-room, which takes
me until 10 o'clock, then dress, seat myself in my corner
on the settee, and give my little ones their lessons, a little
sewing, and a little reading diversify the morning. We
have not had much company as yet, and as I do not intend visiting as many strangers as I did last winter, we
shall not have so much. I do not think Mary could
stand such late hours and constant company as the girls
did, and Ann I am sure can not—indeed we had too much
for pleasure. I expect to pass many of our evenings in
a calm domestic manner—sewing and reading. Mr. S.
is reading the Odyssey. . . . I never wrote more
like a task, and no school girl ever found a task more difficult. You will easily perceive my stupidity. I had best
waste no more paper. Come Mary and fill it—you can
give more pleasure. You may as well write as sit looking out of the window—come along——— Dear sister,
write me soon, a sweet, kind letter and that as I said will
break the spell.[1]

Aunt has left me a little space, dear Mother, to give
you an account of our appearance at the drawing room,
for as I wrote you yesterday little else is left me to say.
I went without the least feeling of trepidation. Mrs. C.'s
party *broke the ice* and I felt quite at my ease. But I

[1] The rest of the letter is by Miss Mary Kirkpatrick, Mrs. Smith's niece.

felt very much disappointed—the ideas I had formed of
the pleasure of the drawing room were not realized.   I
do not however despair of being pleased at some future
time for it was the *thinnest* drawing room that has been
seen.   To see the great and celebrated people of our
country is a very great gratification to me.   I was introduced to Mr. Madison as soon as I entered the room,
but had only the honor of exchanging two or three sentences with him.   Mrs. Madison was extremely polite and
attentive, but looked very ill.   She had on a blue velvet,
blue head dress and feathers with some old finery and
her face look'd like a flame.[1]   With Mrs. Munroe[2] I am
really in love.   If I was a Washingtonian you might say
I worshipped the rising sun—but as I am not, you will
believe my adoration sincere.   She is charming and very
beautiful.   She did me *the honor* of asking to be introduced to me and saying "she regret'd very much she was
out when I called" &c and, tho' we do not believe all these
kind of things it is gratifying to the vanity to hear them.
It would not however have flatter'd me half so much from
Mrs. Madison as from her.   Mr. Neuville[3] and suite were
there in most splendid costume—not their court dresses
however.   Blue coats cover'd with gold embroidery.
The collar and back literally cover'd with wreaths of fleurs
de lys with white underclothes and large chapeaux with
feathers.   The minister's feather was white, the secretaries black, and their dress tho' on the same style not so
superb as his.   Madam and Mademoiselle were very handsomely dress'd in white sattin.   Mr. and Mrs. Bagot[4]

[1] Truth compels the statement—Mrs. Madison painted.

[2] She was Elizabeth Kortright, of New York, daughter of Lawrence
Kortright, a captain in the British army. Her stately manners were in
marked contrast with Mrs. Madison's genial warmth. During her husband's term as President she secluded herself from general society to a
considerable extent because of her ill health.

[3] Hyde de Neuville, French Minister from 1816 to 1822.

[4] Sir Charles Bagot, British Minister from 1816 to 1819.

Mrs. James Madison.

From the steel engraving by J. F. E. Prudhomme, after the portrait by
J. Wood.

were both in complete black. The Abbé Corier[1] the Por-
tugese minister is a venerable old gentleman and a man of
great learning; he speaks five languages perfectly. Commodore and Mrs. Decatur were very brilliant. The Secretaries (except Mr. Munroe) were not there. Mr. Neu-
vill enquired after you and says he regrets his *jolie
bergère,* that a shepherd's life is much happier than that
of a public man. Mr. Bourquinay and Mr. Thierrie (my
favourite) called to see us yesterday morning, the former
improves on acquaintance and look'd quite handsome in
his full dress. I met at Miss Duval's this morning Mr.
Hughes and Mr. Antrobus, the secretaries of the British
Legation. They are sprightly, intelligent young men,
but not to compare with Mr. Bagot. We paid some
visits this morning to Mrs. Seaton and Miss Gales sisters
of *Josey Gales as we say,* Mr. Blake, Mrs. Van Ness and
Mrs. Clay, whose youngest child is very ill with the
whooping cough. Tomorrow evening we are to take
tea sociably with Mrs. Meigs. I feel very anxious to
hear of Elizabeth. I hope by this time she is enjoying
her usual health. Tell me *particularly* how she is and
how your uncle and general health is. My kindest love
to my dear father and the girls and to *all* my friends
individually. How do you like the new divinities, Mr.
Kissgin and does Mr. Vanzant visit you as often as he
did last summer? My next letter will be to Elizabeth if
I can find enough to amuse her. Farewell beloved
Mother—may Heaven bless and preserve you. Mr.
Kent hasent yet arrived.

[1] José Correa da Serra, Minister from Portugal, the most famous wit and
epigram-maker of his day. He it was who called Washington the "city of
magnificent distances."

TO MRS. KIRKPATRICK

January 19, 1817.

This is winter, cold, piercing, winter! I am half frozen, with my back close to the fire and a foot stove beneath my feet. It was so extremely cold that we all agreed not to go to church, for altho' we might have escaped much suffering, our poor coachman would have almost perished. The same consideration kept us at home last night, otherwise we would have enjoy'd ourselves exceedingly at M. de Neuville's, where we were invited to pass the evening.

You were afraid Mary's health would not stand much dissipation. She laid up such a stock at Sidney, that it enables her without the slightest inconvenience to participate in all the gaiety of our gay city. She says she could enjoy being in company every evening. We have seldom exceeded three evenings in the week, altho' we have often had invitations for four or five. This, however, is no great self denial, as we are seldom or ever close at home. Mary has given you I suppose some account of our large party at home. I invited 170, and then offended several families I was obliged to omit; about 120 came. I had 4 musicians from the *Marine Band,* and the goodness of the musick greatly increased the pleasures of the evening. Mrs. Barlowe seem'd about as anxious as if it had been her own party, and wished me to make use of her servants and everything in her house. which could add to the elegance of the party. I accepted but a small portion of what she offer'd; the kind Mrs. Bomford,[1] came early in the morning and assisted

---

[1] A sister of Joel Barlow who was married to Lieutenant Colonel George Bomford, a distinguished officer of the army. Their daughter married Benjamin Lincoln Lear, son by his first marriage of Tobias Lear, Washington's secretary.

in all the arrangements. We had four rooms open, two down-stairs for dancing, one parlour and one supper room up stairs, the table was so arranged that 25 or 30 could sit down at a time and a side board of dishes supplied those that were consumed at table. Such a party could give me no pleasure, but I hope it did others. We were so constantly in company the whole week before, that I was completely tired and half resolved to stay at home the rest of the winter,—but four or five days rest restored me my good health and spirits. I did not go on Monday with the girls to the concert, but on Wednesday accompanied Mary to the drawing-room. I went purely from the desire of pleasing her, but was rewarded for my complaisance, not only by the sight of her pleasure, but by my own enjoyment. Independent of the affections, I know of no pleasure equal to that derived from the conversation of men of genius. And this I enjoy'd in an unusual degree. Governor Barbour[1] (of Virginia) now in the Senate, is a man of fashion, a man of the world, and to all the graces joins the most charming manners and high talents. He has so much ardour and enthusiasm, that one might almost call him *romantic;* he has a beautiful daughter to whom that epithet justly applies, and who is a girl of *Genius,* with all the faults generally attached to that character, but with all its charms. The father and daughter join'd our party for the evening; Gen'l Harrison, (our Western Hero) Col. Taylor, a most agreeable man from S. Carolina and several others, enlarged the little circle, we formed on one side the fire place. But the one who most interested me, was Mr. *Gillmore,* a young Virginian, introduced to me by Miss Barbour. He is called the *future hope of Vir-*

[1] James Barbour, afterwards Secretary of War under John Quincy Adams, and Minister to England 1828–29.

ginia—its ornament!—its bright star! I had a long, animated, and interesting conversation with him, really the
greatest intellectual feast I have long had. He is the
enthusiastic admirer of my dear and revered Mr. Jefferson, and a familiar inmate of his family. During the
last year he has been the traveling friend and pupil of
Abbe Correa, with him he has explored the mountains,
the valleys and rivers of Virginia, and describes its sublime and its beautiful scenery, with all the rapture and
enthusiasm of genius and youth. While I was thus engaged, Mary and Ann were surrounded with their beaux
and lost the pleasure of making the acquaintance of this
interesting young man. I asked him and Govr. and Miss
Barbour to pass the next evening, together with Genl.
Harrison and Col. Taylor,—the two last were engaged.
This evening Mary Ann look'd better than I have ever
seen her. When we first went in, the chairs round Mrs.
Madison were occupied and we seated ourselves on the
opposite side of the fire and were the only party on that
side of the room; few persons had yet arrived, the room
was empty. We had not been long seated when Mrs.
Madison cross'd the room and going up to Mary, took
her hand and after the usual compliments, told her she
had a great secret to communicate, but should not do it,
until the end of the evening. A great deal of rallying on
both sides took place,—when Mrs. M. told her that a
gentleman who had fallen in love with her, who was a
friend of hers, had made her his confidant, that he was
to be there, and she would not tell Mary his name until
she saw how Mary treated him. All this time she held
Mary's hand. The conversation was carried on with so
much animation, that it drew the attention of those
around. Mary's eyes sparkled, she had a brilliant colour,
(which however she always has) she spoke with great

vivacity and look'd really *very* handsome, and more persons than I thought so. Mary's beauty depends almost entirely on expression, manner and colour. Her black eyes and hair, her white teeth and vivid bloom, when heightened by fine spirits, really makes her beautiful and you would scarcely know her to be the same, when silent, quiet, and uninterested. She has always a fine colour and says she never in her life enjoy'd such high health. I asked a friend who was in the way of hearing such things, in what manner Mary was spoken of. She said many called her handsome, but she was most generally admired for her intelligence, her expression and animation—that every one thought her an uncommonly sensible girl and all liked her for the way in which she used her sense, no pedantry, no kind of superiority, but so much good humour and sprightliness! Ann hangs on her arm and smiles, but seldom speaks. She is more inanimate than ever, and alas; not so pretty. On Thursday evening we had a charming little party at home, whom I ask'd in the morning, in a social way. Mrs. Barlowe and Mr. and Mrs. Bomford, Mr. and Mrs. Clay, Mr. and Mrs. Brown[1] (of the Senate) Govr. and Miss Barbour, Mr. Gillmore Abbe Correa, Dr. Tucker and 3 or 4 other gentlemen. I had a long tête-à-tête with the old Abbé, but could not discover any of those charms of conversation for which he is celebrated. We pass'd two mornings this week at the House and could I reconcile it to my domestic duties, I should love dearly to go very often. On Friday evening we went to an intollerable squeeze, at Mrs. Meigs every body I had ever seen in W. was there, foreigners, strangers and citizens. The girls had not been long seated, before I was separated

---

[1] James Brown, of Louisiana, a man of great wealth, with a handsome, fashionable wife. He was Minister to France, 1823–29.

from them by the pressure of the crowd, but from time
to time I saw them, always surrounded with beaux and
to their old acquaintance I saw added Col. Taylor, who
did not leave them the whole evening.   I have not yet
found out whether he is married or single,—he is young
and very agreeable, and seems desirous of becoming an
acquaintance of the whole family.   For my part, I talk'd
a little to a hundred people, but had conversation only
with Genl. Harrison and Abbe Correa.   The former to my
taste is the most agreeable, altho' the other is extoll'd to
the skies, both here and in Philadelphia.   Miss Rush has
been at all the places we have been but seems to produce
no effect and to be little known or noticed.   Next to the
Miss de Kantzows [1] and the other *diplomatiques,* Mary,
I think has most attention.   I include in the above term
the Miss de K.'s, the Miss de Onis' [2] and Miss Louise.
They always sit together, stand together and talk together and never join any of the other young ladies.
At *home* Mary's good humour and good spirits are in-
variable.   We shall be very dull when she leaves us.
Last evening Col. Johnson [3] and Col Fletcher [4] were here
(cold as it was).   Mr. Smith and I play'd chess, Jonathan, mused in one corner, Mary Ann and Col. J. and
Ann and Col. F. amused themselves, very merrily at
least.   I do not see as many love symtoms as I did.
Mary puts no fuel to the flame and you know it cannot
long burn without.   I have seen no stranger this winter
for whom I feel so much interest as Madm. Neuville.   I

[1] Daughters of Baron Johan Albert de Kantzow, Minister Resident of
Sweden and Norway.
[2] Daughter of Luís de Onis, Spanish Minister.
[3] Richard Malcolm Johnson, then a Representative from Kentucky. At
the Battle of the Thames, Canada, October 5, 1813, he killed a powerful
Indian chief in a hand-to-hand fight.   Tecumseh fell in this battle and it
was claimed, although never clearly established, that he was the chief
whom Johnson slew.
[4] Thomas Fletcher, Representative from Kentucky.

could love her, if our intercourse could be social enough
to allow it. They have company I believe almost every
day to dinner, or of an evening. Always on Saturday,—
we have had a general invitation for that evening. I
believe she is completely weary of this eternal dissipation.
I love her for her kindness to Mrs. Stone,[1] she takes every
occasion of showing her kindness and of giving her consequence.

MRS. KIRKPATRICK

23, Novr. 1817, Sidney.

. . . . People seem to think we shall have great
changes in social intercourse and customs. Mr. and Mrs.
Monroe's manners[2] will give a tone to all the rest. Few
persons are admitted to the great house and not a single
lady has as yet seen Mrs. Monroe, Mrs. Cutts excepted,
and a committee from the Orphan Asylum, on which
occasion Mrs. Van Ness first called to know when Mrs.
M. would receive the committee. Mrs. M. said she
would let them know in the course of a few days,—this
she did, appointing the succeeding week for the interview. She is always at home to Mrs. Cutts, and Mr.
Monroe has given orders to his Porter to admit Mr. Clay,
at all times, even when the cabinet council is sitting, and
the other day when he call'd and declined the servant's
invitation into the Cabinet, Mr. M. came out and took him
into the council. Altho' they have lived 7 years in W.
both Mr. and Mrs. Monroe are perfect strangers not only
to me but all the citizens. Every one is highly pleased

[1] A lady whom Mrs. Smith had assisted in starting a girls' school in Washington.

[2] Monroe endeavored to restore to the President's house the stately for-
mality which had prevailed when Washington was President. Mrs. Monroe
paid no visits. Her daughters also paid no visits, and there was a feud
between them and the diplomatic corps in consequence.

with the appointment of Mr. Wirt[1] and Mr. Calhoun,[2] they will be most agreeable additions to our society. Tell Mary Ann that the house of Mr. Brent, opposite to us is occupied by Mr. Walsh and Mr. Corea; I promise myself some pleasure from these new neighbors. . . .

TO MISS ANNA MARIA SMITH

Sunday, between churches, 12 Novr. [1818]

. . . . Yesterday for instance, before I had completed my house hold arrangements, I was called to Dr. Smith, the herb doctor, or as he calls himself, "The Professor in the University of Nature." He brought his Mariner's needle, in which he believes he has made an improvement, founded on a discovery of his own, that will establish his fame and his fortune. He had just come from the President's who had received him most graciously and promised to mention him in his report to Congress. His improvement has been already adopted in our Navy and is highly approved of. The design is, to counteract the variations of the needle, a thing that has puzzled Philosophers and Mariners, ever since the first discovery of the magnet. He does not pretend to have discovered the cause of this variation, that mystery is still unsolved, but to control or to counteract its effects. To have heard him talking to me, you would have supposed I was a mathemetician. I repeatedly assured him of my ignorance, of my utter deficiency in scientific knowledge, and he as repeatedly argued that I was a lady of most philosophical mind and he felt certain, that I could explain his views to others (and he wished them made known) much better than he could. (Poor man he is certainly deficient in language, for although nature

---

[1] As Attorney General.   [2] As Secretary of War.

has given him a most powerful, original and inquisitive mind, she could not give him scientific principles or language.)   He remained at least two hours,—so happy! in having some one to listen to and sympathize with him, that I had not the heart, tired as I was, to send him away, by coldness and inattention, for of course you know I would not do it by words.   Then Mr. Cutts[1] came in, and made a very reasonable visit, and then, after he made his bow, I with great avidity seized my pen and it moved as if it was clothed not only with its own share of feathers, but with the whole of a gooses wing,—it absolutely flew as it transcribed the ideas that oppressed my brain.   But ere one sheet was filled, the door-bell rung and scared my goose away.   . . .

Wednesday, almost dinner time.   Really dear Anna I did expect a letter ere this.   In your last you said I might look for one on Monday.   Till I get it I will proceed with my journal.   Mr. Wood concluded my last page. I arose on Monday morning with more elastic spirits than I have felt since I came into the city.   After breakfast I went forth on a shopping expedition and procured most of the winter clothing for the family, self included.   One article I could not get,—curls, french curls, parted on the forehead, you know how.   You must get them for me either in New York or Phila.   Now remember CURLS! I came home excessively wearied, but unwilling to break in upon another day.   I carried my dress to the mantua makers.   When I came home at dark, found Miss Gallaudet[2] here.   She entertained us with a very minute and well told account of the Hartford Institution, for the Deaf and Dumb.   She is an elderly single lady, very precise in her appearance and plain.   But her language

[1] Hon. Richard Cutts, Mrs. Madison's brother-in-law.
[2] Sister of the father of education of the deaf in America, Thomas Hopkins Gallaudet.

classically correct and elegant. She is fine, intelligent, though neither a very pleasing or interesting woman, is animated and engaged while talking herself, but listless and inattentive to what others say. How very reverse of our friend Lydia. Her object in coming was to consult me about establishing a school here on some improved system,—full of her own views and ideas, she is indifferent to those of others, perhaps this is the characteristic of enthusiasm and that I am as obnoxious to this observation as she is. After tea Mr. Larned and Mr. Bailey came in. Chess, of course, engaged them. Your father and Mr. Bailey, Aunt Ann and Mr. Larned. I was so engrossed by Miss Gallaudet, as not to be able to look over Mr. Bailey's game. It lasted three or more hours. Almost 11 o'clock when it was terminated. Mr. B. as you may suppose, victor. Mr. Gallaudet came in and he and I calculated the expense of a soup-house, we want to establish, in connection with the Howard Institution. The evening if not very amusingly passed rationally with me. When Ann and Mr. L. gave up the chess, Julia arranged a partie for Bayard and Miss Gallaudet (a wretched play, so slow, so precise). Oh how mad he was!—he wanted to have studied Mr. B.'s game and is not very fond of old, young ladies, you know. He begged Julia not to *dispose* of him again. Julia asked Mr. Gallaudet to bring Mr. Noble here this evening (Wednesday) and invited Miss G. to come again. . . .

Sunday morning, Jany. Sidney 1819.

. . . . The next day we went to the city and were received by Mrs. Calhoun[1] with the affection and kind-

---

[1] Mrs. Calhoun was Floride Calhoun, a cousin of her husband. Her mother, Floride Bonneau Calhoun, was of a Huguenot family, and John C. Calhoun acquired wealth and social prestige in South Carolina by his marriage.

ness of the nearest relative or friend. As I had *all* with me, she said she would take no denial to our staying with her until the next day,—this we had to decline. On hearing that Mr. Clay was to speak, I could not resist the temptation and told Susan if she would go home with her father and if he would consent, I would stay.[1] I accordingly went to the Treasury to ask leave and having obtained it, took Susan to Mrs. Bomford's to pass the morning and according to agreement followed Mrs. C. to the capitol-hill, who had gone on before with Julia and Mrs. Lowndes, in order to secure seats. Our little Anna was left in charge with Miss Eliza, who was very kind to her. When I reached the Hall, it was so crowded that it was impossible to join my party, and after much hesitation I consented to allow Mr. Taylor to take me on the floor of the House, where he told me some ladies already were. In the House, or rather, lobby of the House, I found four ladies whom I had never before seen—all genteel and fashionable and under the protection of Mr. Mercer,[2] who shook hands with me. The Senate had adjourned in order to hear Mr. Clay, all the foreign ministers and suites, many strangers were admitted on the floor, in addition to the members render'd the house crowded. The gallery was full of ladies, gentlemen and men, to a degree that endanger'd it,— even the outer entries were thronged and yet such silence prevailed that tho' at a considerable distance I did not lose a word. Mr. Clay was not only eloquent but amusing and more than once made the whole house laugh. Poor Mr. Holmes[3] and Genl. Smythe[4] could not have enjoy'd this merriment as it was at their expense. As you will

[1] Clay's elaborate speech on the Seminole War was made January 20.
[2] John Fenton Mercer, Representative from Virginia.
[3] John Holmes, of Massachusetts.
[4] Alexander Smyth, of Virginia.

read the speech in the paper, I will not detail it, although I could repeat almost the whole of it. But in losing the voice and manner of Mr. Clay, much of the effect will be lost. Every person had expected him to be very severe on the President and seemed rather disappointed by his moderation. To hear the better, I had seated myself on some steps, quite out of sight of the house; when Mr. Clay had finished he came into the lobby for air and refreshment. The members crowded round him, and I imagine by his countenance, what they whispered must have been very agreeable. When he saw me, he came and sat a few minutes on the steps by me, throwing himself most gracefully into a recumbent posture. I told him I had come prepared to sit till evening and was disappointed at his speech being so short; he said he had intended to have spoken longer, but his voice had given out; he had begun too loud and soon exhausted himself. Meanwhile Col. Johnson had risen and was speaking, but the noise of walking and talking and coughing was so loud, it was impossible to hear him. He several times earnestly begged that the little he had to say might be attended to, but in vain. Every one was glad of a little relief after 3 hours, and after speaking without being listen'd to the Coln. begged leave to defer what he had to say to the next day. This was readily granted him. The gentlemen are grown very gallant and attentive and as it was impossible to reach the ladies through the gallery, a new mode was invented of supplying them with oranges etc. They tied them up in handkerchiefs, to which was fixed a note indicating for whom it was design'd and then fastened to a long pole. This was taken on the floor of the house and handed up to the ladies who sat in front of the gallery. I imagine there were near a 100 ladies there, so that these presentations were frequent

and quite amusing, even in the midst of Mr. C.'s speech.
I, and the ladies near me, were more accessible and were
more than supplied with oranges, cakes &c. We divided
what was brought us with each other and were as social
as if acquainted. A great many members came successively to speak to me and Mr. Baldwin[1] and Mr. Taylor
were kindly attentive and staid much of the time near
me,—otherwise I should have felt disagreeable. At dinner, I gave Mr. Calhoun an ample detail of the speech,
which led to a great deal of conversation of men, measures and facts. You know how frank and communicative he is, and considering I was very much animated by
the scene of the morning, perhaps you will not be surprised at our conversing without any interruption until
9 o'clock. I several times after tea begged him to read
or write and make no stranger of me, but this his politeness would not permit him to do. While we conversed,
Mrs. C. and Julia play'd on the Pianno and at chess. At
last I jumped up declaring I would keep him no longer
from business, and proposed to Mrs. C. to adjourn to
our chamber.

TO MRS. KIRKPATRICK

[Sidney,] Sunday, 14 Febr. 1819.

. . . . As for us; we are thank a kind providence
all well. Dear little Anna is I think better than she was
before her illness. We have again resumed our regular
occupations and time passes cheerfully and I hope not
uselessly by. We have until the last 3 days had most
delightful weather; so warm that we could often sit with
the windows open. We improved this charming season
by walking or riding every day, thinking there would yet

[1] Henry Baldwin, Representative from Pennsylvania.

be bad weather enough to keep us within doors at work. I have with the girls passed many pleasant mornings with our friends in the city, have had more company than usual in the country.   Mr. Astley, Mr. Buck, Mr. Wall, Mr. Orplander (?) have at different times dined with us and our good Capt. Riley[1] has been always once and some times twice a week to see us.   When he comes he stays all night and is quite domesticated with us.   Bayard and Anna are reading his narrative, which I read to them two years ago.   It is seldom they do not pay the tribute of their tears to his sad story, at least Bayard, who is a tender hearted little creature.   Since I last wrote I have often seen Mrs. Calhoun and could not resist attending a very large ball she had.   Five rooms crowded. I have seen every one I know for the first and last time this winter.   I was completely weary before the evening was over, so much for habit.   Mrs. C. always enquires very particularly after you, and bade me remember her kindly to you and the girls and to tell Ann to make haste home, or she should not see her for a great while, as she and all her family were going to S. Carolina.

TO MRS. KIRKPATRICK.

Sidney, January 30th 1820   Sunday.
. . . . We have seen but little of Caroline B. She was to have pass'd a week with us, but the Missouri question coming on, she could not absent herself.   She is quite enchanted with the debates and spends all her

[1] James Riley, an adventurous mariner, was shipwrecked on the coast of Africa August 15, 1815, and kept as a slave by the Arabs for fifteen months, when he was ransomed by the British Consul at Magadore.   Mrs. Smith's friend, Anthony Bleecker, prepared from Riley's papers an "Authentic Narrative of the Loss of the American Brig *Commerce* on the Western Coast of Africa" (New York, 1816).

mornings at the Capitol. Our Vice-President[1] was so gallant, that he admitted ladies in the senate chamber and appropriated to them those charming and commodious seats which belonged to foreign ministers and strangers of distinction, but their numbers were so great for some days, that they not only filled these and all other seats, that at last they got literally on the floor, to the no small inconvenience and displeasure of many gentlemen. Nothing could be more brilliant than the audience Mr. Pinckney's eloquence attracted. Every one was in raptures. We intended to have been one of the intruders on that day, but was disappointed by our carriage being broken. Ann and I went one day with Caroline and Mrs. McClean, but were not much amused. Caroline is very affectionate and says nothing but the Missouri question shall keep her from us,—the moment that debate is over, she will come and make a long visit.

TO MRS. KIRKPATRICK

Sidney, April 23, 1820.

. . . . A few weeks ago Mrs. Calhoun[2] lost her infant daughter, about five months old. The moment I heard of its illness I went into the city and offered my services, and staid 2 days and sat up one night. But finding the crowd of visitors so great and the offers of service so numerous and pressing that tho' highly gratifying to the feelings of the parents, they were injurious to the infant. I never in my life witnessed such attentions. Ladies of the first and gayest fashion, as well

[1] Daniel D. Tompkins, of New York.
[2] Calhoun's residence in Washington began when he became Secretary of War in 1817, when his wife and mother-in-law joined him. This child who died March 22 was the second he had lost, the first having died while he was a member of Congress.

as particular friends, pressed their attendance, in a way not to be denied. The President called every day, and his daughter Mrs. Hay, altho' in the midst of bridal-festivities came three evenings successively to beg to sit up and was denied as other ladies were already engaged. I was one night and she came and sat all the evening by the child and reluctantly left it, but told Mrs. C. she should come the next evening, and would take no denial. The next morning Mrs. C. recollecting Mrs. Decatur gave a large party to the bride and thinking Mrs. H. could not with propriety be absent, she sent to beg her not to come, but the President said it was his particular desire that she should, as she was the best nurse in the world and so she proved to be. Mrs. Adams in the like manner and 20 others would attend. This being the case I did not remain, as I found myself none the better for the duties of a sick-room. All this was not a mere tribute to rank, no,—I am persuaded much of it was from that good will which both Mr. and Mrs. C. have universally excited, they are really beloved. Commodore Decatur's death,[1] was a striking and melancholy event. The same day, on which thousands of his fellow citizens attended him to his grave, High Mass for the Duke of Berry[2] was performed in a splendid and solemn manner, in the morning, at which an immense crowd attended, so that the whole day, the whole city, Georgetown and Alexandria were in a commotion, for citizens from both these towns, crowded to the city. The afternoon before, Mrs. Calhoun's infant had been buried, attended by an unusually long train of carriages. This week had been destined to be the gayest of the season, and parties for every night in the week were fixed for the bride, not one of which

[1] He was killed in a duel with Commodore Barron, March 22.
[2] The Duke of Berry was assassinated February 13.

took place, for from the moment Decatur fell, nothing else was thought of. Mrs. Decatur has left the city, house, carriages, &c &c are to be sold, and from all this gaiety and splendor she retires to solitude and melancholy. No one but her friend Mrs. Harper, who was in the house, ever saw her, and even to her, she seldom spoke a single word. More impressively than any words, did these events preach the vanity of honors and pleasures of rank and wealth.

TO MISS SUSAN HARRISON SMITH

Sidney, Sunday evening. [Sept. 1820.]

Your idea has not been a moment absent from my mind, my dearest child since I bade you farewell, except while asleep and even then I dreamt of you. At every hour I have said, "She is now at such or such a place. She has now reached Phila, now is sitting surrounded by such and such friends." Today I have imagined the impression which would be made on your mind, by the sight of so large a congregation, the great concourse of people you would meet in the streets, the sound of so many bells, &c &c. And while at church my petitions rose to the throne of grace with more faith and fervor, from the conviction that at the same hour, you too, were offering up yours.

Never did I hear from Mr. Caldwell and seldom from any one, a more instructive and animating and consoling discourse. It was on the necessity, benefit, and comfort of Prayer. Never having been separated before from my darling child, I feel more depressed and saddened by your absence than I had any idea of. Not an hour passes I do not seem to seek for you, to listen for you, and when

I seek and listen in vain, my heart quite sinks. It is
with a painful pleasure I come across anything that was
yours, and it was not without tears I appropriated your
work-box to myself and fill'd it with my work. These
lonely and sad feelings I know will not last and even
were they more painful than they are I would cheerfully bear them, for the sake of the pleasure and advantage your seperation will procure for you. With a mind
thus soften'd, I heard with peculiar benefit and pleasure
Mr. Caldwell's excellent discourse, and I felt that it was
in prayer we could most tenderly meet, tho' seperated by
such a distance.

I was peculiarly affected with one of the hymns sung
at church this morning, it so truly expressed my visions
and feelings, read it my dear Susan and think of me, it
is the 37th hymn beginning

"Alas what hourly dangers rise."

When you get to Brunswick, you will join the family
Sunday evening concert, sometimes ask your aunt to sing
our favorites, such as "Far from my thoughts etc. . . .

The morning after you left me, accompanied by both
the children, I went to the city, and after a visit to Mrs.
Bradleys, went to Mrs. Calhoun's, intending to stay but
a little while. She would, however, take no denial, but
with friendly force obliged us to stay to dinner. She
gave Bayard calfs' foot jelly, sent for oysters for him,
and then made him lie down on her bed, where he slept
for several hours. When we came away, she loaded him
with jellies and cakes. On Friday I felt so lost, lonely
and desolate without you, that I did not dare to sit down
to my work, but busied myself in the kitchen with making pickles and sweet-meats, and in the afternoon sister
Ann and I walked up to Mrs. Cuttings, who cheer'd us up

with her cheerful conversation and good coffee. When
I came home I still missed my Sue but tried to forget
her in caressing Bayard and Anna. Thursday and Saturday evenings were cold. We had a blaze kindled on
our hearth and enjoyed our first autumnal fire. The
sopha was drawn in its usual place and I took my accustom'd corner. You know how I love this twilight, or
rather fire-light hour, which makes winter dear to me.
The summer then is gone! How like a dream does the
interval appear since I last enjoyed this hour. On Saturday I again accompanied your father to town, Julia
and the children with me, on purpose to visit my two
afflicted friends Mrs. Clifton and Mrs. Tasslet. I spent
some serious hours with them. Poor Mrs. Tasslet is
the ghost of what she was. I never saw anyone so alter'd
in so short a space. We thought her sorrow moderate,
but alas we were deceived by appearances, she took a
pride in suppressing her tears and emotions, but her
sorrow has sunk the deeper and I much fear injured not
only her health but her mind. She says Jane talks continually of Godfrey. When she eats she says, "Mama
give brother some of this, I will save this for brother."
At night she often cries violently and pushes her mother
to the door, saying go mama go for my poor Godfrey,
bring him out of that garden and put him in his cradle.
Godfrey is cold in that garden, mama, for I hear him
crying." This she says almost distracts her. She had
laying by her the last cap he wore, which in his agony
he pulled off his head. She says it shall never be washed
and that it is seldom out of her sight. Poor woman, my
heart bled for her. Old Mrs. Calhoun visits her almost
daily, as she thinks, she is under a *religious concern,* to
use her expression. I much fear in the present distracted
state of her feelings Mrs. C. is not the most useful friend

she could have.   But stop I must, as I have promised to
leave room for a little letter of dear Anna.   Bayard continues to mend rapidly.   Farewell my beloved child.

TO MISS SUSAN H. SMITH

March 19, 1821, Sidney.

.   .   .   .   We are social beings, and the strongest
mind and warmest heart need the stimulus of society—
but not the society of the gay world.   *It* chills the affections, checks the aspirations of the soul, and dissipates
the mind.   You will most sensibly feel the loss of the
social pleasures you have this winter enjoy'd, when you
return to Sidney.   The family you best loved, will have
left Washington.   I mean the Forsythes.   They are to
go to Spain in June, and to New York in the course of
a week or two.   I will ask Julia to try and see you as
she passes through Brenner to bid you a farewell.   Mr.
and Mrs. Forsythe were here this week.   He looks thin
and pale and far from happy.   He has received none of
that public approbation so supporting and gratifying to
men in public life, so absolutely necessary to an ambitious
one.   His resignation I suspect would have been accepted, had it been offer'd, but having no private fortune,
and no expectation of other provision at home, he had,
I suppose, no choice but to return.   Mrs. F. says she
expects they will live in absolute retirement,—this will
not be very agreeable for the young folks.   Indeed none
of them seem pleased with the idea of going.   Thus it is,
my dear Susan, "our very wishes, give us not our wish."
With what eagerness is public employment sought and
yet how few who possess it, are free from the most harass-
ing cares, and severest mortifications.   To fill the vacancy

made by this family, we shall most probably have that of Genl. Brown[1] and of some Commissioners. No one seems yet to have the least idea who they are to be. I have seldom known such absolute silence observed. Not even a conjecture is form'd, altho' it is known from good authority that there have been above a hundred applications from persons of great respectability. Mrs. Calhoun has done her very best to obtain the clerkship of the board, for Mr. Tasslet. She went herself to the President and others, but I fear there is no chance, for a poor man and a foreigner. The son of a Senator is to be the secretary, a place for which many applications have been made, and much interest used even by the person who obtained it. This Florida business has filled our city with strangers. I am told above a 1000 persons are here seeking for some place in this new acquired Territory. The reduction of the army has thrown thousands out of employ. . . .

TO MRS. KIRKPATRICK

[Sidney,] August 17, [1822] Friday morning.

. . . . Our Bayard insists on remaining in the city, even should the cholera prevail there. If duty required it, I would not say a word to change his resolution. I could even encourage him to run any risque, which the duties of public station or humanity might require. But this is not the case. With Mr. Smith it is. He must be at the Bank,—anxious as I shall be. I acquiesce and shall only urge him to use every possible precaution. Several of our neighbours, Mr. Wood among others, are in the same predicament; being in public employ. A considerable degree of alarm and uneasiness prevail in the city,

[1] Jacob Brown, General-in-Chief of the Army from March 10, 1821, till his death, Feb. 24, 1828.

arising from several sudden deaths, chiefly blacks. Our
Police is awakening from its lethargy and are making
preparations. Fruit, especially melons, are prohibited,
much to the discomfort of the farmers and to ours in
particular. We never had such an immense crop of
melons before. The season has been very favorable.
That portion in the garden, under my direction, I have
had destroyed, feeding the ripe ones to the cows and
ploughing up the rest. The girls who stood by to watch
the avidity with which the cows devoured them, said they
could scarcely resist sharing in their feast and quite envied them the fine delicious melons that were thrown to
them. Our farmer will not follow my example, but by
hook and by crook, as the saying is, sells a great quantity,
people come to the field to purchase them. I hope they
will not have cause to rue their obstinacy. We are all
very careful in our diet, yet are none of us free from
occasional disorders of the stomach and bowels. Were
we to consider these as premonitory symptoms, we might
be continually dosing ourselves with medicine. But I
presume until the disease does get to the city, no danger
can arise from these slight complaints, always incident
to the season. With the exception of what you say on
this point your letter is very encouraging and has inspired
me with a confidence I did not before feel. Had I received it earlier, I should have engrafted part of it in a
letter of Maria's, which the persuasions of Mrs. Thornton and Mrs. Bomford to whom I read it, induced me to
publish in the Intelligencer. We always call after church
to enquire after Mrs. Bordeau. Mrs. Bomford does the
same, so our three families generally meet for an hour
or two on Sunday. It was then I read them Maria's
letter. We endeavor to persue our usual routine and
only once or twice have felt depressed or alarmed. The

awful symtoms, described by some of our visitants, produced this effect. Poor Mrs. Cutts is no more. She
has been long extremely ill. Our friend Mrs. Clay, who
while in the city was her daily visitor, awakened her mind
to religious considerations and persuaded her and her
daughters to be baptized. Her whole life has been devoted to the fashionable world. The distinctions it con-
ferred and the pleasures it afforded, the sole objects of
her ambition and desire, until a few weeks before her
death, when her mind was directed to higher objects.
She has been my fellow traveller in the paths of society,
our acquaintances and even our friends were the same.
Mrs. Randolph and Mrs. Clay Mrs. Bomford and Mrs.
Mason were among her most intimate associates and
faithfully discharged the last duties to a sick and dying
friend. Mrs. Van Ness, another contemporary in my
social life, is now dangerously ill of fever. Many of our
citizens have already fled from the expected enemy and
gone to different places in search of safety. . . .

FROM HENRY CLAY

[1822]

MY DEAR MADAM:

Dr. Huntt[1] thinks John[2] better this morning; but his
fever continues, without any alarming symptoms. We
hope to break it to day, and for the purpose of watching
him and seeing that his medicine is properly administered, I shall remain with him and not attend the Senate.

Many thanks for the Jelly &c and especially for your
friendly offer of service. He rests well at night, and
Charles and I sleep in the same room with him, without

---

[1] Henry Huntt, a well-known Washington physician.
[2] Clay's youngest son, born in 1821.

much disturbance to any party.   In the day, he is attended by a good female nurse.   I look moreover to day
or tomorrow for his brother and his wife, who will be
with me a week or ten days.   So that, whilst I am exceedingly grateful for your obliging tender of your personal attention, it will be unnecessary at present to tax
your kindness.   Should a different and unfortunate state
of things arise, I will avail myself of your goodness.

Faith'y yrs,

H. CLAY.

Saturday morning.

TO MRS. KIRKPATRICK

[Sidney,] Oct. 12, 1822.   saturday.

.   .   .   .   Disease and death, are making sad havoc
in many parts of our country, and tho' some are more
dreadfully affected, few are exempt.   Our city is very
sickly.   Billious fevers are universal, tho' not so fatal as
they have been in other seasons.   Lytleton, I am sure, will
sympathise in the general regret all the friends and acquaintances of John Law, felt at his death.   The very week
before I met him, in all the health and enjoyment of youth
and when he smilingly bow'd to me, I pointed him out
to Nicholas, as the young gentleman, whom I had every
day been telling him he resembled,—the next week he
was in his grave.   Poor old Mr. Law, is they say, almost
distracted.   Two months before he lost his darling
daughter and has every reason to fear for the life of his
other son, who is at Pensacola.   Not a family on Capitol-
Hill have escaped disease, and Mrs. Hunter, and Mrs.
Dr. May, are now lying so ill as to afford scarcely a hope
of recovery.   Meanwhile the awaken'd zeal of Mr. Post's
congregation and the other citizens is increasing; there

are large assemblies every night, either at the churches
or private houses. Mr. Caldwell, they say is fast wearing himself out, but as his health decreases, his zeal and
labours increase. All day he goes from house to house,
exhorting and praying, and every night at different meetings. His little daughter Harriet is one of the new converts, and with twenty or thirty other young people, made
a kind of public confession and were prayed over in
church, as they do in methodist meetings. They are introducing all the habits and hymns, of the methodists into
our presbyterian churches, after the regular service is
closed by the clergyman, the congregation rise, and strike
up a methodist hymn, sung amidst the groans and sobs of
the newly converted, or convicted as they call them, then
Mr. Caldwell calls on the *mourners* to come forward, and
he and others pray over them, as they loudly vent their
sorrows. To aid in this *revival,* young Mr. Breckenridge[1] from Princeton, and a Mr. Testen, or Thurston,
or some such name, another navy young man from Phila-
del. have come on. Mrs. Calhoun told me yesterday, her
mother had taken Mr. T. out with her, tho' it was raining
as hard as it could, *"to beat up recruits,"* (that was her
expression) for church that night, and that he never was
known to exhort, (for he is not yet licensed to preach)
without making at least half a dozen converts, that it was
astonishing the number he had converted in the short time
he had been here. A few evenings before, one of our
gayest and most fashionable young ladies, (whose name
I will not now mention) had been converted; that whilst
he spoke, she had been *convicted* and was so overcome
with the violence of her feelings, that she had run forward and thrown herself on him, and lay sobbing and

---

[1] Rev. John Breckenridge graduated from Princeton in 1818, and became
a distinguished Presbyterian divine.

crying on his shoulder, before all the assembly, while he
enquired into her feelings and talk'd most powerfully and
pathetically to her.   Mrs. Bradley, told me that Mr. Post
and Mr. Breckenridge were now labouring in good earnest that they said "they were going through the highways
and hedges, to invite guests," viz., that they went into
every house, exhorting the people, particularly into all
the taverns, grog-shops, and other resorts of dissipation
and vice.   Whether all these excessive efforts will produce a permanent reformation I know not; but there is
something very repugnant to my feelings in the public
way in which they discuss the conversions and convictions
of people and in which young ladies and children, display
their feelings and talk of their convictions and experi-
ences.   Dr. May calls the peculiar fever, the *night fever,*
as he says almost all cases were produced by night meetings, crowded rooms, excited feelings and exposure to
night air.   Mrs. Calhoun, (the old lady) says she means
to bring both the young missionaries out to see us.   Mr.
Breckenridge I really wish to see, as I know his sister
intimately and he knows my friends at Princeton.   She
cannot get her daughter to go to any of these meetings,
who with many others, disapprove of them,—of this number is Dr. Hunter.[1]   *"Revival! indeed,"* said the Doctor,
"I wonder what you mean by a revival?   I call it a *stir up,*
or a *fight,* rather."   *This,* and the Presidential election,
are the two animating principles at present in our city
society.   One or the other is the perpetual theme of discourse.   Every effort is making by Col. McKenny[2] and
his employers to get Mr. Crawford out of the Cabinet.
The discussion is kindling personal feelings, and the
friends of these gentlemen will I fear be made hostile

[1] Rev. Andrew Hunter.
[2] Editor of *The Washington Republican,* Calhoun's organ.

to each other. It was universally *believed,* that Mr. S. would have been appointed in Mr. Meig's place,[1] but he found those whose wishes would have placed him there, have now no influence. And it was only through *him,* that Mr. S. could have had influence on the subject you wrote to me about. You see, therefore, however kind and earnest his wishes for our friend in Phila., he can do nothing. The appointment you wrote about, is deem'd one of *high political* importance, and a high political character is talk'd of. And it will I believe depend on the President. I wish it were prudent to write more openly; as there are at present several points, on which I would wish to write to you. But I have so often experienced that our very "wishes, give us not our wish," that I now endeavour to suppress every desire and every anxiety about the future. We know not what is good for us; therefore I cheerfully resign the destiny of those I love, to an all wise and all good Providence. Anxious! Oh why should we ever be anxious, about a life, whose tenure is so frail and so uncertain! Every day, do we hear of the young, the healthy, the gay and the prosperous, being suddenly snatched from life. Lytleton, I believe knew Dr. Clark, of George Town,—he is dead, and the two young and lovely Miss Beverly's, the sisters of his wife. In the course of ten days, all three, from youth and health and happiness, were torn. And perhaps before another week, his wife, his father-in-law and the young gentleman to whom one of the Miss B's was in a week or two to have been married, may follow them to the grave, for they are all ill of the same disease. Ann Eliza Gales, too, who was likewise to have been soon married, died after a few days illness. Lytleton knew her. Our own family, have

[1] There was an effort made at this time to have Mr. Smith made Postmaster General.

as yet been exempt from sickness, except one of our servant women who is now ill of the prevailing fever.   Our
neighbour Mrs. White died, whilst Nicholas was here.   I
have thus far struggled through the season, not without
many threatenings of disease however, and a degree of
langour, which incapacited me for the least exertion, even
that of writing to you.   Ann's health is much improved
by her morning rides, for she always accompanies the
children to school.   She is in better health and spirits
than I have long known her, which makes me much
happier.

TO MRS. BOYD

Sidney 19, Dec. [1823]

. . . . When shall we see Mr. Boyd? I hope
he will be here when his friend Webster makes his Greek
speech.[1] I shall certainly try to hear it.   And I hope
too when he does come that our friend Crawford, will be
able to see his friends.   He is now shut up in a dark
room and sees very few persons.   That horrible calomel,
with which his whole system is surcharged, is I do believe the cause of all he now suffers.   The inflamation
in his eyes continues, so as to make him almost blind, and
pains, rheumatic pains they call them, have seized on all
his joints.   His head clerk, attends him every morning
and he transacts the necessary business of his office in
his chamber.   His spirits seem unimpaired and warm
weather it is thought will restore him to his usual robust
health.   His prospects are brightening in Pennsylvania.
The *old* Republicans, radicals if you please, disciples of
the Jeffersonian school, are roused from their inactivity
if Pensy goes with Virginia, there can be little doubt

[1] The speech, one of Webster's most elaborate, was delivered January
19, 1824.

of success. Mr. Caln. [Calhoun] and A[dams] seem not such good friends as they were. I can not tell what is the matter, but our politicians think, they will no longer lend each other a helping hand.[1] Whether they must fall without mutual aid, or whether they will get on better, separately, remains to be seen. There is no doubt of Mr. Jefferson's being decidedly for Mr. Crawford,[2] and he is a host in himself. If he were but well! But he has warmly attached friends, not merely political, who seek their own advancement, by favouring his, but personal friends, who love him for his virtues and respect him for his integrity and talents, and he deserves them, for he is a warm and zealous friend, where he possesses friendship. It would grieve me, if when Mr. Boyd came, he did not form an acquaintance with him, which should verify all I say.

Your dispatches will not go to Edward as soon as you hoped. Judge Southard who was here last week, says he has detained the Cyene for Mr. Brown. Mrs. Brown is very averse to a winter passage and good naturedly begged him to have a hole bored in the Cyene, or some other injury inflicted, so that it could not leave port until better season. The Judge told her, that on the contrary, he should hasten matters and begged her to be in readiness. She gave up her house last week and in a few days Mr. Brown departs. I have not called to bid her my adieus. I have given up formalities. Indeed I seldom go to the city and then only to the house of two or three friends. The summer is our gay season. The winter our working time. Your two last letters so inspired me that I have resumed Lucy and write a sheet or two every morning, when not interrupted. . . .

[1] They never did. They were united only in their contempt for Crawford.
[2] Probably a mistake. Jefferson made no intimations to this effect.

TO MRS. SAMUEL BOYD

[Sidney,] Sunday, 11th 1824, April.

. . . . Mr. Crawford[1] has taken Capt. Doughty's farm, which is separated from ours only by the road; he would remove immediately if it were not for business with Congress, but he will come immediately after it adjourns. He was here last week and seems to be recovering his strength. He walked over the grounds and was in fine spirits, and I trust leisure and change of air will soon restore him to perfect health. He talks of travelling north, but is not decided on it and if he finds the air of our hills beneficial, I suspect he will not leave home. Mr. Calhoun has removed to his house on the hills behind George Town and will live I suspect quite retired the rest of the session. He does not look well and feels very deeply the disappointment of his ambition. Mr. Macon and Col. Barton are here and I must close this long letter before Mrs. McClane comes. The gentlemen and Mr. Smith have gone out to walk. The day has cleared and is warm as summer. The peach trees are in bloom, the weeping willows, lilacs, &c &c are in leaf. Adieu,—write soon to

Yours affectionately.

TO MRS. KIRKPATRICK

[Sidney,] Thursday, June 28, 1824.

. . . . But it is natural that you and Maria who are surrounded by so many dear friends and relatives, should not have so much *leisure of the heart,* to think of

---

[1] Crawford had a town house at the corner of Massachusetts Avenue and 14th Street. The historian Schouler (Vol. III., p. 305, "History of the United States") makes the mistake of supposing it to have been his "mansion in the country."

me, as I have, who have no interests beyond my own
family.   I who live as it were in a land of strangers.   To
say this of a land where I have dwelt for 20 years seems
strange and yet is true.   The peculiar nature of Washington society makes it so.   Had the intimate acquaintances I formed when I first came been continued, twenty
years would have ripened them into friendship.   But one
after another have been separated by death, the ocean, or
mountains and water.   Mrs. Wharton and Mrs. Barlow
have long slept in their graves.   Mrs. Pichon, whom I so
tenderly loved and dear Mrs. Middleton, are on the other
side of the Atlantic, as are Mad'm Neuville and several
others that I admired and esteemed and some have been
estranged by differing and conflicting politics.   For instance Mr. Calhoun's family.   You have no idea, neither
can I in a letter give you an idea of the embittered and
violent spirit engendered by this Presidential question.

Our excellent friend Mr. Crawford, has been tried for
the third time, by a committee of men of hostile politics,
and like gold thrice tried in the furnace, comes out more
pure and bright, his most violent enemies, with their keenest researches can find nothing by which they can attaint
the purity of his integrity.   It is surprising to me that his
temper is not soured or irritated by these repeated attacks
of Malevolence and disease; instead of which he is now
more mild and indulgent to his opponents, more patient,
gentle and affectionate to his family than ever.   The
other evening speaking of Edwards [1] "I pity him," said he
with emphasis, "I pity him."   It was just after hearing
an account of the examination, in which his falsehood
had been proved, and his embarrassment and agitation

[1] Ninian Edwards was appointed Minister to Mexico in 1824 and was on
his way to his post when he was recalled in consequence of the discovery
that certain anonymous letters charging Crawford with malfeasance in
office were written by him.

described. "Poor man, I pity him," repeated he while
the moisture of his eyes confirmed the truth of what he
said.   He is now our neighbour, and will, I trust, be
soon quite well.   He told Mr. Smith he would come over
this morning and sit part of the day, he proposed walking, but Mr. S. advised him to ride.   He is so venturesome that I expect he will make himself sick again.   The
other evening when I went over, I found him sitting on
the Piazza, in a thin gingham gown.   But I am going
into details, in which perhaps you take no interest.   This
may be the last year we shall enjoy his society, and if we
lose him we lose our best friend.   But of this I own I
have not much apprehension, as I think his chance much
better than that of either of the other candidates, and
that it will be strengthened by the very means used by his
enemies to destroy him.   But enough of what you care
nothing about.

TO MRS. KIRKPATRICK

[New York] Tuesday morning. [1824][1]

. . . .   We had a charming party at his house,—
he did it to please me, which made me feel a little disagreeable; had he only had Mr. and Mrs. Johnson,
Bleecker, Maria and Mr. Boyd and Cooper[2] and Dr. Mitchel[3] I should have been better pleased, because it would
have been most agreeable to his own feelings.   I did not
go to dinner,—second thoughts made me think it best not.
In the evening, in addition to the above personages were
half a dozen more literary characters, a most interesting

[1] Mrs. Smith was on a visit to her sister, Mrs. Boyd—a rare occurrence,
for she seldom left her home.
[2] James Fenimore Cooper.   He seldom made a good impression on those
who met him for the first time.
[3] Mrs. Smith's old friend, the scientist S. L. Mitchill, whom she had known
when he was Senator from New York.

assemblage to me. Among them Mr. Shaafaer,[1] the
german clergyman. When he enter'd, the Dr. put a
chair next mine for him and he sat by me most of the
evening, gave me a great deal of information. When
Dr. Mitchell came in, he recognized me in his old, cordial
and friendly manner and not being able to get a chair beside me, brought one and placed it right before me, where
he sat a long while, talking with great interest of Washington and Washington folks, and the happy evenings
he used to pass at our house. No uninteresting topics
you will say. "I really did not know how much I loved
Washington until I had left it. I have since found it one
of my greatest pleasures to meet with any one who knew
or cared about it." This gave quite a charm to the
Philosopher's conversation. When he left his seat, Mr.
Cooper directly took it and I had a long conversation with
him conjointly with Mr. Schaafaer. I could not elicite
one bright idea, strike out one spark of genius from
Cooper, he was heavy and common place, no flowing
either of words or ideas,—he is a fine looking man, and
had I not been told, I should have fixed on him as the
author of the Pioneers, in this circle of more than a dozen
literary gentlemen. Dr. Harris,[2] President of the college and two professors were there. Mr. Moore, I believe Maryanne knows. I found him far more agreeable
in conversation than either of the other gentlemen. He
was uncommonly agreeable,—some one has told me he
admired Maryanne very much. I wish the admiration
was strong and mutual. I passed a most charming evening, in the enjoyment of the species of pleasure I most
enjoy. The snow storm and two succeeding days, I sat

[1] Frederick Christian Schaefer, pastor of the St. James English Lutheran
Congregation in New York.
[2] Rev. William Harris, President of Columbia College from 1811 to his
death in 1829.

all the mornings in this nice library. Maria part of the time with me, she says as I have already some of the calamities of authors, I shall enjoy by anticipation some of their privileges and comforts. As I have several days been indisposed, she insists on my laying late in bed, taking my breakfast in the library and lounging part of my morning in my flannel gown on the couch drawn close to the stove. Were you to see me reclining in the midst of my books and papers, you would really believe I was an author in fact. The evenings Mr. Day, Mr. Bleecher and others, pass'd at home with us, and Mr. Boyd and I seldom miss'd having a few games of chess. A number of ladies have call'd to see me. I have at least a dozen visits now on hand. Miss Segwick, the authoress and Mr. Hillhouse[1] the Poet, were both to see me yesterday besides Miss Harrison, Mrs. Lawrence (Miss Smith that was daughter of former senator, whom I knew in Washington) she is a lovely woman. I have promised her an evening if possible. Dr. Mitchel and Mrs. Mitchel called last week and fixed on [*torn out*] for me to pass the evening with them. The friends, Mr. and Mrs. Johnson, Mr. Bleecher and Dr. Stevens were asked to meet me. Maria went with me,—we there met Mrs. [*torn out*] and more than a dozen literary gentlemen. Cooper could not come, but Dr. M. introduc'd another author to me, whose work is now in the press. He put them in the corner of the sopha by me, saying, "here Dr. McHenny.[2] is a lady who will talk of the wilderness and the savages and Braddock's defeat with you, and will talk poetry in the bargain." A singular

[1] James Abraham Hillhouse, of New Haven. His wife was Cornelia, daughter of Isaac Lawrence, of New York. He published a number of long poems, dramas and tales.

[2] Probably this was a Dr. McKenney, but his writings have not preserved his name for posterity.

introduction, but it made us at once quite social. "These are barbarous themes for conversation," said I, smiling, "can you tell why Dr. M. selected them for our discussion?" "Oh, because they are the subjects of the novel I am now writing." Then we talked at large about his work. I knew I could not choose a more interesting topic, and it was one I too felt a peculiar interest in. I questioned him as to his mode of composition, the time he took, &c. "And do you enter into the feelings of the characters you describe?" "So perfectly," said he, "that my paper is often blotted with my tears and I weep, bitterly weep, over sorrows of my own creation." He has likewise published two little poems. The poetry is not very good, but moral and tender. But the poor little author is one of the ugliest of God's creation. Yet he interested me more than Cooper who is a very handsome, fine looking man. He has more heart if he has not more genius. Dr. M. showed us a great variety of natural curiosities but as I told Mr. Smith, *he* is the greatest curiosity in his collection, he was vastly amusing, dressed himself in an indian or mexican mantle with some outlandish crown, and a mexican sword, and enacted Montezuma for us. Afterwards he put all the same savage regalia on Mr. Bleecher, who looked handsomer than I ever saw him in any dress. We called him Pizzaro or Cortes, his black eyes, whiskers, curling hair, and heavy eyebrows, gave him quite the appearance of a spanish grandee. . . .

TO MRS. KIRKPATRICK

[Washington,] Thursday night, 13th January, 1825.

. . . . You must know society is now divided
into separate batallions as it were.[1] Mrs. Adams collected a large party and went one night [to the the-
atre], Mrs. Calhoun another, so it was thought by our
friends that Mrs. Crawford should go too, to show our
strength. Last week I was in the city and the girls
wanted to go. Caroline and I got in the carriage after
dinner, and in one hour collected a party of 10 ladies
and above 20 gentlemen. I called at Mr. McClain's door,
sent for him, told him I was going with the Miss C.'s
and my girls. In a moment he said we should have as
many members and senators as we wanted, he and Mr.
Van Buren would muster them and take the box. With
a strong Crawford escort we went and passed so agreeable an evening that this week they wanted to go again
and the gentlemen said we must let them know in time
and they would display a stronger force. The company
last night agreed on it. So this morning the girls and I
went out to make our arrangements. When we got
there, the senate was sitting with closed doors. We
went for a member who took us in the library and sent
for Mr. Forsythe, Mr. McClane and some other of our
friends, where by the fire on a sopha we made up our
party and a very large one it is. As Mrs. Crawford for
18 months has never been out, scarcely left Mr. C. an

[1] In Washington the chief candidates for the Presidency, all members of
the same cabinet, were Adams, Crawford and Calhoun. Clay also was a
candidate and Andrew Jackson was gathering a mighty following which was
not fully reckoned with by the leaders in Washington. Crawford was a
genial, charming man, and he captured Mrs. Smith completely. He was,
in reality, a mere wire-pulling politician without any real claim to the office
he sought.

hour, I persuaded her to go and promised to stay and keep Mr. C. company, and here I am. We played chess until we were tired, he retired early and I am alone in the house, servants and children excepted, and embrace this quiet and tranquil hour to write to you. Contrary to my intentions I have been drawn more into company this winter than usual. I feel the spirit of society awakened. Never I think did I enjoy it more. It does my heart good to see Mr. C. so well and so happy. His happiness is quite independent of political circumstances, it depends chiefly if not entirely on his family,—he is the fondest father and one of the best husbands I ever knew. There cannot be a kinder or better man, and never had any public character more personal and devoted friends.

The fate of the election is as uncertain as ever,—the friends of each candidate are sanguine of success, and tho' divided and known, as I have said above, yet when they meet, perfectly good natured and polite. And meet they do, at all the parties, and joke together very pleasantly. I cannot perceive any animosity, any bitterness, or suspicion,—every one openly avows his predeliction and does his best to promote the interest of the candidate whose cause he has embraced, but it is all done, (as far as it respects society) in a fair and pleasant manner and I really hope the crisis will pass without turbulence or difficulty of any kind. At Mr. A.'s the other evening, there were Jacksonites and Adamites and Crawfordites all mingled harmoniously together. What a happy government, what a happy country! Since I have been convinced that Mr. C.'s happiness is so independent of success I have become almost indifferent as to the result. If his health is perfectly restored, he and his family will be happy in retired and domestic life. Pardon me for writing so much on this subject about which you cannot care much. It is at present so exclusively the object of public and private interest that I do not think or hear of much else and really just now cannot write of much else. . . .

TO MRS. BOYD

. . . . Another evening had a charming social party at home, viz, Mr. C[rawford']s.[1] He enjoyed himself excessively, it was the first time these two winters he has had a room full of company. He looked perfectly well, and as this is a thing which no one will believe, except those who see him, his friends in Congress are very desirous that he should give a Grand Ball and invite all Congress and all the citizens and strangers and think, seeing with their own eyes, they might perhaps believe that he is no longer a sick man. Mrs. C. feels afraid of the experiment. He has now been secluded from society for 16 or 17 months, and she knows not what effect lights, noise, a crowd and the atmosphere of a crowded room might have. It is to be determined in a day or two. But I wish people would not like Thomas be so incredulous and would believe without seeing, or had good will enough to come and see without invitation. Mrs. C., Caroline and Anne Smith went to the Theatre the other night. We took care to let our friends in both houses know and to ask such ladies as we knew were friendly. The result was there was an overflowing house, very brilliant, and what is better still, with but few exceptions, all Crawfordites. Quite imposing, I assure you. Mrs. C. and party sat in the front box,— it was crowded with members and senators and as Mr.

[1] Where Mrs. Smith was staying, as she had no house in town that winter.

Holmes, who called next day, told us every one was re-
marking how ably Mrs. Crawford was supported. Cobb[1]
and Lowry[2] on one side, Van Buren I believe and I forget who else on the other, with a phalanx behind.   I
went the previous evening and would not go, but staid at
home and played chess with Mr. C.   On every occasion
that offers, his friends show Mr. C. the warmest and most
devoted attachment.   They will adhere to him faithfully.   Whether they will succeed in their endeavours
is doubtful.   Folks here generally consider Genl. J[ack-
son] as having a better chance.   It will soon be determined.   I wish it was over.   Mr. C. seems no way
anxious or impatient, he is always the same, mild, cheerful and affectionate.   The first sound I heard of a morning, was his voice calling to his little children, "Come
here my son, come here my daughter and kiss Papa for
good morning."   He is excessively fond of chess and
plays constantly when not engaged in business.   While
I was there we some times substituted whist, and we all
took turns to read, as he reserves his eyes for business,
to which he attended every morning.   .   .   .

February 11, 1825. Washington.

The contest is last over, and our friend has failed,[3]
this was wanting to show his character in all its light and
brightness.   To me and not only to me but to all those
friends who have seen him as near as I have, he appears
a greater man, than any dignity or office could have made
him.   He heard the decision without any surprise, or
emotion of any kind.   His first words were, "Is it pos-

[1] Thomas W. Cobb, Senator from Georgia.
[2] Walter Lowrie, Senator from Pennsylvania.
[3] Crawford received all the electoral votes of Virginia and Georgia and
some from New York, Maryland and Delaware, but failed of a majority,
and in the election by the House Adams succeeded through the efforts of
Clay.

sible! Well, I really believed from what I heard last night that Jackson would have been elected." The day previous to the election as well as ever since has been stormy weather so that Mr. C. could not go to his office. On the day previous, the girls and Mr. C. brought their work in the parlour, and we read by turns aloud to Mr. C, but we were often interrupted by company. A great many strangers whom curiosity had attracted to Washington, were drawn here by the same motive, wishing to see how the candidate looked at such a crisis. Among others was our old acquaintance Joe Lewis. He asked Mr. Crawford how he expected to spend next summer?—a droll question at such a moment! "Probably in Georgia," answered Mr. C. "but that must depend on events." "True," answered Mr. L. recollecting himself and perceiving his question had indicated his certainty of the result. Soon afterwards, Count de Menou[1] and Mr. Ohner from Baltimore came in. "So," said Mr. O. after some previous conversation, "So, Adams it seems is to be elected." Count de Menou was startled, he looked at me and raised his eyebrows to mark his astonishment and then coming to me he whispered as if in exculpation of his friend's impoliteness, "You see, Madam, what a high respect every one has for Mr. C.'s strength of mind, otherwise no one would have hazarded such a remark just now." Mr. C.'s reply was, "Why, some still hope that Jackson will succeed." There was a succession of company until dinner time, among others Mr. Cambreling brought Mr. Hoar who told me he had recently seen Mr. Boyd.

All the afternoon and evening we played chess. By way of a joke and to increase the amusement and in-

[1] Comte de Menou was Secretary of Legation and Chargé d'Affaires *ad interim* of France.

Andrew Jackson.

From the painting by Sully (1825) in the Corcoran Gallery,
Washington.

terest of the game, "Come" said I, "let it be the presidential game and let us try who will succeed. Which will you be Mr. C?" "Adams, Adams," said he, "for of the two I would wish him to succeed." "I will take the red pieces then and be Genl. Jackson, so take care of yourself Mr. C. for my cavalry can leap over any barrier you may oppose. I shall not be scrupulous I assure you, but take every advantage, not heeding even the constitution of the game." He laughed heartily at the idea and said he would oppose my rashness by his diplomatic skill and political wisdom,—the girls sat round and at every advantage called out "Now Jackson, now Adams." *Stale mate,* we agreed should represent Mr. Crawford. (In truth it was the result in the Presidential game which was anticipated by many of our friends viz., no election). Every game we called one ballot. After five hardly contested games, Adams came off with three. This little conceit gave occasion to a good deal of merriment and will give you some idea of Mr. C.'s state of mind, the night previous to the election. The 9th was a snow storm. Unless you realize the strong hopes of success, which during the last two or three days our friends had felt, and had infused into the mind of Mr. C. and family, you can not realize the state of our feelings. But I cannot go into particulars for I am fearful of trespassing the boundary of confidential or avowed information. But this far I can say, since our friends say it without concealment, and with an indignation which they do not pretend to disguise. The vote of *one* of the gentlemen of your state[1] decided the election. I presume without naming him, Boyd will know him, and this vote was given under the conviction that it was to be thus decisive. "What shall I do," said he to a firm and undaunted

[1] Van Rensselaer. See Mrs. Smith's letter of February, 1825.

friend, with whom for more than two years he had acted,
"the responsibility is more than I can bear."   "Why so?"
replied his friend.   "You are a man in every circumstance of life independent.   There can be no motive except principle to sway your conduct.   You are an old
man.   My vote is equally decisive.   I am a young man,
I risk everything, yet I have no hesitation; take hold of
me and let us stand firm."   This was an hour before the
balloting took place.   "I am determined," answered the
gentleman, "here is my hand, I give you my word of
honor I will not vote for Adams."   Not long after this,
some one told the firm gentleman that the other seemed
irresolute and anxious.   He again went to him and
called your N. Y. Senator[1] to aid him.   Once more he
was confirmed and repeated his promise on his honor.
To give still greater weight, another friend went to him,
as he was passing to take his seat.   To this gentleman he
repeated his promise and said he no longer was irresolute.   Yet ten minutes afterward when he wrote his
ballot, it was for Adams and settled the matter.   The
gentleman who gave me those details and lives in the
same house said for the rest of that day and evening he
was sick at heart, the defeat he could have borne well
enough, but to be thus betrayed, thus deceived in one in
whom he had trusted as in himself, gave him such a disgust to human nature, that he almost doubted the honesty of every man and determined to leave political life,
and retire to the private walks of life.   Thus far I wrote
in the city, and left off friday morning.   The result was
known at three o'clock.   Mr. Dickens[2] who brought intelligence was much affected, more so than any of the
family, soon after, followed Mr. Cobb, the nearest friend

[1] Van Buren.
[2] Asbury Dickens, Chief Clerk of the Treasury Department, who managed
its affairs when Crawford was ill.

of the family, and by dark, many other friends. Mr.
Crawford talked of details of the election, with as much
ease and indifference as a person wholly unconcerned,
and after tea he became so engaged in his game of whist,
that I believe he forgot the recent event,—some of the
company played chess, some talked and laughed. It was
not until eleven oclock we were left alone and I can
truly say this evening was not only cheerful but gay.
"The long agony is over," said Mr. Cobb, laughing and
rubbing his hands, "We have ease and peace at last."
"Well," said Mrs. Crawford, "the thing that reconciles
me to the disappointment, is that it has been brought
about by the hand of God, and not by the designs of men,
and therefore it must be right." She, as well as most of
our friends, think that his ill health prevented his success. The next day, Thursday and Friday and Saturday, the parlour was never empty from ten oclock in the
morning until ten at night, and in the evenings we had
a circle,—one would have thought, instead of the defeated, he had been the successful candidate. On Thursday morning G. Lafayette came and sat an hour, afterwards the old general. The good old gentleman seemed
very much affected for he is very fond of Mr. Crawford,
he pressed his hand between both of his, and then sat
down so close, that I really supposed from his attitude he
was going to *hug* Mr. C. He sat near three hours with
him. On friday morning General Jackson accompanied
by Genl. Swortwout[1] called. I was much pleased with
him. He and Mr. C. shook hands very cordially, he did
so likewise with Mr. Smith who sat near him and conversed freely on common place subjects. The day after
the election, Mr. C. received a polite, frank, and I might

---

[1] Samuel Swartwout, of New York, afterwards Collector of the Port of
New York. His administration of his office resulted in grave scandals.

almost say friendly letter from Mr. Adams, in which he
not only requested, but expressed "an earnest hope and
desire" that he would remain in his present situation, (is
not this a full refutation of all the suspicions Mr. A.
proposed to have concerning Mr. C.'s conduct in the
Treasury). Without waiting to consult anyone, Mr. C.
immediately wrote an answer equally polite and frank,
declining the offer. Every friend who successively came
in and heard his decision approved highly of it,—the
motives he assigned were, that his political views differed
so essentially from Mr. A.'s, that he looked upon it as im-
probable if not impossible that they should ever agree.
To accept a place in his cabinet as an opponent to his
measures he deemed as unpleasant as it would be ungenerous, and to be an accessory to measures he did
not approve, was he thought inconsistent with honesty.
Tho' sensible of the advantage his continuance in office
might be to his young and rising family; tho' he was
going home to comparative poverty, his integrity could
not be shaken. "I cannot *honestly* remain," said he, and
that settled the matter. What a good and great man he
is! To me, he seemed greater at that moment than if
he had been elected President. "Well boys," said Mrs.
C, "only one of you can be a gentleman now. One, may
go to college and the rest of you must turn in to ploughing." "And instead of drawing . . . Miss Caroline"
said Mr. Cobb, "you may turn into the dairy, make butter and cheese, and as for you Ann, you may go to spin-
ning cotton." "And what shall I do?" said little Susan,
"oh you shall reel the cotton yarn. I have a pretty little
reel at home for you, that goes click click." Susan
jumped for joy. "And as for Bibb," continued Mrs. C.
"I can find work for him too." (he is 3 years old) he can
hold the spools, while I wind." All this was said with so

much good humour and pleasantness, that I was almost
tempted to think it was what they preferred.   The whole
family, including Mr. C. are much more gay and cheerful than for many preceeding weeks.   Suspense is certainly more painful, than any certainty.   Saturday evening Mr. Owen of Lanack, passed several hours with us.
He is ugly, awkward, and unprepossessing, in manners,
appearance and voice, but very interesting in conversation.
This has been one of the most interesting weeks of my
life.   I have passed almost every hour of it with Mr. C.
and his family.   He liked to have them all round him
and the evening of the election would not let the little
ones go from him.   Susan had her arms round his neck,
stroking his hair, kissing him and playing with him, while
his little boy sat on his knee, both children encompassed
with his arms and often pressed affectionately to his
bosom.   His feelings, (for he must have felt on the occasion) vented themselves in fondness and caresses of his
children.   It is only through his heart that happiness or
wisdom can reach Mr. C.   Leave him the objects of his
affection and he will be cheerful and happy, whatever
else may befall him.   But this week was a mournful
week too, to me.   I felt as if the approaching separation
was that of death, and as I gazed on him, felt as if taking a last, a farewell look, of one who for many years has
been our kindest and dearest friend.   It required constant
effort to be cheerful, which I wished to be.   One of his
friends, shaking hands with me said,—"between *his*
friends, there must ever be a bond of union.   Yes, even
when we have lost him."   "Such a minority as Mr. C.
has long had," said Mr. McClean to me "never could have
been held together by any motive less powerful than personal attachment.   Never had any man such warm and
devoted friends.   For his sake they were willing to risk

their all;— yea life itself." Nothing could reduce
them.

After church on Sunday, Mr. C. and the rest of the
family, came out with me and spent the rest of the day.
When I shook hands and bid him farewell, "not yet,"
said he smiling. "I shall come to see you again." Various rumours are afloat, concerning the members of the
Cabinet, but without foundation. Mr. A. I do not believe
himself knows. If, (as it is believed) the leading republicans will not accept places, he will be embarrassed, and
must either take federal gentlemen or secondary republicans. As yet, he has shown a great desire to conciliate
and it is said will be a very popular Pred. I hope so. I
love peace and good will with every one. I hope his administration will do honor to himself and good to his
country. All sides show equally good dispositions,—no
personal enmity, no asperity. Genl. Jackson has shown
equal nobleness and equanimity and received equal testimonies of respect and affection. To the honor of human
nature, as much attention has been paid the two unsuc-
cessful, as the successful candidate. For foreigners this
election must have had something new and imposing, and
to every one presented a spectacle of *moral sublimity.*
These agitations and anxieties are now over, for my own
part, I have felt much and rejoice once more to sit down
tranquilly. I shall resume my books and pen without
any wandering thoughts. We now feel fixed for life,
the retirement of Sidney, I have no more to look forward to any change in our mode of living. The few
remaining years of my life, (if indeed years await me)
I will endeavour to improve, as well as to enjoy in endeavours to promote the happiness and welfare of my
children and neighbors. The circle is a very contracted
one, but contains sufficient objects to fill the hands, the

heart, the mind. As for Mr. S. he is always calm.
Nothing has power to disturb his strong and well governed mind. He lives above the influence of the accidents of life.

[Sidney] February 1825.[1]

I have returned home after passing a most interesting
week with one of our best and greatest men—with one
of our kindest and most valued friends. . . .

When I returned to the parlour, the gentlemen were
giving the family an account of the election—the mode in
which it had been conducted and the causes which had
produced this unexpected result. "Falsehood—dam-
nable falsehood," exclaimed Mr. Cobb, "the poor miserable wretch after three times in the course of an hour
giving his word of honor not to vote for Mr. A.—Five
minutes after this last promise—did vote for him and
this gave him a majority on the first ballot." "Do not
say such bad words," said Caroline, "bad words and hard
names, will not alter the matter." "It is enough to make
a saint swear," reiterated Mr. Cobb. "Such treachery
and cowardice!" If Mr. A. had not been chosen on the
first ballot it was calculated—nay, promises had been
pledged,—that three states that voted for him first, would
come over to Mr. C. on the second—and that on each succeeding ballot, his course would have gained strength.
Many who voted for A. did so only in compliance to some
previous engagement with their constituents to make him
their *first* choice, tho' they in their own minds preferred
Crawford, and have since regretted, not following their
own judgments, instead of the instructions of their constituents. It was likewise supposed that when Jackson's
friends lost hope of success, they would prefer C. to A.

[1] From Mrs. Smith's notebook.

and would ultimately vote for him. Such at least was the understanding between the different parties, tho' it never seemed possible to me that Jackson who had so many more states than C. should ever yield to a minority. The only ground for such a hope, was the known impossibility of C.'s friends—who had resolved at all events to vote for no one but him, even tho' there should be no President and that Mr. Calhoun should come in—he being Vice-P. About dusk several other members and senators came in.—The conversation turned on the same subject and every one appeared as much mortified and disappointed as if assured of success previous to the election. Two of the gentlemen proposed going to the Drawing room to see how things appeared there and promised to come back and bring us some account of it. Cards were brought Mr. Cobb and Ann, Mr. Crawford and myself made the game of whist, Caroline and Mr. Lowry played chess and the rest talked and laughed while they looked over our game. That ease which certainty gives the mind after long endured anxiety and suspense, supplied it with pleasurable sensations which for the moment seemed to overbalance the mortification of defeat, and relieved from this pressure the spirits rose with an elastic spring and inspired us with mirth.

This seemed to me the cause. But be it what it might, the fact was certain that we were all very merry and joked and laughed in all honesty and sincerity. Between ten and eleven the gentlemen returned, and gave us an account of the drawing room. "Luckily," they said, they went late, otherwise they could not have got in. Some of the company had gone and made room for the others, but at one time the mass was so compact that they could scarcely move. "Pray Sir, take your finger out of my ear," said some one, "I will, Sir, as soon as I get room to stir."

Some were absolutely lifted from their feet and carried forward without any exertion of their own. Persons who never before had been seen in company, had got in that night, altho' the Marshall who stood at the door of the entrance had done his best to prevent intruders and had actually sent many away. Genl. Scott had been robbed of his pocket-book containing 800 dolls., and much mirth occasioned by the idea of pick-pockets at the Presidents Drawing room. A good anecdote for the Quarterly Review![1] "But when we got there," said Mr. Williams,[2] "the crowd was not so dense. We could see and move. Mr. Adams was not more attended to than usual, scarcely as much so as General Jackson." "I am pleased to hear that," said I, "it is honourable to human nature." "But it was not very honourable to human nature to see *Clay,* walking about with exultation and a smiling face, with a fashionable *belle* hanging on each arm,—the villain! He looked as proud and happy as if he had done a noble action by selling himself to Adams and securing his election. More than one, pointing to A. said, there is our *'Clay President,'* and he will be moulded at that man's will and pleasure as easily as clay in a potter's hands." "When Prometheus made a man out of clay," said Mr. W., "he stole fire from heaven to animate him. I wonder where our speaker will get the fire with which he means to animate his Clay President." "Not from Heaven, I warrant," said one of the gentlemen. "Genl. Jackson," said Mr. Williams, "shook hands with Mr. Adams and congratulated him very cordially on his sweep." "That was a useless piece of hypocrisy," observed Mr. Crawford—"it deceived no one—shaking

[1] The British *Quarterly Review* was generally critical in tone towards the United States. See for example in the October, 1823, number, the review of "Dwight's Travels in New England."
[2] Thomas H. Williams, Senator from Mississippi.

hands was very well—was right—but the congratulatory speech might have been omitted. I like honesty in all things."   "And Van Ranselear[1] was there too," said Mr. Williams, "but tho' he too had a lady hanging on his arm, he looked more in want of support himself, than able to give it to another."

"Poor Devil!" said Cobb, "one cant help pitying as well as despising him."

"Pity!" said Mr. L[owry]—"I have no pity for a wretch like him. If he had not strength to do his duty, why did he not confess it then one would have pitied without blaming him, but to lie—to betray—to give his solemn and voluntary word of honor and five minutes afterwards to violate that word of honor—showed him as destitute of honesty, as he is of strength—such a fellow I cannot pity."

"Well," said Mr. Crawford, "I do pity him, for it was weakness and only weakness that betrayed him; he had no motive, no hope of reward, it was not treachery, but weakness and I pity a weak man, even more than a weak woman."   "Woman!" said Mr. Cobb, "why no old woman in the land would have been so weak."

At this we all laughed, particularly when some one said it was in obedience to women that he had done so, for it was well known his wife had written to him on the subject and that she ruled him with an iron rod.

This I expressed my doubts of, knowing Mrs. V. to be a very mild woman, and whose character I should not suppose calculated to give her such influence.

"You are mistaken madam," said a gentleman, "he refers to her on all occasions.   I remember once dining in a very large company with Mr. and Mrs. Van R.

[1] Stephen Van Rensselaer was the eighth patroon. His wife was Margaret Schuyler, daughter of General Philip Schuyler.

Some one present asked Mr. V. R. if he had read Baron Humbold's late work. He pondered some time on the question, hesitating —'I—I—really am not sure. Have I ever read Humbold's work, my dear?' said he, reaching across a gentleman and speaking to his wife. She looked vexed and hastily replied, 'Certainly, you know you have read it.' "

"Poor fellow, no wonder then," said one, "that he asked her who he should vote for."

"Pshaw!" exclaimed another, "he did not get a letter from his wife during the five minutes that intervened between giving his word of honor and giving his vote."

"No, no," said another gentleman, "But Clay, the grand mover, tempter rather—whispered in his ear, some one told me he saw him leave his chair and go and whisper a few words, just after Van Buren left him."

"That is not so," said another. "I heard it was Webster."

"No, not Webster," said Mr. Vale,[1] "I was in the gallery and with my own eyes saw all that passed, just after he had taken his seat in the New York delegation, and a few minutes before the Ballot box was handed him I saw Scott[2] of Missouri go and whisper in his ear, and some delay certainly did take place when the Box was handed to the N. Y. delegation."

"Well it comes to the same thing," said Mr. Lowry, "it was Clay after all, for Scott was a mere emissary of his, and had previously by his arts secured the votes of this one too. Scott was irresolute, until Clay got hold of him, he had him with him until late last night. And altho his inclination led him to vote for us, Clay had power to persuade him to vote for Adams. 'Ah,' as

---

[1] Stephen Vail, a resident of Washington.
[2] John Scott, Representative.

John Randolph observed after counting the ballots, 'it
was impossible to win the game, gentlemen, the cards
were stacked.' "

"And that," said Mr. Cobb, nodding his head, "is fact
and the people have been tricked out of the man of their
choice."

When the news of his election was communicated to
Mr. Adams by the Committee and during their address,
the sweat rolled down his face—he shook from head to
foot and was so agitated that he could scarcely stand or
speak.   He told the gentlemen he would avail himself
of the precedent set by Mr. Jefferson and give them his
answer in writing.   One of the Committee told me from
his hesitation, his manner and first words, he really
thought he was going to decline.

If success, thus discomposed him, how would he have
supported defeat?

The day of the election was a heavy snow-storm—this
was a fortunate circumstance, as it prevents the gathering
together of idle people, who when collected in crowds,
might have committed some foolish violence.   Indeed in
one ward of the city, Mr. Vale told me, an effigy of Mr.
Adams had been prepared and had it not been a stormy
day, his opponents among the lower citizens would have
burnt it.   This would have excited his friends, (particularly the negroes, who when they heard of his election
were the only persons who expressed their joy by Hur-
ras) some riot might have taken place.   Among the
higher classes of citizens, no open expressions of exultation took place.   Respect and sympathy for the other
candidates, silenced any such expression.

Is there any other country, in which such earnest and
good feelings would have governed the populace?

The clapping in the Gallery of Congress, was short as

sudden—it was silenced by loud hisses, before the order of the Speaker to clear the Galleries could have been heard—silenced by popular feeling. And a simple order, without the application of any force, instantly cleared them. How admirable are our institutions. What a contrast does this election by the House of Representatives form to the elections of the Polish Diet. They were surrounded by foreign armies, controlled by foreign powers. In Washington on the 9th of February not a sign of military power was visible and even the civil magistrates had nothing to do.

While the electoral votes were counting, (which was done by the Senate and House conjointly) foreign ministers, strangers of distinction and General Lafayette were present. But when the Senate rose and the house formed itself into a *Body of States* to elect the President, the Senators withdrew from the floor, and all other persons from the House. "What even General Lafayette?" said I, "Yes," replied Mr. Lowry, "and had General Washington himself been there, he too must have withdrawn." The delegation of each State, sat together and after ascertaining by ballot which candidate had the majority in the State, appointed one of its delegation, to put the ballot for that candidate into the Ballot box.

The whole proceeding was conducted with silence, order and dignity, and after the Ballots were collected Mr. Webster and Mr. Randolph were appointed the Tellers. It was Mr. Webster who with an audible and clear voice announced J. Adams elected.

Such a scene exhibited in perfection the *moral sublime*.

The succeeding day, Thursday, citizens and strangers crowded to pay their respects, not only to the President-elect, but to Mr. Crawford and Genl. Jackson. Mr. Crawford's drawing room was never empty from eleven o'clock in the morning until eleven at night. This morning he did not seem as well as he had done of late. He looked pale, serious and languid, but he conversed with his usual gentleness and cheerfulness. The evening of the election, he kept his little children up later than usual. At twilight they sat on his knees—incompassed in his arms—and he seemed to enjoy with even more than his usual fondness their caresses. I observed him often press them to his bosom and kiss them. Little Susan, kneeling on his lap, hugged and kissed him and stroked his cheeks and played with his hair, until Mrs. Crawford fearing she would tease or fatigue her father, would have taken her away, "No, no," said he, "clasping her and his little son tightly to his bosom, "no, no, leave them with me—they do not fatigue me." And while at cards they were either standing by his knee or on the sopha behind him, bobbing their heads, now here, now there, pressing first one, then the other cheek and playing various little tricks, which on other occasions seemed to disturb him, but this evening, tho' deeply interested in his game, he did not check them, nor would permit them to be sent to bed, but every now and then turned to press their heads and kiss them. Amiable affectionate man! Affection was the most effectual balm to heal any wound disappointed ambition inflicted.

On this day too—Thursday—he had them constantly by him. His wife, his daughters, his younger children and myself were the whole time with him. Even Mrs. Belmoni, the old nurse could not stay away, but often made excuses to come in the drawing room. "Poor old woman," said he, on her leaving the room, "she seems to take it to heart more than any one."

"It is the idea of being separated from the children, and family," said I. "She told me yesterday that she

would never leave you, that whether you would or no, she
would go to Georgia with you and that if you had
nothing but a crust to give her, she would stay with you,
for that it would break her heart to be separated from the
children." Mr. Crawford seemed affected and I thought
I saw his eyes glisten.

How every one who knows this man loves him!

Among the earliest visitors was George Lafayette.
How affectionately he held Mr. C.s hand between both
his, while his countenance beamed with tenderness and
sensibility. His father he said was detained by company, but the moment he was free he should be here.
He sat about an hour. The conversation this morning
was entirely on commonplace subjects—none of the visitors alluded to what had taken place. About one o'clock
General Lafayette came. . . . It was not until four
oclock that Genl. Lafayette left his friend and when Mr.
C. joined us at the dinner table, he mentioned among
other things that he had said, had Jackson been chosen,
Mr. Irving, (former Minister in Spain and a warm
friend of Mr. C.'s then in Paris) would never have for-
given him, but would have attributed his election to him,
at least to the *éclat,* which his arrival in the U. S. had
given to the military. "In order to avoid any such influence," continued the General "and to show that I respected the civil, more than the military power, I have
invariably avoided wearing uniform, and on every occasion since I have been here, have reviewed the troops in
my plain blue coat and round hat." Mr. Crawford expressed his high appreciation of the delicacy and dis-
cretion Genl. Lafayette had shown, not only in this but
in every other circumstance relative to the Presidential
contests.

Before the candles were light, visitors arrived—Col.

and Mrs. Bomford, and Judge Johnson were among the earliest and as soon as we had taken our tea and coffee we commenced our usual harmless game of whist—harmless as we never played for anything.   It was difficult to think up a commonplace conversation, where every one felt so much and cards was a good resource.

Soon after Mr. Van Buren and McClean (of Del) came in.   As soon as the game was finished I gave up my hand to Mr. Van B. and sat by Mr. McClean with whom Mrs. C., Caroline and I had an interesting conversation, as we sat on the sopha, the opposite side of the rest of the company.

"And how do you bear our disappointment?" said I to Mr. McC., who is a particular friend.   "I am sick, sick at heart," replied he.   "I could not come here yesterday—I felt too wretchedly.   I went to bed for an hour or two and when a little calmed, rose and poured out all my feelings in a letter to my wife.   I gave her the whole history and then felt a little easier."

"Why you bear it worse than any one I have seen," said I.

"Oh, Mrs. Smith," said he, "Defeat I could have borne as philosophically as any one, but, falsehood, deceit, treachery, from one in whom I had trusted, with as much fullness and confidence. as I trusted myself, that *I could not bear*.   Mrs. Smith, it has so disgusted me with political men and political life—nay with mankind itself, that I wish I could shut myself up for life and have nothing more to do, with any one but my wife and children. I look around—and exclaim where is there one man I can trust! and I feel there is not one!"

"Why what can have produced such disgust against your species?" asked I.

"Treachery and falsehood," replied he, "where I believed was honor and truth. Genl. V. R. has for two years been one of our mess. He has betrayed those with whom he broke bread. We conversed before and confided in him as one of ourselves. He always professed himself one in our views, our plans, our hopes, and this very morning, not half an hour before he betrayed us, he pledged me his word of honor, that he would not vote for Adams. After the Senate withdrew, some one came and told me he was walking in the lobby, and looked anxious and perturbed. I went to him and asked him what disturbed him. 'McClean,' said he seizing my hand, 'the election turns on my vote—*one* vote will give Adams the majority—this is a responsibility I am unable to bear. What shall I do?'

" 'Do,' said I—'do what honor, what principle directs. General you are an old man. All the circumstances of life place you above the comon temptations of men. You want nothing, you have no motive but duty to sway you. Look at me, I am a young man, I have nothing—I have a large family. *My vote* like yours would turn the scale. I feel a responsibility as mighty; but General, the greater the responsibility the greater the honor. From three we are to choose the man we think the best man. You have often said in your estimation that man was Crawford—why then hesitate? take hold of me, let us march boldly on and do our duty.'

" 'I am resolved,' announced the general, 'here is my hand and I give you my word of honor not to vote for Adams.'

"I then quitted him, but to make assurance doubly sure, I went to Archer and begged him to go and receive the same pledge. He did so, the General repeated to Archer what he had said to me and gave him his word of honor he would not vote for Adams.

"A little while after this, a friend whispered me, that from the General's looks, he was afraid he was again wavering. Another gentleman told me that during this interval, the speaker had been seen whispering with him.

"I then went to Van Buren and begged he would go and talk with him, for the poor old man seemed staggering under the weight of responsibility. When Van B. went to him he was passing round the house to take his seat with N. Y. delegation. He stopped to listen and again to Mr. V. B. repeated his promise on his word of honor, that he would not vote for Adams. After he took his seat next Mr. Morgan, he repeated it to that gentleman and a few minutes afterwards he must have written the name of Adams, which he put in the ballot box. After this, can you wonder that I was sick at heart and disgusted with politics and politicians."

"Have you seen him since?" asked Mrs. C. "Yes," replied Mr. McC. "When the election was over, as I was leaving the House, I saw him coming to me, I hurried forward to avoid him, he hurried after me, when I reached the door I saw a hack, in which were three gentlemen. I jumped in, knowing he could not follow, when I got home, I ran up in my own room, but had not been long there when he followed, he came in, he looked wretchedly, tears were running down his cheeks, 'forgive me, McClean,' said he, stretching out his hand. 'Ask your own conscience General and not me,' said I turning away. Since then he has been in coventry. A similar scene took place with V. B. and the other gentlemen of the mess, we let him continue with us, sit at the same table with us, but we do not speak to him. He is beneath anything but contempt, and he is an old man."

"What possible motive?" inquired I, "can you assign?"
"None," replied Mr. McC, "none, weakness, pure weak-

ness, as he said, the responsibility was more than he could bear."

"He has always," said I, "been considered as a pure and honorable man."

"Always," replied McC., "and even now I do not impeach his purity—it was shear weakness of mind, he never, you know, was thought a man of much understanding, and it is supposed is absolutely governed by his wife and it is said, she has written earnestly on the subject—he might be afraid to disobey."

While we were thus conversing, a servant entered and giving a letter to Caroline, said, it is brought by Mr. Adams Steward. For 18 months Caroline, has opened read and answered all her father's private letters and did not hesitate to do so now.

After reading it, she handed it to McClean, saying, it contains no secrets, only a repetition of an offer already verbally made, or rather a request that my father would continue in his present office. Mr. McC. read it and said it was polite, frank and friendly and asked what were her father's intentions. "To decline" answered she. "I am rejoiced to hear it," said Mr. Mc. "Oh we have but one wish," said Mrs. C, "and that is to return as soon as possible to Georgia, it is absolutely necessary for Mr. Crawfords health and that is all we care for." The letter was laid aside, until the company should go and Mr. McC. advised her not to give it to her father until the next morning, as it was late and he might be fatigued.

Before he left his room the next morning and immediately after taking his breakfast, he answered Mr. A.'s letter. In a frank and friendly manner, without considering the various meanings that might be attached to a word.

Mr. Adams was: "Dr. Sir—I avail myself of the first

moment, since I have been notified of the election of yesterday, to express to you my earnest hope and wish that
you will remain in your present situation, (or retain
your present office) I do not recollect which.   I remain,
Sir, with sincere respect your humble Servt."   To this
Mr. C replied with less conciseness.   "Dr Sir—I have
received and hasten to answer yr friendly letter, But having long since deliberately made up my mind not to remain in my present situation after Mr. Monroe's term
of service expires, You must allow me to decline your
frank and friendly offer, which had it not been otherwise I might have been induced to accept.   With sincere
respect your humbl"

This was written ready to send when two or three
gentlemen, his friends, entered and he showed it to them.
One objected to the word *present* situation, thinking
Mr. Adams might imagine he would accept the office of
State.   As this interpretation might be given, he did not
object to striking out that expression.   That in any circumstances he might have been induced to accept a place
in the office, was a thing these gentlemen deemed de-
grading to him and injurious to the Republican party.
He argued, he meant it as merely complimentary and
he thought the offer on Mr. A.'s part required from him
at least the most obliging mode of declination.   But this
was overruled and one gentleman wished him to say,
that in no circumstances could he be induced to accept
—this he resolutely refused—"friendly letter," was objected to—likewise "frank and friendly offer."   As the
repetition of the word friendly was inelegant and unnecessary he consented to expunge the first friendly; but
insisted on retaining the word in the second place—much
argument ensued and had one of the gentlemen had his
way, a *rude* answer would have been sent.   I was shocked

at such illiberality and narrow-mindedness and glad that
Mr. C. would not yield—the answer contained these, or
nearly these words—

"In acknowledging the receipt of your letter of the
10th I must be permitted, Sir, to decline the frank and
friendly offer it contains and am with high respect your
humble servant." Mr. C.'s frank and generous temper
prompted him to a more courteous answer, but deeming
it a thing of little importance he yielded to this concise
reply.

He was worried by their petty objections, which they
urged and argued about as matters of great importance
and showed more impatience and irritation and yielded
rather because he was wearied and worried than because
he deemed it of any consequence.   .   .   .

When no visitors were present, Mr. C. played whist
and seemed in his usual spirits. A large circle collected
in the evening and as they were particular friends many
details respecting the election took place, by which it was
evident they hoped for ultimate success, could the decision have been delayed; at any rate, they meant had it
been in their power to have prevented an election, thinking it a less political evil to have the vice-President fill the
presidential chair, than either Adams or Jackson. Those
moderate people of their own party think differently and
prefer the present result to a long-contested election, but
all agreed it was Mr. Clay who had decided it, and would
have done it in favour of either of the other candidates to
whom he had given his support.

On Saturday, Congress was not in session, and the
whole morning the drawing-room was crowded with
company, both ladies and gentlemen. The four members of parliament and many other strangers called.

In the evening, among other gentlemen who were there was Mr. Owen of Lanark.[1] . . . He has purchased of the *Shakers,* their establishments at Harmony, consisting of many excellent buildings, manufactures in full operation, Gardens, orchards, vineyards—corn fields —and 30,000 acres of ground.

Mr. Owen cares not how degraded, vicious or ignorant his new colonists may be, as he feels the power of his system to be such, that they can soon be rendered virtuous and educated. At Lanark, he said he had commenced with the *dregs of the dregs* of society. In a population of 2400 criminals and ignorant persons, he had never made any punishments or rewards, beyond a small fine, to restrain vice and encourage happiness which resulted from good conduct and to encourage virtue. In the course of a year the fines had not amounted to quite 40 shillings. "They want nothing and therefore are without tempation—make a man happy and you make him virtuous—this is the whole of my system, to make him happy, I enlighten his mind and occupy his hands and I have so managed the art of instruction that individuals seek it as an amusement. Two of the most powerful moral agents I use, are musick and dancing. Relaxation after labour, and amusement are both physically and morally necessary. Dancing combines both exercise and amusement, and of all pleasures musick is the most innocent and exhilerates the spirits, while it soothes the passions. I require my people to labour only 8 hours out of the twenty-four. Instruction and amusement diversify the intermediate hours."

[1] He was a social reformer of great renown in his day. He delivered a lecture at the Capitol, March 7, 1825, which Monroe and Adams attended. He established a community in Indiana in 1824 which failed in three years. In 1828 he projected a community in Mexico, but the scheme fell through, because the Mexican government insisted the Catholic religion should prevail, and Owen was a freethinker.

"And can you deter from vice and stimulate to virtue without the fear of punishment or hope of reward?"

"Yes," said he, "fear and hope are equally banished, actual enjoyment, which is the consequence or result of good behavior is sufficient."

"If you make the present life so happy, so all sufficient, I fear they will not wish for another." "But," said he smiling, "if their present life prepares them for a future life, is not that sufficient?"

"I have endeavored," said he, "to gather from the experience of others. I avoided all those principles and systems which have failed to make men happy—in other words virtuous. Or rather I have selected from the experiments made in morals, only such as have been proved good and sufficient. And with these materials I am making a new experiment, and feel no doubt of its success. Education is the foundation on which I build—enlighten men's minds and they will discern and understand what will promote their good. Take away want and you take away tempation—make men happy and you make them virtuous—these are my governing principles."

Cool and dispassionate in his manner, slow and even difficult in his enunciation—with a face indicative of a strong mind, but no imagination, it is difficult to conceive that Mr. Owen is a vissionary and enthusiast—yet so he is called. . . .

MR. CRAWFORD AND HIS BARBER[1]

One morning (a few days before Mr. Crawford after his resignation of office left the city,) I was sitting with him and the family, when the servant entered and said,

[1] From the notebook.

Mr. Dickison his Barber, had called and wished to know
if he might come in. "Certainly," said Mr. C. "ask
him in."

The honest man, was accordingly shown in. He was
dressed in his Sunday clothes and evidently came on a
visit, and not on business. He did not approach, but
stood at the door twisting his hat in his hand, not embarrassed, so much as agitated. "Take a chair, take a
chair," said Mr. Crawford, pointing to one near him.
The good fellow obeyed, looked up with eyes full of
tears, but could not for some moments speak, at last
he said, "They tell me, Sir, we are soon to lose you."
"It is true," said Mr. C. "I am going home"—another
pause—"I am heartily sorry to hear it," said he at
last, "every one that knows you is heartily sorry. It is a
long while, Sir. since you've been home, and so I was
thinking your garden might be out o' sorts, which as
you love gardening so, is a pity. No one belikes has
saved good seed for you, and as you know, Sir, mine is
an *extraordinary* good garden, I have been putting up
a parcel of the finest seeds I saved and if you will not be
affronted, should like you to take them with you—and
should consider it a great favour." "Willingly, and
thank you, Dickison," replied Mr. C. On this, the
honest barber's countenance brightened up, he handed
the parcel, saying, "Would to the Lord, I had had as
many votes, they should all have been as freely given to
you Sir"—   Then turning to Mrs. C. and looking at the
children—"And with your good leave, madam, I should
like to cut the young gentlemens hair once again, before
they went." "Certainly," replied Mrs. C. He then
looked first at one, then at another, then at Mr. Crawford, with great emotion, and eyes brimful of tears. He
seemed to be studying for some other mode of expressing

his affection, but could find none, so, slowly getting up and approaching Mr. C., who held out his hand to him, he seized it, and while he held it pressed between both of his, he exclaimed, "Well, God bless you, Sir, God bless you. Yes, wherever you go and as long as you live, may God in his mercy help you!" and unable to say more, he shook hands with the rest of the family, and wiping his eyes with the back of his hand, bowed low and hurried out of the room.

ANOTHER ANECDOTE

While Mr. Crawford was in the country, (the autumn before he left the district) he was too ill to be regularly attended by his barber, when therefore his services were required he was sent for. Such were the exaggerated rumours afloat concerning Mr. C.'s health, that it was impossible to ascertain the truth and both political friends and enemies at a distance were in a constant state of suspense and anxiety. It was an important point to both parties, one endeavoring to lessen, the other to exaggerate the reports of his illness. Persons were sent on the part of his opponents, (who were most apprehensive of deception) to see with their own eyes and hear with their own ears. One morning when two gentlemen of this description, were with him, his barber arrived. He was a good-mannered talkative man, who for twenty years had been chief barber to the whole of Congress, and had for the sake of his amusing gossip been indulged by the members in his communicativeness and familiarity. "What do you think, Sir?" said he to Mr. C., yesterday, "a strange gentleman from N. York came to me. 'Dickison,' says he, 'you are Mr. Crawford's barber I hear, so of course you must know the truth,—they

tell me he is blind, now, my good man, do for God's sake
tell us if it is so—speak the truth and you shall be well
rewarded.' 'Sir,' says I, 'if a blind man can write like
this,' pulling your note out of my pocket and showing it,
'if a blind man can write such a fair round hand as that,
then Mr. Crawford is blind, for that very note did he
write his own dear self.'   La, Sir, I wish you had seen
how disappointed and mouth fallen the fellow looked.
Yes, yes, I knew how it was, right glad would he have
been to have heard you were blind."

"Ha! ha! ha!" echo'd Mr. Crawford.   "Why so I am
blind Dickison, at least too blind to write a single line.
My daughter wrote that note."

The poor barber in his turn looked mouth fallen and
glanced at the two strangers who were present and then
at Mr. C. as much as to say, "but why need you let these
spies know as much."

But Mr. C. would as freely have let the whole world
know, for in this, nor in any other instance, however
trifling would he consent to deceive, or mislead opinion
public or private.   I remember in the winter after his
return, I joined his family in persuading him to receive
his numerous visitants in the drawing room, instead of
his chamber, that he might have less the appearance of an
invalid.   He consented on condition he might have his
large easy chair.

It was placed on the side of the room on which were
the windows, so that the light fell on his back and his
face remained in shadow—what was still worse, the window curtains were of green silk and gave his complexion
a ghastly hue,—ensconced in this great high backed chair,
tinted with these green curtains, he looked ill, very ill, almost corpse like, at the very time when his health was
almost restored and his complexion far from pale.

The most unfavorable impressions respecting his health were made—on all such as saw him only in his great chair and the worst reports consequently circulated. I urged him to dispense with the chair and substitute a sopha, and to have the green curtains changed for crimson. He laughed heartily at what he called my female artifices, and told me he could not play the coquette even to win the favour of his mistress,—the public. At last we worried him into compliance, so far as to exchange the chair for a sopha—but never could prevail on him to change the curtains, so that through all this eventful winter, he looked in much worse health than he really was and even some of his friends thought, he was incapacitated by disease for being President.

But to return to our honest Barber, who was continually giving proofs of his enthusiastic regard for Mr. C. on some such occasion, I asked Mr. C. what had given rise to such an uncommon attachment. "That is more than I can tell," said he, "but of my own liking for the good natured fellow it occurred oddly enough. I had lost one of my carriage horses and was looking out for a match. One day as I was riding along Pennsyl. Avenue, I met Dickison mounted on precisely such a horse as I wanted. I stopped and calling to him, asked if he would part with it and at what price.

" 'To you Sir,' said he 'at no price.' 'How so friend?' said I, 'why not to me—have I ever done you any harm?' 'No, Sir,' replied he, 'you have never done me harm, but you have done your country great harm by the vote you gave yesterday in Congress, and if you were to lay me down your whole fortune you should not have my horse.'

" 'Well done my brave fellow," said I, holding out my hand to him. 'I wish every man was as honest as you and happy thrice happy would our country be.' From

that day I employed him as my Barber and we have ever
since been as good friends as honest freemen can be."

TO MRS. KIRKPATRICK

[Sidney,] March 12, 1825.

. . . .   Yesterday we bade farewell to our excellent friend Mr. Crawford and his amiable family. To me,
it was an affecting sight to see this truly good and great
man, quitting the theatre of his ambition and his activity,
to retire to comparative obscurity, inaction and poverty—
voluntarily quitting it, rather than to remain in a situation in which he said he could no longer do good to his
country. He immediately and unhesitatingly declined
Mr. Adams invitation to retain his place in the Cabinet,
and when I suggested to him the interests of his family
and his own gratification as motives for continuance, "I
cannot do it honestly," replied he, and that settled the
matter. "I cannot support measures I do not approve,
and to go into his cabinet, as an opponent, would be very
ungenerous." It is said, that no man is a great man,
when seen near. In Mr. C.'s case, this is not true, for
it is only when seen near, that all his great qualities are
discernible. In the privacy of domestic life, and in the
unguarded hours of social and confidential intercourse,
he discovers dispositions of the heart and powers of
mind, which public occasions do not call forth. It is
easy to put on a smiling countenance and to assume
cheerfulness for a few hours; particularly when public
applause stimulates and rewards you. But it is not easy
to be really calm amidst difficulty, conflict and suspense,
to be cheerful when hope is blasted, when wishes are disappointed, when pride is mortified, when the object of
ardent desire, of strong effort, of long continued exer-

tion, of exclusive thought, is suddenly wrested from you.
The full and crowded mind is suddenly left a void, and if
not a strong mind, it would sink. Not so Mr. C. The
object that occupied his mind, for eight, perhaps more
truly for twelve years, is snatched from him, and disappointment inflicts so little pain, that it is hard to believe
that hope could have given much pleasure. I passed the
whole week of the election with him and studied his
character with the care and attention with which a
painter would have studied his features. He betrayed no
anxiety, while in suspense, and no defeat in faction when
disappointed. He was uniformly cheerful and the only
difference I perceived was an increase of tenderness to
his children. To me, this was one of the most interesting weeks in my life. Deep interest, strong excitement,
produced by a great object, were circumstances of rare
occurrence and offered me a proportionably rare enjoyment. Every day, or rather evening, I was in company
with some of the most distinguished actors in this interesting drama. I knew the causes of their circumstances and the motives of their actions, on which public
opinion speculated and so often misinterpreted. It was
curious and amusing to compare rumour and truth, and it
was highly interesting to watch not only the development
of characters, but of events. To this speculative and
moral interest was added that of friendship and affection
and I enjoyed that pleasure, (a pleasure which life so seldom affords) which a full mind and a full heart only can
yield. In these large objects, individual interest was
scarcely felt—selfish, I should have said. I thought so
much of others that self was forgotten. Perhaps it is to
this cause I must ascribe the indifference I have felt as to
the fate of Lucy[1] and other things of the same nature.

[1] One of her stories.

My thoughts and feelings generally run in one channel.
When divided into separate streams they lose their force.
This winter Mr. C.'s circumstances and character have
been more interesting to me than my enemies. Our
families have almost lived together and I have passed so
much time in the city since we left it. I have been in
more society than I have been in for many years, and
never enjoyed it more. But this is all over now! The
dissolution of such an intimacy, the separation from such
friends, inflicts almost as much pain, as the death of those
we love and esteem. The cessation of an interest so
deep and so lively leaves a vacuum in the mind, which
common objects cannot supply. Madam Pichon, my
first friend in Washington, after eight years intimate intercourse, was taken away. Mrs. Barlow succeeded;
she too is gone, but not more completely lost to me,
tho' divided by death, than Md. P., and good Mrs. St.
Gêmmes, tho' separated only by the Atlantic. Mrs. Middleton[1] promised to supply the place of these friends to
me. The ceremonious intercourse of strangers had
given place to the confidential intercourse of congenial
minds and kindred feelings; from whence was springing
up an intimacy, which in time might have ripened into
tender friendship. But she, too, is placed by circumstances on the other side of the ocean. Mr. Crawford
and his family more than supplied her place. The others
were exclusively my friends, but these last were the
friends of my husband and children and our intercourse
had all the kindness and intimacy of relationship. But
again, we are bereft of what we most valued in our social
circle and thrown once more upon ourselves for all the
pleasures, which intimate and confidential society affords.

[1] Wife of Henry Middleton, of South Carolina, Minister to Russia, 1820–
1830. She was a regular correspondent of Mrs. Smith.

Well, few are as rich as I still am, few as happy in their homes, and less dependent on society. I enjoy society with the keenest relish, and so I do retirement,—each has its peculiar delights. One is left me, and I am determined not to allow the enjoyment of what I possess, to be lessened by the want of what I cannot obtain. "This was very wise," you will say, "but not very easy." For me it is easier than for most folks. Such is the conformation I have received from nature, that present objects only affect me in a deep or lively manner. Out of sight, out of mind, is pretty true, when applied to me. It is a defect, I know that, yet it is one I rejoice in, since it spares me great pain. However accute my sorrows are, they are soon over. I have had some that have kept me waking, but few, if any, that a sound sleep has not cured. I have ever found sleep to be a lethean draught, —in it I lose not only the sensation of pain, but the ideas which cause pain. This argues a great deficiency of sensibility. I know it well, and always have said, nature had given me only a deep sensibility to pleasure. Monotony and quiet are the foes dangerous to my happiness. Stagnation is like death. Stagnation of the mind is one of the worst of evils.

TO MRS. BOYD

[Sidney,] January 12, 1827.

. . . . As Dr. Stevens once said to me, when complaining of nervous affections and restlessness of mind, "You have almost passed the stormy part of life and are entering on a calm and tranquil state, when all these complaints will vanish." His prediction is accomplished and I am often astonished at the contentment and serenity I enjoy. Not that I can possibly imagine

this arising entirely from physical causes. My health
indeed is better, and not subject to the violent attacks I
then was subject to, but I hope more may be ascribed to
mental discipline, and tho' I fear, Maria, you do not like
to hear me ascribe such effects to philosophical reading,
yet in the truth I believe this the cause. For the last two
years my reading has been almost exclusively of moral
subjects as treated of by the ancient philosophers, and
in their writings there is a calm and tranquilizing and at
the same time elevating influence, that has a most delightful effect on the mind. But do not connect with
philosophy, anything adverse to religion. As I once said
the philosophy of Socrates, Cicero and Seneca, has no
resemblance to that of the modern school. The immor-
tality of the soul and the government of God is enforced
with an eloquence that charms while it convinces and
their system is no ways incompatible with that of re-
vealed religion, nor have I found that it undermined my
faith in Christian doctrine. I wish you would read
Cicero's essay on *old age,*—every person advanced in life
would I think derive advantage from it. My pen you
see, will wander. I meant not this digression.   .   .   .
   Last week I went in to pay some necessary visits and
dined at Mrs. Thornton's. After dinner I sent for
Brother and after passing the twilight hour with Mrs.
Bourdeaux and Thornton, I took him with me to Mrs.
Johnson's,[1]—this little woman improves exceedingly on
acquaintance. I tell her she is too good for a mere fashionable lady and I believe her heart tells her so too, for
since the birth of her son, she does not go into half as
much company as she used to do. She has great simplicity of manners and her living and dressing in the

---

[1] The wife of Mrs. Smith's old friend, Colonel Richard Mentor Johnson,
now Senator from Kentucky.

highest style and the consequent flattery and attention
she receives has not in the least spoil'd a natural kind and
sensible disposition. I like her more and more. We
spent an agreeable hour with her and staid to tea, when
finding I *would* go to Mrs. Clays she said she would go
with us. It had been three weeks since I had been
there. Brother who had dined there the day before in
a large company, said he was much more gratified by this
social visit. Mr. C.[1] was very agreeable. I joked him
a good deal on the learned judge he had appointed in
Jersey.[2] "At first," said I, "he was a sadler, then a store
keeper and then when made a justice of peace, he under-
took to read Blackstone, the only law-book it is said he
has ever read. What a learned judge and chancelor he
will make!" "Stop, stop," said Mr. C., "you do not know
Mrs. Smith I was a store-keeper." "I did not," said I,
"but I know without your telling me that your studies
were not limited to Blackstone." He took my raillery in
very good part and defended the appointment very skill-
fully and brought me to acknowledge it was impossible
to please every body. The next evening I was engaged
at a large and splendid party at Mr. Wirt's, and as Mrs.
Clay said etiquette allowed of my so doing I asked brother
to go along and appointed him to meet me at Mrs. Clay's
at 7 oclock. The next evening I went in, Ann with me
and Mrs. C. and party waited until near 8 for brother.—
As he did not come, she told me I had best call for him
at the President's where he dined. I did so, but he had
just left the house. Mr. Clay had left word for him to
follow us and I was afraid he would not, but staid in the
reception room waiting for him and soon saw his face
through the crowd and making my way found him and

---

[1] Clay was then Secretary of State.
[2] William Rossell had just been appointed United States District Judge.

introduced him to Mr. and Mrs. Wirt, and kept his arm through the evening introducing him to all my acquaintances. It was a charming party and I enjoyed it the more for having his company. Mrs. Barbour[1] asked me and all the family, brother included, to spend the next day socially with her and to pass the evening. She always receives company on Saturday evening. We agreed. The next day, was as you may believe a very interesting one to me and the girls. Mr. Smith on that day, read his memoir on Mr. Jefferson before the Columbian Institute. There was unexpectedly a great many ladies. The President of U. S. being likewise Pres'd of the institute, presided on this occasion. I felt absolutely sick from anxiety, as my dear husband is totally unaccustomed to speak in public, but every thing went off very well,—no hesitation or embarrassment, tho' from inward emotion his voice was low and indistinct. When you read the memoir, which I shall send you, you will have a new proof that my husband is no courtier, indeed, without servility I think I urged him to make some mention of J. Adams,—but he confined himself wholly to the subject of his memoir and tho' Genl. Brown, our good friend sat close before him and he did not spare military power and glory.

Brother seemed really charmed with Gouv'r Barbour's eloquent and amusing conversation,—certainly few equal him in colloquial powers. Being engaged early in the evening at Mrs. Rush's, brother left us when we rose from table and we ladies retired to dress for the evening. You know Mrs. Barbour is almost as great a talker as myself, being both in very high spirits, which the girls declared were increased by champayne, we passed really a merry hour or two during the unceremonious ceremony

[1] Wife of James Barbour, Secretary of War.

Henry Clay.

Secretary of State 1825-1829.

From the portrait by Edward Dalton Marchant.   In the State
Department, Washington.

of dressing. Between 7 and 8, the company began to assemble and tho' an uninvited and social meeting, the rooms were soon filled. Mr. Smith, for a wonder, made his appearance for a little while on his way to sup with the Typographical Society on its anniversary. Mr. Gales and 4 or 5 stranger editors, mostly members of congress went with him and did not return until after twelve, when as all the company were gone, to beguile the time I was playing chess with Gouv'r Barbour. Thus passed another most agreeable evening. We returned home, all of us in fine spirits. If I could, I would have gone on Wednesday to Mrs. Clay's drawing room, but Mr. Smith had an engagement in the city and I gave it up. However, we were as happy at home, sitting round a cheerful fire and reading English history and sewing, so much interested in the adventures of Prince Charles, that we could not close the book until past 11 o'clock. Thus at home or abroad we are quite happy. We have frequent and agreeable and long visits from College friends and our winter evenings are as pleasant as summer days. On Christmas we were very happy, as well as gay. Dear Mrs. Bomford and all her family came early in the morning and staid until late at night. In the evening about 20 young people joined us and musick and dancing and games enabled our young folks to have a merry christmas. . . .

TO MRS. BOYD

[Sidney,] Decr. 21st 1827.

. . . . Next week there is to be a Fair, for the benefit of the Orphan Asylum. Every female in the City, I believe, from the highest to the lowest has been at work for it. Mrs. Van Ness spares neither time or

expense and Mrs. Lovel for three weeks has been working night and day and enlisted her husband and sisters
who have painted &c, &c, besides begging for scraps
and pieces of all kinds to dress dolls and make pin-
cushions. From knit-stocking, clergyman's bands, to
hats, caps, tables, and dresses the ingenuity of our ladies
has been employed. Carrusi, the Italian musick master
whom you saw here has lent his large elegant assembly
room. Col. Henderson, (of the Marine Corps) lends the
whole band of musick and his men are to decorate the
room with greens and flowers. The Speaker of the
House[1] has promised to patronize it. There are to be 30
tables arranged in a semi-circle at each of which is to pre-
side one married and 2 young ladies, wearing some badge
to distinguish them. I took little interest because I had
heard little of it, until last week when I went into the city
to pay some visits. I found the zeal which prevailed
there quite contageous and my enthusiasm was immediately excited. Having nothing to give that was of any
worth that depended on the expenditure of money, it all
at once occurred to me, one of my MS might be turned
to account.[2] I went in search of Mrs. Bomford, who was
in the city, met her, got into her carriage, communicated
to her my design, in case she approved it. She was
absolutely delighted, thought it would give great eclat
to the Fair, to have a new novel to sell. As I did not
visit Mrs. V. Ness, yet thought it right that the offer
should be made to her, as Chief Directress, Mrs. B. vol-
unteered to go to her and to stay in the city and go
with me to dine at Mrs. Thornton's. We called at the
War Department to let Col. B. know, and then as I did
not wish to go to Mrs. V's. she proposed getting out at

[1] Andrew Stevenson, of Virginia.
[2] " What is Gentility or, The Brothers," was published for the fair.

the gate and leaving me in the carriage.   While she was in the house, Genl. Van Ness came up and discovered me, an awkward circumstance.   Mrs. Van N. was equally delighted with the project and said nothing could have come more apropos, as that very moment she was writing to Mr. Pishey Thompson, to request his aid in making up a literary table.   She promised to call at Mrs. Thornton's after dinner to see me and arrange the affair.   The time was so short, that only three printers who printed papers had hands and materials sufficient to do it.   Mr. Gales was applied to, but declined.   Duff Green[1] agreed to do it but could not promise to have it done for the Fair and his terms were very high.   I left the business entirely in Mrs. V.'s hands, and have not heard on what she has decided.   That evening, Friday, Ann and I returned with Mrs. Bomford and staid all night.   The next morning she carried us to the city where we were engaged to dine with Mrs. Southard.[2]   Ann and I passed a quiet, comfortable morning with Mrs. Clay, who is not well and talks of returning home, in a year's time as a thing, now certain and on her own account is pleased. At three we went into Mrs. S.'s who for the last year has been kindness and sociability personified.   Before we rose from the table, Mrs. Clay came in and looking at new caps and gowns and other articles of dress amused us until tea time when Mrs. and Miss Cutts joined us and soon after Col. and Mrs. Bomford who came to take us home with them.   Mrs. Clay made us promise to go to church and spend the next day with her.   This we did,

---

[1] At the time he was editing the opposition newspaper.

[2] Samuel Southard, of New Jersey, was Secretary of the Navy from 1823 to 1829.   His family and the Smiths were on terms of intimacy for many years.   It was Mrs. Smith's brother-in-law, Chief Justice Kirkpatrick, who twitted Mr. Southard with his ignorance of naval affairs when he was first appointed Secretary by asking him if he could honestly assert he knew the bow from the stern of a frigate.

and a most agreeable day we passed.   Two or three gentlemen were there and Mr. Clay was more cheerful,
frank and agreeable than I have seen him for six months,
whether this proceeded from any new views or hopes, or
a relief from suspense and uncertainty, I cannot tell.

TO MISS SUSAN H. SMITH

[Sidney,] Tuesday, Febr. 1828.

.   .   .   .   Have you read, or heard read the debates
in Congress,—those I mean on Retrenchment,—they
were very inflamatory and I think disgraceful to both
parties.[1]   I should like to hear Mr. Kirkpatrick's remarks on them, yet, notwithstanding, I could not approve, I certainly was entertained.   Anna Maria read
several long speeches aloud; particularly Mr. Everett's
and Mr. Hamiltons.   On opposite sides and both marked
by superior talents.   Randolph too has been very amusing, but old Kremer exceeded every thing, his cackling
hen will never be forgotten.   But it is a sad thing to see
Congress giving way to such merely personal interests,
when it is the nation they should think of and feel for.
Poor Mr. Clay, the Telegraph gives him no rest.   It
has got up the story of Col. Morrison's legacy to the
College in a new and more aggravated manner; I think
he must now come out and defend himself.   We have
not seen Mrs. Clay since Mrs. Southard's party three
weeks ago.   The weather and roads render intercourse
impossible.   The weather now however is fine and if it
continues a week, the roads will be good, yet even then
I shall not expect to see our city friends and particularly

---

[1] They *were* disgraceful.   George Kremer, a Representative from Pennsylvania, a reckless demagogue and freak, was the father of the false cry
that Clay had sold his vote to Adams for the Secretaryship of State.

Mrs. C. who is overwhelmed with company, besides a very large dining company every week and a drawing room every other week.   She says when Mr. C. dines at home, he never dines alone but always has a social company in a family dinner, which however is really the trouble of a large one.   She is obliged to go to other peoples parties, sick or well, for fear of giving offence, a thing more carefully avoided now than ever.   .   .   .

FROM MADAME PICHON[1]

Paris, rue Blanche, April 12, 1828.

DEAR AND TRUE FRIEND:

I am finally about to write to you after a long silence, and in order to be able to tell you more I write in French, as it goes faster.   I have but one hour to write this letter and wish to employ it well.   It will be deliver'd to you by a young man whom I recommend to you.   He will reside in New York in a commercial house.   He leaves a father and mother and sisters who love him.   I have learned by experience that nothing can mitigate the grief felt at such a separation except the hospitality which I received in your good and admirable country.   However, in order to find this hospitality it is necessary to show that one deserves it.   Mr. Hervey belongs to a respectable family.   He is very genteel and well bred.   His father loves science and is a good patriot, which are good recommendations in your country.   Treat him, you and Mr. Smith, as you did us.   This is the most fortunate thing I can wish for him.   Introduce him to all our common acquaintances, and if he sends you this letter before going to Washington, please give him some let-

---

[1] Translation from the French.

ters for your friends in New York and Wilmington. I wish for his sake that Miss Bayard were there.

So many misfortunes may happen in one year that I do not dare speak to you about any one in America, but will talk to you concerning ourselves first. I will say that if I have not written to you it was not because I had forgotten either you or yours, as you have done with me, for I received from Mr. Warden (who gave it to me) a work written by you, which I read with keen interest and which adorns my library to the great satisfaction of my personal pride, which is flattered by the talent of my friends. I have a daughter 21 years old, Henrietta by name, about whom I have already spoken to you, who, like myself, appreciates merit above all else. In consequence of this she was married a year ago. She refused what the world calls excellent matches in order to marry a very amiable young *savant,* who is an eloquent and most distinguished professor of physics, well educated in literature and political economy, a good son and good brother, witty and gentle (two qualities hard to find together), and whom we have known for over 6 years. He kept my head turning for two years. I was thoroughly tormented, dear friend, and I thank God for not having more than one daughter for I should lose my head if I had the anxieties to go through for another which I experienced for this one. You know how economical and industrious Pichon and I are, and that he understands business and attends to his own. In the positions he has filled we have made some savings which he invested well in property which has doubled in value. He has unraveled the affairs of my parents and thanks to his efforts my mother now enjoys a nice little fortune. We operated a farm for five years. It was a poor one but we have improved it and sold it at a good profit.

We have bought the house we live in, have enlarged it, and instead of 3,000 francs income which the farm yielded in good years we now have 8,000. This enabled us to give Henrietta a snug little dowry, which, in our opinion, warranted our consenting to her marriage with a man of merit, pursuing an honorable career, and whom she loved, even though he had no fortune of his own. One of our friends who had acted as father to Mr. Pouillet (now my son-in-law) ever since he arrived in Paris, at the age of 17 years, ought to have known us well enough to suppose that our least objection was the lack of a fortune (for with talent and good morals one can always be acquired). Mr. Pouillet ought to have supposed that I thought too much of my daughter to receive a young man who was amiable, well formed, and with interesting features, as I received him, if my husband would not accept him as a son-in-law, provided he became attached to Henrietta. This was simply good sense. We did all we could to cause our friend to guess what we thought, but nevertheless they understood the contrary, and when the position of Mr. Pouillet, appointed professor at the faculty of sciences, became improved and enabled him to marry, and when Henrietta had reached 19 and I thought he would ask me for her, she fell seriously ill and was between life and death for 7 days. Pouillet ceased to come and my poor daughter, who has an elevated soul, persuaded herself that she hated him. This hatred made me shudder and I interpreted it as another sentiment. It took her two whole months to recover. Her character had changed. She was on the point of marrying a stupid fellow, convinced that she would not suit a man of merit—she whose careful mental education and imagination are so well fitted to render happy the man who is capable of appreciating it. Pouillet was also on the verge of forming a ridiculous union, in order to forget Henrietta. All this lasted 10 months. You who are a mother may judge of my torments. I could no longer sleep and shed many a bitter tear. My husband was in despair and blamed me for everything. If I had occasion to go out I went on foot, however tired I was, in order to meet Pouillet, convinced as I was that there was some misunderstanding which one word would clear up. However, a mother can not speak in such a case.[1] Finally, when about to marry, Pouillet felt that the sacrifice would be too great and found a pretext to break the engagement. I had used all my skill in breaking that of Henrietta and in estranging forever the poor young man who could never suit her, for an intellectual woman married to a fool is to me a monstrosity. Breaking off the engagements was not all. How were they to see each other again? My elder son met his dear professor of physics, who was enraptured to see him again, as you may suppose. Theodore went home with him and then Pouillet came again. Dear friend, a mother feels for her daughter. When I saw him I was overcome and felt that the fate of my poor Henrietta, consequently more than mine, depended on that visit. My husband, enraptured, kissed me and told me to provide for everything, to agree to the marriage, and to offer a dowry. In a word, after two months of fears, of reticence, and new misunderstandings, Pouillet came and asked me whether I thought that Pichon would give his consent if he asked for Henrietta. I suppose you think my troubles were o'er. Not at all. Henrietta, enchanted, did not wish to admit to her father or brother that she had been mistaken and that she did not hate her husband. Her father thought that he had

[1] Besides, I did not meet him.

been mistaken and that she did not love him any
more than the fool that she had come near marrying.
Theodore, being persuaded that his sister only married
Pouillet because it was my wish, grew desperate, although he used to like him as a brother. Thus, dear
friend, this marriage took place in the midst of fears
and reproaches to me, and while parting with a charming daughter, my best friend, I had the sorrow of seeing
my husband and son reproach me with having sacrificed
her by making her marry a man she did not love, and
with having deprived them of her without having secured her happiness. For a year, however, she has been
the most happy of women, and that consoles me. Pouillet's celebrity is increasing every day. His heart and his
personal pride are satisfied. Their pecuniary situation
is good. . . . I assure you that I believe it is fortunate for my sons to have a brother-in-law who shows
them that labor and talent are the surest roads to domestic
happiness and fortune. Theodore is a man of parts, but
lazy. He would have wished his sister to marry a man
he did not like as well as this one, but who would have
had sufficient influence to secure him a position so that
he would not have to learn any profession. He is studying to be a lawyer and may become a distinguished one
by working. He will then have glory, independence, and
fortune. Jerome, the younger, is witty and full of ardor.
He is studying all he can in order to enter the polytechnic
school. I hope he will not come out of it a soldier, in
spite of what he says about it, and that he will acquire a
taste for science and enter the department of mines or of
bridges and highways, for I do not like military men.
They would sell their country for a cordon. They do not
understand liberty and are veritable despots. My son-
in-law has a grand quality which I must not refrain from

mentioning to you: he admires your country and you in particular. He read your ode five years ago and has been scolding me ever since for not writing to you oftener, for he is convinced (and rightly) that correspondence with you must be a great pleasure. Oh, how you would like my young married couple! There is wit, patriotism, the morals of the golden age, imagination, extensive knowledge, and Henrietta knows English and German well and plays well on the piano. All this is happiness for me, is it not? And besides, they love me tenderly. My mother, who is over 84 years old, has preserved all her physical and moral faculties. She lives in our house. Unfortunately my children are away from home, but as I have excellent health I often go to them and they come to see me as often as they can. We gain by seeing one another as often as possible while we are able to live near or with them. . . .

Good-bye, dear friend, and you and all who are dear to you please accept the assurance of my affection and that of Pichon, as well as his regards.

                             A. Emilie Pichon,
                                 née Brongniart.

Mr. Jefferson's death caused us much grief. Such men are a loss to humanity and the glory of the human race.

TO J. BAYARD H. SMITH

                          Monday. [1828]

Yesterday, my dear Bayard, I passed some hours so agreeably that I must give you some account of them.

---

[1] Jonathan Bayard H. Smith, Mrs. Smith's only son, was born July 9, 1810, graduated at Princeton in 1829, taking second honors. He practiced law in Washington till the civil war broke out, when, being a Southern sympathizer, he went to Baltimore. He died in California, August 20, 1889.

Mr. Owen of Lanark, passed the day here. Never have I met with any one whose whole heart seemed so full of benevolence, whose mind was so exclusively occupied with schemes for the promotion of the happiness of mankind, his time, his thoughts, his feelings, his fortune are all devoted to this all absorbing idea (for alas, he is but a visionary) that thus fills his mind, heart and time, with a confidence so sanguine as to banish every doubt of its possibility. In his ideal system of perfect virtue, and consequently perfect happiness, he loses sight of the inherent principles of human nature, and builds his scheme of happiness on an angelic nature. Or rather, he denies that there are any inherent principles of action in man, and asserts that he is the mere creature of circumstances. "Man," says he, "is the effect, not the cause. It is not his natural virtue or his natural vice, which makes his happiness or misery. It is the good or the bad circumstances by which he is surrounded which make him virtuous or vicious. Circumstances form his nature." Here is his first error. To convince us, however, of the truth of his hypothesis, he gives as an example: an infant born among Quakers and raised among them to manhood, and asked if the same individual raised from infancy to manhood among Jews or among savages, would not in each state be a totally different character. I allowed that he would be a different character, but not a different being, viz. that his opinions as to government, his faith as to religion, his mode of conduct, of living, of dress, his pleasures and occupations, would all be modified by the condition in which he was brought up, and as to external circumstances, each of these individuals would be perfectly different one from the other, and yet, all would be as man the same identical being, that the Quaker, the Jew, or the savage, would love and hate, be revengeful or merciful, proud or humble, ambitious or lowly-minded, irrascible or gentle,—in fine, that under all these modifications, he was still the same being.   To this Mr. Owen would not assent, but asserted that under a certain modification of circumstances, he would be exempt from hatred, revenge, malice, pride and anger, and this belief in his mind amounts to absolute conviction, the effort of his life had been and always will be, to bring about such a combination of circumstances, as should necessarily make man a perfectly virtuous and therefore perfectly happy being.   He asserted that he had made a successful experiment at Lanark, where he had taken children from two years of age to 12; among many hundreds there was not an instance of jealousy, rivalship, anger or hatred, in any degree; that to effect this, he banished alike, hope or fear, and had neither rewards or punishments, the actual pleasure of doing right was a sufficient reward for success and a sufficient stimulus to effort; That those who witnessed the effects of his system of education, said it was magical.   "But, my dear Sir," said I, "did you ever see any of these little angels, after they grew up to be men and women?"   He acknowledged he never had.   "You knew them then only while their wills were controlled and directed by yourself, while in fact they were mere machines.   I fear, Sir, when their passions were developed and their wills were allowed free action, you would find, after all, your angels were but men and women,—even pigs are pretty clean little animals, but when grown into hogs, are ugly, dirty creatures."   Mr. Owen laughed at my exemplification, but denied my inference.   Another of his fundamental principles is, *man cannot believe or disbelieve at will.*   Yet, in every state of society, viz. in all religions, Brahmin, Mohamedan, Jewish or Christian, this *moral impossibility* is required of him, and non-compliance produces an ideal criminality, which in all countries subjects man, either to suffering or hypocracy and by separating virtue from action, and by attaching it to *Faith,* it perverts the moral instinct, and subverts morality, and in so doing lays a foundation for vice.

That belief does not depend on volition, is a fact I have too forcibly learned from my own experience to deny, and I therefore agreed with him in the deductions he drew from this his 2d fundamental principle, but could not carry them out as far as he did, which was to *believe nothing,* as it respected religion.

His scheme is to equalize property, or throw it into a common stock, so that no one will be very rich, and *none* poor. In order to accomplish this he would have society divided into communities,—no community to exceed 2000 individuals, nor be less than 800. This community, instead of living in towns or cities, should form a kind of village, extending over ten miles square,—each community should have within itself schools, manufactures, agricultural grounds, &c sufficient for the abundant supply of every comfort, nay every luxury of life, and I suppose ten miles square in the fullest cultivation, would do this. The perfection to which machinery is brought, lessens manual labour in such a great proportion, that instead of labouring 12 and 14 hours a day, as mechanics are now obliged to do, in order to gain a competence, it would not be necessary for them to labour six or eight hours and would thus leave them a great portion of their time for intellectual and moral improvement and likewise for amusement, which he thinks absolutely necessary for the perfection of morals, so much so that dancing, musick and other pleasures, are at Lanark and other places where he has tried his experiment as much a part

of his system as the arts, sciences and mechanics. He
would allow of no *system* of religion being taught, but
would leave all men absolutely free to believe or disbelieve
whatever they chose. Marriage is to be released from its
present fetters and when a couple grew weary of each
other, they would be allowed to separate and form new
connections, and as his system is totally to exterpate
every evil passion and there would be neither hatred,
rivalship, jealousy, anger, or animosity of any kind, he
thinks these separations would not frequently occur.
Such are the outlines of his scheme for universal virtue
and happiness and uninterrupted peace,—a scheme in
which he has undoubtedly faith and which he not only believes *may be,* but *will be* realized. All the world divided
into small communities! The whole race of man to be
perfectly virtuous and perfectly happy! I told him it
would be nothing more than the Christian milenium, and
I believed such a time would arrive as well as he did, but
then I expected it would be brought about by very different means. He is extremely mild and instead of being
offended by opposition or difference of opinion he is
pleased with free discussion and even bears being laughed
at, with great good nature. However eroneous and per-
nicious his opinions may be, he, himself, I think a truly
benevolent and good man. This bright vision fills his
mind, to the exclusion of common sense and universal
experience,—he is an amiable mad-man. Yet such is his
influence, that he has obtained from the Mexican Government (from whence he has just returned) the grant
of a province of very rich, beautiful and nearly uninhab-
ited land, (part of Texas) where he means to establish
his system, which is to serve as a model, for the rest of
the world, and he calls it his model-government. His
whole soul is filled with this scheme. It was really very

interesting to hear him and I hope this letter will be interesting to you.

TO MRS. BOYD

Charlott's Ville, Saturday evening August 2d, 1828.

. . . . We are at a spacious and elegant hotel, have a drawing-room on the second floor, with our bed-room opening from it and Mr. Smith's adjoining ours, for Anna lodges with me, the bed-rooms open on a piazza from which we see mountains rising all round us. The nearest is Monticello on the north-west, over there in the south-west rise the Alleghany, or Blue-ridge, reposing in their blue and misty grandeur on the horizon and looking like vast masses of clouds. From our drawing room windows, a beautiful country beyond the Court-House and some of the private dwellings of Charlottsville, with mountains in the distance. Dear Monticello! my chief inducement to take this long journey, was once more to visit its revered shades and to weep over the grave of one of the best and greatest of men and of a friend loved and venerated. Mr. Smith had business here. Mr. Monroe's vast landed estate in this neighborhood being made over to the Bank of the U. S. in payment of his debt to that institution, Mr. Biddle expressed a wish to Mr. Smith, that if such a journey should be agreeable to him, he should come in and superintend the sale, which is to take place on Monday. The Court is then to meet, and it is expected hundreds of people will then be here, as politics, law, justice and business of all kind are transacted at Virginia Courts. As I had not been very well, he thought a journey and mountain air might be of use to me. As Anna had never been from home, excepting to Heywood, I chose her as my companion and fille de

chambre and nurse, should any of my attacks of fever,
render one necessary. To make the journey easy, we
came in our own carriage and to vary the scene and
avoid some very bad roads, we came as far as Fredericksburg in the steam-boat, having the carriage on board.
This place is 70 miles from Fredericksburg and by rising
with the sun, we have performed the journey with great
ease in two days, stopping to rest two hours at breakfast
and 2 at dinner. From the Potomack, to this elevated
spot, there is a continued rise, hill after hill. I do not
believe in the whole distance we ever found 2 miles of
level at a time—generally it was up one hill, down and
up another. Some of them tremendously precipitous to
such a rare traveller and great coward as myself. Yesterday we passed by a turnpike, one end of a mountain,
the assent was almost too much for my courage. Today
I suffered but little from fear and when we past the ridge,
it was through a gap along the banks of the Ravenna, a
mountain river, rocky and enclosed in overhanging and
picturesque banks. It was a kind of defile through which
the road wound, high hills on each side, the sun hot and
scarcely a breath of air. We suffered from the heat, but
it enhanced our enjoyment on reaching this height and
taking possession of our cool, airy apartment, together
with the luxury of a bath. I felt so well and so happy,
when after bathing and changing my dress, I seated myself at the pleasant window that as usual I longed to participate with those I love, and as Anna wished to be the
writer home, I determined to avail myself of the pro-
pitious moment to write to you. Our supper table is set
and Mr. Smith waits for me, so good night. I will only
add, I had a short and pleasant interview with Jefferson
Randolph as he was passing through this place, with his
two daughters, the great grand children of Mr. Jefferson.

Monday evening. Yesterday morning, we were informed Mr. Mead,[1] one of the best and most pious preachers in the Episcopalean Church, was in Charlottsville and would preach. We went to hear him and were both edified and gratified. There was a very large and respectable congregation. At least 20 private carriages were at the door, as many of the gentry from the country even from the other side of the mountain had assembled to hear this popular preacher.

Mr. Hugh Nelson, late Minister to Spain, was one and many other of the most respectable men of the place were among the communicants. There were six tables. I have never before since I left your part of the world seen so many communicants. From this circumstance I should suppose much greater attention was paid to religion, than I had been led to expect in Virginia. We had an excellent sermon and the whole service was solemn and affecting. In the afternoon, we went to the University. It is about 1 1-4 miles from town. Never have I beheld a more imposing work of Art. On a commanding height, surrounded by mountains, rises the Rotunda, or central building, forming one side of an oblong square, on two other sides running from north to south are the Pavillions, or Professor's houses, at about 60 or 70 feet apart, connected by terraces, beneath which are the dormitories, or lodging sleeping rooms of the students. The terrace projects about 8 feet beyond the rooms and is supported on brick arches, forming beneath the arches a paved walk, sheltered from the heat of summer and the storms of winter. A vast wide lawn separates the two rows of pavillions and dormitories. The south end at present open and standing there gives a noble and

[1] This was the famous William Meade, afterwards Episcopal Bishop of Virginia, the author of "Old Churches, Ministers and Families of Virginia," the greatest storehouse of local Virginia history in existence.

magnificent view of the buildings. There are 12 Pavillions, each one exhibiting the different orders of architecture and built after classic models, generally Grecian. The rotunda is in form and proportioned like the Pantheon at Rome. It has a noble portico,—the pillars, cornice, &c of the Corinthian. We went to the house of Professor Lomax, who is a near relation of William Washington, and were most kindly and hospitably received. He has a very large family, wife and daughters friendly and agreeable. We sat in the Portico of his Pavillion and feasted our eyes on the beauties of the surrounding scenery, then walked through the buildings, visited the Rotunda and the library, a magnificent apartment, larger and more beautiful than the library in the Capitol, but I cannot go into details. The whole impression on my mind was delightful, elevating, for the objects both of nature and art by which I was surrounded, are equally sublime and beautiful. We returned to our Hotel by sunset and soon after Mr. Nelson and one or two other gentlemen and a lady whom we knew called and passed the evening with us. We promised this amiable family to return and take a more minute survey this morning. They asked us to dine, but Mr. Smith's business did not permit our accepting the invitation. We promised to be there by 9 o'clock, but before that hour young Mr. Lomax was here to accompany us. He returned with us and has just gone, not having left Anna Maria's side ten minutes at a time. I have been joking her on her attractions. The whole family received us like old friends and near relations. Professor Lomax is a charming man, in every respect, looks, voice, manners, so like Mr. Wirt that he might be mistaken for him. He and I sat in the Library looking over books and conversing on literary subjects for more than two hours, while the young people were roaming about and climbing to the dome or roof of the Rotunda. I have seldom passed two hours more agreeably. I felt sorry Mr. Smith could not participate in my pleasure, but business detained him in the Town. A violent shower prevented our going up one of the adjoining mountains on the top of which the observatory is built. Anna Maria was positively enchanted and I could scarcely get her away. When we returned to our Hotel we found the space between it and the Court-House filled with hundreds of people and amused ourselves the rest of the day in watching the various and curious groups and hearing the various cries, for the Court is likewise a kind of fair and sales of various kinds going on, while that of Justice was going on within the Court House. In the afternoon Professor Lomax, came to see us, soon afterwards Mr. Rives,[1] member of Congress and several other persons called on us and agreeable conversation passed away the time. Mr. Rives insisted on our calling at his house and we have promised to pass tomorrow night. We shall go in the morning to Monticello, and from there in the afternoon to Mr. Rives', which is 14 miles further on and the next day to Mr. Madison's.

Thus far, my excursion has been far pleasanter than I expected. I have seen more persons and the scenery has been more beautiful than I anticipated. This hasty sketch will give you a very imperfect idea of the pleasure I have enjoyed. An hour ago, we had one, which it would require a whole sheet to describe. We heard a pleasing voice, delivering what we thought an animated oration on the pavement before the house. On looking out of the window we discovered it to be Phillip Bar-

[1] William Cabell Rives, of Castle Hill, statesman, diplomatist and author of a mighty fragment in three large volumes, of a " Life of James Madison," covering only part of his career.

bour,[1] the member of Congress. He was sitting on the
pavement surrounded by a dozen or twenty gentlemen
and more, whom he was entertaining with a history of
events, debates and scenes which took place in Congress-
Hall. Roars of laughter followed some of his stories
and attention waited on all. I mean to commit one or
two of his anecdotes to paper. They were original and
piquant.

It is now late, and I conclude my letter with my visit
to Charlottsville and shall when I return home, write to
you again and give you an account of the rest of my adventures. Last summer you and sister sent me sketches
of your excursions and I now unexpectedly have an opportunity of returning the compliment. But good night
my dear sisters.

TO MRS. BOYD

Sidney, Aug. 12, 1828.

. . . . Before this I presume you have received
my hastily scribbled letter from Charlottsville. I am almost sorry that I wrote so carelessly under the excitement
of feeling, my little journal would have been better had
it been quietly and more carefully written at home. It
proved at least that the idea of my dear sisters is ever
present and enhances what pleasures fall to my lot. I
entirely forget where I left off, but if not mistaken it
was after I had been at the University of Virginia, one
of the finest specimens of art and the most magnificent
institutions I have ever seen. It has a most imposing
effect. In a city, or land cultivated country it would not
be so impressive. But on a landscape so rich, varied and

---

[1] Philip Pendleton Barbour, brother of James Barbour, Mrs. Smith's
friend. He was afterwards Judge of the Supreme Court. He lived at
"Frascati," about fifteen miles from Charlottesville.

beautiful, so remote from any city, there was something novel as well as grand in its locality, that certainly had a strong effect on the imagination. Were I a young man and a student there, methinks the place alone would purify and elevate my mind. The discipline of the Institution has been greatly improved, and Mr. Madison, who is no visionary or enthusiast, says he does not believe more orderly habits or purer morals are to be found in any other college in the U. S. Some years ago, when some riot broke out among the students, originating in a mere frolic, in which the faculty interfered and were resisted, they had to call together the Rector, (then Mr. J.) and some of the nearest visitors or Trustees. The students previous to their arrival had determined not to yield, or give up each others names, but if it became the alternative, to submit to expulsion in a body. Mr. Jefferson and several of the visitors assembled. The students called before them, stood erect, and looked defiance. There was a silence and pause of expectation, waiting Mr. J.'s rising. He sat amidst them with his bent form and grey hairs, like a Father amidst his children. He looked upon them with the tenderness of a father and it required an evident struggle to repress his emotions. At last he arose, his lips moved, he essayed to speak,—burst into tears and sank back into his seat. The shock was electric. The proud spirit of youth yielded to the tenderness of youth and one and all submitted, acknowledged their faults, and without the least equivocation answered all the interrogotories put to them. To be sure Chapman Johnson, finding Mr. J. could not speak, arose and addressed them, but as one of the young men told me, it was not his words, but Mr. Jefferson's tears that melted their stubborn purpose. If I recollect aright, 20 or more were expelled, the discipline reformed, since which time no disorder, no rebellion of any kind has occurred. The Episcopalian and Presbyterian Ministers alternately preach at the University on Sabbath afternoons, and the students are allowed to attend in the mornings any of the churches in town their conscience or inclination lead them to. After passing 2 1-2 pleasant days at Charlottsville we set off on Tuesday for Monticello. I cannot stop to describe the windings of the road among the mountain scenery. Near the summit, a little off the road, we got out of the carriage to visit the grave of Jefferson. A rude stone wall encloses a small square, left in a state of nature, full of forest trees and rocks and wild plants, amidst which is Mr. J.'s grave between that of his wife and daughter. Were I to describe all the feelings which swelled my bosom while standing by the side of that lonely and lowly grave in the solitude of the mountains, or the reflections on human life and human greatness, which rushed on my mind, I should leave no space to say anything of the interesting family this great man has left behind him—left poor and afflicted. I will, then, restrain my pen and carry you with me to the summit of the mountain, on which his now desolate mansion stands. How different did it seem from what it did 18 years ago! No kind friend with his gracious countenance stood in the Portico to welcome us, no train of domestics hastened with smiling alacrity to show us forward. All was silent. Ruin has already commenced its ravages—the inclosures, the terraces, the outer houses. But we drove to the door, ascended the steps, knocked, and after a while a little negro girl poorly dressed open'd those once wide portals. We entered the hall once filled with busts and statues and natural curiosities to crowding, now empty! Bare walls and de-

faced floor, from thence into the drawing room, once so
gay and splendid, where walls were literally covered with
pictures like the Hall,—bare and comfortless.   The furniture pictures, statues, servants, all gone, sold, yes sold!
not descended to the survivors.   But Mrs. Randolph
came, came with open arms and an affectionate countenance and seemed like the spirit of the place, that had
survived its body.   Yet no, the Master spirit, the animating spirit was gone.   And yet it was not gone, but
seemed to be invisibly hovering near.   Yes, I felt, tho' I
could not see its presence.   After a few moments emotion,
conversation took place.   Mrs. R. called her children,
now women and her grand children, the size and age of
what the others had been when I last saw them.   Scarcely
chairs to sit on!   "You will excuse all that is wanting,"
said she.   "You know all that has passed."   What a
sweetness, dignity, resignation,—nay cheerfulness.   And
such a reserve!   But her soul is superior to the accidents
and incidents of fortune.   It is only where these changes
touch her heart, she feels their pressure.   The family
dependent on her, consists of 4 daughters, all women, 4
sons, the youngest 12 yrs old, 4 grand-children, the husband of her eldest daughter Mr. Trist, and old Mrs.
Trist his grand mother, in her dotage, with no home but
what Mrs. R. can give her.   Mr. Triste [1] is very young
and not yet in business.   Her youngest son she has left
at Cambridge.   Her eldest is married; has 7 daughters,
and lives on his father's farm which he has purchased.
Mrs. R. and I rambled alone to a distant part of the
grounds.   How affecting was her conversation! the details of the last few years.   "Oh, Mrs. Smith," said she,
speaking of her eldest son, "Jefferson is my treasure!

[1] Nicholas P. Trist, afterwards Assistant Secretary of State and a distinguished diplomatist.

Never was there such a son, he is my support,—nay he is the father of us all, he was the joy and support of his grand father's declining years and the comforter and consolation of his father's dying hour!" He does indeed appear to be a most exemplary man and is very interesting in his looks. I enquired into her future plans, they were not yet fixed. In a few weeks she must leave this dear and sacred spot for in a few weeks Monticello must be sold. She still vacillates between Philadelphia and Washington as her future place of residence. She will chose that which she thinks will be most advantageous to her children. Mr. Trist has studied law and intends practicing it. One of her boys is on a farm with his eldest brother. Should she come to Washington, what a precious and interesting addition will she and her family be to our little circle of friends. It will be an important event to me. Next to my sisters, I know not the woman I could so entirely esteem or so tenderly love. She unites a strong and highly cultivated intellect, with a soft, tender heart and a frank, communicative disposition. Oh, I earnestly hope she may determine on Washington!

TO MRS. BOYD

[Sidney,] Monday, 17th August.

Several days have elapsed, since I began this letter. A little fatigue and over excitement brought on an attack of fever. I am now quite well and resume my journal. With a new sheet I will commence a new subject, one the reverse of the one I wrote of on the last page.

We left *Monticello*. We walked from the very top to the bottom of the mountain, between 2 and 3 miles.

The road was so rugged and broken, that the carriage passed it with difficulty. We travelled about thirty miles, generally through woods and up and down steep hills. Mr. Smith told us very seriously, that he begged we would not be prevailed on to stay beyond a few hours at Mr. Madison's, as his business required his immediate return. Anna and I felt very sorry, but of course determined to be governed by his wishes,—however we did not the less heartily wish that rain or some other incident might occur to detain us at Montpelier. After breakfast, the next morning, we resumed our journey and after having lost ourselves in the mountain road which leads thro' a wild woody track of ground and wandering for some time in Mr. Madison's domain, which seemed to us interminable, we at last reached his hospitable mansion. We had scarcely entered on his estate, before our wishes were granted and it began to rain, at which Anna and I rejoiced, and I do not believe Mr. S. was sorry. We drove to the door. Mr. M. met us in the Portico and gave us a cordial welcome. In the Hall Mrs. Madison received me with open arms and that overflowing kindness and affection which seems a part of her nature. We were at first conducted into the Drawing room, which opens on the back Portico and thus commands a view through the whole house, which is surrounded with an extensive lawn, as green as in spring; the lawn is enclosed with fine trees, chiefly forest, but interspersed with weeping willows and other ornamental trees, all of most luxuriant growth and vivid verdure. It was a beautiful scene! The drawing-room walls are covered with pictures, some very fine, from the ancient masters, but most of them portraits of our most distinguished men, six or eight by Stewart. The mantlepiece, tables in each corner and in fact wherever one could be fixed, were filled with busts, and groups of figures in plaster, so that this apartment had more the appearance of a museum of the arts than of a drawing room. It was a charming room, giving activity to the mind, by the historic and classic ideas that it awakened.

After the first salutations were passed, Mrs. M. invited us to a chamber, where we might make ourselves comfortable, as she said. She led the way to an elegant little chamber, on the same floor and adjoining her own, furnished with crimson damask and looking out on the beautiful lawn. She sent a maid to attend us and said she would return by the time we had exchanged our damp clothes. This we soon did and she then carried us in to her own chamber. It was very large and commodious and furnished with every convenience and much elegance. Before a large sopha, lay her work. Couches, easy-chairs &c invited us to ease and comfortable indulgence. I told her I had no notion of playing lady visitor all day and sitting prim in the drawing room with our hands before us and if she would resume her seat and her work, we would sit with her and work too. It was so agreed. She drew Anna on the sopha beside her and gave her half a dozen pretty books to look over, while drawing a french arm chair, or fauteuil (what charming things they are!) close by her, I reclined at my ease, while we talked,—and oh how we did talk. We went over the last 20 years and talked of scenes long past and of persons far away or dead. These reminisences were delightful. She certainly has always been, and still is one of the happiest of human beings. Like myself, she seems to have no place about her which could afford a lodgement for care or trouble. Time seems to favour her as much as fortune. She looks young and she says she feels so. I can believe her, nor do I think she will ever

James Madison.

From a picture by Gilbert Stuart in the possession of
T. Jefferson Coolidge.

look or feel like an old woman.   They are seldom alone,
but have a succession of visitors, among whom are a
great many foreigners.   Few visit our country without
visiting Monticello and Montpelier.   She gave me an
entertaining account of the visit of the three members of
parliament, who passed several days with them.   I could
scarcely credit my senses, when dinner was announced
and I found it to be four oclock!   So rapidly had the
morning passed away.   We did not rise from table until
six oclock.   Mr. Madison was chief speaker, and his
conversation was a stream of history, and continued so
until ten oclock, when we separated for the night, so
rich in sentiments and facts, so enlivened by anecdotes
and epigramatic remarks, so frank and confidential as
to opinions on men and measures, that it had an interest
and charm, which the conversation of few men now living, could have.   He spoke of scenes in which he himself had acted a conspicuous part and of great men, who
had been actors in the same theatre.   No common-places.
Every sentence he spoke, was worthy of being written
down.   The formation and adoption of the Constitution.
The Convention and first congress, the characters of
their members and the secret debates.   Franklin, Washington, Hamilton, John Adams, Jefferson, Jay, Patrick
Henry and a host of other great men were spoken of
and characteristic anecdotes of all related.   It was living
History!   When I retired for the night, I felt as if my
mind was full to over-flowing, as if it could not contain
all the new ideas it had received, as if I had feasted to
satiety.   And this entertaining, interesting and communicative personage, had a single stranger or indifferent
person been present, would have been mute, cold and
repulsive.   After dinner, we all walked in the Portico,
(or piazza, which is 60 feet long, supported on six lofty

pillars)[1] until twilight, then retreated to the drawing
room, where we sat in a little group close together and
took our coffee while we talked. Some of Mr. M.'s
anecdotes were very droll, and we often laughed very
heartily. I wish my letter was large enough to contain
a few of them, which I am sure would make you laugh
too. He retains all the sportiveness of his character,
which he used to reveal now and then to those whom
he knew intimately, and Mrs. M. says he is as fond
of a frolic and of romping with the girls as ever. His
little blue eyes sparkled like stars from under his bushy
grey eye-brows and amidst the deep wrinkles of his poor
thin face. Nor have they lost their look of mischief,
that used to lurk in their corners, and which vanished and
gave place to an expression ever solemn, when the conversation took a serious turn.

In the course of the evening, at my request Mrs. M.
took me to see old Mrs. Madison.[2] She lacks but 3
years of being a hundred years old. When I enquired
of her how she was, "I have been a blest woman," she
replied, "blest all my life, and blest in this my old age.
I have no sickness, no pain; excepting my hearing, my
senses are but little impaired. I pass my time in reading
and knitting." Something being said of the infirmities
of old age. "You," said she, looking at Mrs. M., "you
are *my* mother now, and take care of me in my old age."
I felt much affected by the sight of this venerable woman.
Her face is not as much wrinkled as her son's who is only
77 years old. Mr. and Mrs. Madison urged our passing

[1] The original house at Montpelier was built between 1756 and 1760 by
Madison's father and was a plain, rectangular brick edifice of four rooms.
It was enlarged at different times and various improvements made, the most
important being in 1809 by Dr. Thornton. Latrobe also lent assistance
in adding the wings. The house was one of flawless taste architecturally
when Mrs. Smith paid her visit.
[2] She lived in a wing of the Montpelier house where she had a separate
establishment from her son. She died in 1829, aged 99 years.

several days with them, and on our declining told us we
must come soon again and stay longer. Anna Maria
was highly gratified and delighted and says if she lives
to be as old as the venerable mother, she will never lose
the impression this visit has made on her mind. She
listened to the conversation with the greatest interest and
was charmed with Mrs. M.'s affable affectionate manner.
Mrs. M. called her nothing but "my little girl" and talked
a good deal to her. One time on the portico, she took
Anna by the hand, saying, "come, let us run a race. I
do not believe you can out run me. Madison and I often
run races here, when the weather does not allow us to
walk." And she really did run very briskly,—it was
more than I could do, had I attempted it, which I did not,
however, as I preferred listening to the gentlemen's conversation. We parted with them the next morning after
lingering until a late hour over the breakfast-table. The
rest of our journey, 50 miles by land and 70 by water,
was quiet, commonplace, every day pleasure, which it is
not worth detailing. We reached home on Saturday
after 10 days absence. Eleven days of agreeable travelling, during which we had seen three grand and interesting objects, the University, Monticello and Montpelier.
Anna says it will be an epoch in her life, to which she
shall always recur with the most pleasurable feelings.
I paid the penalty I always pay, for a deeply excited interest or very lively emotion,—a fever. It confined me
three days to my bed, but when the pain was subdued,
I found pleasure in my confinement to a bed surrounded
by my dear attentive children. . . .   Farewell.

TO MRS. KIRKPATRICK

Washington, Nov. 21, 1828.

. . . . Two weeks have passed since we located ourselves in our new habitation.[1] Never in my life have I been so comfortably and agreeably fixed. My wishes are completely satisfied. Our house, a delightful one, in the best part of the city, surrounded with good neighbors, good churches and good pavements which enable us to visit both neighbors and churches in all weather. You will recollect the situation of the Department of State &c—it is opposite to this. A broad pavement leads one way to Capitol Hill and another to George-Town, besides cross paved ways in every direction. We could keep up a very social intercourse now, without a carriage, but this, tho' not a necessity is a very agreeable convenience and will add greatly to our pleasure. Mrs. Clay, Mrs. Southard, Mrs. Lovel, Mrs. Cutts, Mrs. Newal, Mrs. Cashier Smith, (cashier for Bank) Mrs. Barret, Mrs. Lawyer Jones, Mrs. Genl. McComb, Mrs. Johnson, Mrs. Andrew Smith, (formerly Miss Graham) Mrs. Rush, Mrs. Wirt, Mrs. Thornton, are our neighbors, viz is within two squares; the most distant is not more, and many are on the same square and some within a few doors. Excepting Mrs. Barret, (who we are told is a charming woman and our nearest neighbor) all are old and familiar acquaintances some of them my most intimate. Mrs. Genl. Porter, Mrs. Seaton, Miss Vale and several other old and agreeable acquaintances tho' farther off, are still within walking distance. These I have named and twenty others have already been to see

---

[1] The new house occupied the square between Pennsylvania Avenue, 15th Street and H Street, and faced on 15th Street, opposite what is now the Barton Hotel.

us.   Some of them have been three or four times, setting
an example of the sociability to which they invite us.
Having so totally given up society, I had no idea that
the persons whom I had for so many years declined visiting would have come to see us, and expected to have had
(what I really wish for) a very small circle, at the largest
not exceeding a dozen families.   But this part of my plan
I must relinquish, unless I wish to give offence.   At least
30 families have already visited us and I am over head
and ears in debt.   Yet I hope to limit habits of intimacy
and not allow my time to be wholly taken up by society.
If it depends on me, a very few, very few, will be on
the list of intimates, but among them shall be sweet Mrs.
Wirt and her lovely daughters.   Instead of a formal
morning call, she and the girls came in the afternoon and
urged us to follow their example.   Mrs. W. and her two
eldest daughters, Elizabeth and Catherine, last winter
joined the church, and tho' they participate in the general
amusements of society it is with that moderation, which
fulfils the precept of St. Paul, to use the world, but not
abuse it.   She is however a domestic woman, visiting
as little as her situation will allow.   The whole family
are refined and intellectual and derive their chief amusements from books, music and conversation.   Catherine
is in such delicate health, that she is never to go out of
an evening.   She is one of the loveliest and most interesting creatures I have ever met with, and so tender, so
carressing, so delicate and soft in her manners.   But
more of her another time.   Mr. Wirt has taken two pews
in the church in which we have taken ours and for the
same reason, Mr. Campbel's being the pastor.[1]   It was
under his ministry that the girls made an open profession

[1] John Nicholas Campbell, pastor of the New York Avenue Presbyterian
Church.

of religion. He had a bible class they diligently attended. He is a great favorite and friend of the family and this summer has been traveling with Mr. Wirt and his daughters. I am not personally acquainted with him, but am prepared to admire and reverence him, altho' a very young man. As Mrs. W.'s is the family I feel more desirous of intimacy with, both on my own and my girls account, I have said more of them than any other and hope during the winter to have much more to say. Since my arrival in the city, most fervently have I wished Mr. Adams would remain in office. The prompt kindness and friendly attentions showed us by many of those whose continuance depends on Mr. Adams induces this wish. But the question is otherwise decided and notwithstanding Mr. Smith's political satisfaction I feel great personal regret. I shall lose not only agreeable acquaintance but a tried friend, for such has Mrs. Clay been, and of late Mrs. Southard and the Judge have been to us like near relatives. But above all shall I regret the loss of the Wirt family. The mother and father all I wished as friends for myself, and the daughters the very characters I would have chosen among thousands for my daughters friends, and they showing as they have done, similar desires of intimacy with us. Oh that Genl. Jackson may leave the Attorney General with us, whatever other changes he makes. Mrs. Johnson[1] of Louisianna, is Ann's favorite. She is not only the fashion but the Ton, yet admiring and admired as she is, and the gayest among the gay, she has a simplicity and frankness and kind heartedness about her, that is very attractive, and there is no one Ann likes as well. She buys every new book and they are all at our service. She sent me a dozen the other day. As

---

[1] Wife of Josiah S. Johnston, Senator from Louisiana.

for Books, we shall be at no loss. The library of the
Dept. of State, is close to us, and the city library and I
count on access to the Congress Library as in times of
old, when as Mary Ann may recollect I used to have
members names signed on blanks for me to fill out at
my pleasure. The only difficulty will be to find time to
read. I will tell you our plan of living—our parlours
open into each other with folding doors—fire in both
is made before breakfast. After breakfast I come into
the front parlour, a table with my india writing and
work-box is on it, and books and paint-box &c, stands in
the middle of the room, always ready for me to write,
read or sew. The breakfast things are directly removed
to the kitchen, which is light, nice and comfortable, where
the house keeper goes to attend to her duties, the other
girls sit in the dining-room, at their work or reading until
one oclock. Then we visit, and walk if the weather is
good, or receive visitors, or join our circles and while one
reads aloud the other works. Excepting three rainy
days, we have not been alone a single day, having a reception of visitors from one oclock until bed-time. After
tea, Mr. Smith sits alone in the dining room until 9 and
then joins us, when Ann, myself, or some of our guests
play chess with him, unless prevented by the pleasures
of conversation. We are engaged in reading aloud, the
Lady of the Manor and Mrs. Hemer's dramatic pieces.
Each of us have different books of a more instructive cast
for our individual study. Until one oclock we do not
visit and hope to be able not to receive visitors. Sunday
is a delightful day to us all, especially the servants. My
arrangements are such, that only one of the women remains at home and that, only till dinner is over, the other
woman and William, Lawrence and Mary Ann go to
Sunday school and then three times to church. The girls

have already commenced their sunday school labours.
We have to rise very early, but so much the better. Mr.
Gallaudet (you must I think remember the old gentleman
when we lived in Phila) is to be their constant Sunday
beau, to take his tea here and then accompany them to
evening-church.

This is the second day it has rained without interruption, to me it is pleasant weather and I enjoy the uninterrupted quiet it affords us. After finishing this letter
I shall sit down and read the American Review some
articles of which require close attention. We made two
new acquaintances this week, Mr. Burrel Randolph,
(brother of Beverly) and Mr. Triste, a young gentleman
married to a grand-daughter of Mr. Jefferson's just from
Monticello. Mr. Clay has given him an appointm of 14
hundred a year. He brought me an interesting letter
from Mrs. Randolph, who from motives of economy will
not remove to this place until next autumn. I wish I
had had a letter of yours to answer and mine should
not then have been so full of egotism. Let me intreat
you to write soon to your affectionate sister.

TO J. BAYARD H. SMITH

[Washington,] Sunday evening, Novr 23, 1828.

. . . . Mr. Triste is a very interesting man and
when he conversed of Mr. Jefferson I listened to him with
delight. He drew me a plan, designed by Mr. J. for the
family grave yard and speaking of his grave, asked me
if I had observed a venerable oak tree which shaded it.
"Beneath that tree," said he, "Mr. Jefferson when a
young man was accustomed to sit and muse, and when
he and Dabney Carr, his early and bosom friend, rested

from their rambles it was at the foot of this tree. Here he enjoyed these outpourings of the soul, that perfect sympathy, which a friendship so fond and true only could afford. On one occasion they mutually promised each other that who ever died first should be buried under this tree and that the surviver when his turn came should lie by the side of his friend. Mr. Carr died at a distance from Monticello, while Mr. J. was absent, I believe in Europe. On his return he had his friend's body taken up and brought to the appointed spot. Mr. J.'s wife was laid near; a place between his friend and wife was reserved for himself, and there he now rests beneath his favorite oak." I wish my letter would admit of my giving you other interesting details, but it does not. Tuesday it snow'd, and falling weather continued until Thursday afternoon, when the sun shone forth brightly, previous to setting. We took advantage of the fine weather next day to pay a great many visits. We were all out and I did not expect to find any body at home. Mrs. Rush was, and her room was so comfortable and charming and she was so agreeable that I paid a most unfashionable visit. After dinner Ann and I went out again. We meant only to make calls, but they turned into social and pleasant visits. First at Mrs. Southard's. She told us Judge Southard had just gone to see us. We staid to tea and soon afterwards he came in and said he had taken his tea with Mr. Smith and the girls. He talked very frankly of his removal next March and his future plans and from this subject we reverted to inaugurations of all the Presidents and their attendant circumstances and went, that is I went, into a history of Washington from the time the government first came. Some of our recitations were quite amusing and when I rose to depart, Judge S. said, I had better sit still and talk over old times. We wished however to pay an evening social visit to Mrs. Wirt. We were ushered into a very large and elegant drawing room, in the middle was a round table, cover'd with books, engravings, work-boxes &c &c lit by a splendid lamp. Round the table was seated the young ladies and 2 young gentlemen. A rousing hickory fire blazed in the chimney and diffused warmth and cheerfulness through the room. On one side of the fire Mrs. Wirt, with a small table and candles by her, sat reading. I have never seen such a union of comfort and elegance, I might say splendor. Ann joined the young people at the table and I sat on the sopha by Mrs. Wirt. Coffee was immediately brought in and afterwards dried fruits. But the best part of the entertainment was intellectual. The girls brought me their albums to look over, full of beautiful paintings, and original poetry—they were quite a treat. Mr. Wirt and Mr. King soon joined us and the conversation was so agreeable, that fond as I am of music I regretted the interruption it gave to conversation. Catherine played on the harp and sung to it some sweet songs; afterwards she accompanied Elizabeth on the piano, with her harp in some very fine pieces. Mr. Wirt listening in apparent rapture and requiring the harp to be tuned and retuned, till as he said it was within "half a hair's breadth" the same tone as the piano. At last the piece concluded and we bade this charming family good night and found to our astonishment when we reached home that it was near 11 o'clock.

The domestic habits, style of living, and character of this family, come nearer to my beau-ideal, than that of any other I know. I have endeavored to describe it, in my Seymour Family; for you know Mr. Wirt was the model of my Mr. Seymour.

TO J. BAYARD H. SMITH

[Washington,] Sunday evening, 30 Nov. 1828.

. . . . I told Genl. P.[1] I was a self constituted delegate from the young ladies of Washington, to beg he would use his authority and forbid the ferocious Winebagos from assaulting the girls in the manner they did. They have run after several young ladies and others they have caught in their arms and kissed, till decent young women are nearly afraid to walk out. He promised he would attend to my request and have such improper liberties repressed. While discussing this subject, Governor Cass[2] came in, and Mrs. Porter told him the complaints I had brought against his Indians. He would not allow they could be justly censured and vindicated them with great warmth. However, next day he went to their lodgings, enquired into the business and gave strict orders to have them properly watched. You have no idea, what a general dread they inspired. On Tuesday Mary Miller and Caroline Breckenridge came to dinner, and in the afternoon Virginia Southard, Esther Smith, our neighbor, The Seatons were asked but did not come. I sent for James Doughty Mr. Ellison, Dawes Elliot and Edward Cranch wishing to introduce our friends to Mary Miller. These were the young folks, Mrs. Clay and Mrs. Southard, Mr. Claibourn[3] and Governr Cass the old folks. I expected Mrs. Bomford and Mrs. Thornton and Mrs. Johnson and their husbands. The gentlemen of the Cabinet who were to come received a summons to attend the President at his dinner, on business and could not get away until 9, when they adjourned

---

[1] Peter B. Porter, of New York, Secretary of War, a distinguished officer in the War of 1812.

[2] Louis Cass was then Governor of Michigan Territory.

[3] Nathaniel H. Claiborne, Representative from Virginia.

to Mrs. Johnson's where they had been previously engaged to supper. I introduced all your young friends to Mary, Dawes Elliot, seemed to be *very* much pleased and conversed almost the whole evening with her. Mrs. Southard asked all the ladies present to spend the next evening with her, and never did I spend a merrier evening. As Mrs. Seaton said, she heard there was no one there above 15 years old. We certainly all acted like girls, excepting myself. I did not dance, but played chess, tho' not with much gravity I must confess. Perceiving Mary M. did not enjoy the dancing, I asked her to play. Mr. Shaler, our Consul at Algiers and an old acquaintance of mine, sat near and alternately helped us. Afterwards I played with him and then with Dr. Lovel. But there was such a laughing and talking around me, I could not help joining in the mirth, losing my game. The girls had no beaux and in order to set them a dancing, Mrs. Clay, Mrs. Johnson, Lovel, Jessup and others danced with them and were as merry as a parcel of girls. Mr. Clay, had been dining out, and did not come in until 9, but in such spirits, that he added to those of the company. I never saw him so gay and agreeable. Indeed all the defeated party, appear as if they had thrown down heavy burdens and felt light of heart. Mr. Adams has rented Commodore Porter's house for Mrs. Adams, whose health will not allow of her residing in Boston, and many people think he will likewise remain here, as his rupture with his old friends and party, will make Boston a very unpleasant home for him. Mr. Wirt, it is said, will settle in Baltimore and the other gentlemen return to their respective homes.

On Wednesday we passed the morning in visiting and paid off some of our debts, but on our return found we had incumbered new ones. This morning visiting breaks

up all my sober plans. I will struggle hard to have
more time to myself, for the girls and myself are already
wearied of so much going out. Wednesday evening we
had to ourselves and passed it in work and reading.
Thursday, Julia Seaton spent the day here and in the
afternoon Col. and Mrs. Bomford came and staid until
11 oclock. Mr. and Mrs. Seaton called on their return
from the President's where they had taken tea and passed
the early part of the evening. Friday, a delightful rainy
day, we passed in reading and work. Saturday went to
see the Indian Dance, in the afternoon to see Mrs. Clifton
and in the evening at home. Mr. Triste came in to tea
and sat until near ten with us. We have had a great
deal of morning company which has lengthened our list
of acquaintances far beyond my wish. Govr Cass is the
most agreeable new acquaintance I have formed. He is
very frank and communicative and his conversation interesting.

Tomorrow Congress opens. I expect and hope we
will have a quiet, tranquil winter. Our city is rapidly
filling, not only with members but with strangers. In
my next, I shall, I suppose have something more interesting to say.

It is with difficulty I have written thus far. John
Scott (his first visit) and William Bryan and the ———
were talking all around me and I scarcely know what
I have written. I shall watch anxiously for your next
letter. If you are well, write immediately on receipt
of this, which I suppose will be Wednesday evening and
if you write on Thursday I shall get your letter on Saturday. The girls join me in affectionate remembrances.
Tell me whether you see Mary Miller and what she tells
you about Washington, how she likes us, &c &c. Good
night dearest Bayard.

TO MRS. BOYD

[Washington,] Decr. (20, I believe) 1828.

. . . . You ask how the administration folks look since their defeat. They all with one consent, do what I think dignity and self respect requires,—appear cheerful and good humoured, mix freely and frankly with the triumphant party and in Congress all is harmony I am told. Mr. and Mrs. Adams have gone a little too far in this *assumed* gaiety at the last drawing room they laid aside the manners which until now they have always worn and came out in a brilliant masquerade dress of social, gay, frank, cordial manners. What a change from the silent, repulsive, haughty reserve by which they have hitherto been distinguished. The great audience chamber, never before opened, and now not finished was thrown open for *dancing,* a thing unheard of before at a drawing-room! The band of musick increased the hilarity of the scene. All the folks attached to the administration made a point of being there. The ladies of the Cabinet in their best bibs and tuckers. Most of them in new dresses just arrived from Paris. Every thing in fact was done to conceal the natural feelings excited by disappointment and to assume the appearance not only of indifference, but of satisfaction. As one of the opposition members observed, "The Administration mean to march out with flying colours and all the honors of war." Well, I think I would do so too, only not carry it so far as to betray affectation. In private and social intercourse, among themselves, where no false assumption is necessary, I have, I must say, seen the same good humour. They treat their defeat as one of the chances of war, which happen to the most brave and

John Quincy Adams.

From the portrait by Jean Baptiste Adolphe Gibert.   In the State
Department, Washington.

skilful, as well as the weak and ignorant.   We have been
asked in a social way to all our neighbors.   Mrs. Clay,
Mrs. Southard, Mrs. Wirt, Cutts, Porter, &c, where we
met the same folks and without a single exception all
seemed in a good humour.   Mr. Clay seems in better
health and spirits than he has been for many months.
Genl. Porter is in fine spirits, as well as his charming
wife and seems determined to keep open house and extend his hospitality equally to both parties.   We were
at a crowded party there this day week, asked to meet a
few friends, and found at least 200.   This morning I
have received another invitation for this evening,—when
from what I hear there may be five hundred, so none of
us wish to go.   Last week we had invitations to 4
parties, but I went only to Mrs. Porter's and this week
shall confine ourselves to Mrs. Clay's drawing room and
company one evening at home.   Mrs. Porter will be very
popular.   Frank, gay and conversible, she is cordial
with every one, and pleases every one.   And so odd, an
absolute original.   The first rainy day I can find time
I mean to draw her portrait and record some of her
sayings and phrases, to add to my collection of *original
pictures*.   I like her very much, but shall see little of her,
for she is now in for it, up to the very ears in the bustle
and business of company.   She has hardly time to eat
or sleep she says.   I went out one morning visiting with
her, her list of visits to be returned, already amounted
to 500 and all who call on her, she is obliged to invite
to her parties.   As Mr. Cox[1] of your city, who preached
for us said, "Is the Lord a hard master, is his work
drudgery.   No I tell you, his yoke is easy and his burden light.   It is the world that is a master and let you do

---

[1] Probably Samuel Hanson Cox, a Presbyterian divine, one of the founders
of the University of the City of New York.

what you will, slave yourself to death, give health, give fortune, give time and all you have and still you can never please him." And this is true, Oh hard and exciting world, *I* will not be thy slave.

TO MRS. KIRKPATRICK

[Washington, January, 1829.]

Wednesday morning: We had a most agreeable evening without the aid of other amusement than what the intellect afforded. Conversation never flagged a moment, but until 12 o'clock was sustained with such animation that every one expressed surprise on discovering it was so late. Dr. and Mrs. Lovel, Dr. and Mrs. Lindsay, several ladies you do not know, Gen'l. Van Rensalaer, Mr. Henry, Mr. Wood, Mr. Chase, three literary and agreeable single men and a number of married ones, Mr. Campbell, accustomed in the circle of his wife's family, to gay and fashionable society (she was the sister of the rich Miss Bowling Sam Bayard courted) appears quite like a man of the world in company,—his manners polished and refined. It was the most agreeable party we have as yet had at home and just such as I wish to have, far more to my taste than the other occasion when I had Mrs. Clay and the other Secretaries' families, Mrs. Johnson, Cutts, &c., with cards and dancing. We all enjoyed ourselves, the young folks clustered around the center table and played *Insertion,* the game you taught me and which I so called, wrote rhymes, etc., and were merry without being silly—but someone rings.

Thursday: A happy New Year to my beloved sister and each individual of her dear family! How are you this morning? Would that I could wrap my arms

around you and give you the kiss of gratulation. The
girls you say are to pass this gala day in New York
and Maria with so many young people around her will
be younger than usual. I picture you and Mr. Kirkpatrick seated at this moment alone and quiet by a big
blazing fire in your comfortable parlour—each with your
books.   As it is dark and cloudy here it may be tempestuous with you. Our city is as alive and bustling as
New York—There are few persons who are sitting
quietly at home—everyone is thronging to the President's—to the last Levee of Mr. Adams carriages were
rolling incessantly past. I am seated with Julia in the
front parlour by a good fire of Lehigh coal. Mr. Smith
and the other gentlemen are surrounding a wood fire
in the dining room, they being disinclined to see company who may call. All are reading except myself and
my book is by me, but before I open it I could not
resist the impulse of my heart to write to you. I have
again read your last letter and feel interested in the
account you give of your society—The only public charity of whose beneficial influence I feel no doubt is the
education of the poor. This goes to the root of the
evil; in giving instruction, you give to the poor the
means of avoiding poverty. Most other public charities,
by relieving their present wants, take from them the
most powerful incentive, that of necessity, to provide
for the future by their own exertions.—They depend on
the relief benevolence extends to them and do little for
themselves. I shall participate in the pleasure success
will afford you and were I nearer would as gladly participate in your labours. Mrs. McClane of Delaware has
come. I passed two hours with her and then had fairly
to run away, for she talked at such a rate it was difficult
to get off. "How many children have you brought with

you," said I—"Let me see—three and a half—am I not
venturesome to come with half finished work?"   She is
in excellent spirits—animated and political—her husband has staked everything on his political measures,
his practice injured, his popularity in his own state gone [1]
—Jackson's election affords him something more than
mere triumph.   I have no doubt he builds on it hope, nay
almost certainty of office.   But alas! I fear disappointment awaits him, as well as many other supporters of
Jackson.   *All* cannot be in the Cabinet—Those who are
not what will they do?   Turn against him?   One of his
warmest partisans speaking about Mr. McClain last night
said he must remain in the Senate.   They will not spare
him, for certainly as his seat was vacated an administration man would be put in—After the example of your
state, who mean, we are told, to turn out Gov'r. D. and
put in Mr. Southard.   The aim of the defeated party
certainly is to get a majority in the Senate and thereby
to control the President.   Tonight Gen'l. Eaton, the
bosom friend and almost adopted son of Gen'l. Jackson,
is to be married to a lady whose reputation, her previous
connection with him both before and after her husband's
death, has totally destroyed.[2]   She is the daughter of
O'Neal who kept a large tavern and boarding house
whom Littleton knew.   She has never been admitted into
good society, is very handsome and of not an inspiring
character and violent temper.   She is, it is said, irresistible and carries whatever point she sets her mind on.
The General's personal and political friends are very
much disturbed about it; his enemies laugh and divert
themselves with the idea of what a suitable lady in waiting Mrs. Eaton will make to Mrs. Jackson and repeat the

[1] Louis McLane, of Delaware, was appointed Minister to England, 1829,
Secretary of the Treasury, 1831, and Secretary of State, 1833.
[2] See Mrs. Smith's letter to Mrs. Boyd, spring of 1829, *infra*.

old adage, "birds of a feather will flock together." Dr.
Simm and Col. Bomford's families are asked. The
ladies declare they will not go to the wedding, and if
they can help it will not let their husbands go. We
spent the evening at Dr. Simm's last night. All present
were Jacksonians—Dr. Simm the most ardent and devoted. He had lately received a letter from Gen'l. J.
which he promised to show me. I wanted to see it
immediately, suspecting, as I told him, if he deferred
showing it, it would be with the intention of correcting
the orthography. He laughed and joked on the subject
very good naturedly and about Mrs. J.[1] and her pipe in
the bargain. What a change will take place in our
society—how many excellent families shall we lose. I
told the Doctor I should cry all day long on the 4th of
March, for my politics were governed by my heart and
not my head—To dismiss Mr. Wirt! Where will he
get such another man? Oh, how sorry, very sorry I
should be. Our intimacy is progressing and time might
transmute it into friendship. But these miserable fetters
will deprive me of this hope. For eight years how I did
love to go to the President's house on this day. The
gracious countenance that then beamed on the thronging
multitude, the sweet mild voice, the cordial pressure of
the hand, I could no longer meet and therefore I will not
go. How much goodness and greatness then dwelt
there—now shrouded in the cold and narrow grave—the
home of all men. Thither we are hastening, the humble
and the ambitious, the poor and rich, the vanquished
and the triumphant. How trivial and inconsequent are
the rivalships and conflicts which now make such a stir.
A few years and the eager, animated actors on the present scene shall be still and silent and forgotten—and we

[1] It was well known that Mrs. Jackson smoked a pipe.

too, my sister,—for my part I look not for a return of
this day. I feel astonished that I am still here, but now
that my long secretly indulged wish of having my girls
fixed in the city is fulfilled I am ready—I am willing to
leave them. They will not now be left in the inactivity
and desolation of solitude. I enjoy life, but I have had
enough of it. Were it not for the constitutional and
merely animal gaiety of my disposition I should be dreadfully weary of this twice told tale. But these spirits
bouy me up on the calm surface of life's sea and give to
my exterior an appearance of enjoyment, often delusive.
Serious reflection and deep feeling float not on the surface. I therefore am not known or even suspected. At
this moment how little would a visitor who should enter
and with whom I should rattle away on the occurrences
of the day, how little would my own children who sit
around me imagine the subject of my thoughts and feelings during the many wakeful hours of last night—
thoughts and feelings which still occupy mind and heart
—Yes, at this moment I would rather shut myself up in
my own room and weep than sit in the parlour and
entertain company—I hear someone coming, a carriage
stops.

Friday.—A right down snow storm! The first one
we have had this season—it was very complaisant to wait
until the gaities of the holidays were over. Last night
the incessant rolling of carriages sounded like continual
peals of thunder or roaring of the wind, and every carriage having lights the appearance was very singular.
The night was dark and the lights darting and flying
about in every direction (for nothing but the lamps was
visible) appeared like brilliant meteors in the air. Mr.
Smith called me to the door to look at them. The pavement, indeed street, in front of the English Minister's

house[1] was light as noonday, a line of torches being
placed along the pavement. The street was full of carriages, about 400 it is said, all with lights and in motion.
His ball was given, it is said, to the President's family
and was more brilliant than any former. We kept our
resolution and would not go—neither to a ball in Georgetown to which we were asked. Sent. Eaton's wedding
likewise took place last night, so that the streets were as
light and as full as in the morning. This is a long New
Year's letter. I indulged myself in scribbling so much
because the gents being away from you I wished as far
as I could to amuse your solitude and supply their place.
On reading over these two crowded sheets I fear they
will tire you, but at least they will prove how much I
think of you. Good day, dearest sister—now for an
uninterrupted morning's reading. I shall enjoy it.

Yours tenderly.

TO J. BAYARD H. SMITH

[Washington, January, 1829]

. . . . We talked—my goodness, how we talked,
so fast and so loud we could scarcely hear each other.
"Tell us all about the gay world," said Mrs. Clifton.
"We *poor* people know nothing of it but by rumour."
So we told of all the gay and great folks and great
parties, and marriages and deaths, funerals and festivals,
we knew anything of, while we sat round the table and
drank our tea. Scarcely could we get away from these
attached friends. But the sun had set and we had other
visits to pay. On our way back we stopped to see an
old friend Mr. Ingham and his lady, who arrived a few

---

[1] Charles Richard Vaughan was then British minister.

days ago—and then proceeded to Mrs. Clay's, where I
reproached myself for not being oftener, considering
the present state of affairs. We were conducted up
stairs, the door of the little drawing-room opened. All
was bright with splendid furniture, lamps and blazing
fire, but no smiling faces like those we left in the little
kitchen mingled their light with the surrounding objects.
Mrs. C. was mournfully walking the room and as we
entered, held up her finger, to impose silence, and pointed
to the sopha. "He sleeps," whispered she. I felt a shock
on turning my eyes as she spoke, on the sopha was
stretched at full length Mr. Clay face and all, completely
cover'd with a dark cloak, which looked like a black pall.
We took our chairs, without speaking and sat silent.
Our entrance however had awakened him and after a
minute or two, he slowly rose and putting the cloak aside
reclined in one corner with his feet stretched along the
sopha. I had not seen him for three weeks and was
shocked at the alteration in his looks. He was much
thinner, very pale, his eyes sunk in his head and his
countenance sad and melancholy—that countenance
generally illumined with the fire of genius and animated by some ardent feeling. His voice was feeble
and mournful. I cannot describe dear Bayard what
melancholy feelings were excited in my breast. But
I had come purposely to try and cheer my excellent
friend Mrs. Clay, who I knew was sick and sad, so I
resisted my melancholy tho' I could not help continually
contrasting the little kitchen and its inmates, with this
present scene. There gaiety had been spontaneous, here
it was forced. Still I was, if [*torn out*], at least cheerful
and said everything I could think of to amuse my *great
friends,* with far less success however, than with my
poor friends. Gentlemen came in and enquiries were

made about the other sick members of the Cabinet. Mr.
Rush, who has been alarmingly ill, for a week past, is
not it is fear'd yet out of danger. The first symptoms of
disease were altogether in the head. Mr. Southard, tho'
just out of his room, after three weeks confinement, is
appointd acting Secretary of the treasury. He is so
feeble that I fear this added labour will produce a re-
lapse. Mr. Clay has not been out for a week and is
scarcely able to sit up. Last week Mr. Wirt had two
attacks, to which they gave no name, a vertigo, followed
by a loss of sense or motion. One attack, he remained
three hours, insensible, the gentlemen all agreed, the only
chance he had for prolonged life was his relinquishing
his practice. During a week or more, Genl. Porter, was
almost blind from inflamation of the eyes and went to
his office with two blisters on, one behind each ear. Mr.
Adams always appears in fine spirits, but it is said, is so
feeble as to be obliged to relinquish his long walks and
to substitute rides on horseback—this, I give from hear-
say, for I have not seen him. How strange it is, that
every individual of the administration, should be ill. I
really feel very anxious about Mr. Rush and Mr. Clay.
You, from your connection with his sons, will feel most
for Mr. R. and I need not caution you not to mention
what I have said, lest you alarm them, as it is probable
they are not informed of the worst symptoms. You
will know, sooner than I shall, the result of election of
Senator. From the last news, I fear Judge Southard
will lose his election and Mr. Ewing be chosen.[1] I shall
be sorry. I hoped we should keep this amiable family.
The thought of losing so many old and agreeable acquaintances, not to say friends, makes me feel sad,—

[1] Theodore Frelinghuysen was elected. On his retirement from the Navy
Department in 1829 Judge Southard became Attorney General of New
Jersey.

the time is rapidly approaching.   Mrs. Clay's next drawing-room, closes this social scene, intercourse between
these families and general society.   She says, she shall
not go out any more and immediately after next Wednesday, begin to pack up and make preparations for
going home.   The President, in the course of ten days
or two weeks is going to leave the President's House
and remove to Commodore Porter's House, which he
has rented.   What a change, what a change will there
be in our city.   On no former occasion has there been
anything like it.

Saturday morning.   Susan and I, accompanied by
Mrs. Barnet went last evening to Mrs. Lovel's, where
we met a much larger company than we expected, but
very agreeable.   It is a right down snow storm to-day.
After closing this letter I shall write a long one to your
aunt Boyd.   You know I love to write on a stormy day.
If the weather does not prevent I expect a small chess
party to meet here this evening.   Do you not wish you
were with us.   Good morning dear Bayard.   Now you
have answered the others my turn comes and I shall look
impatiently for a letter.

TO MRS. KIRKPATRICK

[Washington] January 12, 1829.   Monday.

.   .   .   .   Rank, honors, glory, are such unsubstantial empty things that they can never satisfy the desires
that they create.   You would not wonder at these reflections, if living as I do in the midst of a defeated
and a triumphant party—in the midst of men who have
expended health of body and peace of mind, a large
portion of their lives, who have watched and worked,

toiled and struggled, sacrificed friends and fortune, and domestic comfort, and gained what? Nothing, that I can perceive, but mortification and disappointment, the best part of their lives passed in pursuit of that which in possession was embittered and vexatious, and in the loss leaves nothing behind. Every one of the public men who will retire from office on the fourth of March will return to private life with blasted hopes, injured health, impaired or ruined fortunes, embitterd tempers and probably a total inability to enjoy the remnant of their lives. Poor Judge Southard has been very ill, is still confined to his room and looks wretchedly. Mr. Rush totally secludes himself; nobody sees him. Mr. Clay still keeps on the mask of smiles. Genl. Porter less hackneyed and worn out worried or weakened looks and I suppose feels the best of all, but even he, hospitably as he lives and universally as he entertains, must injure his private property. Yet with these examples before their eyes, others eagerly seek for the same places, indulging the same high hopes, which will be followed by like disappointments and vexations. Such are the irresistible allurements of ambition! But oh what a gloom is cast over the triumph of Genl. Jackson, by the death of a wife fondly and excessively loved! of a wife who it is said, could control the violence of his temper, sooth the exacerbations of feelings always keenly sensitive and excessively irritable, who heal'd by her kindness wounds inflicted by his violence, and by her universal charity and benevolence conciliated public opinion. It is said that she not only made him a happier, but a better man. I fear not only the domestic circle, but the public will suffer from this restraining and benign influence being withdrawn. Affliction generally softens, but sometimes it sours the human heart,—should it have the latter effect the public councils and affairs will have reason to deplore this awful and sudden event. She died the day before the one on which the festival of triumph was to take place at Nashville,—feasting was turned into mourning, the festival into a funeral, the cannons and drums that were to proclaim the victory of political party sounded only to proclaim the victory of death. To die was the common lot, but to die in such peculiar circumstances and at such a moment is an event rare as it is solemn and carries with it such a deep conviction of the impotency of honor and grandeur and power that the impression can not be easily effaced from a reflecting mind. On mine it has made a deep and I hope a salutary one. . . . Strange that a single woman, possessed of goodness tho' destitute of talents, could thus influence the destiny of nations! A similar case will occur to your mind perhaps in recollecting the history of Greece. It was Themistocles (I believe) who said, My little son governs his mother, his mother governs me,—I govern Athens, Athens governs Greece, Greece governs the world. So my boy governs the world. . . . One morning Mrs. McClain of Delaware, who you know is a great favorite of mine, Mrs. Clay, Mrs. Cutts and Mrs. Holly sat a long time with me. Mrs. McC. is so entertaining and agreeable that time literally flies, when I am with her. She and Mrs. Porter are extremely alike in character,—gay, frank and intelligent. But Mrs. P. has a warmer heart and no one can know without loving her. I have seen a great deal of her lately and propose passing this evening with her. Every other Monday (which I call her great Monday) she sends out hundreds of invitations, has the band of musick and opens four rooms. The intervening, (or as I call it, her little Monday) she sees any friends who choose to go, but without particular invitations. We have been invited to all, but have declined going on the Great Mondays. I promise myself much pleasure this evening.

Last week we were asked for the 2'd time to Mrs. Dickens[1] and as she said it was a small social party I and Susan went, but half, if not all Congress and their wives were there and the people almost a solid mass,—it was with difficulty, I secured a comfortable seat in a corner of the room for Susan and myself. For the beginning of the evening we knew not a creature in the room,—they being the strangers and visitors in the city. About 9 o'clock Mr. and Mrs. McClain entered; she spied me, and as glad of a comfortable seat as myself, a vacant chair next me. We laughed and talked so merrily as to attract Mrs. Porter, who with difficulty broke away from the crowd of gentlemen that surrounded her and came to us. She made Susan get up and give her her chair, much to poor Sue's regret who (a most terrible thing to her) had to stand. With the Secretary and Senator's ladies, our corner became the most attractive spot in the room, next to the Pianno, where the Miss Fultons (from New York) were playing and singing in high style—Italian in perfection. Madam Garcia over again. But charming as the musick was, it could not interrupt our conversation. Several gentlemen gathered round the great ladies and the rest of the evening I passed very pleasantly. I knew not who gave most delight Mrs. P. or Mrs. McC. I should call them both Rattles if they were not something so much better,—they are charming women. Mrs. P. had asked me to find her a poor girl, who would be willing to go to New York with her as a servant. Last week I was called to visit a family, in the extremity of want and sickness,—6 chil-

[1] Wife of Asbury Dickens.

dren, 4 of whom were girls. Their necessities were so far beyond my ability to relieve, that it occurred to me to recommend one of the girls to Mrs. P. and to make known to her the situation of the family. It was dark when I went and bitterly cold. Mrs. P. was going in the evening to Baron Krudener's[1] Ball, but the moment I described the condition of this family, she called her servant, had bread, candles, &c put up, tied a hankerchief over her head, put on an old plaid cloak, jumped into our carriage and went with me to see them. The next day when I went to see them, I found on her return home she had sent them a blanket, meat, meal, and other articles. Who that looked at her that evening, gaily dressed, charmed and charming, flattered and carressed, would have imagined her as she had been an hour before, wrapped in an old cloak, seated by the bed-side of a dying woman in a cold, miserable room, surrounded by half naked and starved children? But could they have witnessed the contrast, how would delight and admiration have been converted into love and esteem, or rather the one added to the other. Can you wonder at my loving this woman? Truly, I would rather General Jackson should not come, than that such a woman should go away. There is no one in the city so popular. The New York papers have celebrated her and say she throws Mrs. Clay completely in the shade.

FROM MADAME PICHON [2]

Paris, January 26, 1829.

My Dear Friend:

Since I received your last letter, together with the charming work which you sent me and which I read with

---

[1] Russian Minister 1827 to 1836.
[2] Translation from the French.

great pleasure, two events have happened in my family
in which your mother's heart will take part. My daughter, after long suffering, was successfully delivered of a
pretty daughter who promises to be large and strong.
She suffered at first in nursing, but as she embraces our
principles, she took courage and suffering yielded to
maternal perseverance. Her little one who is 2 months
old is beginning to know her mother and even her father,
who quits his scientific labors to come and rock his
daughter when he hears her cry. It is a great happiness
for me to be a grandmother and to see my mother still
able to come to my daughter's house and dance my
daughter's daughter on her lap. However, this happiness is mingled with a very keen sorrow, for Theodore,
who will soon be 24 years old, is endowed with agreeable
physical features, has a fine pronunciation, and has done
some remarkable work at studying, was going through
his last year preparatory to becoming a lawyer, and had
already pleaded with some success, but he did not like
this occupation, which is so independent and which I
should so much have desired that he would pursue. His
father often expressed regret before him that he had
ceased being employed by the Ministry of Foreign Affairs, where he might have secured a position for him.
Having been born at sea, hearing constantly of traveling,
being surrounded by men of learning who had made some
interesting voyages, and having himself passed three
years in Germany in a very agreeable and brilliant manner during his childhood, poor Theodore opened his eyes
and tormented his father to assert his former rights in
that Ministry in his favor. Well, Pichon was recently
charged with a negotiation with the Republic of Hayti
with Mr. Esmanyart. Their two sons have been appointed secretaries of the commission. Good bye plead-

ing and the lawyer's robe, for he no longer thinks of anything but the embroidered coat of secretary of legation.
The commissioners are not going away any more, for the
negotiations are being attended to in Paris, but my Theodore has persuaded his father to ask the Count de la
Feronais, who is very kind to my husband, to have him
appointed pupil vice consul in Haiti.   He has gone, he has
left father, mother, brother, sister, and his little niece who
already smiled at him.   He has gone, seeing happiness
in a foreign land where I lost my brother-in-law of yellow
fever.   He takes the place of the son of a lady whom I
knew well during my childhood, and who just perished
also of that terrible disease.   He embarked after arrival
at Brest without having time to write to us except a
word to my mother, whom he will probably never see
again.   There he is in the midst of the dangers of the
sea, and the climate, the child whom God had given me
to take the place of Louis!   The same fate perhaps
awaits him.   Oh, my friend, do you feel all I suffer?   I
have not the courage to go into society.   I dread those
satisfied countenances which will greet me and congratulate me on the fine career of my son, on the great success
he will achieve, and all those commonplaces—nonsensical
ideas of people who do not understand real happiness.
I thought I had prepared things for my old age; I
thought I had inspired in my children, by dint of care and
tenderness, enough affection for me to create in them
a leaning toward some profession which would enable
them to live honorably near us.   Well, Theodore, if I
keep him, will go from one consulate to another, and
when he comes to Europe I shall think that I am near
him.   He will probably marry a woman that I do not
know, and his children will be strangers to me!   Is
that where my dreams of happiness and the cares which

I bestowed on him as a child were to lead me? In order
to part with him as late as possible, I had been his first
Latin teacher. His father had put him into a college
near to our house. We saw him very often, and yet
when, after his vacation, he had to return there and
leave the paternal roof after we had passed 6 weeks together, what tears we shed together! Yet he is leaving
us now perhaps forever, and his young brother, who had
fever three days owing to his grief at his departure, and
who also seemed to love us so tenderly, is thinking of
nothing but studying to enter the Military School of
St. Cyr! How mothers who have sons are to be pitied!
A gentleman was saying the other day that those who
had only sons were like hens that had hatched nothing
but ducklings. It is a true image: The poor hen resting
on the shore while her offspring find pleasure in an element which makes her tremble for them. I am very
happy, at least, that my Henrietta has inherited my
tastes, perhaps even in an exaggerated degree. She
likes nothing but domestic life. She has married a man
of intellect, who enjoys great celebrity in sciences and
who loves me as his own mother. She will bring her
daughter up well, and out of four children I shall have
that one, and she will have procured a son for me, while
those whom I nursed are leaving me! I hope very fervently that Theodore will go to the United States some
day. He will see you and that will be a consolation for
me. He might have gone to New York with Mr. Dannery, but the consulate general of San Domingo is a
legation, there is no minister, and Theodore having been
secretary of the commission, is acquainted with the negotiations and is almost secretary of legation, which is more
interesting for a mind like his, for political affairs have
more interest than the purely commercial ones of the

consulate.   May God protect him and preserve him from
sickness, and he may be happy, for he is sacrificing everything for a brilliant future.   He has some great advan-
tages.   He knows three living languages—English, German, and Spanish; he has ideas enough about science
to derive agreeable pastime from them, and by working
he ought to become a very distinguished consul.   As
for myself, I must learn to be happy to have a son whose
name will be in the gazette, and I must not think of the
fact, when I receive a satisfactory letter two months after
it was dated, that two months have passed since it was
written!   I am falling into old age with all the anguishes
of my youth.   Alas!   I will support them with courage,
believing them to be a sacrifice necessary to my future
happiness.   Where is that happiness so dearly bought?
My poor husband is exhibiting fortitude, but tenderness
is getting the better of his fatherly pride and he is suffering keenly at this departure.   However, political events
and the world distract him.   I, on the other hand, am
constantly brooding over my grief, and see nothing but
my son, ill and deprived of my care!   But, my friend, I
wished to speak to you of the pleasure I derived from
your pretty story about "What is real gentility."   It is
charming.   It is a very faithful depiction of the character of Mr. and Mrs. Madison.   It seemed to me that
I saw her.   The visit of Mrs. Madison to the good
mother who falls and breaks her pipe is a picture made
from nature.   And I have made the acquaintance here
of a young American lady who is so great a woman of
fashion that I believe she prides herself on imitating the
fickle and unrepublican character which you so wittily
depict.   Your country worries me; it is becoming spoiled;
there you have a military President; it is an attack
against your liberty!   You are spreading out; the taste

of high society and rank is being formed; take care! Titles and nobility are at your doors. You were getting on so well without the aristocracy necessary to the old world! As to us, we are gaining more than you are losing, and we have more freedom than I ever saw in France. I do not speak of the time when Bonaparte had given us a mute legislative chamber, spies everywhere, and imprisonment for talking in our own houses, without our friends' knowing we were there, not to speak of the evils of war. The parties are beginning to merge together, and if a few ambitious persons are discontent, we must hope that they will not succeed in depriving us of the peace and liberty which we are now finally enjoying.

It is late and I will leave you, asking you to embrace the opportunity offered by Mr. Dannery's stay in New York to let me hear from you as well as from Mr. Smith and all your family. We occasionally see Mr. Boyd. He wanted me to help him choose some books for his young children, but the preparations for the departure of Theodore have thus far deprived me of this pleasure, though I have not given it up.

Accept, dear lady, the assurance of my sincere affection and the respects of my husband, and remember me to Mr. Smith and our common friends.   Yours truly,

A. EMILIE PICHON.

TO J. BAYARD H. SMITH

[Washington] Friday Jan. 30. [1829.]

. . . . I was interrupted by the entrance of company, and if the truth were known, I dare to say, you are glad I was broken in upon a subject more serious than pleasant. Well, I will resume my letter, but not my sub-

ject, but continue my journal from my letter of last week.
I then told you we were going to have a small party, a
small, but very select and agreeable one it was. Mr. and
Mrs. Calhoun, she as friendly and social, he as charming and interesting, as ever Mr. and Mrs. Gilmer, (our
Crawford friends) Mr. and Mrs. Rives, both talented
and superior folks, Phillip Barbour, of whose eloquence
and coloquial talents you have heard your father and me
talk. Col. and Mrs. Bomford, Dr. and Mrs. Lovel, Mr.
and Mrs. Seaton, Dr. and Mrs. Simm,[1] Genl. Porter and
the ever admired and charming Mrs. P. with Miss
Moris, Caroline Breckenridge and about a dozen more,
Senators and Members. Conversation flowed without interruption, every one was gay and animated. Some
played chess, some sat by the table and talked, but most
conversed in groups. Every one did as they pleased.
For a wonder, in a Washington party, they could *sit,* as
well as stand.   There were above 40 in the room, yet it
was not the least crowded and I received many compliments on the greater rationality, as well as pleasure
of such a small select party, than the usual squeezes and
crowds. I enjoyed myself more than on any previous
evening this winter. I conversed by turns with all my
guests, but longest with the two I most admired, Mr.
Barbour and Mr. Calhoun. The limits of a letter will
not allow all, otherwise I should like to detail what was
said by these gentlemen. Mr. Barbour conversed about
Mr. Jefferson and the University of Virginia and gave me
some interesting information, Mr. Calhoun about the late
election and the characters of some of the leaders on both
sides.   I really ought to commit observations such as his
to paper, but I can not find time. When Mrs. Porter and

[1] Dr. Thomas Sim, who after the death of his first wife became engaged
to Mrs. Smith's sister-in-law, was one of the founders of the Medical
Society of the District of Columbia and its second president.

her large party entered, she as usual created quite a sensation. All crowded round her. She had a nod for one, a smile for another and good humour and gaiety for all. While with Mr. Calhoun and afterwards with others she carried on a sprightly conversation, to which all around listened with delight. Every gentleman then in the room was a Jacksonian, some violent, but she rallied them so charmingly, that had they been enemies they must have become friends. "Oh," said she, in reply to some remark on her going to every party, "I have not long to stay, so I am determined to see and enjoy all I can. If my time is short, it shall be sweet, as the proverb says, short and sweet. But no matter," added she nodding her head significantly,—"If we must go now, we will be back in 4 years, so take it yourselves." The gentlemen laughed and said they would not relinquish so soon as that. "We'll see, we'll see," said she nodding good humourd'ly. "At least we will both do our best, one to keep in, the other to come in" or something to that effect. "What a pity it is," observed Mr. Calhoun to me, "that all the ladies can not carry it off (their defeat) as charmingly as Mrs. Porter, but some I hear take it much to heart." "The gentlemen more than the ladies," said I. "All the Secretaries are sick. One day last week, with the exception of Genl. P. all were confined to their beds." "After all," said Mr. C., "these things are, as it were, the mere charity of war and triumph of defeat, change sides and every one takes his turn, so that one ought not to feel great elevation or great depression, but in either case take the result with moderation, but above all, as far as possible to avoid mingling *personal,* with political feelings. There is nothing from which I have really suffered in the late conflict of parties, but the division it has created between

me and personal friends; as for the enmity and abuse of
political opponents, that is *nothing,*—wounds which leave
no scars."

But I must check my pen, the detail of conversations
is endless. It was near twelve when the company dispersed. We had several invitations which we declined,
that to Miss Williams wedding, one. This party was
not only a crowd, but a *crush;* some folks were nearly
hurt. It is supposed a thousand invitations were given
and actually above 700 accepted and the house not large.
On Saturday evening the bride saw company. We had
two other invitations for that evening, to a musical party
at Mrs. Wirt's and a chess party at Mrs. Burnels, besides
which Anna Maria was asked to a cottillion party at Miss
Sutherland's and a party to the theatre with Mrs. Seaton.
She preferred the last and went to Mrs. Seaton's where
she staid until Monday morning, happy, as she always is,
with these friends. *Your father,* yes your father, went
with Susan and myself to see the Bride, and well worth
was she to be seen. *Beauty itself.* I could do nothing
but look at her, nor Mr. Vaughn (the english minister)
either. He seemed as if he could eat her up and if
eyes could have eaten, he would have devoured her.
Persico, the Italian Sculpter, has begged permission of
her father to take her bust, which he says is faultless,
perfectly classical. Her next sister is as pleasing, almost as beautiful, tho' not so classically or symetrically
proportioned. The groom is a handsome and pleasing
young man. I conversed a good deal with him. If
such a thing as perfect felicity ever is found on earth,
surely this lovely young couple possess it. So young,
so beautiful, so virtuous and so loving and beloved,—
their first love, and that approved by parents and friends
and crowned with affluence. What is wanting? May

this rare example of human felicity long remain unimpaired. An agreeable, but not large company was assembled, and we remained until 3 o'clock. Then, after leaving Susan at home and taking up Julia, we went to Mr. Barnels, where we found all the company engaged at chess. They soon found partners for your father and myself. Mr. Bailey, member of Congress and famous chess player, for your father, and Mr. Barnel and I. Those who did not play conversed together, and even we chess folks, with the exception of Mr. Bailey and your father, took the liberty to laugh and talk a little. I came off victor in two games, and had it not been for the entrée of oysters, your father thinks he would have gained one game of Mr. B. But oysters, ham, wine, porter, &c sadly distract one's attention you know. We played until 11 o'clock and I could have gladly played an hour or two longer, but yielded to *propriety*. . . .

TO J. BAYARD H. SMITH

[Washington] Thursday, 5 Febr. 1829.

. . . . After tea, about 8 oclock, we went. Unless you had seen it, you can have no idea of the crowd. I should say more than a 1000 people. Mr. and Mrs. Clay were not well, but supported this trying ordeal admirably—for trying it was—to be cheerful when the heart was aching and the health impaired, and to smile on defeat; tho' surrounded by the victors, yet all this they did. I could scarcely help crying and to avoid so awkward a delemma, laughed a great deal. Oh, the world, the world, what a masquerade it is. The drama of the Adams administration is now closed, the curtain dropt, it has been a kind of tragic-comedy, as indeed the whole of life is.   I do not suppose any of the members will be seen any more in the social circle.   As soon as possible after the 4th of March, they will take their departure. There was a rumour in the drawing-room that Mr. Wirt was again ill and had just had another severe attack. Dr. Hunt who came from his house, said he had been with him for three hours.   Mr. Wirt is rather better.   I shall call at both places this morning.

Anna, went with Julia and me last evening.   She was highly delighted with the scene and enjoyed it excessively.   Julia, looked very well and both the girls had more attention paid them than usual and of course could not fail being gratified.   We did not get home until after 11 oclock.   Col. and Mrs. Ward came with us and as we were a little hungry or so, we had pickled oysters, cold beef, &c &c and laughed and talked until 12 oclock. Mr. Ward has been here this morning to enquire after our healths.

In a day or two Genl. Jackson will arrive—he declines all parade and instead of the grand display that was expected, I suppose he will make a quiet entrée which I shall be glad of on account of our old friends.   The carriage is ready for me to go out—so good morning.

Wednesday morning.   It is a week today since I began this letter, and not one half hour have I had to finish it.   Engagements of various kinds at home and abroad, occupy every moment, leaving me no time to read even a novel.   One evening I passed most pleasantly at Mrs. Clay's in company with Mrs. Porter, her brother Mr. Brekenridge[1] and his wife and a few others.   I am delighted with Mr. B. and conversed a great deal with him—the next morning he and Mr. Danforth, another

---

[1] Probably John Breckenridge, Chaplain of Congress in 1822–3 and afterwards pastor of the 2d Presbyterian Church of Baltimore.

clergyman and Dr. Collins were with us a long while. One whole morning Mr. Campbell spent with us and every morning and every evening Mr. Ward has been here.   He is almost an inmate of our family—who it is he is pleased with it is impossible to tell, his attentions are so equally divided.   I do not think therefore that love is the attraction.   He brings us new books very often and is in every way agreeable. I shall quite miss him when he goes, the 4th of March.

We were preparing to go to the House to see the votes counted for President, but the weather is unfavourable.   General Jackson has arrived.   Preperations were made and crowds would have gone to meet him, but he eluded them all, and came in early this morning—4 hours before the expected time.   Your father just stepped in to tell us, to prevent our going among others to see the parade.   But now I hear cannons firing, drums beating and hurraing—I really cannot write, so adieu for the present.

Monday 16 Feb.   I might as well have finished my letter as gone down on the avenue with the girls.   Nothing but boys—everything has been so quiet, that if one did not hear of the fact, no one would know Genl. J had arrived.   It has made no change whatever even in the hopes and fears of the expectants and the fearers—both tremblingly alive to what may happen—his most intimate friends, the very persons who are candidates for office, do not yet know who are to form his cabinet—meanwhile parties have stopped, the old administration have closed their houses and no others yet open.   A universal dullness pervades society—or rather gloom—at least among those with whom I most associate.   Judge Southard has had another and more dreadful attack.   I saw him on Saturday—he looks to me as if he had not long to live.

Genl. Porter, has likewise been very ill and kept his room most part of last week and is not yet out. Mr. and Mrs. Clay will not visit, and see only a few friends. We, viz, our family, are however as gay as usual and constantly engaged in little social parties at home or abroad.

TO MRS. BOYD

[Washington,] Friday 6th Febr. 1829.

. . . . I do not believe we have been a single day alone since we came to the city. We literally live in society and that of a very agreeable kind. We have greatly enlarged our acquaintance among the members of Congress and several begin to visit in a social way. Since I last wrote we have had several agreeable parties at home—the largest about 40 persons, was made in compliment to our old friends, Mr. and Mrs. Calhoun. By accident most of the company were of Mr. C.'s politics, altho' an equal number of administration folks had been asked. Mrs. Porter and her family came, but really they mingle so frankly and sociably with the Jacksonians, that their opposing sentiments are often forgotten. She is the most popular woman we have ever had here since Mrs. Madison. Gay, frank, communicative, kind. She is a universal favourite and it seems like no party at all, if she is not present, and when she is, she is so surrounded, notwithstanding which she makes out to notice every body and to make every body feel as if they were particularly noticed. A nod, a smile, and shaking of the hand, answer the purpose, for the smile or nod of a Secretary's lady have a wonderful charm. Noah,[1] in his paper, has puffed her at a great rate, on several occasions

[1] Mordecai Manuel Noah in the *National Advertiser*.

I am told. But what is better than all this, she is truly kind-hearted and charitable, without any ostentation whatever. A family of 8 persons whom I made known to her, because I was unable to give them the relief they required, she has now entirely supported for the last month or six weeks. One of the children, by her orders, daily carries a basket to her kitchen which is regularly filled. Her good nature equals her benevolence. The last large party she had, she bade the two girls bring their basket at 9 oclock in the evening, and told them they might stay in the back room (where the refreshments were prepared), see the ladies as they went and came thro' the hall and gather up the fragments of the cake, blanc-mange, jelly, etc. The poor mother when she told me of this the next day seemed absolutely far more grateful and delighted than by the more substantial donations she had received.

Three days have elapsed since I commenced this letter. Every day I have sat down to it, but not been able to write more than a few lines without being interrupted. Yesterday, the moment I had swallowed my breakfast, I came into this parlour and as usual left the girls in the dining-room, seized my pen, determined to have a long talk, about many things with my own dear sisters. Before the above page was written, Mr. Leon, Anna's excellent and amiable french-master came to pay *me* a visit and soon after my good neighbor Mrs. Andrew Smith, an hour afterwards Mr. Ward, a young Bostonian, a great favorite with us all, who has absolutely domesticated himself in our family. Then Mrs. McClean of Delaware,—kindly, charming and interesting. Each and all staid most of the morning, and before they went my friend Lydia English, who staid all day and night and is still with us, and in the evening some gentlemen. Not a single minute from ten oclock in the morning, until 11 oclock at night, had I leisure to read or write, and this is the history of every day, with the variation of different persons. . . . .

I have tried and other friends have tried, to procure a clerkship for him.[1] Mrs. Porter did her very best and I used all manner of persuasion and argument with the kind, good natured secty of War.—"My dear Madam, what am I to do? When we ask Congress for more clerks in the Dept and tell them the present number is insufficient for the duties of the offices, the reply is, If you continue to fill the offices with *old men,* no number will be sufficient. Get young men and fewer will answer and the work be better done. This is too true, the public benefit is sacrificed to private interest and charity. The Departments are literally over-stocked with old, inefficient clerks. I cannot serve your friend, consistently with duty."

TO MRS. BOYD

[Washington] Febr 16, 1829.

. . . . I have been a great deal in Mr. Clay's and Southard's family, both ill,—so ill, I do not think either has long to live. Yet, they think not so, and attend to business, tho' they decline all company at home and never go out. I never liked Mr. Clay so well as I do this winter, the coldness and hauteur of his manner has vanished and a softness and tenderness and sadness characterize his manner (to me at least), for I know not how it is in general society—that is extremely attaching and affecting,—at the same time, perfect good humour, no bitterness mingles its gall in the cup of disappointment

---

[1] A Mr. Andrew Smith, who had failed in business and whose wife was a friend of Mrs. Smith's.

and I often hear him, when only two or three friends are present, speak of Genl. Jackson and the present state of affairs in a good humour'd sprightly way. He has a cause of domestic affliction in the conduct and situation of his son[1] a thousand times more affecting than disappointed ambition. We all went to the *last* drawing room,—we did it to show our respect. My heart was heavy, very heavy, that word *Last!* Immense crowds filled the room, crowds of the triumphant party. I could not bear it as well as Mrs. Clay. I staid close to her, knowing she was so sick she could scarcely stand and that both she and Mr. C. for three previous weeks had been made very wretched by their domestic grief,—indeed for two weeks Mr. C. had not been able to sleep without anodynes. I stood behind her and watched the company. She received all with smiling politeness and Mr. C. *looked* gay and was so courteous and gracious, and agreeable, that every one remarked it and remarked he was determined we should regret him. My heart filled to overflowing, as I watched this acting, and to conceal tears which I could not repress, took a seat in a corner by the fire, behind a solid mass of people. Mr. C. saw me, and coming up enquired if Mr. Smith had come. I answered in the negative. "But *you* are," said he taking my hand and looking sadly affectionate. "This is kind, very kind in you, Mrs. Smith." I returned the pressure of his hand, and without reflection said, "If you could see my heart, you would then think so." "Why what ails your heart?" said he, with a look of earnest interrogatory. "Can it be otherwise than sad," I answered, looking at Mrs. Clay, "when I think what a good friend I am about to lose?" For a moment he held my hand pressed in his without speaking, his eyes filled

[1] His eldest son was insane and confined in an asylum.

with tears and with an effort he said, "We must not think of this, or talk of such things *now*," and relinquishing my hand, drew out his handkerchief, turned away his head and wiped his eyes, then pushed into the crowd and talked and smiled, as if his heart was light and easy. Alas, I knew, what perhaps no other among these hundreds knew, that anguish, heart-rending anguish, was concealed beneath that smiling, cheerful countenance, and that the animation and spirits which charmed an admiring circle were wholly artificial. Judge Southard has all manner of disappointments to sustain, as well as repeated severe attacks of disease and pain. He had until within a week of the election, every reason to believe he would be chosen Senator, but his friends betrayed him, and one friend, old, tried and who was under great obligations. Oh, ingratitude is sharper than a serpent's teeth. He had just recovered a little strength, when owing to Mr. Rush's extreme illness, he was appointed Secr. of the Treasury pro tem.; scarcely able to discharge his own business, the addition was too much for him, and a few nights ago, sitting late and hard at work, he was seized with what his Physician called spasms in his stomach,— for six hours he suffered agony, which even opium could not allay, until taken in great quantities. Yesterday, when I saw him, he was sitting up surrounded with papers, his eyes sunk to the very back of his head, the sockets black and hollow, while the eye burnt with unnatural brightness. "Oh do not kill yourself," said I, as I held his burning hand, "put away those papers. You are too ill to attend to business." "I must," replied he, "if I die at my post," and there I verily believe he will die,—he looks awfully. He had his heart set on the exploring voyage and had the preparations for it in such forwardness, that he thought it impossible Congress would prevent it, by refusing the necessary appropriation. But it is said, they will. Hard things are said of him on the floor, motives attributed, which I do not believe ever actuated him. Oh how I pity these public men, and as I look at Mr. Clay particularly, how often have I repeated the apostrophe of Cardinal Wolsey, "Oh had I served my God, half so devotedly as I have served my King, I should not now in my old age, thus have been left," etc. Mr. Rush and afterwards Mrs. Rush have been very ill, and are exceedingly depressed,—they have not gone out, or received company this winter. Mr. Wirt, too, has been ill, but is now better. . . . Phillip Barbour was here the day after the General's arrival and warm Jacksonian as he is, I told him his success would cost me too much grief, to allow me to participate in the gratulations of the political party to which my husband belonged. "I shall cry more than I shall laugh on the 4th of March," said I. Mrs. Porter is the only one of the administration party, who has been in spirits this winter. It is partly constitutional with her and, I suspect, part policy. It is impossible when one sees her so attentive and even cordial with the Jackson party not to suspect, she has some hopes of propitiating them. Yet it may be genuine good humour and good spirits. She is a charming woman, and what is still better, she is a good woman. I have seen a great deal of her, indeed, we are on the terms of old friends and relatives. We have been asked at least once every week to a party there, last week to two,—one a gay company, the other serious, religious folks to meet her Brother Mr. Breckenridge. Oh what a zealous, saint-like man *he* is! he is indeed a burning and shining light but he is burning fast away, flesh and blood can not sustain such exhausting and consuming labours. How I wish I could sit under his ministry. How cold and lifeless our Pastor seems, compared to him. Speaking of Mr. Campbell, among other things, all however kind and Christian, he made use of those expressive words, "I wish he was more steeped in the spirit." I had some delightful communion with this apostolic man. Surely he is in all things like the beloved disciple, so full of love. Such a christian would I desire to be, and until I am, until this divine love takes full possession of my soul, I shall never be as happy, as I feel I have the capacity of being. It is good to see the world, as I see it. Oh Maria, its splendid out side, its gaiety and glitter, amuse but do not deceive me. How can they, with such striking proofs before me, of the bitterness and heartlessness within. And yet I am amused, and very much interested in the characters and scenes around me, but it is the interest and amusement one finds at the theatre. I look upon life as a stage, and on men and women as mere actors. One drama is just finished, the curtain has dropped, the actors have left the stage and I have followed them behind the scenes, where their masks and dresses are thrown off and I see them as they are, disappointed, exhausted, worn out, retiring with broken fortunes and broken constitutions and hearts rankling with barbed arrows.

Another drama is preparing. New characters, in all the freshness and vigour of unexhausted strength, with the exhileration of hopes undaunted by fear, of spirits intoxicated with success, with the aspirations of towering ambition are coming on the self-same stage. Will public favour cheer their closing, as it inspires the opening scene? Time must show, but most probably, they in their turn will drink the cup of honor to the bottom and find its dregs nauseous and bitter. I hoped this cold morning to have been alone, but one set of ladies have just gone and here stops another carriage. I wish I could be alone one morning.

TO J. BAYARD H. SMITH

[Washington] Wednesday 25th February, 1829.

With what anxiety and impatience have thousands looked forward to the present period, and crowded from all parts of the union, to our metropolis to witness the splendour of Genl. J.'s reception and his inauguration—Poor souls—disappointment has awaited them—The General would allow no parade—as I told you in my last he entered the city and was in it, many hours without its being known—and his being here has made no change in the aspect of society and would be unknown, were it not for the anxiety and curiosity of expectants and aspirants and *fear-ants* (a new word). As for gaiety—there is none—even the cotillion parties and public assemblies, theatres and concerts fail to attract citizens or strangers. I never witnessed such a dullness, nay gloom as that which pervades society. The party, who are withdrawing from office, sick and melancholy, will not mix in society and the private parties given are uninteresting to strangers, because there are no Secretaries or public characters there—Genl. Jackson and his family, being in mourning,[1] decline all company, so that a Party must be grave and sober, to be à la mode. The crowds of strangers who are here, having no drawing-rooms, no parties, or levees to atend, surge about *guessing* for news and spreading every rumour as it rises and every day gives rise to new rumours about the Cabinet. Last week it was considered certainly fixed—

[1] Mrs. Jackson died in December, 1828, just before he left for Washington.

Van Buren, for state depart'n; Ingham, for the Treasury, Genl. Eaton for the War, Gov'r Branch for the Navy, and Mr. Berrian, attorney Genl.—Astonishment and disappointment filled the minds of friends and foes —with the exception of Van B—— the cabinet was pronounced too feeble to stand and every one said such an administration must soon fall—Remonstrances were made by the Tennesee delegation in a body, (so it is said) against Genl E——'s appointment, and after difficulty and hesitation *the General,* who it was said, firm as a rock, was never known to change, found I suppose, that the authority of a President, was very different from that of a military chief and *must yield* to council— A change was then said to be made, and Judge McClean, put in the cabinet, and Genl. Eaton in his place as postmaster—But even this, it is said, does not satisfy public opinion which will not allow of Genl. Eton holding a place which would bring *his wife* into society—(for this is the difficulty)   Every one acknowledges Genl. Eaton's talents and virtues—but his late unfortunate connection is an obstacle to his receiving a place of honour, which it is apprehended even Genl. Jackson's firmness cannot resist—It is a pity—Every one that knows esteems, and many love him for his benevolence and amiability.   Oh, woman, woman!—The rumour of yesterday was, that he was to have no place at home, but be sent abroad—so it was added (tho' evidently only for the joke of it) that he was to be minister to *Hayti* that being the most proper Court for *her* to reside in— I repeat these are rumours—The Cabinet mentioned first, was I believe—official—No one doubted it—the changes I mention are doubtful—Van Buren, it is generally supposed, will not serve with these gentlemen— there being no personal respect or liking between them.

If he declines it will be difficult to find another equal to
the place, for Tazewell of Virginia[1] is to go to England—
Everyone thinks there is great confusion and difficulty,
mortification and disappointment—at the *Wigwam*—as
they call the *General's* lodgings.　Mr. Woodbury,[2] looks
glum as well as several other disappointed expectants.
He was the only Eastern man, of sufficient consequence
among the Jacksonians and he has not a place in the
Cabinet—the first time since the Constitution was
adopted in which New England was not represented in
the Cabinet.　Such a disregard to New England it is
supposed will alienate many of the Jacksonians in that
quarter.　Our friends at Kalacama too are sadly disappointed.　Mr. Baldwin confidently expected to be
Attorney-General, and it is said now he will get absolutely *nothing.*　Our friend Louis McLean of Del. is
likewise left in statu quo—though his friends had not
a doubt of his being in the Cabinet—there are hundreds
of offices thro. the Union, vacant, which the Senate will
not fill, viz—sanction Mr. Adams nominations—but defer filling them until after the fourth of March—All
the subordinate officers of government, and even to the
clerks, are full of tremblings and anxiety—To add to
this general gloom we have had horrible weather, snow-
storm after snow-storm—the river frozen up, and the
poor suffering the extremity of cold and hunger—Some
instances of death from want of fuel, were discovered,
and awakened public sympathy, and exertion—Mr.
Gales issued orders for subscriptions to be taken up for
the relief of the poor, and appointed three persons in

---

[1] Littleton Waller Tazewell of Norfolk did not go to England, but remained Senator from Virginia till he resigned in 1833 "from pure disgust
of Federal politics."

[2] Levi Woodbury of New Hampshire was then Senator.　In 1831 he became Secretary of the Navy and in 1834 Secretary of the Treasury.

each ward to receive contributions of any and every
kind—to visit all the dwellings of the poor, and to relieve their sufferings—Congress gave 50 cords of wood
to the poor—The Treasury department, not having a
right to give, sold at first cost (not one fifth the present
price of wood) 50 cords.—The War department ordered
all that could be spared to be given on the same terms—
and members of Congress, officers of government,
strangers, and citizens have I am told very liberally subscribed to the relief of sufferings induced by this un-
precedented severe weather—Today is a dismal day—
no high and cutting winds make you sensible of the
cold—but a silent, still freezing is going on, that takes
one unawares and unprepared—It is raining—the drops
fall slowly and sound like heavy fall of shot, as if they
fell, one by one, and they rest on the window panes
as if so chilled they could not run off—But notwithstanding the weather your father has gone to Captain
Tirgy's funeral[1]—It would have been a splendid military one—but I take it for granted this weather must
curtail the parade—This puts me in mind of an annunci-
ation in the paper—viz, that *the General* declines any
military parade on the 4th of March, and means to walk
to the Capitol, to take the oath of office—Our streets are
now deep in slush—snow, mud, mire!—and if they continue so, until the 4th of March, a pretty procession
will it be on foot!—a grand sight—for the strangers to
behold, who have flocked here from the East, the West,
the North and the South—But yet I like *the General* for
his avoidance of all parade—It is *true* greatness, which
needs not the aid of ornament and pomp—and delicacy
too—I like the suppression of military attendance—but
really think the good old gentleman might indulge him-

[1] He died February 23.

self with a carriage—I think I shall like him vastly, when I know him—I have heard a number of things about him which indicate a kind, warm, feeling and affectionate heart.—I hope sincerely, he may get safely over the *breakers* which beset his entrance into port, and when in—God grant the good old man a safe anchorage in still waters. . . . We have had a pleasing visit from Mr. Josiah Quincy—an old and valued friend—which to me was the most interesting incident of the week— Mrs. Clay's furniture is to be sold this week—the fair is to be this week—Mr. Danforth's new church is to be dedicated this week, and the Inauguration is to be next week—and then a general dispersion—Mrs. Clay, Mrs. Porter, Mrs. everbody I care for will be going—and such dreadful weather! ! !

TO MRS. BOYD

[Washington,] Spring of 1829.

. . . . Mr. Clay, has this winter, been such an object of interest to me, For to me *intellectual power,* is more facinating and interesting, than any other human endowment. And never in any individual have I met with so much, as in him. Yes, he has a *natural,* power and force of mind, beyond any I have ever witnessed. In Mr. Jefferson, Madison, Crawford, and other great men I have known, much of their intellectual strength, was derived from education and favoring circumstances, a combination of which carried them forward in the career of greatness and raised them to the elevation they attained. Not so Mr. Clay. Whatever he is, is all his own, inherent power, bestowed by nature and not derivative from cultivation or fortune. He has an elasticity and buoyancy of spirit, that no pressure of external circumstances, can confine or keep down. Nay, occasional depressions seem to give new vigour to this elastic power. For instance his late defeat. So far from disheartening, it has been positively exhilorating in its effects. He began to weary of the measures pursued in the last campaign, it closed, to be sure, in his defeat, but its termination freed him from weights and shackles, which had connections or duties, and like the Lyon, breaking the net, in which he had been entangled, he shakes from him all petty encumbrances and rises in all the majesty of intellectual power and invigorated resolution. He is a very great man. I have seen him, this winter, *as a man,* not a politician or stateman, but studied him, undisguised from any of the trappings of official form and conventional respect. Certainly, one of the most interesting days I have ever passed, was last Sunday. He and Mrs. Clay passed it with us. We had no other company to dinner, and I am certain he enjoyed being thus alone with a family he had known for 18 years, and feeling the triumph of personal regard, over the respect paid to office. He knew that for the last 8 years Mr. Smith had been his political opponent, and felt pleased with finding himself treated with the cordiality of friendship, in such circumstances. Whether it was this, or any other cause, I know not, but whatever the cause might be, the effect was to produce an openness, communicativeness, an affectionateness and warmth and kindness which were irresistibly captivating. We lingered long round the dinner table. He and Mr. S. conversed on past times and characters, long since passed from the scene of action. In the afternoon and evening, Genl. McComb, Mr. Ward, Mr. Lyon (another domesticated beau) and several other gentlemen came in and until past 10 oclock at night the conversation flowed in an unbroken stream and if committed to writing would prove interesting to those yet unborn, for the topics were national, subjects suited for history. Mr. Clay was the chief speaker. He was animated by his heart as well as genius. Reclining on the sopha, from which he occasionally in the warmth of argument, would rise or stretch out his arm, his attitude as well as countenance would have made a fine picture. But enough of one individual. I will only add, if his health is restored, we will see him more efficiently active than ever. Elizabeth says you wish for a description of the Inauguration, and for some account of the new Cabinet,[1] of the President and his family. On these topics I have but little to say. Bayard will transmit to Sister Jane and she to you, my last long letter to him, containing a full account of that *grand spectacle,* for such it was, without the aid of splendid forms or costumes. Of the Cabinet, I can only say the President's enemies are delighted and his friends grieved. It is supposed wholly inefficient, and even Van Buren, altho' a profound politician is not supposed to be an able statesman, or to possess qualifications for the place assigned him. Yet on him, all rests. Mr. Ingham, is the only member with whom we are personally acquainted, —him we have known long and well. He is a good man, of unimpeachable and unbending integrity. But no one imagines him possessed of that comprehensiveness and grasp of mind, requisite for the duties of his new office. He will be faithful, this, no one doubts. Whether he will be capable, experience only can show. Of the others, we know absolutely nothing, the people know nothing, and of course can feel little confidence. As for

[1] Martin Van Buren, Secretary of State; Samuel D. Ingham of Pennsylvania, Secretary of the Treasury; John H. Eaton of Tennessee, Secretary of War; John Branch of North Carolina, Secretary of the Navy; John H. Berrien of Georgia, Attorney General.

the *new Lady*,[1] Elizabeth enquires of after a thousand rumours and much tittle-tattle and gosip and prophesyings and apprehensions, public opinion ever just and impartial, seems to have triumphed over personal feelings and intrigues and finally doomed her to continue in her pristine lowly condition.   A stand, a *noble* stand, I may say, since it is a stand taken against power and favoritism, has been made by the ladies of Washington, and not even the President's wishes, in favour of his dearest, personal friend, can influence them to violate the respect due to virtue, by visiting one, who has left her strait and narrow path.   With the exception of two or three timid and rather insignificant personages, who trembled for their husband's offices, not a lady has visited her, and so far from being inducted into the President's house, she is, I am told scarcely noticed by the females of his family.   On the Inauguration day, when they went in company with the Vice-President's lady, the lady of the Secretary of the Treasury and those of two distinguished Jacksonian Senators, Hayne and Livingston,[2] this New Lady never approached the party, either in the Senate chamber, at the President's house, where by the President's express request, they went to receive the company, nor at night at the Inaugural Ball.   On these three public occasions she was left alone, and kept at a respectful distance from these virtuous and distinguished women, with the sole exception of a seat at the supper-table, where, however, notwithstanding her proximity,

---

[1] The famous Peggy O'Neil, daughter of a tavern keeper in Washington, widow of a paymaster in the navy, and now bride of the Secretary of War, a fine appearing woman, whose reputation had unfortunately for her been made in Washington.   Van Buren was the only man who stood by her. She was finally driven out and her husband left the Cabinet.

[2] Robert Y. Hayne of South Carolina, anything but a Jacksonian when the nullification issue came up, and Edward Livingston, then a Representative from Louisiana, soon to be a Senator, then Secretary of State and finally minister to France.

she was not spoken to by them.   These are facts you
may rely on, not rumours—facts, greatly to the honor of
our sex.   When you see Miss Morris, she will give you
details, which it would not be proper to commit to writing.
She and I have become very social and intimate and
have seen each other often.   I hope she will call on you
and talk over Washington affairs.   Dear Mrs. Porter,
her departure cost me some bitter tears.   And so did
good Mrs. Clay's.   Mrs. Ingham professes a desire to
be very social with me, "the oldest friend," as she says
her husband has in the city, but a friend of 18 years is
a thing I shall never *make* now, it is too late in the day.
We visited the President and his family a few days since,
in the big house.   Mr. Smith introduced us and asked
for the General.   Our names were sent in and he joined
the ladies in the drawing-room.   I shall like him if ever
I know him, I am sure,—so simple, frank, friendly.   He
looks bowed down with grief as well as age and that idea
excited my sympathy, his pew in church is behind ours,
his manner is humble and reverent and most attentive.

Mrs. Sanford[1] and I interchanged several visits and
she passed an evening with us, but she did not interest
me.   For your sake, dear Maria, I will visit Mrs. Hamilton, tho' I have resisted many inducements to make new
acquaintances.   I have too many already.   But I shall
drop most of them when I return into the country, then
I shall regain my freedom, and do as I like.   The last
six weeks have been far less gay, but much more interesting than the first part of the season.   We went less
out and had less company at home.   Mr. W.'s daily
visits, Mr. Wood's and Mr. Lyon's, almost as frequent,
and the new books they brought us, fitted up our evenings far more pleasantly than common-place visitants.

[1] Wife of Nathan Sanford of Albany, Senator from New York.

Mr. Wood, who is goodness personified, remains, he is our fellow citizen, and we look for his smiling benevolent countenance, daily as the evening returns. Mrs. Thornton has been very ill and I have been a great deal with her. Dear Mrs. Bradley has gone, and she went rejoicing to a better world. Capt. Tingey too. Our first kind friend and acquaintance. Mrs. Clay is as much lost to me as if separated by death, and Mrs. Porter. For ten days I was taken up with sick and dying, and departing friends. The last two weeks have been melancholy weeks to me. Judge Southard continues too ill to move, his little daughter is ill too, their furniture is all sold, and it is melancholy to visit them, but it is a duty I often perform. Mr. Wirt's family go in a few weeks. Mr. Rush, it is said, is to be sent to England by the Canal-company, with a good salary, and the family are in good spirits. Mrs. Calhoun goes home, not to return again, at least for 4 years. Mrs. Ingham will not be back until autumn. All our citizens are trembling for fear of losing offices. Mrs. Seaton is very ill. Gales and Seaton, I fear ruined. In fact never did I witness such a gloomy time in Washington. I hope things will brighten. My paper is full.

TO MRS. KIRKPATRICK.

[Washington] March 11th, Sunday [1829.]

. . . . Thursday morning. I left the rest of this sheet for an account of the inauguration. It was not a thing of detail of a succession of small incidents. No, it was one grand whole, an imposing and majestic spectacle and to a reflective mind one of moral sublimity. Thousands and thousands of people, without distinction of rank, collected in an immense mass round the Capitol,

silent, orderly and tranquil, with their eyes fixed on the
front of that edifice, waiting the appearance of the
President in the portico. The door from the Rotunda
opens, preceded by the marshals, surrounded by the
Judges of the Supreme Court, the old man with his grey
locks, that crown of glory, advances, bows to the people, who greet him with a shout that rends the air, the
Cannons, from the heights around, from Alexandria
and Fort Warburton proclaim the oath he has taken and
all the hills reverberate the sound. It was grand,—it
was sublime! An almost breathless silence, succeeded
and the multitude was still,—listening to catch the
sound of his voice, tho' it was so low, as to be heard
only by those nearest to him. After reading his speech,
the oath was administered to him by the Chief Justice.
The Marshal presented the Bible. The President took
it from his hands, pressed his lips to it, laid it reverently
down, then bowed again to the people—Yes, to the people in all their majesty. And had the spectacle closed
here, even Europeans must have acknowledged that a
free people, collected in their might, silent and tranquil,
restrained solely by a moral power, without a shadow
around of military force, was majesty, rising to sublimity, and far surpassing the majesty of Kings and
Princes, surrounded with armies and glittering in gold.
But I will not anticipate, but will give you an account of
the inauguration in mere detail. The whole of the preceding day, immense crowds were coming into the city
from all parts, lodgings could not be obtained, and the
newcomers had to go to George Town, which soon over-
flowed and others had to go to Alexandria. I was told
the Avenue and adjoining streets were so crowded on
Tuesday afternoon that it was difficult to pass.

A national salute was fired early in the morning, and

ushered in the 4th of March.   By ten oclock the Avenue
was crowded with carriages of every description, from
the splendid Barronet and coach, down to waggons and
carts, filled with women and children, some in finery and
some in rags, for it was the peoples President, and all
would see him; the men all walked.   Julia, Anna Maria
and I, (the other girls would not adventure) accompanied
by Mr. Wood, set off before 11, and followed the living
stream that was pouring along to the Capitol.   The
terraces, the Balconies, the Porticos, seemed as we
approached already filled.   We rode round the whole
square, taking a view of the animated scene.   Then
leaving the carriage outside the palisades, we entered the
enclosed grounds, where we were soon joined by John
Cranet and another gentleman, which offered each of
us a protector.   We walked round the terrace several
times, every turn meeting new groups of ladies and
gentlemen whom we knew.   All with smiling faces.   The
day was warm and delightful, from the South Terrace
we had a view of Pennsylvania and Louisiana Avenues,
crowded with people hurrying towards the Capitol.   It
was a most exhilirating scene!   Most of the ladies preferred being inside of the Capitol and the eastern portico,
damp and cold as it was, had been filled from 9 in the
morning by ladies who wished to be near the General
when he spoke.   Every room was filled and the windows crowded.   But as so confined a situation allowed
no general view, we would not coop ourselves up, and
certainly enjoyed a much finer view of the spectacle,
both in its whole and in its details, than those within the
walls.   We stood on the South steps of the terrace; when
the appointed hour came saw the General and his company advancing up the Avenue, slow, very slow, so impeded was his march by the crowds thronging around

him. Even from a distance, he could be discerned from those who accompanied him, for he only was uncovered, (the Servant in presence of his Sovereign, the People). The south side of the Capitol hill was literally alive with the multitude, who stood ready to receive the hero and the multitude who attended him. "There, there, that is he," exclaimed different voices. "Which?" asked others. "He with the white head," was the reply. "Ah," exclaimed others, "there is the old man and his gray hair, there is the old veteran, there is Jackson." At last he enters the gate at the foot of the hill and turns to the road that leads round to the front of the Capitol. In a moment every one who until then had stood like statues gazing on the scene below them, rushed onward, to right, to left, to be ready to receive him in the front. Our party, of course, were more deliberate, we waited until the multitude had rushed past us and then left the terrace and walked round to the furthest side of the square, where there were no carriages to impede us, and entered it by the gate fronting the Capitol. Here was a clear space, and stationing ourselves on the central gravel walk we stood so as to have a clear, full view of the whole scene. The Capitol in all its grandeur and beauty. The Portico and grand steps leading to it, were filled with ladies. Scarlet, purple, blue, yellow, white draperies and waving plumes of every kind and colour, among the white marble pillars, had a fine effect. In the centre of the portico was a table covered with scarlet, behind it the closed door leading into the rotunda, below the Capitol and all around, a mass of living beings, not a ragged mob, but well dressed and well behaved respectable and worthy citizens. Mr. Frank Key, whose arm I had, and an old and frequent witness of great spectacles, often exclaimed, as well as myself, a mere novice,

"It is beautiful, it is sublime!" The sun had been obscured through the morning by a mist, or haziness. But the concussion in the air, produced by the discharge of the cannon, dispersed it and the sun shone forth in all his brightness. At the moment the General entered the Portico and advanced to the table, the shout that rent the air, still resounds in my ears. When the speech was over, and the President made his parting bow, the barrier that had separated the people from him was broken down and they rushed up the steps all eager to shake hands with him. It was with difficulty he made his way through the Capitol and down the hill to the gateway that opens on the avenue. Here for a moment he was stopped. The living mass was impenetrable. After a while a passage was opened, and he mounted his horse which had been provided for his return (for he had walked to the Capitol) then such a cortege as followed him! Country men, farmers, gentlemen, mounted and dismounted, boys, women and children, black and white. Carriages, wagons and carts all pursuing him to the President's house,—this I only heard of for our party went out at the opposite side of the square and went to Col. Benton's lodgings, to visit Mrs. Benton and Mrs. Gilmore. Here was a perfect levee, at least a hundred ladies and gentlemen, all happy and rejoicing,—wine and cake was handed in profusion. We sat with this company and stopped on the summit of the hill until the avenue was comparatively clear, tho' at any other time we should have thought it terribly crowded. Streams of people on foot and of carriages of all kinds, still pouring towards the President's house. We went Home, found your papa and sisters at the Bank,[1] stand-

---

[1] Branch Bank of the United States of which Mr. Smith was president. It stood at the corner of 15th Street and Pennsylvania Avenue.

ing at the upper windows, where they had been seen
by the President, who took off his hat to them, which
they insisted was better than all we had seen. From
the Bank to the President's house for a long while, the
crowd rendered a passage for us impossible. Some went
into the Cashier's parlour, where we found a number
of ladies and gentlemen and had cake and wine in
abundance. In about an hour, the pavement was clear
enough for us to walk. Your father, Mr. Wood, Mr.
Ward, Mr. Lyon, with us, we set off to the President's
House, but on a nearer approach found an entrance impossible, the yard and avenue was compact with living
matter. The day was delightful, the scene animating,
so we walked backward and forward at every turn meeting some new acquaintance and stopping to talk and
shake hands. Among others we met Zavr. Dickinson
with Mr. Frelinghuysen and Dr. Elmendorf, and Mr.
Saml Bradford. We continued promenading here, until
near three, returned home unable to stand and threw
ourselves on the sopha. Some one came and informed
us the crowd before the President's house, was so far
lessen'd, that they thought we might enter. This time
we effected our purpose. But what a scene did we witness! The *Majesty of the People* had disappeared, and
a rabble, a mob, of boys, negros, women, children,
scrambling fighting, romping. What a pity what a pity!
No arrangements had been made no police officers
placed on duty and the whole house had been inundated
by the rabble mob. We came too late. The President,
after having been *literally* nearly pressed to death and
almost suffocated and torn to pieces by the people in their
eagerness to shake hands with Old Hickory, had retreated through the back way or south front and had
escaped to his lodgings at Gadsby's. Cut glass and

china to the amount of several thousand dollars had been
broken in the struggle to get the refreshments, punch
and other articles had been carried out in tubs and
buckets, but had it been in hogsheads it would have
been insufficient, ice-creams, and cake and lemonade, for
20,000 people, for it is said that number were there,
tho' I think the estimate exaggerated.   Ladies fainted,
men were seen with bloody noses and such a scene of
confusion took place as is impossible to describe,—those
who got in could not get out by the door again, but had
to scramble out of windows.   At one time, the President
who had retreated and retreated until he was pressed
against the wall, could only be secured by a number of
gentlemen forming round him and making a kind of
barrier of their own bodies, and the pressure was so
great that Col Bomford who was one said that at
one time he was afraid they should have been pushed
down, or on the President.   It was then the windows
were thrown open, and the torrent found an outlet,
which otherwise might have proved fatal.

This concourse had not been anticipated and therefore
not provided against.   Ladies and gentlemen, only had
been expected at this Levee, not the people en masse.
But it was the People's day, and the People's President
and the People would rule.   God grant that one day or
other, the People, do not put down all rule and rulers.
I fear, enlightened Freemen as they are, they will be
found, as they have been found in all ages and countries
where they get the Power in their hands, that of all
tyrants, they are the most ferocious, cruel and despotic.
The nosiy and disorderly rabble in the President's House
brought to my mind descriptions I had read, of the mobs
in the Tuileries and at Versailles, I expect to hear

the carpets and furniture are ruined, the streets were muddy, and these guests all went thither on foot.

The rest of the day, overcome with fatigue I lay upon the sopha. The girls went to see Mrs. Clay and Mrs. Southard. Mrs. Rush was at Mrs. C.'s—Mrs. Clay's furniture all sold, the entry full of hay, straw, and packages, and in her little back room, scarcely a chair to sit on and she worn out with fatigue. "This being turned out, is a sad, troublesome thing, is it not?" said Mrs. Rush. "Coming in, is troublesome enough, but *then,* one does not mind the trouble."

After tea, Mr. Ward, Mr. Wood, Mr. Lyon, and Warren Scott, came in and staid until past 11 oclock. Mr. S. and I talked of Brunswick friends and of old times. Col. Bomford has been here, just now and given me an account of the Ball, which he says was elegant, splendid and in perfect order. The President and his family were not there. The Vice President and lady and the members of the new cabinet were. Mrs. Bomford was in her grand costume,—scarlet velvet richly trimmed with gold embroidery, the large Ruby, set in diamonds, for which Col. Bomford has refused five thousand dollars, and which I believe you have seen, she wore in her turban. Mr. Baldwin,[1] notwithstanding his disappointment, for he confidently expected a place in the Cabinet, was, Col B. says, excessively merry. During all this bustle in the city, Mr. Adams was quietly fixed at Meridian Hill, to which place he and his family had removed some days before. . . . Everybody is in a state of agitation,—gloomy or glad. A *universal removal* in the departments is apprehended, and many are quaking and trembling, where *all* depends on their places.

[1] Henry Baldwin of Pennsylvania. He was appointed a Judge of the Supreme Court in 1830.

The city, so crowded and bustling, by tomorrow will be silent and deserted, for people are crowding away as eagerly as they crowded here. Mrs. Porter goes on Saturday, Mrs. Clay on Monday, Mrs. Wirt and Southard in the course of the week. We are asked to a party at Mrs. Wirt's tonight, but shall not go,—the funeral of the morning leaves us no disposition for company.

TO J. BAYARD H. SMITH.

[Washington,] March 12th, 1829.

The winter campaign is over—the tents are struck and the different parties are leaving the field—Congress has adjourned—and the hosts of strangers who but a few days ago, swarmed our streets and crowded the public houses, are gone too—the bustle of a busy throng —the rolling of many carriages have ceased and the busy and animated scene, is comparatively silent and deserted. . . . Our friends, too, Mrs. Porter, Mrs. Clay, and many others are gone or going, and these continual partings with those we love and esteem, have thrown a sadness over the last week, that I in vain try to dispel. Never before did the city seem to me so gloomy—so many changes in society—so many families broken up, and those of the first distinction and who gave a tone to society. Those elegantly furnished houses, stripped of their splendid furniture—that furniture exposed to public sale. Those drawing-rooms, brilliantly illuminated, in which I have so often mixed with gay crowds, distinguished by rank, fashion, beauty, talent— resounding with festive sounds—now, empty, silent, dark, dismantled. Oh! tis melancholy! Mrs. Clay's, Mrs. Porter's, Mrs. Southard's houses exhibit this spectacle—They are completely stripped—the furniture all sold—the families, for the few days they remained after the sale—uncomfortably crowded in one little room. The door shut on company and only one or two intimate friends admitted—Nor does the Entry, of the triumphant party, relieve this universal gloom—Alas! it only adds to it—General Jackson's family in deep mourning—secludes them from society,—they are not known, or seen, except at formal morning visits—They quietly took possession of the *big house,* where if they choose they may remain invisible, and as much separated from social intercourse, as if on the other side of the mountains—But what most adds to the general gloom—is the rumour of a general proscription—Every individual connected with the government, from the highest officer to the lowest clerk, is filled with apprehension. Men whose all depends on the decision, await it in fear and trembling—Oh how dreadfully must a parent feel, when he looks on his children gathered round him, and knows that one word spoken by a stranger, may reduce them to beggary—Such is the situation of hundreds at the present moment—and of men too far advanced in life, to be able to enter on new paths of industry. Last Sunday Mr. and Mrs. Clay passed with us, in a social, domestic manner—Never did I see this great man, (for in native point of mind, I never knew his equal) so interesting—nay fascinating. I had heard of his possessing this power of captivation, which no one who was its object could resist, and I have before seen and felt its influence, but never in the same degree, as on this occasion. At dinner he sat next to your father, next to one he knew to be opposed to his late political course and whom for many years he had, consequently, seldom seen, but the little differences of party were forgotten; the patriot to the patriot, who, however they might differ in the means, had the same end in view. Meeting on this common ground and avoiding the late field of combat they conversed on general yet interesting subjects, connected with past events. The characters and administrations of Jefferson and Madison were analized, and many private anecdotes were drawn from the memory of each. Mr. Clay preferred Madison, and pronounced him after Washington our greatest statesman, and first political writer—He thought Jefferson had most genius—Madison most judgment and common sense—Jefferson a visionary and theorist, often betrayed by his enthusiasm into rash and imprudent and impracticable measures, Madison cool, dispassionate, practical, safe. Your father, would not yield Jefferson's superiority and said he possessed a power and energy, which carried our country through difficulties and dangers; far beyond the power of Madison's less energetic character. "Prudence and caution —would have produced the same results," insisted Mr. Clay. After drawing a parellel between these great men, and taking an historic survey of their political lives, they both met on the same point, viz. that both were *great* and *good,* and tho' *different,*—yet *equal.*—We lingered long around the table, after dinner was removed, listening to this interesting conversation.—When we returned to the parlour Mr. Clay left us, to take his usual walk, and Mr. Ward, Mr. Lyon, and General McComb unexpectedly entered—The weather without was gloomy, cold and cloudy, but the circle around our bright fire, was not only cheerful but gay and witty. It was twilight—rather fire-light when Mr. Clay returned— Anna Maria relinquished to him, his favorite seat on the sofa, on which he threw himself, reclining, rather than

sitting—How graceful he looked!—his face was flushed
with exercise and his countenance animated with some
strong emotion. After a while without any previous
observation, half rising from his recumbent position, and
stretching out his arm, "There is not," said he, "at Cairo
or Constantinople, a greater moral despotism than is at
this moment exercised in this city over public opinion.
Why a man dare not avow what he thinks or feels, or
shake hands with a personal friend, if he happens to
differ from the powers that be." I shook my head observing, "Not all, Mr. Clay." "Yes, *all,*" said he, "who
have anything to lose—and I should not this day be in
your house, if Mr. Smith was not safely laid up in the
Bank."—We all laughed, while I replied "You would not
say so, if you believed *so* Mr. Clay"—"If the fact were
true," said your father, in his sternest manner "such
men deserve to lose their places, and I would have them
all turned out"—"Oh, Mr. Smith" replied Mr. Clay, his
countenance, his manner, his voice softening into the
most tender and persuasive expression "Oh, Mr. Smith
—we must forgive them—remember they suffer not
alone—their families, their children—think of them, and
who is there would not excuse their timidity." Language cannot describe the manner and look with which
this was said—No doubt, his first remark, was elicited,
by some neglect he himself had felt, during his walk—
but how soon was momentary indignation conquered by
generous and tender feelings—He has from nature a
fund of tenderness and sensibility, which even ambition,
that all-absorbing passion, has not had power to dry
up—"The politician has no heart" says *Sallust* then, even
yet, Henry Clay, is not a thorough politician, for on
many an occasion have I witnessed the irrepressible tenderness of a feeling heart—Never can I forget the tears

he shed, over his dying infant, as it lay in my lap, and he
kneeled by my side—With what deep tenderness did he
gaze on it, until, unable to witness its last agonies, he
impressed a long tender kiss on its pale lips—murmur-
ing out "Farewell, my little one"—and left the chamber
—and the next morning when obliged to speak to me
about the funeral, he walked the room, for some time,
in mournful silence, as if struggling to compose his feelings, so as to be able to give his directions with calm-
ness—"My only difficulty" said he at length, "is to decide on what is my duty—I would fain remain at home
this morning—but I believe it will not do—I have no
right to allow private concerns to interfere with public
duty—No—I must go to the House," (he was then
Speaker) I combatted this, and told him I was certain
the members would not expect him—He still walked the
room in doubt how to act—when the Sergeant at Arms
was announced, and on his entrance, brought him the
condolence of the House, and an offer, if he wished it,
of attending the funeral—"Thank the gentlemen for me,
and tell them I am truly grateful for their indulgence in
excusing my attendance this morning—beyond this I
have nothing to wish and beg they will not put themselves to inconvenience—it is an infant—and I wish only
the attendance of my family, and the few friends who
are with us."—This winter, when he first learnt the
result of the election, instead of depression of spirit his
mind seemed inspired with new vigour and animation as
if relieved from some heavy burthen—*suspense* was *over*
—and to a person of his nature, ardent, restless temper-
ament, suspense is the least endurable of all sufferings—
New scenes, new projects opened on his view—like a
wrestler, who had been thrown, but not disabled, he
started up, shook off the dust, and wiped off the sweat of

the first conflict, and gathering up new strength and resolution—prepared for another combat for the prize of,
glory—Such has he seemed to me, since the election was
decided—more elastic, more vigorous, more high
spirited—and I verily believe he is actually happier than
if calmly and securely seated in the presidential chair—
for then there would be none of the activity, energy, and
power of conflict brought into play—excitement is as
necessary to his moral, as stimulus is to his physical existence—Henry Clay was made for action—not for rest.
—Such was the result of his political *affliction*—How different its effects from those of private, domestic sorrow!
—When he heard of the excesses of a profligate but still
beloved son—when he heard that son was in prison—
his heart sunk within him—disease was increased by
distress—health and rest forsook him—I alluded to this
in a former letter—the circumstance was then a secret,
and I told you not of it—since, I have discovered it to be
generally known, and therefore tell it you.—For several
weeks Mr. Clay told me, sleep totally forsook him, and
he could procure none but through the aid of anodynes.·
It was a knowledge of this secret sorrow, at the time of
the last Drawing-room that so tenderly excited my sympathy, that I had to retreat to a corner to conceal tears
I could not repress—(but I believe it was to your aunt,
and not to you I described that scene)—When I am writing on a subject that interests me I cannot stop my pen.
—but from this long digression, let me try and get back
to our own fireside, and the admiring circle that surrounded Mr. Clay—So interesting was his conversation,
so captivating his frank cordial manner, that I could
almost have said with Mr. Lyon—"I could have listened
all night, and many nights with delight"—and with Mr.
Ward have exclaimed "What a treat! It is indeed the

feast of reason, and the flow of soul."—Washington,
Jefferson, Hamilton, Burr, and many other conspicuous
actors in our National drama were the subjects of discussion—not only their character, but their actions, and
their motive of action—To read history, is cold, stale,
and unprofitable, compared with hearing it—the eloquence of language, is enforced by eloquence of the soul-
speaking eye and persuasive voice—It was past ten
o'clock before Mrs. Clay, usually so early in her hours,
rose to depart—Altogether, this day and evening have
been the most interesting that have occurred this winter—Yesterday, your father accompanied us on a visit
to our new President—I imagine we were the only
ladies, who had not, long before hastened to wait on his
family—but I felt too much on losing my old friends, to
be in haste to pay my respects to their successors—After
sitting awhile with Miss Easton, Mr. Smith asked if the
President saw ladies—She said she would inquire, and
left the room for that purpose—In a few minutes after
she sent our names, General Jackson entered. Mr. S.
introduced us, and he shook hands cordially with each
of us. I asked very frankly of his being unwell, and attributed his indisposition to having too much to do—
the Senate being impatient to rise, and he consequently
having to work night as well as day. Was not this frank
—He shook hands again with each when we went, and
I must say I was much pleased—A carriage—interrupted
—Tuesday 17th.

Two days have passed since I commenced this letter,
during which nothing interesting has occurred—All the
citizens, more or less, have been engaged in the bustle of
the winter, and are glad of quiet—at least all that I
know—There is a complete cessation of *parties* and visiting—the weather has been bad, another cause for staying

at home—I have enjoyed this quiet, read and written more the last week, than in a whole month, before— We shall remove into the country the beginning of next month, if the weather allows when will you be here?

TO MRS. KIRKPATRICK

[Washington] [1829]

. . . . Mr. Campbell[1] seldom visits us. His mind seems wholly engaged with his affair with Mrs. E. [aton]—he has injudicious friends who keep alive his irritation of mind and temper and are urging him on to make an Exposee of facts which tho' they would free him from the imputation of a false calumniater, would embroil him with the present party, throw him into the arms of the opposition and in fact make a political tool of him. The facts he possesses might ruin (it is said) the Secr. and his wife, but what then. Would it raise him in public estimation and thereby increase his usefulness? I think not, and have said so to him, and by so doing, show less sympathy in his excited feelings, than those who appear to enter so warmly into his interests and urge him to publish a book, while in fact I believe they use him, to promote their own views.

Mrs. E. continues excluded from society, except the houses of some of the foreigners, the President's and Mr. V. B.'s. The Dutch Minister's family have openly declared against her admission into society. The other evening at a grand fête at the Russian Minister's Mrs. E. was led first to the supper table, in consequence of which Mrs. Madm. Heugans and family would not go to the table and was quite enraged,—for the whole week

[1] George W. Campbell of Tennessee was not in office at this time, nor did he attain national prominence again.

you heard of scarcely anything else. And it is generally
asserted that if Mr. V. B. our Secr. persists in visiting
her, our ladies will not go to his house. We shall
see. . . .

TO MRS. KIRKPATRICK

[Sidney] Tuesday, Aug. 16, 1829.

. . . . Tell him I am really surprised he has not
come on to see his President. I can not take to the new
folks. The Presd. and his family sit in the pew behind
us, and I often have the pleasure of pinching his fingers,
as he has the habit of laying his hand on the side of the
pew and I have the habit of leaning back. The first two
or three times of his coming to church, he bowed and I
curtisied after church, and the same with the ladies, but
now we never look at each other. Neither Mr. S. or I
have ever called but once at the White-House and besides representation (we are told) has been made that Mr.
S. is a *Clayite,* so that we are not in favour at court, and
as little acquainted with the other members of the administration. Those citizens who wished for an acquaintance, obtained it very easily, for never before was
the Palace so accessible,—persons of all ranks visit very
sociably I am told, and in return the family accept all invitations and visit the citizens in the most social manner,
and live on more equal and familiar terms, than any other
Presd. family ever has. All my sympathies attach me to
the ex-party.

TO MRS. KIRKPATRICK

[Washington] Thursday, 27, Nover. 1829.

. . . . From mere curiosity I have commenced an
account of our visitors and every morning set down the
number of the previous day. It is three weeks since I

began and the number already amounts to 197,—not all
different individuals, but the aggregate of each days
visitors, who are often the same persons. We have at
least 6 or 7 young gentlemen friends, who are frequently with us. An accidental concurence of circumstances has obliged us to have more invited company
within this period, than we generally have within treble
that time. Mrs. Randolph I believe I told you was settled among us and very near our house. I see her almost
daily, and feel it incumbent upon me, in her present
altered condition, to pay her every possible attention. I
therefore had a party for her, wishing to make known
to her and her to them, my most agreeable acquaintances.
On this occasion I opened both rooms and did my best to
give her an agreeable party. Then came Mr. Biddle,
President of the Bank, and Mr. Smith had to give him
a dinner party. (I would rather give a dozen evening
parties.) To this we asked Mr. Gallatin and some of the
members of the Cabinet. Mr. Berrian, whom we all admire, nay almost love, was one. Truly he is a most
charming man. We shall, I expect, be quite social neighbors, as Mr. Smith is as much taken with him as any
of us. . . . .

Dear Mrs. Randolf! How I wish my dear sisters
that you knew her. Whenever she has visits to return,
I call for and accompany her. Several mornings have
been thus engaged. Yesterday I went with her to the
President's to introduce her to Mrs. Donaldson.[1] She
was very much affected on entering the house, and with
tender emotion pointed out to her daughter, the different apartments. "That was my dear Father's cabinet,
that, his favorite sitting room, that—was my chamber
and that, girls, was your nursery." Thus, as we passed

[1] Wife of Andrew Jackson Donelson, the President's private Secretary.

through the Hall and long passages, to the Lady's drawing-room on the second floor, did she designate each
room.   When we were going away, I enquired of Mrs.
Donaldson, whether we could look into the East-Room,
she answered in the affirmative and had she known a
little more of the usages of good society, she would have
accompanied Mrs. R. to that and other apartments.   But
she let her go without this attention.   Mrs. Donaldson
had previously called on Mrs. Randolph, not waiting for
the first visit.   The President too, called to see her, in
all due form, the Secr. of State wrote a note to Mr.
Triste enquiring of him, if Mrs. Randolf would be at
home at such an hour, on such a morning, when, if at
home, the President would do himself the pleasure of
waiting on her.   And so he did, accompanied by the
Secr. of State.   He demonstrated great kindness and expressed his hopes that she would be a frequent visitor at
his house.   The next day the ladies of his family called
on her.   She has been very generally visited and her visiting list is filled as fast as she empties it.   I shall as far
as is in my power give her the use of our carriage and do
every thing I can to prove the tender regard and high
esteem I feel for her.

TO MRS. KIRKPATRICK

[Washington] Decr 27, 1829.

.   .   .   .   She[1] and Mrs. Randolph are the only
women here, with whom I wish, in addition to my old
friends, Mrs. Thornton and Bomford, to cultivate an intimate acquaintance.   Mrs. Randolph and her family I
see almost daily.   The round of company in which she
has been involved lately has made her sick.   I passed part

[1] Mrs. Rush.

of a morning this week by her bed-side. Some reference was made to Monticello. Her father's image which is seldom absent from her mind, was thus recalled. "This" said she, taking up the down cover-lit, which was over her, "was the one he used for 40 yrs. and this bed was his."—The one, I imagine, on which his last hours were past, for she stopped, choked by emotion and could not restrain her tears, tho' she concealed them by drawing the bedclothes over her face.

Never have I known of a union between any two beings so perfect as that which almost identified this father and daughter. I am sure you would love Mrs. R.,—so soft, gentle, mild and affectionate, in disposition, voice, and manners, with a mind so refined and cultivated and a character firm and energetic. It is a pity that her extreme modesty throws a veil over her virtues and talents, which is withdrawn only by great intimacy. She has been treated with the greatest attention and respect by all the citizens as well as the officials. When she dined at Mr. V. B.'s he led her first to the table, even before the ladies of the President's family, and at the President's house, Genl. Jackson led her before the Senator's or Secrs. ladies. And as our system of etiquette is more rigidly observed than it ever was before, Mrs. R. is thus placed at the head of society.

TO MRS. KIRKPATRICK

[Washington,] Janur. 26. 1830.

 . . . . The wind is blowing high and cold, the streets filled with clouds of dust. We have had no weather all winter so cold. I have fixed myself close by a blazing fire to write to you this morning without

much fear of being interrupted, for almost everyone
is thronging to the capitol to hear Mr. Webster's reply
to Col. Hayne's[1] attack on him and his party. A debate on any political principle would have had no such
attraction.   But personalities are irrisistible.   It is a
kind of moral gladiatorship, in which characters are torn
to pieces, and arrows, yes, poisoned arrows, which tho'
not seen, are deeply felt, are hurled by the combatants
against each other.   The Senate chamber, is the present arena and never were the amphitheatres of Rome
more crowded by the highest ranks of both sexes than
the senate chamber is.   Every seat, every inch of ground,
even the steps, were *compactly* filled, and yet not space
enough for the ladies—the Senators were obliged to
relinquish their chairs of State to the fair auditors who
literally sat in the Senate.   One lady sat in Col. Hayne's
seat, while he stood by her side speaking.   I cannot
but regret that this dignified body should become such
a scene of personality and popular resort, it was supposed yesterday that there were 300 ladies besides their
attendant beaux on the floor of the Senate.   The two
galleries were crowded to overflowing with *the People,*
and the house of Reprs. quite deserted.   Our government is becoming every day more and more democratic,
the rulers of the people are truly their servants and
among those rulers women are gaining more than their
share of power. One woman has made sad work here;
to be, or not to be, her friend is the test of Presidential
favour.   Mr. V. B. sided with her and is consequently
the right hand man, the constant riding, walking and
visiting companion.   The P—— and his friend Genl.

[1] The great debate between Webster and Hayne took place January
15–26, and on the day Mrs. Smith wrote Webster delivered his most famous
speech.

E., while the other members of the cabinet, are looked on coldly—some say unkindly and enjoy little share in the councils of state. Mr. Calhoun, Ingham, his devoted friend, Branch and Berrian form one party, the Prd., V. B., Genl. E. and Mr. Bary[1] the other. It is generally supposed that, as they cannot sit together, some change in the Cabinet must take place. Meanwhile, the lady who caused this division, is forced notwithstanding the support and favour of such high personages to withdraw from society. She is not received in any private parties, and since the 8th of January has withdrawn from public assemblies. At the ball given on that occasion, she was treated with such marked and universal neglect and indignity, that she will not expose herself again to such treatment. Genl. E., unable to clear his wife's fair fame, has taken his revenge by blackening that of other ladies, one of whose husbands (——) has resented it in such a manner, that it was universally believed he would receive a challenge. But Genl. E. has very quietly pocketed the abuse lavished on him. This affair was for two weeks the universal topic of conversation. Mr. Campbell, as the original cause of all this uproar and difficulty, felt so miserable for a whole week, while a duel was daily expected, that he said it wholly unfitted him for everything else. It is only as it regards our young pastor, that I take any interest in this affair. On his account I greatly regret it, for so completely has it occupied his time and his mind that it has rendered him incapable of attending to his ministerial or pastoral duties, to such a degree as to produce great dissatisfaction in his congregation. He has received a call from Albany, with the offer of a salary of $2000, and I rather

[1] William T. Barry, of Kentucky, appointed by Jackson Postmaster General.

think he will accept it, if he does we shall lose a good *preacher* but nothing more. The admiration excited by his sermons has spoiled him for a faithful Pastor,— a humble minister of the gospel. He is an elegant, polished, agreeable young man, of brilliant talents, of bland and pleasing manners. He seldom visits us, and none of that intimacy and confidence and interest has taken place, which I would desire should connect me and mine with our Pastor.

Since Christmas we have, comparatively to what we were before, been quite retired and domestic. The *gay season,* then commenced—large parties, every night— these we do not like. Gov. Branch's crush-party sickened me of them and we have declined 12 or 13 invitations. We have three for this week but shall not accept of one. But most folks are fond of them and our neighbors and beaux among the rest, so that instead of participating of our fire-side pleasures they sought these of drawing rooms and Balls. The less we go out the less we are inclined to go out, so that we shall soon, if we go on at this rate, live as retired as we did at Sidney. Yet it is seldom we are quite alone; when we are, one of the girls reads aloud and thus pleasantly beguiles the evening. I have visited but few strangers. Mrs. Frelinghuysen is among that few. I want to ask her to pass an evening, but if I do there are so many others that I must ask, and I feel so little inclined to give a party, that I fear to undertake it; as for a plain tea-drinking, she would not think it worth while to get a hack to come to one. The city is thronged with strangers, fashionable ladies from all quarters, a great many mothers with daughters to show off, a great many young ladies coming to see relatives and to be seen by the public and all coming in such high ton and expensive fashions, that the poor citizens can not pretend to vie with them and absolutely shrink into insignficance. We have made no interesting acquaintances. I promised myself more pleasure than I have realized in my intercourse with Mrs. Randolph. Her family is so very, very large that I can never see her alone; besides she and her 4 daughters are continually, almost every night in company and when disengaged are happy to find rest and quiet by themselves at home. Our young folks do not take to each other as I hoped. Her daughters can bear no comparrison to her, tho' they are very amiable and intelligent. When all this turmoil of gaiety is over, I hope to see more of her. She is completely wearied, but thinks it advantageous to her family to mix in society. My Julia is quite recovered and we are all quite well and I think quite contented, which is the highest degree of happiness we should expect. May you dear sister and those you love be blessed with it.

TO MRS. KIRKPATRICK

March 31st, 1830.   Washington.

. . . . Since I began this letter I have had several interruptions,—first came Joseph Dougherty, the favorite and confidential servant of Mr. Jefferson, while he resided in Washington. He is an Irishman, and has all the glow of affection and enthusiasm peculiar to his nation. With a good education and natural intelligence he acquired in his long service a degree of elevation and refinement of feelings and views, seldom or ever found in his class. He sat at least an hour, talking of the dear old Man, as he called him, and telling me anecdotes about his private life, which only a favorite domestic

could tell. He was in the midst of a minute detail of
Mr. J.'s distribution of every hour of the day, from sun
rise until bed time, when Mrs. Cutts entered. "Well,"
exclaimed he, "here are three of us, who can testify of
the good old times!" When Mrs. Randolph arrived in
the city, he waited on her, and after urging his services
(gratuitous and friendly) he finished by saying, "Do,
madam, make me of use to you, and believe me, I will
now be a more faithful and devoted servant to you, than
I ever was while you lived in the President's house."
He is never weary of reciting Mr. J.'s praises. "His
whole life was nothing but good," said he,—"it was his
meat and drink, all he thought of and all he cared for,
to make every body happy. Yes, the purest body." He
was sure nobody could know without loving and blessing
him. The entrance of other company, made him withdraw, and after Dr. Seawell and Mrs. Brown went, Col.
Bomford came in and sat more than an hour. Thus has
my rainy morning been stolen from me, which I had
appropriated to letter writing.

I have been much engaged lately in reading Mr. Jefferson's correspondence.[1] Seated at my chamber window
from whence I could see the President's house, terrace
and garden. I often withdraw my eyes from the book
to look at the place which once knew him, but knows him
now no more. "And is it possible," I said to myself,
"that I have been the familiar companion of this man
who will be hereafter looked upon, as we now look upon
Cicero, and other great men of antiquity,—that I have
conversed with him of the events recorded in these pages,
and which will constitute some of the most important
facts in the history of mankind?—that I have walked

---

[1] "Memoirs, Correspondence, and Miscellanies of Thomas Jefferson," by
Thomas J. Randolph (4 vols. Boston, 1820).

with him on that Terrace, sat by his domestic fire-side
and been with him in the still more sacred seclusion of his
daughters sick-chamber?" How like a dream it appears.
I wish every body would read these letters, and not a few
selected ones, most unfavorable to his character. Take
them all in all, and they present examples of candour,
impartiality, benevolence, and wisdom, seldom, if ever
equalled. Cicero's correspondence can bear no comparison as to intellectual excellence. Whatever his opinions on religion were, they were not negligently made
up. His researches were deep and extensive. And the
result of these researches, was conviction of the truth
of the system he adopted, but at the same time of the most
perfect tollerance towards other men's opinions. "I
judge of every man's faith, by his life," said he in a letter
to me, "and I wish my fellow citizens to judge of mine
by the same test." Mrs. Randolph has lent me, one work
of his, that shows the interest he took in the subject of
religion. It is selections from the four Gospels, so arranged as to give the complete history of the life, pre-
cepts and doctrines of Jesus Christ, without the repetition
which is found in the different gospels. His mode was
to cut out of each portions which by being connected gave
in one view a more clear and complete account, than
when found scattered through the different gospels, and
this not in one language, but in Greek, Latin, French
and English. He always speaks of Christ as one of the
greatest of reformers and wisest and best of men, and
his system of morals as the most pure and sublime of any
ever given to man. His religion he considers to be pure
deism. The worship, purely spiritual, independant of all
external forms. Never was a death more serene and
happy than Mr. J.'s. Mrs. R. not only detailed every
particular and word of the last hours of his life, but has

shown me the last lines he ever wrote.   They were addressed to her, written during his last illness, when every
hope of life was fled,—entitled "a death-bed adieu."
He put them in her hand the day before his death, saying with a placid smile and tender voice, "that is for you,
my daughter."   She did not open the little pocket-book
in which they were enclosed until some days after his
death.   In these lines which are in verse he bids her not
to weep at an event which would crown all his hopes,—
that his last pang would be in parting from her, but that
he would carry her love and memory to the two happy
spirits (her mother and sister) who were waiting to receive him.

TO MRS. KIRKPATRICK

August 1st, 1830.   Sidney.

. . . .   I am sorry for your sake Mr. W.[irt] did
not remain in B.   His conversation would have charmed
you as much as his oratory,—his manners in the domestic circle have a charm peculiar to himself.   The last
evening I passed with this charming family, previous to
their leaving Washington, he appeared in a more amiable and affecting light than I had ever seen him.   He
was reclining in one corner of a sopha, and while he conversed with me in the most animated manner, he would
occasionally turn to his lovely daughter, whose head was
leaning on his shoulder, and who with playful fondness
was patting his cheek, or twining her fingers in the curls
that shaded his temples, and look on her with a pride
and tenderness words could not have expressed.   There
is a great deal of this caressing manner between him and
his children; they seem to love one another, as compan-

ions and friends of the same age love each other and yet
without any dereliction of that respect which accompanies affection for a parent.   In truth I never met with
a family like them,—every individual bears the stamp of
genius—genius, with all its ardent affections, enthusiasm and eccentricity.   There is as much heart as there
is brain in their composition; were it otherwise, one
might admire without loving them.   Mrs. Wirt has least,
perhaps *none* from nature, but she could not live 30
years with Mr. W. without catching some portion of his
powerful and glowing genius.   She is a woman of sound
common sense, a great manager and economist and has
made Mr. Wirt the useful and respectable character he
now is.   "Yes," said an old friend, who was giving me
the family history, "all he now is, he owes to his wife."[1]
Genius is too often a meteor that dazzles the blind, an
ignis fatuus that lures to danger, instead of guiding to
safety.   Such, in his youth, it proved to Mr. W.   He
was an almost lost and ruined man, both in morals and
fortune, when he married the excellent wife, whose prudence and affection snatched him from the dangers that
surrounded him and has since been his guard and support.   I wish she had accompanied him and you could
have become acquainted with her.   Yet, this could not
have been done, in one way, not in many interviews, her
disposition is too reserved to allow of her being easily
known.   I never heard of any one that was confidentially
intimate with her, or indeed, at all intimate, yet such is
the sweetness and softness of her manners, that she con-
ciliates affection in spite of her coldness and reserve.
She is wholly devoted to her husband and children,—to

[1] She was Elizabeth Gamble, second daughter of Col. Richard Gamble, a
merchant of Richmond.   Wirt was a widower twenty-nine years old when
he married her in 1802, after he had been put on probation for a period by
Col. Gamble before he would give his consent.

live in them and for them—and does not disguise her indifference to all other things and persons, so that with
all her merit, she is not popular in general society, but
is proportionably dear to the few to whom she is well
known and to whom she unveils herself.   Lovely as her
daughters are, I often fear for their happiness; they are
hot-house plants, that will never bear an exposure to the
cold and rude air of common life.   Their health seems
as fragile, as their characters are delicate.   I cannot
reconcile Mrs. W.'s artificial and refined system of education, with that sound, practical common sense, which
she has discovered in her other duties.   .   .   .

TO MRS. KIRKPATRICK

August 29, 1831, Sidney.

.   .   .   .   What does Lytleton *now* think of Genl.
Jackson? The papers do not exaggerate, nay do not detail one half of his imbecilities. He is completely under
the government of Mrs. Eaton, one of the most ambitious,
violent, malignant, yet silly women you ever heard of.
You will soon see the recall of the dutch minister announced. Madm. Huygen's spirited conduct in refusing
to visit Mrs. E. is undoubtedly the cause. The new Cabinet if they do not yield to the President's will on the
point, will, it is supposed, soon be dismissed. Several of
them in order to avoid this dilemma, are determined not
to keep house or bring on their families. Therefore, not
keeping house, they will not give parties and may thus
avoid the disgrace of entertaining the favorite. It was
hoped, on her husband's going out of office, she would
have left the city, *but she will not.* She hopes for a com-

plete triumph and is not satisfied with having the Cabinet broken up and a virtuous and intelligent minister recalled, and many of our best citizens frowned upon by the President. Our society is in a sad state. Intrigues and parasites in favour, divisions and animosity existing. As for ourselves, we keep out of the turmoil, seldom speak and never take any part in this troublesome and shameful state of things. Yet no one can deny, that the P.'s weakness originates in an amiable cause,—his devoted and ardent friendship for Genl. Eton. . . .

TO MRS. SAMUEL BOYD

Sidney, August 29, 1831.

. . . . I called the other day to see Mrs. McClean, I found her precisely the same frank, gay, communicative woman she ever was. She pulled off my bonnet that I might be more at ease, threw herself on the sofa and made me lounge by her, where we had a long talk about England, viz., she had, while I listened, well pleased. She mentioned you and your kind invitation. She is evidently very much elated with her past and present dignity, but her self-complacence is united with so much good humour to others, that it is not offensive. She will have as difficult a part to play in society as her husband will in office, as she, as well as he, must be under the influence, I was going to say, despotism of the President's will. And altho' I sincerely believe him to be a warm, kind-hearted old man, yet so passionate and obstinate, that such a subserviency must be very galling and hard to bear. In truth, the only excuse his best friends can make for his violence and imbecilities, is, that he is in his dotage. His memory is so frail, that he can scarcely remember from one day to the other what he says or what he does;[1] but while his mind has lost its vigour, his passions retain all their natural force, unrestrained by the only power that ever could restrain them, his good and most beloved wife. Van Buren stood them as long as he could, but unable to govern or direct judgment so weak and passions so strong, he escaped from the increasing difficulties of his station, and *most kindly and disinterestedly* changed places with his *friend*. Before many months are over, I suspect that friend will not thank him for his *disinterested* kindness. It is said the gentlemen of the present cabinet, mean to act in strict unison and thus by their *united power* oppose all injudicious, foolish or injurious measures, hoping this union will make their power irresistible, but I suspect the secret, continually applied influence of Mrs. E. will continue to govern and direct the feelings and will of the good old man. We will see. Mrs. E. can not be forced or persuaded to leave Washington. Her triumph, for so she calls the dissolution of the cabinet, her triumph she says is not yet complete. All her adversaries are not yet turned out of office, to be sure, three secretaries and a foreign minister are dismissed, but Mr. and Mr. and Mr. remain, they too must go, and she *must be* received into society, and she hopes and believes that next winter the present Cabinet ministers will open their doors for her. Mrs. McClean has already committed herself on this point. Previous to her going to England, when on a visit here, in direct violation to the most violent asseverations previously made, she visited this lady, and instantly became a great favorite with the Pres'd. If she follows up this system, she will doubtless gain great influence with

---

[1] Mrs. Smith was never more mistaken in her life.

him, but will lose proportionately in society. I am sorry she so committed herself, for the question in society is not so much about Mrs. E., as the principle, whether vice shall be countenanced. And she has placed herself in the sad predicament of acting in the affirmative to this important question. Alas, what will not ambition do with the very best of us? I am glad I have not been brought to the trial, for when I see such a high minded woman yield to its delusive power, I would not answer for myself. She is now looking for a house, and when one is found, means after going home, to return next month and form her establishment. Were it not for the E. affair, I think she would make a very popular lady-secretaress, almost as much so as dear, good, lovely, and lamented Mrs. Porter. Oh how every one loved that woman! I do not anticipate any intimacy. Our husbands are too different in their views and feelings, and I fear she and I will be equally so. Yet she is a charming woman and I am always entertained and delighted in her society, but I every year am more and more wearied from the world of fashion, more and more attached to our fire-side circle. My ambition is, I think, conquered. I have philosophised myself out of its enthralling power. The shifting scenes I have gazed on for thirty years have convinced me of the emptiness and vanity, and unsatisfactory nature of the honors and pleasures. What changes have I witnessed! What is popularity, what is celebrity, what is high station? Objects of painful anxiety in pursuit, of dissatisfaction and disappointment, when attained, and when lost, empty and unsubstantial as a dream. Domestic Life! There alone is happiness. I have tried all the pleasures of the gay world and never found any half as satisfying and enduring as these I have enjoyed in my solitary chamber with my

books and pen.   Such are my views and feelings in the
country, God grant, the city may have no power to
change them.   Farewell dear Maria, my paper admits
not of another line.

TO MRS. KIRKPATRICK

Washington, 1831.   Novr. 7th, Sunday afternoon.

.   .   .   .   But how changed our circle since the first
winter! There are none now in the city, Mrs. Thornton,
Seaton and Bomford excepted, that we care one half as
much for as those that Genl. Jackson displaced.   We
have several new neighbours.   How we shall like them,
time must determine.   An Empress, an ex-Minister's
widow and Mrs. Secretary McClean are among these
nearest to us.   Madame Iturbide, the former Empress
of Mexico, is close to us.   We could, were we so inclined,
almost shake hands from our back windows.

Sister Gertrude,[1] the nun, who last spring escaped from
the convent at George Town, is an inmate of her family,
in fact, an adopted daughter and has the whole charge of
her three daughters.   Sister Gertrude I knew well in
her childhood, saw now and then through the convent
grate and on one occasion when accidently alone with
her, offered if she wished to leave it, to communicate her
desire to her relatives, but she then said she was confined more by her own inclination, than by her vows, or
the walls that surrounded her.   I shall try to renew our
acquaintance.

My dear Mrs. Randolph, has removed far away,

[1] She was a Miss White, of Montgomery Co., Md.   She never disclosed
her reasons for leaving the convent, and continued to attend the Catholic
Church.

Mrs. William Thornton.

After a water-color by Dr. Thornton in the possession of J. Henley Smith, Washington.

almost to George Town,—quite out of my walking capacity. She has been absent since May, but is daily expected back.

With the exception of good Mrs. Newal's family, all
my other neighbours are gayer folks than we have any
desire to be, for this in every sense of the word is the
West end of the city. Elizabeth Wirt, now Mrs. Edds-
borough arrived a few days since. She is to live in her
father's former house, and I suppose some of the family
will always be with her. Mrs. Wirt and Catharine accompanied her. We called yesterday, the Bride, groom
and bridesmaid, (viz. Catherine) were all in deep black,
but they were quite gay and happy. I did not see Mrs.
Wirt. She had been so much agitated by meeting her
friend Mrs. Lear, that she could not venture to see any
other of her friends. She returned yesterday to Baltimore. Mr. Farley, Catherine's disappointed lover, lives
in a house exactly opposite to Eddsbourough. I wonder if such close neighbourhood, will not reunite the
lovers. . . .

TO MRS. KIRKPATRICK

[Washington] Friday, Decr. 9th, 1831.

How little did I imagine when I closed my last letter
to you my dearest sister, that more than two weeks
would pass without my resuming my pen and commenc-
ing the journalizing letter I promised. But so it is,—
my time does not seem at my own command, it is stolen
from me by the force of circumstances, yet—circumstances so insignificant as not to deserve being recorded. My
visiting list is one of the smallest of any lady in Washington,—yet to keep up an interchange with only 70 or

80 persons consumes almost all my morning hours. One day when I was visiting with Mrs. Porter and remarked incidentally here is the list of visits I owe, at least 50, " Oh how happy you are," said she, " only look at mine, it exceeds 500." Now this does not appear to you a more silly custom than it does to me. But what is to be done? Why, either to give up society, or conform to its established customs, at least partially and moderately conform, and that is all I do,—and had I not young persons in the family, I really would give it up and live ————.[1] Being a stormy day I thought I should write without interruption, but two have occurred since I began writing, —one a poor and worthy woman with whom I had a long talk, the last one of the most amiable and agreeable young men,—Lieut. Farley,[2] the discarded lover of Catharine Wirt. He is handsome, highly informed, in fact an intellectual man and of most exemplary morals. Catherine is here, living close by him, and is said to be very unhappy. He is so indignant at the treatment he has received, that it is said his love is conquered and to all appearance he is as happy as ever. But I rather think it is only pride gives him this appearance.

Our good friend Mrs. Clay has arrived. Altho' it was a snow storm the day after her arrival, Ann and I hastened to welcome her back and sat the whole of a long morning with her. She looks ill and unhappy, and much cause has she, poor woman, for her unhappiness. Her two eldest sons are living sorrows to her, which all who have had the trial, say are the most difficult afflictions to bear. One, irreclaimably dissipated, the other insane and confined in a hospital. Mr. Clay is borne up

---

[1] So in the MS.
[2] John Farley, who did not renew his suit to Miss Wirt, but married Anna Maria Pearson of Washington. He resigned from the Army and entered the Coast Survey.

by the undying spirit of ambition,—he looks well and animated, and will be this winter in his very element,— in the very vortex of political warfare. With his unrivaled and surpassing talents, his winning and irresistibly attractive manners, what is it he cannot do? We shall see, but I shall think it strange if he does not succeed in all his aims. He has been received with marked deference and respect, and altho' the President of the Senate is an administration man, he has been placed on some of the most important committees. Mr. Adams[1] in the lower House [receives] still more marked and cordial attentions. Judge Wayne[2] told me yesterday, it was really gratifying to see party-spirit so subjugated to a better feeling,—that every day, men of all parties, crowded round him to testify their respect and good will.

Govr. Barbour and his family are likewise here. We called yesterday to see them,—it is really a great pleasure to meet those with whom we had lived so cordially and agreeably. How glad I should be to get all our old friends back again and not to feel as we now feel, surrounded by strangers,—with hostile feelings or absolute indifference. Mrs. McClane sat some time with me yesterday, poor woman,—her new honors are not without thorns, and she feels them acutely.

Mrs. Livingston[3] takes the lead in the fashionable world and Mr. L. is trying to take the lead in the political. Neither Mr. or Mrs. McC. are people who will willingly follow, and it is already rumoured that much conflict and dissatisfaction exists in the Cabinet. The President has

---

[1] John Quincy Adams was elected a Representative in 1831 by the Anti-Mason party.

[2] James Moore Wayne, then Representative from Georgia, appointed Judge of the Supreme Court in 1835.

[3] She was Louise D'Avezac, the widow of a Jamaica planter, Moreau, and had married Mr. Livingston in New Orleans in 1805.

had a nuptual fete in his family, on the marriage of his adopted son, which gave rise to some difficulties respecting etiquette. He, (the Presd.) communicated to Mr. McC. his design that the Secretary of State should always take precedence of the foreign ministers at table, but that the rest of the Cabinet should follow the foreign ministers. Mr. McC. said this was an arrangement which he could not yield—that in the Council chamber as the Secretary of State was constitutionally entitled to the first seat next the President, he had no hesitation in yielding it to him, but in all other places, he claimed absolute equality and could not yield to so marked a distinction as the President proposed, that he considered the Cabinet as a unit. The argument was carried on some time. At last the President consented that *all* the members of the Cabinet should precede the foreign ministers, and that the President should lead Mrs. Livingston. This order was settled, and announced by his Private Secr. to the company. On learning it, the French minister urged the Dutch minister, as the oldest resident, to resist such an innovation and to maintain the right of precedence for the foreign ministers. Accordingly Mr. Huggins, remonstrated with the Private Secr. (the company all standing, dinner having been announced). The Private Secr. communicated the difficulty to the President. He at once, good humouredly said, "Well, I will lead the Bride, it is a family fête,—so we will wave all difficulties, and the company will please to follow as heretofore."

Now, triffling as this affair will appear, it may have serious political consequences. The Presd. and foreign ministers are dissatisfied with the Secr. of the Treasury, and the poor man is not of a temper to conciliate dissatisfactions,—and then too, the Secr. of State will resent the

Dr. William Thornton.

After a water-color by himself in the possession of
J. Henley Smith, Washington.

resistance made to the honor designed him by the President, and the ill will thus engendered between the two
first members of the Cabinet will doubtless influence their
deliberations.   And the Presdt. himself, never yet could
bear opposition.   The Bank question has been another
point of controversy, so much so, that joined with various
little matters, a member of congress told a friend of ours,
he should not be surprised at another blow up.   If these
details do not amuse you and the girls, I am sure they
will Lytleton, and as he is an invalid, I should be glad to
make him smile amidst his pains, but bid him remember
they are very confidential, and might bring me in a scrape
if made known, for folks would guess his informer.   Mrs.
Eaton's affair, at the beginning, was but a spark, but
what a conflagration did it cause.—Good morning, I am
called to dinner,—it is four oclock, and my fingers are
numbed,—the ground is covered with our fifth fall of
snow and the clouds look heavy with another,—what a
winter!

Saturday morning.   I had just seated myself by the
centre table in the parlour,—my usual seat, and taken my
pen to write you a few lines, when Mr. and Mrs. Everet[1]
came in,—they are very sensible, agreeable people, but
would be still more so if not so formal and precise.   Mrs.
Van Ransalear, in describing Mrs. E. to me the first
winter she was here, said the gentlemen called her a
hoity-toity woman.   In our formal morning visits, I have
seen nothing of this kind, she is the perfect lady, in appearance and manners, without pretensions of any kind.
The girls sit of a morning in the dining room, which
opens from this, where they read and sew together, seldom coming in to receive company, unless it is some one
whom they particularly wish to see, with the exception of

---

[1] Edward Everett was then serving in the House.

Julia, however, who always sits by me. After dinner and through the evening, all the girls come into the parlour and Mr. Smith and Bayard sit and read and write in the dining room. When we are alone, which is seldom the case, one of us reads aloud and the others sew, but few evenings pass without one, two or more visitors, and then chess, musick, back gammon &c. take the place of books and work. Last evening it was such bad weather, that we were certain of being alone and were comfortably seated with our books and work, when the bell rung and Mrs. Gurley and Mr. Colton, (a young clergyman) came in. She had brought her work, and Mr. C. wanted to play chess with me; so our circle was enlarged, without putting aside our work. Mr. Gurley,[1] (the model of my Sidney Jones) and Secretary to the Colonization Society is a most interesting man; in his books, a hero of romance; in his temper and life, one of the most perfect Christians I ever knew. He is our near neighbour and were he not so constantly and laboriously engaged would be a frequent visitor, for he seems to like us as much as we like him. His wife is very young, very beautiful and ingenuous and simple as a child,—not much mental strength or improvement but truly lovable. Mr. Colton is a so-so Yankee, a chaplain in the navy. Last night they staid until eleven, but at 9 oclock I, as usual, slipped out of the room with my Sue and went to our room, for she sleeps in my chamber. She has been so well for some weeks past, that when amused, she has generally sat up as late as the family. She is much better than I expected or even hoped. If the cough would yield, I should be quite easy, as in other respects she is better than she was last winter. She does not like to be treated as an invalid, and will not let me have any little delicacy pre-

[1] Ralph Randolph Gurley, a Presbyterian, one of the founders of Liberia.

pared exclusively for her and when I make jelly or
blanc mange, will not eat it unless all the family partake
of it.   Never did I know any one so little selfish.   She
gets wearied of sitting up and sewing and to lie down on
a sopha and read is the only indulgence she allows herself, and reproaches herself with laziness for doing that.
She has a small bed at the foot of mine, enclosed in a
screen.   She drinks red pepper tea through the day and
takes the syrup of squads mixed with paragoric at night,
and always carries a box of hoarhound candy or jujube
of which she uses a great deal.   I at times can scarcely
believe she is the subject of a dangerous disease.   Surely
of all the diseases that assail the human frame, this is
the most easy, as it is the most insidious,—no pain, no
uncomfortable feelings, for the slight and occasional
fever is pleasant and exhilerating.   Is it possible it is
undermining life?   I cannot at times realize it.   My
hopes of her recovery are much strengthened of late,—
at least of the continuance of life for many years.   I have
heard of so many similar cases, where the patient lived
for 10, 15, 20 years.

Ann has gone out this morning on her society duties,
to distribute clothes to the poor.   We have several families under our care in whom we take peculiar interest.
Good Mrs. Brush and her grand daughter, is the one that
we most care for.   In her old age, she is totally depend-
ant on her friends for support, being disabled by sickness
as well as old age from doing anything for herself.   So
humble, so pious, so cheerful, so contented,—I never saw
such a sufferer.   Her life is an eloquent sermon, it is
practical christianity.   Through how many hours of illness has she attended me!   And Mrs. Lawyer Jones[1]

[1] Wife of Walter Jones who was a leader of the District bar for many
years.

and Mrs. Seaton, she was with the latter at the successive deaths of five children, and she endeared herself
to us all. So you may believe in her helplessness, she
wants for no comfort. Another interesting sufferer is
an old English woman, 84 years old, without a single
acquaintance or relation on whom she has any claim, excepting such as humanity supplies. She is a mysterious
personage, a woman of fine education and delicate appearance,—report says, the daughter of a nobleman, who
eloped in early life with a husband of inferior birth.
Last week when I visited her, she was in such a dreadfully nervous state, that all the usual remedies failed;
after administering laudanum and ether, ineffectually, I
at last forced her to lie down, and succeeded in keeping
her in bed, and finally soothed her into tranquillity by
reading,—at first I tried the Bible, but that had not that
continuity of subject that fixed the thoughts,—she said
she loved poetry and that Pope was her favorite, so I
sent to my friend Mr. King, who lived near, and had
recommended Mrs. de la Plane to my care, for a vol and
read three books of the Essay on Man. This lulled and
composed her. Often she exclaimed, How beautiful,
how true, how sublime! When I read the line, the pur-
port of which was, "He reasons best, who can his soul
submit." "Oh," said she, "that I could submit, then
all would be easy, would be right!" In the evening
Mr. King called to make enquiries. "Did you not
think me crazy," said I, "when I sent for a vol of
Pope for a poor woman?" "Almost," said he laughing, "at least, thought I to myself, nobody but Mrs. Smith
would think of such a thing!" "Extraordinary cases
require extraordinary remedies." "True," he replied,
"and yours by its success proves it was judicious." I
acted from experience, for often and often, when every-

thing else has failed, I have been relieved from dreadful
nervous attacks by poetry. "Saul was relieved by
musick," observed Mr. King. These nerves——a carriage——It was Cornelia Barbour, daughter of Govr. B.
late minister to England. Her mother and father are
confined to the house by influenza, but I doubt not he
will find his voice to make a long speech in the Convention. I bade Cornelia, exert her eloquence and the
power of her charms to get Mr. Clay chosen. Oh, how
glad should I be to have old friends back again! Cornelia was as gay, charming and carressing as ever, she
hugged and kissed us heartily. As she went, my friend
Wood came in, his wife is worse. He brought me the
lines I had given him, (for I let him have whatever I
write, he takes such a lively interest in my pen-work)
which I hastily wrote for Louisa Bomford-Leay,—I mean
one evening she was here, to a little party Anna Maria
gave her. The bridal cake was crowned with a pair of
doves (in sugar) This device suggested the lines which
I hastily wrote and twisting the paper with some roses,
suspended it from the united bills of the doves. The
cake was first carried to Louisa. I stood near and told
her the doves had a message for her,—she disengaged
the billet-deux and found these lines:

> Gentle Doves, fly, fly away
> Swift, to the lovely Bride convey,
> Love's own emblem in this flower,
> To bloom in her domestic bower.
> Her joys be like the winter rose,
> Blooming 'till life's last season close.

The Bride and company professed themselves charmed
with the compliment, which at least was something new.

The morning is over, dinner is ready. I have found
so much pleasure in thus chatting with you that my work

and book have remained untouched. Another week too has closed. Closed after 7 days of cheerfulness and peace, be grateful my heart for so many mercies. Dear sister adieu until next week.

TO MRS. KIRKPATRICK

[Washington] Thursday, 15 Decr. 1831.

. . . . Mrs. Clay just calls. It is really impossible to get this letter finished. I promised to go out with her, so adieu.

Friday morning. 17th. The morning was so excessively cold yesterday, that I did not dream of any one's going out that could stay at home, and had seated myself to write to you, as I thought for the whole morning, when Mrs. C. came to claim my promise of making a course of morning visits. I did not find it so cold out as in the house and was on the whole better for my ride. Altho there is no probability of Mr. C.'s being chosen President,[1] yet the enthusiasm and unanimity with which he was chosen as a candidate by the convention could not but be gratifying. Mrs. C. has been quite sick; the first day she left the house, she came and sat most part of the morning with us and asked Ann to go with her to choose a bonnet &c for she seems to consider us as relatives. Wherever she went yesterday she was received with demontrations of affection; the fact is tho' a very plain and unadmired woman either in mind or manners, she is so kind, good, and above all, discreet, that I do not think during the many years she lived here she ever made an enemy, tho' she was not as popular and admired as other ladies have been. . .

[1] He was now in the Senate.

FROM MISS SEDGWICK[1]

New York 1 March 1832.

. . . . My dear Mrs. Smith I fear that while I was in your city I must have appeared to you very cold and unmoved by your cordial and constant kindness. I was not so. I saw so much that was new to me, had so many new subjects of curiosity and interest opened upon me, that I was the passive recipient of a multitude of impressions, without being able on my part to make any demonstrations of feeling. I assure you I brought with me and shall retain a deep sense of your cordiality and effective benevolence towards me. I have had much pleasure in reading your parting gift. You have delineated very common infirmities in our society in a natural and unoffending manner. It is a great matter to avoid alarming the pride of the class you would mend. Of all writers the *moral* writer has the most difficult task. The religious teacher comes forth invested with authority and armed with panoply divine, but he who would shoot folly as it flies rushes amidst a hostile army, and for the innocent brush he has given, may receive a cloud of arrows dipped in gall. I some times think with Molière who says somewhere in two very pithy lines, that there is no folly equal to his who attempts to mend the world. And yet the best of every age from the Divine Author of our religion down to the humblest but sincere follower have been engaged in this *mending* work. Then let us believe it a noble one and do not you, my dear Mrs. Smith, be faint hearted in it. . . .

Mr. Calhoun's pamphlet has here,[2] as I presume every

---

[1] Catherine Maria Sedgwick wrote a number of successful novels and sketches, one of which "Redwood" (1824) being published anonymously was translated into French and attributed to J. Fenimore Cooper.

[2] In reply to General Jackson's charges in the Seminole affair.

where, produced a great sensation. I am not addicted to political reading but the atmosphere of Washington was still about me, for to tell the honest truth I believe it was the light of Mr. Calhoun's splendid eye still lingering in my imagination, and I read this with interest or at least I'll swear to every word of Mr. C.'s letters. They are written with the pen and spirit of a true gentleman, a spirit of rectitude, delicacy and refinement, and I trust he will break the net his enemies have been weaving around him. The impressions of the unprejudiced seem to me to be all in his favor, and it is the few and not the mass, in our part of the country, who look thro' the witching glass of party darkly. Mr. C.'s face charmed me, it is stamped with nature's aristocracy, and with honest Caleb I am a thorough believer in "visnomy." But are we not a happy people to be sitting by our parlor fire-sides and getting up an agitation with such topics when the nations of Europe are about to pour their blood like water and tears like rain for political existence? . . .

TO MRS. KIRKPATRICK

Monday, September 3rd 1832.
[Sidney]

Summer has gone! It departed in a violent storm and autumn commenced with weather almost as cold as it concludes. It is a rainy, a right down rainy day, such as I love. Seated by my window looking out on the beautiful hills and on the close surrounding trees, listening to the pattering of the rain and watching the waving of the boughs in the wind, I could truly enjoy this aspect of nature, were it not for the thought of the hundreds and hundreds of my fellow citizens who must suffer, alas, fatally suffer from exposure to this weather. Since the hard rain on Friday and the cold which succeeded it, many poor creatures have perished with the cholera. Although it is two weeks since it made its appearance in the central part of the city, not a case had occurred in the eastern or western extremeties. About the middle of last week a number of cases appeared in the western part, viz. near Georgetown, in the vicinity of Rock Creek, the mouth of the Tiber and the canal,—all around our friend Dr. Sim. He spent the day with us yesterday and went with us to Rock Creek church. When he left the city there were within his knowledge eleven lying dead and five or six who must die in the course of the day, in that part of the city. We found the hearse in the church yard, and persons digging the grave of an old neighbor, but late resident in the city. On Saturday morning after eating a hearty breakfast she was taken ill and at 4 oclock in the afternoon was dead. Although our city has none of the narrow streets and alleys and filthy wharves, etc., of a commercial city and of a dense population, it has other local circumstances as unfavorable to health and as prolific in cases of disease peculiar to itself. This season especially, several large public works are going on—The Canal, the McAdamizing Pennsylvania Avenue, and the opening the ground for the conveyance of water; the latter of which requires digging for miles and through hills, as the source of the water is distant and far below the level of the reservoir on Capitol hill. It is a great work, which added to the others, has drawn to the city at least a thousand laborers, in addition to our own, most of them Irish. Boarding as they must among our poorest citizens, they are crowded into wretched cabins, where in some cases they have been found without bedding, seats or tables,—literally lying, sitting and eating on the floor, so closely packed that they had only room to stretch themselves out; this is the worst, but others are not much better off. Thus are they lodged at night after, being exposed all day to the open air. Bayard says it makes his heart ache as he goes along the avenue, to see the poor creatures sitting on piles of stones in the burning heat of the noon day sun, after having been exposed to the cold fogs of the morning, their heads sunken on their bosoms, their eyes never raised to the passers by, looking so sad and diconsolate. For how can they be otherwise, strangers as they are, working in the midst of disease, in continual apprehension of its attack, and without any hope beyond that of being, when attacked, thrown in a cart and carried to a Hospital, which they fear as they fear the grave itself? So averse are the poor generally and they in particular to going there, that they conceal the first symptoms, so that when the last stage comes on, it is commonly fatal. Even then, they are carried by force, for voluntarily they will not go. Last week about 400 Swiss citizens arrived in the city; not being able to find better employment, they were obliged to go to cracking stones on the avenue. Poor souls, when I think of the hopes that led them from their far off country, across the wide Atlantic, and the dreadful reverse they have met with, my heart bleeds for them. The population of our city is made up of individuals from all parts of America,—I was going to say the world, for we have a great many foreigners, all, in some way or another, dependent on the government and changing with the changing administrations, each family standing as it were by itself and caring only for itself, unconnected by any of these ties of common interest, which unite the permanent inhabitants of other cities, and without the bonds of kindred, long acquaintanceship or connections which form the cement of society, destitute of that pride of citizenship, that love of country, that home feeling, which stimulates the people of other cities, to make exertions and sacrifices for the common good.   Now, when assailed by a common calamity, each individual thinks only of his own security.   Efforts are making to awaken public sympathy, to arouse the principle of humanity. As yet the disease has attacked only the poor foreigners, labourers and blacks.   When it reaches a more respectable class, it will doubtless awaken a deeper interest and livelier sympathy.   But we have no funds, and the administrators of the general government do not feel at liberty to apply public money to the present necessities of the city.   Our papers will give little information as to the prevalence of the disease.   No regular reports are made by physicians and cannot be of interments, when the poor and the blacks can without expense or trouble bury their own dead in the commons.

Friday evening, Sept. 7. . . . . The disease is increasing and spreading to all parts of the city, but the proportions of deaths have greatly decreased.   The system of depletion has been found very successful,—bleeding and calomel, the chief agents.   *No stimulants whatever.*   He [Dr. Sim] brought me a lancet to-day and gave me instructions how to use it.   Of course, only in cases where medical aid could not be procured and the risque of not bleeding was greater than its being done by me.   I know not whether in any case I could muster courage, but it will do no harm to have the lancet.   He told us of some wonderful cases affected by bleeding and calomel, the doses, immense.   It is dark and I must finish this tomorrow morning.

Saturday morning, 8th.   I feel this morning, to use

a very vulgar, but very expressive comparison, as limber
as a wet rag and as tremulous as an aspen. For not
only all day and every day are our nerves thus excited,
but often at night. . . . .

Bayard, by Dr. Sim's express direction, left the city
on Tuesday and is now with us. The cholera was all
around him and no longer confined to the intemperate
and the poor, but extending to those of regular habits
and comfortable circumstances. It is now for my dear
husband only that I have to fear and tremble. Several
cases have occurred near the Bank. If tranquillity of
mind is a preservation, he will be safe, for never did I
see him more calm and firm. He goes into the city
every day, rain or sunshine, and does not come home
until four oclock. While in the city he keeps in his own
room. Poor William who drives him in is dreadfully
afraid, and no wonder, as the disease is so fatal to the
blacks. I suppose three times as many are victims to it
as whites; they and the foreigners, Irish and Swiss are
its peculiar mark. I know not whether you remember
Brown, whose family Mr. Smith bought and whose
daughter died that August you were here. He died
after a few hours illness, and his son who attended on
and buried him, came out directly afterwards to us. He
was not well, I gave him medicine and he is now free
from complaint. All our black people are very much
down-cast, particularly Priscilla, having among the victims to this pestilence lost several friends. I do all I
can to cheer them, for which they are very grateful.
As long as this north-west wind blows, our neighbors
think we are secure, but fear a southern wind would
bring it into the country. . . . .

What may almost be called a revival, prevails among
them. Great attention to religion is awakened, num-

bers have, or are to join the church next Sabbath and I
sincerely hope a great and permanent reform will take
place among our poor labouring class. You will see
in the National Intelligencer, (which I believe Lytleton
takes) notice of Mr. Colton's attendance in the hospitals.
He really does seem like another Apostle. He has a
wonderful influence in the city, although it is but 5 or
6 months since he took Mr. John's place in Trinity
church. He has warmed all his congregation with his
own zeal for the present sufferers. The ladies have
formed themselves into societies, some to make up
clothes for the poor, sick, some to prepare the food for
them and others to take charge of orphans. The two
Miss Tayloes, hitherto the gayest of the gay, most fashionable and world-devoted among our young ladies, are
said to have become very serious under his preaching,
and will most probably join the church. He is a delightful preacher. I shall try and make his acquaintance if
we live to meet next winter. But he looks as if he would
not last so long. Consumption seems to have marked him
for her own. His voice is sepulchral, and very, very
solemn. Last week he preached three times at Rock-
Creek, without neglecting his weekly and Sabbath services in the city, and since has been continually occupied
in visiting and comforting the sick. I cannot hear a
word of our minister's being thus engaged. His wife is
a sickly-timid woman, and I fear will use her influence to
keep him back from this trying duty. The spirit of
benevolence during this past week has been completely
aroused in the city and is in active exercise. I feel my
present uselessness and inactivity painfully. . . . .

Monday morning. Yesterday we had an overflowing
congregation. Old Rock-Creek was crowded. The
circumstances were solemn and affecting. A great

many young persons joined the church, with ceremonious not usual in the Episcopalian church. Quite Methodistical. Dr. Sim, did not accompany us, but came during the service and the girls all rode home with him, in his carriage. No doubt, most of the neighbors, think they are married. He could not pass the day,—some of his patients were to ill to spare him so long. The disease continues rapidly to extend and increase but has become so manageable that not many deaths occur. My fine collection of stimulants of all kinds, set out in order on my mantle piece, bundles of linen &c., &c., are pronounced worse than useless.

TO MISS ANNA MARIA H. SMITH

[Washington] Saturday morning, 15th Decr. 1832.

. . . . What do you think of Septemea's having become a Catholick? It is even so and I believe she will soon publicly join that church. Mary Ann Graham has done so, likewise Jeanette Hart, and Mrs. Tucker told us Mrs. Hall too, but I have heard it from no one else. Mr. Pise[1] is carrying all before him. His zeal, his eloquence and his personal beauty combine to give him an influence no priest has before had amongst us. When he preaches, the church is so crowded, that not only the seats but the isles are crowded. You will have seen by the papers that he is chosen chaplain to the Senate. Mr. Poindexter who called here yesterday, said the motive was to show the universal toleration of our government. Mr. Palfrey has been to see us, but our own clergyman Mr. Smith has not been inside our

[1] Charles Constantine Pise, a Catholic priest of great renown in his day. He was a friend of Henry Clay, who secured his appointment as chaplain to the Senate. He is the only Catholic who ever held the post.

door since we came to town.   He visits no one and his
sermons are growing more and more metaphysical and
political and becoming more and more a mere student.
When Mrs. McComb[1] came to the Dorcas Society the
other day, she took the same occasion to pay me a long
visit, and I liked her better than usual.   I see very little
of Mrs. Thornton.   It is now ten days since I have been
there, the weather and my pen engagements have prevented my going out, except to see sick neighbours.   Mr.
King was here last night and had a long talk with Ann,
on religious subjects.   The room was so warm that my
head turned, I was dull and could not entertain him,
being more inclined to go to sleep.

TO MRS. KIRKPATRICK

[Washington,] Christmas, 1832.

.   .   .   .   The ambition some felt for its honors
exists no longer, and this was one of the strongest stimulants to activity and exertion I ever felt.   But a life in
Washington cures one of ambition for honors and distinctions, by exhibiting them in all their vanity, instabil-
ity, and transitoriness, and unveiling at the same time all
the pains and some vexations appertaining to them.   I
wonder if Mr. Clay realizes these things and can learn
to be content with the portion he possesses.   Were we to
have a peep into his bosom what a lesson we should
learn.   And Mr. Calhoun,[2] will his high soarings end
in disappointment and humiliation or be drowned in
blood?   However he may now err, he is one of the

---

[1] Wife of Major General Alexander Macomb, commanding the army.
[2] He was in the midst of his efforts to apply the nullification theory.

noblest and most generous spirits I have ever met with.
I am certain *he* is deceived himself, and believes he is
now fulfilling the duty of a *true patriot*.   What a happy
nation we were !   Alas, and may we not write, *we are?*
The impending political storm, as you may easily suppose
is almost the exclusive object of interest and conversation.   .   .   .

TO MRS. KIRKPATRICK

[Washington,] January 17, 1834.

It is a rainy day, and therefore I may hope it will be
free from the continual interruptions to which I am subject on fine sunshiny days—though as *they* have been
rare this winter, you may imagine according to that
rule that most of my days were interrupted leisure.   But
I know not how it is, I have very little leisure for either
reading or writing; interchanging visits with above
100 people consumes a great deal of time—now and then,
most agreeably, as for instance one day this week, out
of 12 visits which I paid, 3 were pleasant, 2 interesting.
With Mrs. Gorham[1] I sat I am sure more than an hour,
and when I left her, thought to myself our conversation might have furnished two entertaining biographical
sketches, with the effect of perfect contrast.   She began by making inquiries about Mrs. Clay, which from
the interest she took in the subject led me into many
details and gave a continuity to speaking, which made
Mrs. Gorham only a listener; but we exchanged our
parts and she became the speaker, I the listener, when
she entertained me excessively with the account she

---

[1] Wife of Benjamin Gorham, a Representative from Boston, son of
Nathaniel Gorham.

gave of Mrs. Otis—the dashing Mrs. Otis.[1] Mrs. G. is
one of the most sensible, best informed, frank and agreeable women that have ever been in Washington. I hope
to improve our acquaintance into intimacy, particularly
if, as she hopes, Miss Sedgwich comes on to stay with
her. I afterwards called on Mrs. Wirt, scarcely, however, hoping to see her, as she has within this month lost
her eldest daughter Mrs. Randal. But she sees her
friends. I found her quite composed. She and her
two daughters were in the parlour dressed to receive
company and though serious, not melancholy. Here I
had an interesting visit. In the evening we went round
to drink at Mrs. Thornton's and Mrs. Wayne living
next door, I determined to step in, and pay her a social
visit. She looked so comfortable, so homelike and at
the same time so elegant, and as usual she was so
pleasant, that had I not been engaged to Mrs. Thornton I should have liked to have passed the whole evening with her. A handsomely furnished room, was
cheerfulized by a large bright fire. She, her daughter
and son were sitting by the centre table reading, on one
side the fire place, drawn forward, was a handsome
pianno, on the other side a comfortable sopha. How
delightfully she does converse! Her daughter, though
a sweet, modest girl, will never be a belle, or have half
her mother's attraction. The son has neither the modesty of the sister, nor the animation of father or mother.
Being in deep mourning, she does not go out, but Judge
Wayne with his daughter and son go to all the parties;
of which however there have not been as many as usual.
Mrs. McClane as lady of Secty, of State, has come out
splendidly, every week having a dinner and evening

---

[1] She was Eliza Henderson Bordman, married Harrison Gray Otis, of
Hartford Convention fame, in 1817, and became a social leader and authoress.

party. We do not visit now. I could not submit to her
capricious ways. She invited us to one of her parties
last week, but as she had not returned my last visit we
would not go, so I suppose that will end our social intercourse. Neither do we see the other ladies of the administration. Indeed our society is divided by the two
political parties which divide our government, and in
society, as well as in politics the opposition, I think,
carries the day. Mrs. Clay, Mrs. Webster, Sprague and
many others are ladies of the opposition—and among
the citizens, with few exceptions all the most respectable
and fashionable people. The General and his friend
Van Buren are going out of fashion and I suspect out
of place—Their popularity, if all I hear is truth, is rapidly decreasing. Mr. Clay is in fine health and spirits;
frank, cordial and good humored. I cannot help indulging some presidential hopes in his favour. Mrs.
Clay is the same kind familiar friend and comes every
day or two and passes part of the morning with us—but
her health is indifferent. Last evening we went together to a large party at our neighbour, Mrs. Taylor.
She called early and sat an hour with us before we went
to the party. James Bayard was here, too, but could
not as he had intended, accompany us, as he had severely
sprained his arm by a fall. The party was as gay and
splendid, as it could be where the close packed living
mass concealed all the beauty of the inanimate objects
in the room. Miss Wharton of Phila. is the reigning
Belle. I made my way through the dense mass to get
a view of her, pioneered and guarded by Col. House,
but after all my trouble, was disappointed in her exceeding beauty. Virginia Southard, I think much handsomer. The noise and crowd was too great for conversation, and I soon grew weary and was glad at 11

o'clock to get home. I was gratified by Julia's good looks. She was dressed in plain white satin and pink and white flowers on her head—her hair arranged by a hair dresser. But in such a crowd it mattered little how one was dressed. I shall not again go to such a large party—I cannot bear them, and expected this to have been a small one.

TO MRS. KIRKPATRICK

Washington, Febry. 10th, 1834.

How often, how very often on awakening, have I said, before I arose, "This morning I will pass in writing to my dear sister," and then arranged in my mind all I had to say. But something would occur some necessary piece of work must first be dispatched, some errand, some visit or some visitor interfered and the intended letter was put off for tomorrow; tomorrow and tomorrow have come and gone, till in their accumulation they have become weeks, instead of days, and yet on retrospect seem like nothing. Pleasantly however have they passed, and if marked by no event that stamp'd a character on the days to come they have produced present content and left agreeable impressions. Compared with our acquaintances, we lead quite a retired and domestic life, viz., we neither give parties, nor go to parties, yet we are seldom or ever alone. Sometimes one, sometimes a dozen are added to our family circle. Last evening, for instance, when Genl. Taylor went away, he observed, "you have had a charming little party this evening," "Party," said I, "it was no party, viz., no one was invited, but all came in accidently." "Really," replied he. When he entered, Mrs. Barret

and Mrs. Smith were playing chess at a little table, on
one side of the fire, Mr. Barret and I, at the other side,
and round the centre table were clustered Virginia
Southard, Mrs. Bryan, Mrs. Brooks, Ann, Julia and
Bayard; in the corner of the sopha sat Anna and George
Bomford winding worsteds, and when Genl. T. and his
young friend Capt. Duval entered, the room looked full.
And during the day, from eleven oclock, it had not been
empty.   Virginia is passing some days with us, and yesterday Mrs. Barret came early to spend a social day.
You should have seen us, how comfortable we looked
and how industrious, Virginia and Anna doing their canvas work in frames; Ann and I doing ours on our hands,
each with a little table before us, covered with worsteds
of every shade and colour.   Mrs. Barret and Julia working muslin, all circled round a blazing fire, while without
doors it was cold and lowering.   The bell rings,—it is
Mrs. Clay, who feeling at home, sat down among without
disturbing us.   The bell rings,—some ladies you do not
know, who put us a little out, but they did not stay long.
Some shade of colour was wanting, the shop was distant, but the difficulty was surmounted by Mrs. Clay's
telling the girls to take her carriage, she would sit with
us till they returned.   Virginia and Anna ran up stairs
for bonnets and cloaks and just as they got down, Mr.
Bryan entered, bringing with him a very handsome
young man, whom he introduced, but finding the girls
on the wing, he handed them into the carriage, jumped
in with them, and let the handsome stranger find his
way on foot, (a love-struck partner of Virginia's, as we
afterwards found) Mrs. Clay took up one of the girl's
work and our needles were resumed, when the bell again
rung, and Mr. Calhoun came in.   It seemed quite like
old times to have him and Mrs. Clay together, separated

as they have long been, not only by distance, but still more by politics. I dare say he sat near an hour and we had a talk of old times, as well as present times, but said not a word of the future, where collisions of interest may again separate these once friends. After he went, Catherine Smith came in, to show us a screen she had just finished, the canvas was worked over white velvet and the threads afterwards drawn out, which has a beautiful effect. It was the finest specimen of the worsted work I have seen and our exclamations of admiration were re-iterated. This work is becoming quite a mania here, even I could not resist, but I cannot work after a pattern, or count stitches and have astonished the girls with my fine bunch of flowers, done al fresco. I compose the flowers as I proceed, one after the other, fitting them in as suits. I am as much delighted with this work as with painting. Virginia, Ann and Anna are all working ottomans for Mrs. Clay and I am doing her lamp and stands. At Lowel a present of a great quantity of worsted was made her and we are thus helping her to use them. She does the filling up, the girls only do the flowers, for which they had gone to seek for some peculiar colour. But when once in the carriage and knowing Mrs. C. was comfortably fixed with us, they took the opportunity to make some other calls and it was almost three oclock when they came back, so I could not but ask my cousin Bryan to stay to dinner and soon after Bayard came in and brought George Bomford, as he often does, to dinner too. Well, n'importe, we were all friends and relatives, it was only adding two more plates and another leaf of the table. Mr. Bryan is devoted to Virginia, he has eyes, ears and tongue for no one else. Whether it is love or flirtation I know not. For as Virginia is quite ton, young men distinguish themselves by being in her train, and self-love is often the cause of the devoted admiration they profess for great Belles. But Virginia is worthy of admiration for herself alone. She really looks beautifully, —the latter part of last evening she went to a party at Mrs. Webster's. Anna and I sat up until after 11 for her, and when she came home, her father, her almost idolizing father with her, she looked not only lovely, but splendid, so sparkling were her eyes, so radiant her countenance and so brilliant her complexion. I suppose she had been greatly admired, for Mr. Southard looked so pleased, so delighted. The diary of this day will give you some idea of most of our days, though it is seldom our visitors are as interesting and agreeable, too generally they are commonplace and indifferent, and I would prefer being alone with my family and books. As for parties, I could not stand them. I went to two, but love my own fireside too much to go to any more. Anna is almost as averse. She has been likewise only to two or three this winter. Although we have invitations to most, if not all that are given. Julia is the only individual in the family, that really likes to go out. Ann is very much engaged in her various societies and the visitations and duties they render necessary, and I have several interesting families to visit. The one in which I take most concern is that of a young woman in the last stage of consumption, both she and her mother are destitute widows. The invalid is young and very pleasing in her appearance. I love to sit with her. There is a great deal of suffering and sadness this winter among the labouring class, and how society is to form a system that will give permanent, or even regular relief to a class, who depend on daily labour and never make provision for a day beyond, I know not. The very remedies provided by benevolence seem to increase the evil by making them still more improvident. What is to be done? Employment would do, but Houses of Industry require not only great capital, but great, very great perseverance, zeal and integrity in the administrators. Few if any have succeeded. Besides the labouring class, there are other poor, still more to be pitied, sudden reverses, such as dismisal from office produces in one day reduced from competence to poverty, as our acquaintances the Elgars. The blow to them was quite unexpected—occasioned by some disagreement with the President. The family will leave the city in the spring and I believe retire to a little farm in Ohio. How little suited will the girls be for a farm in Ohio where female servants are scarcely to be had. Pecuniary distress is extending to every class and every part of our country. The present state of affairs, unless some compromise between the opposing parties take place, will go on from bad to worse. And what is the point in dispute? Not any great political principle, but the rival pretentions of two or three individuals to the Presidency, for disguise it as they will, the point to be decided is, Who shall be President? Mr. Van B. hoped to make himself so, by destroying the Bank and its vast political influence, which had exerted hostility to him. And his opponent, whoever it may be, hopes by establishing the Bank and securing its influence to put down Mr. Van B. and his party. Thus the ambition of individuals, is the main spring of the great political machine which we call *The Government*.

TO MRS. BOYD

Washington, Feb. 19th, Wednesday.   1834

. . . . Diverging as I have to other subjects, the idea of poor Dr. S[tevens][1] has not for a moment been absent from my mind, pray write soon again and tell me how he supports his affliction.   Perhaps I more sensibly feel it, from that preparation of the mind for such impressions, produced by the death of Mr. Wirt.   He died yesterday.   Most solemnly have I felt this affecting event.   He never recovered from the loss of his dear daughter Agnes.   His whole system was shaken by it.   His mind detached earthly interests and eagerly and ardently fixed on heavenly.   Preparation for the awful event which has now taken place, has been his chief business for the last two years.   On one Sabbath he attended public worship, on the next he was on his dying bed.   His daughter, Mrs. Randal, died about a month ago.   I have not heard how Mrs. Wirt is supported under this sore affliction.   Never were any couple united by a fonder or stronger affection.   Such a man could not but be loved with ardent and exclusive affection.   Great, good, amiable beyond his fellows, kind and loving in his disposition, frank, gentle and cordial in his manners, he could not be known without being loved.   I was last evening reading over some pages he had written in my book of souvenirs, on the eve of his leaving Washington.   The reflection there traced suited the occasion and what he said of his departed friends and the vain pursuits of life, applied to him so forcibly, that I felt as if though dead, he still spoke, as if I heard his voice.   . . .

[1] Alexander Hodgson Stevens, a great surgeon in New York.

FROM MRS. MADISON

Montpellier Augt. 31, 1834.[1]

I have received with due sensibility my dear friend your kind letter of the 29th and can assure you that if a Biographical sketch must be taken, its accomplishment by your pen, would be more agreeable to me than by any other to which such a task could be committed, being persuaded not only of its competency, but of the just dispositions by which it would be guided.

Dolly and Mary are now with us, but if I had known your wish as it regards my letters to them, and some of mine to their mother [*torn out*] have thrown light on the early occurrences of my life, but that they contain my unvarnished opinions and feelings on different subjects. As it is I will have them sent here, when the girls return to the city, in order that I may select those, at all worthy of your attention.

My family are all Virginians except myself, who was born in N. Carolina, whilst my Parents were there on a visit of one year, to an Uncle. Their families on both sides, were among the most respectable, and they, becoming members of the society of friends soon after their marriage manumitted their Slaves, and left this state for that of Pennsylvania, bearing with them their children to be educated in their religion—I believe my age at that time was 11 or 12 years—I was educated in Philadelphia where I was married to Mr. Todd in 1790, and to Mr. Madison in 94, when I returned with him to the soil of my Father, and to Washington, where you have already traced me with the kindness of a

---

[1] This letter, the editor assumes, was the basis of the sketch of Mrs. Madison in Herrick and Longacre's National Portrait Gallery, printed anonymously but doubtless written by Mrs. Smith.

Sister. In the year 91, and after the death of my Father, my Mother received into her house some Gentlemen as boarders—and in 93 she left Philadelphia to reside with her daughter Washington—afterwards, with my sister Jackson, and occasionally with me.—I am sensible that this is but a general answer to your. Should any particular information be desired, I will endeavor to furnish it.—

I am sorry to add that Mr. Madison's health has not been and is not now so advanced, as might be inferred from occasional references to it in the newspapers.— The effect of his severe and protracted rheumatism has been increased by other indispositions—one of which still hanging on him he is happily however, exempt from much pain, and every favourable change in him, brightens my hope of his recovery. He unites with me in every good wish and affectionate remembrance for yourself, Mr. Smith and your daughters.

Your constant friend.

TO MRS. KIRKPATRICK

[Washington] [1834]

. . . . If I dared to say so, I would say that the subject of a heriditary monarchy have a better chance of well-being and tranquillity. But this would be treason. The Senate chamber is now the centre of attraction, not only of political interests, but of the fashionable world likewise. It is daily crowded by all the beauty and fashion of *our* great world—crowded almost to suffocation. There never were so many strangers, especially ladies, before in the city and these, having no other occupation, or place of display, every day resort to this arena, where our intellectual gladiators exhibit their various and gigantic powers, not simply for the good of the country, but for the entertainment of the audience. The atmosphere and crowd are so oppressive, that it is an exhibition I cannot partake in, otherwise the real eloquence of the present Senate, would prove irresistibly attractive. Genl. Preston's[1] was of the most popular kind and charmed every one that heard it. But as to producing change of opinion, or conviction in the minds of the hearers or readers, all this eloquence might have been spared for *personal, individual* interest, only, will opperate this affect. Place, not principle is now-a-days the object contended for. And after all, when the highest place is attained, is the successful occupant happier? For no sooner is it obtained than he becomes the object of abuse, and feels himself tottering in place and reputation.

Rumours prevail of an approaching change in the Cabinet. Poor Mr. McClane[2] after all the sacrifices of private and domestic comfort, after all his labours and strivings, to retain his hard earned place for so short a time! If I supposed our political intrigues and parties amused you, I could give you a little vol. of such sketches. From hear say, however, for Mr. Smith is wholly disconnected with politics and I take no further interest in them, than personal regard for some of the actors inspire. I cannot help, anxiously wishing that Mrs. Clay, may once more be a resident amongst us. She is such an affectionate, sincere, kind friend, such a good woman, that her being here, adds very much to our social enjoyment. It is seldom that two days pass

[1] William Campbell Preston, Senator from South Carolina from 1832 to 1842, a brilliant orator and a follower of Calhoun.
[2] Louis McLane retired to his country place in Cecil County, Maryland, this year.

without her coming to see us and after sitting an hour
or two asking one or the other of us to ride and visit
with her which this winter is peculiarly convenient and
agreeable. Her health is so bad, that she never goes
out of an evening. While I think of it, let me give you
Mrs. Bordeau and Mrs. Thornton's kindest remembrance to you. . . . Mrs. Bomford, we do not often
see, she has at present so large a family (her house
being full of friends and relations) that she cannot often
leave home, but when she does come to see us, her cordial kindness is refreshing to ones heart. As to our
domestic matters, my dear sister, I have gratefully to acknowledge they are more comfortable and cheerful than
they often have been. We all enjoy good health and
good spirits, subject only to transient and occasional
interruptions. . . .

TO MRS. KIRKPATRICK

[Washington] Wednesday, 12th 1835 January.

. . . . They all paid long visits, and this morning,
just this minute, Miss Martineau.[1] At so early an hour
I expected no one and was so engaged in this letter, that
I scarcely raised my head, when the door opened and
two plain looking ladies (one of the ladies, was Miss
Jeffries, her friend and companion) walked in. They
had walked and I had not attended to the ringing of
the door bell, not expecting visitors at this hour. "I
have come early," said she, "to make sure of finding
you at home, and because it is my only disengaged time.
I yesterday planned a quiet sitting of two hours with
you, but I found it impossible." She is a woman you

[1] Harriet Martineau came over in the summer of 1834, when she was 32
years of age and in the zenith of her fame.

would love, so plain, unaffected and quiet in her manners and appearance, yet animated in conversation.
She brought me a letter of introduction from Mrs. Eck-
art, and sent it with her card, the day after her arrival,
otherwise I do not know whether I should have called
on her, under our present plan of domesticity, and the
feelings thereby induced, for when one lives out of company one shrinks from it. Accompanied by the girls I
called on her, sent in my name. There were three or
four other ladies in the room, but her advancing to
receive us, was a sufficient indication that she was Miss
Martineau. She was sitting in a corner of the sopha,
which supported the arm and hand, which held the
speaking-tube to her ear, she handed it to me saying,
"Do you know the use of this?" I answered affirma-
tively by an inclination of my head and putting the tube
to my lips, soon forgot I held it, and conversed as easily
as if not through this, it must be confessed, awkward
medium. As I had always understood she was of the
Liberal if not radical party, the advocate of the poor
and of the working-class, I did not anticipate the reception she has met with from our dignitaries and fash-
ionables. But the English minister was the first to wait
on her, introduced her into the Senate, to the President, &c., &c., which at once made her *Ton*. She has
literally been overwhelmed with company. I have been
told that the day after her arrival near 600 persons
called, (an exaggeration I suppose) but the number
was immense. Poor I had been planning to show her
the same kind of friendly, plain attentions I had done
Mrs. Brenton and Miss Sedgwick, and offered to call
with the carriage and accompany her to Congress, to
make her calls of ceremony, &c., &c. When I found
these calls had been dispensed with, and the President's

family and Secretaries ladies had first called on her, I told her I did not give nor go to large parties, but should be glad to see her in a social and domestic manner. This I repeated this morning and told her when the hurry of her gay engagements was over, I would ask a quiet day. "Name what day you please after this week, and it shall be reserved for you," replied she. Yesterday she dined at the President's, and in the evening went to a large party. Today she dines at Sir Charles Vaughan's[1] and in the evening a party at Mrs. Butler's[2] (the attorney general) two large evening parties to which she had promised to go, violent headaches, induced by the crowds of company during the whole day, obliged her to send an appology. Her health is very delicate. During the last year she has been laboriously employed, to such a degree as to impair her health. Absolute relaxation and change of scene were prescribed, and she thought she could obtain both these remedies by making the tour of U. S. But if followed by such crowds, her aim will be defeated. From her manners and appearance no one would believe it possible she could be so distinguished, celebrated, followed. The drollest part of the whole is, that these crowds, at least in Washington, go to see the lion and nothing else. I have not met with an individual, except Mrs. Seaton and her mother, who have read any of her works, or knew for what she is celebrated. Our most fashionable, exclusive Mrs. Tayloe, said she intended to call, and asked what were the novels she had written and if they were pretty? The gentlemen laugh at a woman's writing on political economy. Not one of them has the least idea of the nature of her work. I tried to explain them to Mr. Frelinghusen, Clay, Southard and others.

[1] The British Minister.   [2] Benjamin F. Butler of New York.

Harriet Martineau.

But enough of Miss Martineau for the present. If she interests you, tell me so and I will give you what further details. But perhaps like your Bayard you may think it all ridiculous. . . . .

FROM MR. AND MRS. MADISON

Montpellier Jany. 17, 1835.

Be assured my dear friend that we reciprocate all the good wishes which your letter has so kindly conveyed to us this day—for yourself—Mr. Smith, and your amiable family—and truly, your observations on our acquaintances accord also, with my feelings on the subject—my experience teaches, that our hearts recur and cling to early attachments, as the most happy of our lives. I ought now to offer many apologies for my silence, and if I was not acquainted with your goodness and forbearance, I should despair of forgiveness— but I trust in a simple statement of facts to shew you that my delinquency has not proceeded from want of love, and confidence in your friendship, nor am I without explanations, which will at least mitigate it. My letters to my sister Todd at the closing scenes of the War, happen to be with her in Kentucky, and I was unwilling to have them exposed to the mail, if I had been sure of their arrival in time, and that they contained anything worthy of being extracted. I might plead also my constant engagements of different sorts at home, which have not permitted me to search our papers, and bring my mind to the revival of scenes, or circumstances that might possibly throw a faint interest over a recital of them, and lastly I must in candour say, that I have felt more than a mere reluctance in being a Judge and witness, of incidents if existing, that might be worthy of the use to be made of them.

Your enquiries after my dear Husband will be partially answered by himself. He is better in health than he was two months ago, tho' still feeble and confined to his rooms—we trust however that with great care against the cold of this Winter, he will be able to take exercise in his Carriage when the Spring season shall cheer us again. I have been afflicted for the last two weeks with Influenza, the violence of which seems slowly passing away, altho' the cough continues.

I send you an engraving from Stuart's portrait, which tho' indifferently executed, is a better likeness than Mr. Wood's, which I would send also, but that the *stage* has ceased to run to and from Orange C. House for a few days, on account of bad roads.

I hope the efforts of our friend Mr. Clay, in his interesting report, to keep "sweet peace" without a loss of honour, may prove successful. A war between the United States and France that would cost both so much, for a cause apparently insignificant, would be a *spectacle* truly deplorable, in the present state of the World.

Ever affectionately yours,
D. P. MADISON.

I am very thankful, my kind friend, for the interest you take in my health. It is not good, and at my age, nature can afford little of the medical aid she exerts on younger patients. I have indeed got through the most painful stages of my principal malady, a diffusive and obstinate Rheumatism, but I feel its crippling effects on my limbs, particularly my hands and fingers, as this little effort of the pen will shew. I owe my thanks to

Mr. Smith also, for the friendly lines which accompanied
your former letter to Mrs. M. and the good wishes conveyed in your last.   Assure him of the continuance of
my great esteem and cordial regards.   May you both
long enjoy the blessing of health, with every other
necessary to fill the measure of your happiness.

                    JAMES MADISON.[1]

TO MRS. KIRKPATRICK

                    Washington, Febr. 4th 1835.

. . . . Friday 5th. And now for Miss Martineau,
since you desire to hear a little more about her, particularly of the day she passed here. But I really must
give you a previous scene which amused me extremely
and will not be without some diversion for you. The
day previous to our little dinner party, I sent for Henry
Orr, whom I had always employed when I had company and who is the most experienced and fashionable
waiter in the city. He is almost white, his manners
gentle, serious and respectful, to an uncommon degree
and his whole appearance quite gentlemanly. "Henry,"
said I, when he came, "I am going to have a small
dinner party, but though small, I wish it to be peculiarly
nice, every thing of the best and most fashionable. I
wish you to attend, and as it is many years since I have
dined in company, you must tell me what dishes will
be best. "Boulli," I suppose, "is not out of fashion?"
"No, indeed, Ma'am! A Boulli at the foot of the table
is indispensable, no dinner without it." "And at the
head?" "After the soup, Ma'am, fish, boil'd fish, and
after the Fish, canvas-backs, the Boulli to be removed,

[1] He died June 28, following.   His letter is in a painful trembling hand.

and Pheasants." "Stop, stop Henry," cried I, "not so many removes if you please!" "Why, ma'am, you said your company was to be a dozen, and I am only telling you what is absolutely necessary. Yesterday at Mr. Woodbury's there was only 18 in company and there were 30 dishes of meat." "But Henry I am not a Secretary's lady. I want a small, genteel dinner." "Indeed, ma'am, that is all I am telling you, for side dishes you will have a very small ham, a small Turkey, on each side of them partridges, mutton chops, or sweetbreads, a macaroni pie, an oyster pie"—"That will do, that will do, Henry. Now for vegetables." "Well, ma'am, stew'd celery, spinage, salsify, cauliflower." "Indeed, Henry, you must substitute potatoes, beets, &c." "Why, ma'am, they will not be genteel, but to be sure if you say so, it must be so. Mrs. Forsyth the other day, *would* have a plum-pudding, she will keep to old fashions." "What, Henry, plum-pudding out of fashion?" "La, yes, Ma'am, all kinds of puddings and pies." "Why, what then must I have at the head and foot of the table?" "Forms of ice-cream at the head, and a pyramid of anything, grapes, oranges, or anything handsome at the foot." "And the other dishes?" "Jellies, custards, blanc-mange, cakes, sweet-meats, and sugarplums." "No nuts, raisons, figs, &s., &c?" "Oh, no, no, ma'am, they are quite vulgar." "Well, well, Henry. My desert is, I find, all right, and your dinner I suppose with the exception of one or two things. You may order me the pies, partridges and pheasants from the French cook, and Priscilla can do the rest." "Indeed, ma'am, you had best"—"No more, Henry," interrupted I. "I am not Mrs. Woodbury." "Why to be sure, ma'am, her's was a particular dinner on account of that great English lady's dining with her." "Did Miss M.

dine there?" "La, yes, ma'am, and I was quite delighted to see the attention Mr. Clay paid her, for indeed ma'am I consider Mr. Clay the greatest and best
man now living, and sure I should know, for I served
him long enough. Oh he is kindness through and
through and it was but proper, ma'am, that the greatest
man, should show attention to the greatest lady. He
sat by her at dinner and talked all the time just to her,
neither of them eat much. I took particular notice what
she eat, so I might know another time what to hand
her, for she dines everywhere, ma'am, and I see her
taste was very simple. She eat nothing but a little
Turkey and a mite of ham, nothing else, ma'am, and
Mr. Clay hardly as much, they were so engaged in conversation. I listened whenever I was near and heard
them talking about the national debt. Mr. Clay told
her our debt was paid off and she told him she hoped
their debt would soon be paid off too, and they con-
sulted a great deal about it." "Why is Miss M. such
a great woman, Henry?" "Why, they tells me, ma'am,
she is the greatest writer in England and her books
doing monstrous deal of good." "Well, Henry, it is
for this Lady my dinner is to be, but it is a family dinner, not a ceremonious one. She is to spend the day
just in a social friendly way with me." "Why, ma'am,
that is just as it should be, as you are a writer too.
But indeed, ma'am, if not another besides her was invited, you ought to have a grand dinner. I should like
you, ma'am, to do your best. It is a great respect ma'am
she shows you and a great kindness you show her, and
I dare say, ma'am, she'll put you in one of her books,
so you should do your very best." But I carried my
point in only having 8 dishes of meat, tho' I could not
convince Henry, it was more genteel than a grander

dinner.✗ He came the next day, and leaving him and
the girls as his assistants (for Anna absolutely locked
me out of the dining room) I sat quietly in the front
parlour, as if no company was expected. Mrs. Randolph,
Mrs. Coolidge (Ellen Randolph that. was), James Bayard and B. K.[1] were the only additional guests to Miss
M. and Miss Jeffrey her companion. About 3, B. K.
came. I only was in the parlour, the girls were dressing, presently Ann. came down, and told me Miss M.
and Miss J. were up stairs in my room. "And you left
them there alone?" exclaimed I. "To be sure answered
Ann, with her usual nonchalance. I have never been
introduced to them and they asked me to show them
to a chamber." "And you let them go in alone!" "To
be sure." I hastened up stairs and found them combing
their hair. They had taken off their bonnets and large
capes. "You see," said Miss M., "we have complied
with your request and come sociably to pass the day
with you. We have been walking all the morning, our
lodgings were too distant to return, so we have done
as those who have no carriages do in England, when
they go to pass a social day." I offered her combs,
brushes, etc. But showing me the enormous pockets in
her french dress, said they were provided with all that
was necessary, and pulled out nice little silk shoes, silk
stockings, a scarf for her neck, little lace mits, a gold
chain and some other jewelry, and soon without changing her dress was prettily equipped for dinner or evening company. We were all as perfectly at our ease as
if old friends. Miss M's toilette was soonest completed
and sitting down by me on the sopha, and handing me
the tube, we had a nice social chat before we went down
stairs. I introduced Mr. Smith, my nephews, and son

[1] Bayard Kirkpatrick, her nephew.

&c. Mr. S. took a seat on the sopha by her, and I on a chair on her other side, to be near to introduce others. It was quite amusing to see Mr. S. He took the tube and at first applied its wrong cup to his lips, but in the warmth of conversation perpetually forgot it, and as he always gesticulates a great deal with his hands, he was waving about the cup, quite forgetful of its use, except when I said, as I continually had to do, "Put it to your lips." But Miss M. has admirable tact and filled up the gaps of his part of the conversation, made by the waving of the tube, by her intuitive perception and talked as fluently of Lord Brougham, Lord Durham and other political personages, of whom Mr. S. enquired as if she had heard every word. A little after 4, Mrs. Randolph and Mrs. Coolidge came. I was glad Mrs. R. was so handsomely dressed (in general she disregards her toilette) and looked so dignified and well, for I wished Miss M. to see the daughter of Jefferson to advantage. Mrs. C. looked lovely and elegant. I gave Mrs. R. a seat next Miss M. But she said but little and afterwards told us, the very touch of the Tube, put all her ideas to flight. She went to the contrary extreme of Mr. S., and kept the cup pressed so tightly on her lips, that she could scarcely open them. Mrs. Coolidge managed better, and conversed with perfect ease and great fluency until dinner, which was not served until five oclock, when the curtains being drawn and shutters closed, the candles on the table were lit and made every thing look better. Miss M. sat next me, Mrs. R. below her, Miss Jeffries led in by B. K. sat between him and Mr. S., and was, they say, extremely entertaining. J. Bayard sat all the time by Mrs. C., the old friend of his sisters and seemed delighted with her. Dinner went off *very well*. I conversed a great

deal with Miss M., as Mrs. R. would not. Our conversation was very interesting and carried on in a tone
that all the rest of the company could hear. One fact
was new and strange. Speaking of the use of ardent
spirits by the poor, she said its high price precluded its
use, there were now few gin-shops. Opium had been
substituted by the poor for gin, and apothecaries boys
kept constantly busy, making up penny and ha-penny
worths of opium. It was taken not in sufficient quantities to exhilerate, but only to stupefy and satisfy the
cravings of hunger. What a wretched state of society
does this imply! Her conversation is rich in most interesting illustrations of manners, facts and opinions
and what she said at dinner, if written down would fill
4 or 5 such pages. While at table, a note from Mr. Clay
was handed me, so handsomely written and so full of
cimpliments for Miss M. and regrets from being prevented joining our party in the evening, that I handed
it to her and she then burst forth in an eloquent eulo-
gium of him. It was near 7 when we returned to the
parlour, which was brilliantly lighted, (as I think light
a great promoter of social pleasure). Mr. King was
lounging in the rocking chair, quite at his ease. He
knew Miss M. and instantly sat down on one side of her,
I on the other. Mr. King[1] engaged her in details about
the English affairs and great men. She was copious
and interesting in her details. I wish I could relate
a hundredth part of what she said, but it is impossible.
She pronounced Lord Durham (Mr. Lambton, that was)
to be the greatest man now in England. "He will soon
be our premier, he will be the savior of England!" said
she with enthusiasm. He is her greatest and most intimate personal, as well as political friend. All the other

---

[1] Probably John Pendleton King, Senator from Georgia.

distinguished men passed in review. It was a rich treat
to hear her. Her words flow in a continual stream, her
voice pleasing, her manners quiet and lady-like, her face
full of intelligence, benevolence and animation. She
always leans back in the corner of the sopha, seemingly
unconscious of the presence of any one except the person
she is talking with. Mr. & Mrs. Frelinghusen and Mrs.
Burgess (a most lovely young widow), Mrs. Thornton,
Mrs. Bomford and her family, Mr. & Mrs. Calhoun and
her 3 young ladies, the Southards, Mr. Palfrey, the
unitarian clergyman (ours was asked but did not come)
and about a dozen gentlemen, made up the evening
party. Mr. Frelinghusen and Mr. Calhoun both sat and
conversed a great deal with Miss M., and most of the
company by turns sat a while by her. Mr. Calhoun is
one of her greatest admirers, his Mess gave her a dinner, Mrs. Bomford was unexpectedly pleased because
unexpectedly she felt herself at ease with Miss M. She
is so simple, plain, good-natured and unaffected, that
I wonder every one does not feel at ease. Ease and
animation pervaded the whole of the company, we had
some delightful singing from the young ladies, Scotch
songs to perfection. It was 11 oclock before the party
broke up. Every one gratified at an opportunity of
meeting Miss M., in such a quiet, social manner. The
next day, by appointment, I accompanied Miss M. and
Miss J. to Kalorama. Anna Maria went with us. In
a carriage she needs not her tube, but hears distinctly
without it. In a carriage, too, sitting so close one feels
so confidential. We rode about from 12 until past three
and our conversation would fill several sheets. I enquired about her early life, her motives for embracing
literature as a pursuit, the formation of her mind, habits
and opinions, all of which she freely gave me the his-

tory, and an interesting history it is. "Do tell me," said I, "if praise and celebrity, like everything else do not lose their relish?" "I never," said she, "had much relish for general praise; the approbation of those I love and esteem or respect, I highly value. But newspaper praise or censure, are perfectly indifferent to me. The most valued advantage I have gained is the facility which it gives me to gain access to every person, place or thing I desire, this is truly a great advantage." Speaking of the lionizing of celebrated people, "Well," said she, laughing, "I have escaped that, to my knowledge, I have never been made a show of, or run after as a lion." Of course, I did not undeceive her. I asked her how I should understand an expression she several times used. "Since I have been employed by government." She said, two of the subjects she had illustrated in her stories, had been by the request of Lord Brougham and Lord Durham, who supplied her with the materials, or principles, viz., the Poor-Laws, on Taxation. She was employed by them to write on these two subjects, on which account she and her mother had removed to London, as the transmission of Phamphlets by the mail, became too burthensome, frequently requiring her to send a wheel-barrow to the Post office. For the last two years she and her mother have resided in London, have a small house adjoining the Park, which is as quiet and pleasant as in the country. Here she had daily intercourse with the members of the Cabinet and leaders of the whig party, particularly the above-named gentlemen. She never makes visits and receives them only at 2 specified hours every day, but while Parliament is sitting, dines out (at night, remember) every day. Once, while at Lord Durham's in the country, at table, a gentleman sitting next her observed, "There is one

subject, Miss M., I think your genius admirably calculated to illustrate." "What is that," said she, with eagerness glad to be instructed. "The Poor Laws" replied
he. "Why exclaimed Lord D., in what corner of England have you been living, that you do not know, this is
the very subject on which she has most ably written."
"I did, I candidly own," said Miss M., when she told
me this, "I did feel completely mortified." My paper
will hold no more. I will soon write again, but as I
cannot write all this over and it may amuse Maria, I
wish you would send it to her. Oh how tired my head
and hands are! The girls are equally so of holding their
tongues.

TO MRS. BOYD

[Washington] February 14, 1835.

. . . . Hearing that Congress had placed the Nu-
midian Lion, at the disposal of the President, she[1] instantly hurried to him, obtained a private interview, and
asked him to bestow the Lion on the Orphan Asylum.
The old general showed so much warmth and kindness
in acceeding to her request, that she says she was so
overcome, that she burst into tears and seizing his
hand, kissed it in the excess of her delight and gratitude. He immediately drew an order on the Secretary
of State and signing it, gave it to her. She hastened
to us with the glad tidings and could not tell her story
without tears. It is for both the Asylums, Protestant
and Catholic. This morning she has been here to consult on the best mode of using the bounty. Capt. Riely,
was here last evening and gave us his opinion, which
I detailed to her. She took Ann with her and is now

---

[1] Mrs. Bomford, chief directress of the orphan asylum.

gone to call on the different Managers, to collect their opinions, and will be out I dare say, until 3 or 4 oclock, although it is snowing. Whatever she does is with her whole heart, in private kindness and friendship she is equally zealous. I do love her, and so does every one.

Last evening we had a delightful fire side circle. All were so animated. Mrs. Thornton and Bordeaux, Mrs. Newman and Mrs. Woodyer, (Mr. King's relations) Mr. King, Mr. Reide and last but not least Capt. Riely. He came so apropos to tell us about the Lion. Mrs. Newman was delighted to see him and wanted to hear from his own mouth his African adventures,[1] so I made him put his chair in front of us and tell his story to Mrs. Newman, who listened with the simplicity and eagerness of a child. On the other side was a party at whist and in the centre of the circle gentlemen talking politics. We frequently have these little tea drinkings of a dozen or so.

Miss Martineau has been likewise an exciting object lately. I wrote sister a long account of her, and to spare myself the repetition requested her to send the letter to you. No stranger, excepting La Fayette, ever received such universal and marked testimonies of regard. At first our great men were disposed to laugh at her, but now they are her most devoted admirers and constant visitants. Mr. Webster, Mr. Clay, Mr. Calhoun, Preston, Judge Story and many others often visit her and when she goes to the Senate or Court-Room leave their seats to converse with her. Besides these attentions, they show still more personal evidences of regard. Mr. Clay insists on her making his daughter's house at New Orleans and his own house in Lex-

---

[1] He had just returned from a voyage to Morocco and had brought the lion as a present from the Sultan to the President.

Dear Mrs Smith.

Miss Jeffery & I are sorry that we have not been able to come near your end of the city, this long while. Between the attractions of the Capitol & a succession of friendly visitors at home, we are so engaged that we think ourselves in a fair way of forgetting how to put one foot before the other. But you will see us again before we leave the city.

I thank you for the kind

method by which you have testified your regard for me. You must feel as strongly as myself how impossible it is for me to appropriate what you say; but the kindness of your feelings is an independent affair; & I thank you for it.

Miss Jeffery joins me in kind regards to your circle. Believe me, dear Madam,

truly your obliged

Harriet Martineau.

Feb'y 7th

ington her residence while in these places, and Mr. Calhoun, by his letters, will ensure her every kind attention in Charleston. Yet all this does not seem to turn her head in the least, and so frank, modest and simple are her manners and appearance that to meet her in company, no one would dream she was so distinguished a personage. Perhaps you have seen in the Intelligencer my political address to Harriet Martineau.[1] If you have not, let me know and I will send you a copy, or will ask Sister to send you the one I send her. I cannot, just now at least, copy it again. You must let me know what you think of it. I sent Miss M. a MSS copy, in return she wrote me a very simple, unpretending and kind note. On coming home yesterday I found her card to take leave, so I shall not see her again. She is really interesting in conversation and character, though not in appearance. A most original and powerful genius, and apparently as good as she is great. Anna Maria who is not very susceptible of quick impressions, says she cannot help loving her. Our winter is almost over. With us, with me, it has passed as pleasantly as it has rapidly. Unmarked by any deep or lasting interest, it has glided by like a dream leaving no vestige behind. Congress, too, has hitherto been very tranquil. Mr. Calhoun's report,[2] however, yesterday has broken its quiet. There was great agitation,—some personal violence it is said in the Senate, even a duel apprehended. The Senate chamber was crowded to crushing with ladies. I never go on such squeezing occasions.

Every day brings us as invitation to a Ball or Party,

[1] It was one of a number of addresses in verse to Miss Martineau. The one she enjoyed most was to her famous ear-trumpet which was apostrophized "beloved horn!"
[2] On the use of patronage by the President.

three cards for next week are now lying on the table, but we decline all. The gaiety is increasing and so is luxury and European habits, hours and fashions. We are quiet spectators of the bustling scene, without the slightest desire of being actors. I am every moment expecting Mrs. Bomford back, her young ladies are to remain all day with us and if the weather permits a large party of young people are to meet here and go in the evening to the exhibition. But I rather think the threatening clouds will not disperse, the snow has stopped but the clouds are dark and heavy. My paper is full and my hand tired, so I will with every kind wish, bid you my dear Maria, adieu.

TO MRS. BOYD

[Washington] March 11th, 1835.

. . . . Mr. Jacob Abbott[1] came with Dr. S. to see me in the morning. His book is much more interesting than his conversation. Yet in a short visit one cannot fairly judge. The Corner Stone, I like better than any work on the same subject I have ever read. I like the *temper* in which it is written, a truly christian temper, and consequently felt drawn to the author. I wish I could have seen more of him. His book (which you sent me) has been travelling ever since from friend to friend. I quite want to see it again. I thank you for the *House Keeper,* but have not yet had time to read it, I received it only yesterday.

Are you not sorry you have finished the life and correspondance of Hannah Moore? I felt as if separated from her after a long personal intercourse. I imme-

---

[1] The author of innumerable children's books, including the " Rollo Books."

diately got a large volume of her works, but this did
not supply the loss. Do you know I am disappointed in
them. I had read all, as they successively appeared and
remember I then remarked they are too verbose, they
are often heavy, and after reading Practical piety, you
have little else to learn from her other works, which
contain precisely the same sentiments and opinions under
a different title and in language a little varied. But
after reading her memoirs, I concluded I must be mistaken. Such universal and lavish praise. Such rapid
and extensive sales and numerous editions,—such high
reputation, could only have been effected by intrinsick
and rare and superior genius. Yes, genius, for simple
goodness and piety, could not have ensured such success. I therefore resolved to re-peruse her works and
set eagerly about it. The result is the same,—they are
very good, but very heavy, the sentiments so heavily
laden with words, that they drag extremely, and one
grows weary. The same truths conveyed in fewer
words would be far more striking and impressive. The
letters written to an author, are no certain indications of
the writer's real opinion. When one sends you a book
you must praise it. It is a pity that so large a portion
of the Second Vol. is taken up with these complimentary
letters. You should read Mrs. Montagu's letters, Mrs.
Carter's life and other cotemporaneous works to keep
up with the delightful society to which Miss Moore introduced you.

I have read Stewart's sketches[1] and agree with you in
thinking there was an indelicacy in addressing the let-

---

[1] Charles Samuel Stewart, a chaplain in the navy and a noted traveller.
"Residence at the Sandwich Islands 1823–25" appeared in 1828, "Visit
to the South Seas" (2 vols.) in 1831, "Sketches of Society in Great Britain
and Ireland in 1832" in 1834, the last-named being the book to which Mrs.
Smith refers.

ters to dear Virginia, whether a betrothed or not betrothed. The family, Mrs. Southard especially, absolutely and seriously deny there being any truth in the
rumour of any designed connection. The letters are
very inferior to those Mr. Stewart wrote from the Sandwich Islands. One reason, Virginia says, is, that they
are all mutilated. None of them are given as they were
written; the most interesting and confidential parts were
omitted. I am sorry I did not write by Capt. Riley but
I did not know until he called to bid us farewell, that he
was going to New York. When I mentioned you to
him, he said if I wrote, he would with great pleasure
carry my letter over to Brooklyn and go to see my sister. He is a kind, warm-hearted man and since his
first introduction to me by my dear Mr. Bleecher, has
felt like a friend and been quite domesticated in our
family. He has no talents for conversation and needs
being drawn out. A general dispersion of the recent
inhabitants has taken place and Washington is now as
quiet as a village. How many of the hundreds who
have separated will never meet again. Ours is a strange
state of society, made up of persons from all parts not
only of this country, but of Europe thronging here in
crowds, eager, bustling, agitated by various and often
conflicting interests. No monotony here, every season,
nay every week and month brings change and variety.
New faces, new interests, new objects of every kind,
in politics, fashions, works of art and nature, for ex-
hibitions of all descriptions are here displayed. When
lo, Congress adjourns, the curtain drops, the drama is
over, all is quiet, not to say solitary. To our family it
makes less difference than to those who live the year
round in the city. In April we retire from all bustle
and society. The time for our retreat draws nigh and

I look to it with pleasure. We are as punctual as the
seasons and with the return of the first of April, go into
the country. I hope your husband's intended little visit
will be before our leaving the city, as we can in that
case have him with us and see more of him than at
Sidney. . . .

TO MRS. KIRKPATRICK

Sidney, 16 April, 1835. Thursday.

. . . . Since I last wrote, two of my earliest acquaintances in Washington have been taken from life,
Mrs. Thurston and Mrs. Diggs. In former years I was
intimate with both, as well as with Mrs. Cutts and Mrs.
Van Ness, all conspicuous members of the social and
fashionable circle of that day. We have been travelling
the same road and about the same age. They have finished their journey,—am I near the end of mine? How
many of my cotemporaries have quitted the Stage of
Life. Some who in youth were united in the same pursuits and by the bond of strong interest and kind feeling.
Mr. Bleecker, Mr. Woodhull, Mr. Finlay among many
others. Friends of my youth! Little did I expect to
outlive either of these. My dear Mrs. Randolph is, I
hear, very ill. She has been during the whole winter in
a suffering state of health. I had some interesting rides
with her on some of the pleasant days of last month.
The day she dined with Miss Martineau at our house
was the only visit she has paid for a year, and except
when I called for her to ride, she never went out. The
last time, we conversed much of her father. She often
had to turn aside her head and wipe her eyes. I never
saw her so much affected by the subject on any previous
occasion. I was urging her to write an account of the
last week of his life and the closing scene, which she

only could entirely and truly do, as she never left him for an hour. She only shook her head and wept. I wish I could be with her in her illness, but with her five daughters around her, I fear there will be no room for me. The family this winter has been very large, 8 grand-children with her. One has long been dangerously ill and another is now attacked with a similar disease. They are lovely interesting children, the eldest not eight years old. In all she has 24 grand and 3 great grand children. I have no friend here whom I more tenderly love, and at present suffer much anxiety on her account. . . .

Friday 17. I left off yesterday to read to the girls. Marriage, by the author of Inheritance, amused without much interesting us and made our needles fly more quickly. The parlour looked like a work room, (not littered however) 4 females at work, when a carriage drove to the door,—in the country quite an event, but it was no fashionable visitor, but Mr. Herring, the Editor of the National Portrait Gallery, who for a year past has been a correspondent of mine. As some return for an article I wrote for him he brought me two volumes. or sets of this beautiful work, containing 12 numbers a vol. He passed several hours with us. He has come on to paint some portraits for his Gallery. I am very partial, you know I always was, to Painters. Not long before I left the city, I made the acquaintance of Durand, the Engraver, and likewise a portrait painter,—one of the most agreeable acquaintances I made the whole winter, more so than Miss M. He is so very modest and reserved a man that only those who take pains to draw him out, would discover his intelligence. He left me a little momento of his visit by a beautiful drawing in my album of the head of Jefferson. . . .

TO MRS. BOYD

[Washington] Christmas day, 1835.

. . . . Poor Mr. Clay, was laughing and talking and joking with some friends when his papers and letters were brought to him; he naturally first opened the letter from home. A friend who was with him, says he started up and then fell, as if shot, and his first words were "Every tie to life is broken!"[1] He continued that day in almost a state of distraction, but has, I am told, become more composed, though in the deepest affliction. Ann was his pride, as well as his joy and of all his children his greatest comfort. She was my favorite, so frank, gay, and warm hearted. Her husband was very very rich. Their plantation joined Mr. Clay's and afforded a daily intercourse. Of five daughters, she was the last, and now she is gone and poor Mrs. Clay in her declining age is left alone and bereaved of the support and comfort which daughters and only daughters can afford. I now, cannot realize that you or I can ever be so bereaved, we are so far advanced towards our journey's end. . . . .

FROM HENRY CLAY

Washn, 31st Decr 1835

DEAR MADAM

I rec'd your kind letter of this date. From no friend could condolence, on the occasion of my recent heavy affliction, have come more welcomely; but dear Madam all the efforts of friendship or of my own mind have but little effect on a heart wounded as mine is. My

[1] The story was that he fainted.

daughter was so good, so dutiful, so affectionate; her
tastes and sympathies and amusements were so identical
with my own; she was so interwoven with every plan
and prospect of passing the remnant of my days, that
I feel I have sustained a loss which can never be re-
paired.   Henceforward, there is nothing before me in
this world but duties.

My poor wife has suffered beyond expression; but
she has in affliction a resource—a great resource—which
I have not.[1]   I will transmit your friendly letter to her
which, I have no doubt, she will receive as a fresh tribute from a friendship which I know she has ever highly
appreciated.

With true regard
I am sincerely y'rs

Mrs. M. H. Smith.   H. Clay

TO MRS. BOYD

[Washington] Feb. 6, 1836.

. . . . . I last week for a *wonder* went to a large
party.   It was given by our neighbour Commodore
Rodgers,[2] who has always been a great favorite of mine,
and as it was so near I ventured.   I passed my time very
quietly and pleasantly, for after looking for a while on
the crowd in the ball room and ascertaining the fashions
of the season and contemplated the *Lions,* Mr. Welles
and Mr. Power, found a delightful comfortable fauteuil
in the reception room, where I lounged quite at my ease,
conversing by turns with my acquaintances.   Mrs.

---

[1] Later in life he was confirmed as a member of the Episcopal
Church.

[2] The great John Rodgers, first of the line of the family of distinguished
navy officers.

Wilkes,[1] by her own desire was introduced to me, and told me as an old acquaintance of her mother's she had wished to be acquainted and would without ceremony have called to see me first had she not feared being intrusive. Of course I must now go to see her, which I should be most pleased with doing, (as I found her uncommonly pleasing) were it not for her living so far, far away from our neighbourhood, too far for me to walk. I am ging this morning, likewise to call on the Bride, Mrs. Smith, Marion Clark that was. We were invited to the wedding party, but only Bayard went. The invitations were very general, including strangers as well as citizens and the crowd consequently excessive. There was scarce a possibility of moving and much less of seeing the individuals of this splendid crowd, for the dresses I am told were unusually rich and elegant. The supper was as rare and as brilliant as our best artists and unlimited expenditure could make it. The company in small parties went up to look at the table, to feast their eyes before its beauty should be destroyed by going up to feast their palates. The next morning both bride and groom received company. A table as elegantly and profusely spread as the night before, with a superabundance of the finest wines, (champagne inclusive) were provided up stairs for the gentlemen, while wedding cake &c., &c., were served in the drawing room for the ladies. The throng in the morning equalled the one on the previous evening. Expecting this would be the case, I deferred my visit, as my head dare not venture into crowded places. Dr. and Mrs. Rodgers, Virginia Southard and some others of the bridal train, hence inmates of the family. Mrs. Rodgers I am told has

---

[1] Wife of Charles Wilkes, afterwards Rear-Admiral in the Navy, the officer who intercepted the British steamer "Trent" in 1861.

astonished the natives, by the brilliancy and costliness
and elegance of her wardrobe. "Did you hear of the
fatal accident that occurred at Mrs. Clark's Saturday
morning?" said my lady informant, with a long melancholy countenance. "Fatal accident? No, what was
it?" "Poor Mrs. Rodgers, only think how unfortunate,"
and she paused and looked so mournful that I really felt
alarmed and exclaimed, "Was she hurt?" "No, but her
exquisite pocket handkerchief that cost 60 dols was burnt
up,—a spark flew on it, and the cob-web texture was
instantly in flames, from which her superb dress likewise suffered irreparably." We laughed heartily at the
finale of the mournful story. The same lady told us
such dresses had never before been displayed here. Do
you know I am half afraid to go this morning to see
this fine lady, but as a hundredth cousin, I suppose I
must, seeing as how she is staying with Mrs. Clarke,
who requested me to call on her. The increasing luxury
of dress and living in this place, will soon oblige the
poor-gentry to form a separate association. . . .

TO MRS. KIRKPATRICK

[Washington] Wednesday afternoon, March 28, 1837.

. . . . Another object of deep interest which has
engaged me lately, is Mr. Pettrich, the German Sculptor.
The choice of the Artist who is to do the work in the
Capitol, is left to the President, and Persico[1] and Pettrich
are the competitors. Their friends are making all the
interest they can, (for every thing goes by favor). Mrs.
Taylor and I are the most zealous suitors on his behalf.
She with the Presd—I with his bosom friend Mr. Butler.
I have written him two letters containing Mr. Pettrich's

---

[1] Persico was the artist selected for the tympanum of the Capitol.

history &c. Mrs. Butler came to see me in consequence, and seemed so tenderly interested, that I have great hopes, though she says Mr. B. can say nothing at present. I drew up an account of Mr. Pettrich which appeared in the Globe and Intelligencer and which Mrs Tayloe is going to send to the New York Mirror. She and I have kept up a correspondence of notes for a week past and are both of us solicitous and impatient for the President's decision, as we have both during the last winter seen poor Mr. P. almost daily. She has been able to do much more for him than I have and most liberally assisted him in the pecuniary way for he has fallen into great difficulties. I cannot tell you how much I feel for him and his poor little wife. He has such a warm grateful heart that no one can know him without being interested for him. I think Mr. and Mrs. Butler will be his assisting friends, in case he does not get work, for they are most benevolent people—sincere zealous Christians. The more I know the beter I like this lovely family. Most happy is Mr. Van B. in having such a friend and adviser. . . . .

FROM MRS. MADISON

Montpellier Sept. 10th 1838.

Yours, of the 6th my ever dear friend has come to make me blush for my delinquency, nor will I now add a long apology for an ungracious silence, as is sometimes done in such cases, but simply tell you that on my arrival at home after a warm and dusty ride, I found myself involved in a variety of business—reading, writing, and flying about the house, garden, and grove—straining my eyes to the height of my spirits, until they became inflamed, and frightened into idleness and to quietly sit-

ting in drawing-room with my kind connexions and
neighbours—sometimes talking like the *farmeress,* and
often acting the Character from my rocking chair; being
thus obliged to give up one of my most prized enjoy-
ments that of corresponding with enlightened and loved
friends like yourself.

I rejoice to hear that you, Mr. Smith, Anne, Julia and
your son, have been well, and wish you could have been
all here. In truth, I am dissatisfied with the location
of Montpellier, from which I can never separate myself
entirely, when I think how happy I should be if it joined
Washington, where I could see you always, and my
valued acquaintance also of that city, among the first of
whom is dear Mrs. Bomford.—I rejoice too that my dear
Hannah is safe from the eating of *grapes*—be pleased
to give her an affectionate kiss from me as well as her
little daughters. I am gratified at Dr. Sewall's remembrance, and but for *recreant* eyes, I should have enclosed
him a book ere this.

I cannot express dear friend how much I was affected
at your observations on past attachments, and events,
unless by showing my resemblance to you, in the devoted and lively affection I bear to my early friends and
associates—I must refrain however from *writing* much
more now, than that I will apply to Mrs. Willes and
some of my own people for the nurse you desire and if
a suitable opp'y should offer, send her to you—The one
I loaned Mrs. Randolph was totally unfit for the service of small children.

Anna has gone to a large party for the day and evening but I hope will return in time to add her respectful
love for you, with mine for Mrs. Smith, Anne and Julia
—for your son too when he returns. A. and myself
never enjoyed better health than now, and we shall take

Mrs. James Madison.

After a water-color by Dr. William Thornton.

heed of your good counsel by preserving all sorts of fruit, which with us has been abundant, as well as vegetables, tho' the prospect for a winter store of them, is not good.

When you see our amiable neighbours, of the whole square, present me most kindly to them—also to Mrs. Lear Mrs. Thornton and Mrs. Graham.

I left some things of great value to me in my house and am glad to find from John's account that the depredation did not amount to more than petty larceny.

Ever your own
D. P. Madison

FROM J. BAYARD H. SMITH

White Sulphur Springs
Greenbrier Court, July 29, 1839

My Dear Mother:

On Sunday afternoon the day I last wrote you I bade adieu to Montpelier and its kind and hospitable mistress, having spent a few very pleasant and quiet days. Miss Payne is as amiable as ever. Two afternoons were spent in riding on horseback with Mr. Todd.[1] We took such long rides that we did not return until 9 or 10 oclock. Mrs. Madison appears to live quietly, as while I was with her there was no company, tho' she said that the house had been full most of the time since her return. On the first day she had twenty to dine. We did not reach Charlottsville until 12 ocl. that night, having in our little stage five persons, two seats and only two horses. How inferior the travelling in the South is in every respect to that in the North. Here we have bad horses, bad vehicles, bad roads, bad public houses, bad bedding,

---

[1] Mrs. Madison's graceless son, John Payne Todd.

dirty, miserably clothed negroes to wait, nothing wearing the appearance of comfort or neatness; even in the
little villages you pass every thing bears the aspect of
the want of comfort and tidiness and finish, the houses
unpainted, no glass in the windows, and the question is
often asked of yourself how such houses &c can send
forth such well dressed and gentlemanly persons. In
the North the reverse holds good in every instance.
The traveller sees not only comfort, plenty, prosperity,
activity, energy, but luxury and elegance and this in
much newer settled countries than the South. Can it
be that the existence of slavery creates this difference?
I remained one day, Monday, in Charlottsville for the
purpose of visiting its two grand objects of attraction,
Monticello and the University. These I need not describe to you who have already described them much
better than I could. Mr. Todd at parting gave me a
letter of introduction to Dr. Griffith one of the Professors, but upon going to the U. I was informed that he
was absent and as my letter was an open one I took the
liberty of sending it to one who remained, Dr. Cabel
who very politely showed me every part. It is a beautiful institution and in its arrangements &c. surpasses
any other I have seen. Its library is quite large, a person dying in Richmond lately left it an addition of 5 or
6 thousand volumes.

My feelings upon reaching the summit of Monticello
and entering the house, took me completely by surprise.
I rode up the hill at a gallop without thought, but when
I alighted and looked around me the associations of the
place began to rush upon my mind and all were melancholy and sad. Around me I beheld nothing but ruin
and change, rotting terraces, broken cabins, the lawn,
ploughed up and cattle wandering among Italian mould

ering vases, and the place seemed the true representative of the fallen fortunes of the great man and his family. He died in want, almost his last words were that if he lived much longer a negro hut must be his dwelling. His family scattered and living upon the charity of the world, and to complete the picture the simple plain granite stone that marks *his* resting place defaced and broken and not even a common slab or piece of wood to distinguish the grave of his loved daughter, nothing but the red clay, and all his estate even the dust of his body the possession of a stranger.[1] It was with difficulty I could restrain my tears, and I could not but exclaim, what is human greatness. At Montpelier and Mount Vernon no such feelings obtruded themselves. All wore the appearance of plenty and no change or misfortune had overwhelmed them. . . .

PRESIDENT'S HOUSE FORTY YEARS AGO

[1841]

"Walls," it is proverbially said, "have ears," had they likewise tongues what important, interesting and amusing facts could the walls of the President's House reveal. What a variety of characters, of events, of scenes, recurs to the mind of one who has watched the mutations which have taken place in this dwelling of our chief magistrates! Each successive administration seems like a complete and separate drama performed by new sets of performers. How changed in every respect, both externally and internally is this National Theatre. The unfinished and comfortless condition of the presidential mansion is well describel by Mrs. Adams, in her recently

[1] From the note book.

published correspondance. It stood on the wide uncultivated common, without any enclosure, shelter or ornament, and so pervious was it to the weather, that rain and wind found access even to its best sleeping apartments. But Mrs. Adams had to endure these discomforts for only a short season, and whatever her husband might have felt on descending from his high station, she, it may be easily imagined, was glad to return to the comfort and tranquility of her own happy home. Then came Mr. Jefferson. Borne on the full tide of popularity, sustained by a strong and triumphant party, with what exhileration of spirit must he have entered on his new theatre of action. His cabinet was formed of men of the highest talents, who were not only political, but personal friends, whose opinions, interests and principles were so identified with his own, that the different views necessarily taken by different minds of the same subjects, never produced a discordance destructive of unanimity of action. Often has Mr. Jefferson been heard to declare this distinguishing characteristic of his administration, was the one which he most highly appreciated. "In fact," said he to a friend, " we were one family."

When he took up his residence in the *President's House,* he found it scantily furnished with articles brought from Philadelphia and which had been used by Genl. Washington. These though worn and faded he retained from respect to their former possessor. His drawing room was fitted up with the same crimson damask furniture that had been used for the same purpose in Philadelphia. The additional furniture necessary for the more spacious mansion provided by the government, was plain and simple to excess. The large *East room* was unfinished and therefore unused. The apartment in which he took most interest was his cabinet; this he had arranged according to his own taste and convenience. It was a spacious room. In the centre was a long table, with drawers on each side, in which were deposited not only articles appropriate to the place, but a set of carpenter's tools in one and small garden implements in another from the use of which he derived much amusement. Around the walls were maps, globes, charts, books, &c. In the window recesses were stands for the flowers and plants which it was his delight to attend and among his roses and geraniums was suspended the cage of his favorite mocking-bird, which he cherished with peculiar fondness, not only for its melodious powers, but for its uncommon intelligence and affectionate disposition, of which qualities he gave surprising instances. It was the constant companion of his solitary and studious hours. Whenever he was alone he opened the cage and let the bird fly about the room. After flitting for a while from one object to another, it would alight on his table and regale him with its sweetest notes, or perch on his houlder and take its food from his lips. Often when he retired to his chamber it would hop up the stairs after him and while he took his siesta, would sit on his couch and pour forth its melodious strains. How he loved this bird! How he loved his flowers! He could not live without something to love, and in the absence of his darling grandchildren, his bird and his flowers became objects of tender care. In a man of such dispositions, such tastes, who would recognize the rude, unpolished Democrat, which foreigners and political enemies described him to be. Although Sir Augustus Foster[1] in his notes lately published has

[1] In the Quarterly Review, 1841. Henry Adams in his History of the United States (vol. 1, p. 186) quotes it, but it is without doubt a caricature of Jefferson.

thus depicted Mr. Jefferson, he candidly says, he believed his careless toilette and unceremonious manners to be mere affectation, assumed to win popularity. The picture this gentleman has drawn of Mr. Jefferson is a mere characature, in which those who personally knew him cannot discover a trait of resemblance. If his dress was plain, unstudied and sometimes old-fashioned in its form, it was always of the finest materials; in his personal habits he was fastidiously neat; and if in his manners he was simple, affable and unceremonious, it was not because he was ignorant of, but because he despised the conventional and artificial usages of courts and fashionable life. His simplicity never degenerated into vulgarity, nor his affability into familiarity. On the contrary there was a natural and quiet dignity in his demeanour that often produced a degree of restraint in those who conversed with him, unfavorable to that free interchange of thoughts and feelings which constitute the greatest charm of social life. His residence in foreign courts never imparted that polish to his manners, which courts require, and though possessed of ease, they were deficient in grace. His external appearance had no pretentions to elegance, but it was neither coarse nor awkward, and it must be owned his greatest personal attraction was a countenance beaming with benevolence and intelligence.

He was called even by his friends, a national man, full of odd fancies in little things and it must be confessed that his local and domestic arrangements were full of contrivances, or *conveniences* as he called them, peculiarly his own and never met with in other houses. Too often the practical was sacrificed to the fanciful, as was evident to the most superficial observer, in the location and structure of his house at Monticello. "What could have induced your father," asked a friend, "to build his house on this high peak, a place so difficult of access, where every drop of water must be brought from the bottom of the mountain and where the soil is so parched and sterile that it is to be feared his lawn, his shrubbery, his garden will be all burned up." "I have heard my father say," replied his daughter, "that when quite a boy the top of this mountain was his favorite retreat, here he would bring his books to study, here would pass his holiday and leisure hours: that he never wearied of gazing on the sublime and beautiful scenery that spread around, bounded only by the horizon, or the far off mountains; and that the indescribable delight he here enjoyed so attached him to this spot, that he determined when arrived at manhood he would here build his family mansion."

The same fanciful disposition characterized all his architectural plans and domestic arrangements; and even in the President's House were introduced some of these favorite contrivances, many of them really useful and convenient. Among these, there was in his dining room an invention for introducing and removing the dinner without the opening and shutting of doors. A set of circular shelves were so contrived in the wall, that on touching a spring they turned into the room loaded with the dishes placed on them by the servants without the wall, and by the same process the removed dishes were conveyed out of the room. When he had any persons dining with him, with whom he wished to enjoy a free and unrestricted flow of conversation, the number of persons at table never exceed four, and by each individual was placed a *dumb-waiter*,[1] containing everything

---

[1] Mrs. Smith describes the dumb-waiter in "A Winter in Washington" Vol. II, p. 34.

necessary for the progress of the dinner from beginning
to end, so as to make the attendance of servants entirely
unnecessary, believing as he did, that much of the domestic and even public discord was produced by the mutilated and misconstructed repetition of free conversation
at dinner tables, by these mute but not inattentive lis-
teners. William McClure and Caleb Lowndes, both
distinguished and well-known citizens of Philadelphia
were invited together to one of these dinners.   Mr. Mc-
Clure who had travelled over great part of Europe and
after a long residence in Paris had just returned to the
U. States, could of course impart a great deal of important and interesting information with an accuracy and
fullness unattainable through the medium of letters.
Interesting as were the topics of his discourse, Mr. Jefferson gave him his whole attention, but closely as he
listened, Mr. McClure spoke so low, that although seated
by his side, the president scarcely heard half that was
said. "You need not speak so low," said Mr. Jefferson
smiling, "you see we are alone, and *our walls have no
ears.*" "I have so long been living in Paris, where the
walls have ears," replied Mr. McClure, "that I have contracted this habit of speaking in an undertone." He
then described the system of espionage established
throughout France whose vigilance pervaded the most
private circles and retired families, among whose servants one was sure to be in the employment of the
police.

At his usual dinner parties the company seldom or
ever exceeded fourteen, including himself and his secretary. The invitations were not given promiscuously,
or as has been done of late years, alphabetically, but his
guests were generally selected in reference to their
tastes, habits and suitability in all respects, which atten-

tion had a wonderful effect in making his parties more agreeable, than dinner parties usually are; this limited number prevented the company's forming little knots and carrying on in undertones separate conversations, a custom so common and almost unavoidable in a large party. At Mr. Jefferson's table the conversation was general; every guest was entertained and interested in whatever topic was discussed. To each an opportunity was offered for the exercise of his coloquial powers and the stream of conversation thus enriched by such various contributions flowed on full, free and animated: of course he took the lead and gave the tone, with a *tact* so true and discriminating that he seldom missed his aim, which was to draw forth the talents and information of each and all of his guests and to place every one in an advantageous light and by being pleased with themselves, be enabled to please others. Did he perceive any one individual silent and unattended to, he would make him the object of his peculiar attention and in a manner apparently the most undesigning would draw him into notice and make him a participator in the general conversation. One instance will be given, which will better illustrate this trait in Mr. Jefferson's manners of presiding at his table, than any verbal description. On an occasion when the company was composed of several distinguished persons and the conversation earnest and animated, one individual remained silent and unnoticed; he had just arrived from Europe, where he had so long been a resident, that on his return he felt himself a stranger in his own country and was totally unknown to the present company. After, seemingly, without design led the conversation to the desired point, Mr. Jefferson turning to this individual said, "To you Mr. C, we are indebted to this benefit, no one more deserves the gratitude of his country." Every eye was turned on the hitherto unobserved guest, who honestly looked as much astonished as any one in the company. The President continued, "Yes, Sir, the upland rice which you sent from Algiers, and which thus far succeeds, will, when generally adopted by the planters, prove an inestimable blessing to our Southern states." At once, Mr. C. who had been a mere cypher in this intelligent circle, became a person of importance and took a large share in the conversation that ensued.

When Mr. Jefferson took up his residence in Washington, on becoming the President of the U. S. he did not forget that he was a fellow citizen of its inhabitants. While Congress was in session, his invitations were limited to the members of this body, to official characters and to strangers of distinction. But during its recess, the respectable citizens of Alexandria, George Town and Washington were generally and frequently invited to his table. On one occasion the Mayor of George Town and his wife were among the guests and the place of honor, on Mr. Jefferson's right hand was assigned to her. She was a plain, uneducated woman, but wishing to do her prettiest, she thought she must talk to the President and having heard his name in some way, though she knew not how, coupled with Carter's mountain, she made a still more awkward inquiry of him, than Madm Talleyrand made of Volney when he dined at her husband's table, for turning to Mr. Jefferson, she asked him if he did not live close by Carter's mountain."[1] "Very close," he replied, "it is the adjoining mountain to Monticello." "I suppose its a very convenient pleasant place," per-

---

[1] During the revolution the British under Tarlton invaded Charlottesville where the legislature was temporarily sitting, and Jefferson, who was Governor of Virginia at the time, fled to Carter's Mountain to avoid capture. His enemies said he was a coward, but he would have been a fool if he had not run away.

sisted the lady not observing the significant frown of her
husband, or the inexpressible smiles of the rest of the
company.

"Why, yes," answered Mr. Jefferson, smiling, "I certainly found it so, in the war time." Being puzzled by
this reply and catching a glimpse of her husband's countenance, she forbore any further inquiries on the subject, and not being able to think of any else to say in
which the President might be interested, she remained
silent during the rest of the entertainment.

One circumstance, though minute in itself, had certainly a great influence on the conversational powers of
Mr. Jefferson's guests. Instead of being arrayed in
strait parallel lines, where they could not see the countenances of those who sat on the same side, they en-
circled a round, or oval table where all could see each
others faces, and feel the animating influence of looks
as well as of words. Let any dinner giver try the experiment and he will certainly be convinced of the truth
of this fact. A small, well assorted company, seated
around a circular table will ensure more social enjoyment, than any of the appliances of wealth and splendour, without these concomitants.

The whole of Mr. Jefferson's domestic establishment
at the Presidents House exhibited good taste and good
judgement. He employed none but the best and most
respectable persons in his service. His maitre-d'hôtel
had served in some of the first families abroad, and
understood his business to perfection. The excellence
and superior skill of his French cook was acknowledged
by all who frequented his table, for never before had
such dinners been given in the President's House, nor
such a variety of the finest and most costly wines. In
his entertainments, republican simplicity was united to

Epicurean delicacy; while the absence of splendour ornament and profusion was more than compensated by the
neatness, order and elegant sufficiency that pervaded the
whole establishment. ⅄

He secured the best services of the best domestics,
not only by the highest wages, but more especially by
his uniform justice, moderation and kindness and by the
interest he took in their comfort and welfare.   Without
an individual exception they all became personally attached to him and it was remarked by an inmate of his
family, that their watchful cheerful attendance, seemed
more like that of humble friends, than mercenary meni-
als.   During the whole time of his residence here, no
changes, no dismissions took place in his well-ordered
household and when that time expired each individual
on leaving his service, was enabled by his generous inter-
ference, to form some advantageous establishment for
themselves, and in losing him felt as if they had lost
a father.   In sickness he was peculiarly attentive to their
wants and sufferings, sacrificing his own convenience to
their ease and comfort.   On one occasion when the family of one of his domestics had the whooping cough, he
wrote to a lady who resided at some distance from the
city, requesting her to send him the receipt for a remedy,
which he had heard her say had proved effectual in the
case of her own children when labouring under this
disease.   This lady relates another instance of his kind
consideration; she noticed a piece of furniture, of a
rather singular form as she was passing through a small
parlour leaning on his arm and struck by its beauty as
well as novelty, stopped to enquire its use.   He touched
a spring, the little doors flew open, and disclosed within,
a goblet of water, a decanter of wine, a plate of light
cakes, and a night-taper.   "I often sit up late," said he,

"and my wants are thus provided for without keeping a servant up."

The place of coachman, was little more than a sinecure, as his handsome chariot and four beautiful horses, were never used except when his daughters visited him. He paid no visits and when he took his daily ride, it was always on horseback and alone. It was then he enjoyed solitude, surrounded only by the works of nature of which he was a fond lover and great admirer. He used to explore the most lonely paths, the wildest scenes among the hills and woods of the surrounding country, and along the high and wooded banks of the Potomac. He was passionately fond of botany, not a plant from the lowliest weed to the loftiest tree escaped his notice, dismounting from his horse he would climb rocks, or wade through swamps to obtain any plant he discovered or desired and seldom returned from these excursions without a variety of specimens of the plants he had met with. . . .

He was very anxious to improve the ground around the President's House; but as Congress would make no appropriation for this and similar objects, he was obliged to abandon the idea, and content himself with enclosing it with a common stone wall and sewing it down in grass. Afterwards when the *grisly Bears*, brought by Capt Lewis from the far west, (where he had been to explore the course of the Missouri,) were confined within this enclosure a witty federalist called it the President's *bear-garden*. How the federalists delighted to turn all Mr. Jefferson did or said into ridicule! In planning the improvement of these grounds, it was Mr. Jefferson's design to have planted them exclusively with Trees, shrubs and flowers indigenous to our native soil. He had a long list made out in which they were arranged according to their forms and colours and the seasons in which they flourished. To him it would have been a high gratification to have improved and ornamented our infant City. But the only thing he could effect, was planting Pennsylvania Avenue with Lombard Poplars, which he designed only for a temporary shade, until Willow oaks, (a favorite tree of his) could attain a sufficient size. But this plan had to be relinquished as well as many others from the want of funds.

By his desire, our Consuls at every foreign port, collected and transmitted to him seeds of the finest vegetables and fruits that were grown in the countries where they resided. These he would distribute among the market-gardeners in the City (for at that time there was abundant space, not only for gardens, but little farms, within the City bounds), not sending them but giving himself and accompanying his gifts with the information necessary for their proper culture and management, and afterwards occasionally calling to watch the progress of their growth. This excited the emulation of our horticulturilists, and was the means of greatly improving our markets. For their further encouragement, the President ordered his steward to give the highest prices for the earliest and best products of these gardens. There were two nursery-gardens he took peculiar delight in, partly on account of their romantic and picturesque location and the beautiful rides that led to them, but chiefly because he discovered in their proprietors, an uncommon degree of scientific information, united with an enthusiastic love of their occupation. Mr. Mayne, a shrewd, intelligent, warm hearted Scotchman, rough as he was in his manners and appearance, could not be known, without being personally liked. It was he who introduced into this section of our country, the use of the American Thorn for hedges. This was the favorite, though not exclusive object of his zealous industry. Rare fruits and flowers were his pride and delight: this similarity of tastes made Mr. Jefferson find peculiar pleasure, in furnishing him with foreign plants and seeds, and in visiting his plantations on the high banks of the Potomac. Although the President made no visits in the city, he would often call on acquaintances, whose houses he passed in his rides, and show a lively interest in their rural improvements; with such he would always share the plants and seeds he received from abroad. Mr. Jefferson was known in Europe as much, if not more, as a philosopher, than as a politician. Mr. Jefferson's acquaintance in this wide and distinguished circle in Paris, made him well known throughout Europe, and when he became President his reputation as a Philosopher and man of letters brought many literary and scientific foreigners to our country. Among others Baron Humboldt, one day in answer to some enquiries addressed to this celebrated traveller, he replied, "I have come not to see your great Rivers and Mountains, but to become acquainted with your great-men." Of these, he held Mr. Jefferson in the highest estimation. Soon after the Baron's arrival on our shores, he hastened to Washington, and during his visit to our city, passed many hours of every day with Mr. Jefferson. Baron Humboldt, formed not his estimate of men and manners, by their habiliments and conventionalisms, and refined as were his tastes, and polished as were his manners, he was neither shocked or disgusted, as was the case with the British Minister (Mr. Foster) by the old fashioned form, ill-chosen colours, or simple material of the President's dress. Neither did he remark the deficiency of elegance in his person, or of polish in his manners, but indifferent to these external and extrinsic circumstances, he easily discerned, and most highly appreciated the intrinsic qualities of the Philosophic Statesman through even the homely costume, which had concealed them from the ken of the fastidious diplomat.

Were all travellers like Baron Humboldt, they would obtain much more correct and extensive information of the countries and people they visited, than is too commonly the case. He was most truly a citizen of the world, and wherever he went he felt himself perfectly at home. Under all governments, in all climes, he recognized man as his brother. Kind, frank, cordial in his disposition, expansive and enlightened in his views, his sympathies were never chilled, his opinions never warped by prejudice. The varieties of condition, of character, of customs he met with among the nations he visited, were never subjected to the test of his own feelings and perceptions, but tried by the universal standard of abstract principles of utility, justice, goodness.

His visits at the President's-House, were unshackled by mere ceremony and not limited to any particular hour. One evening he called about twilight and being shown into the drawing room without being announced, he found Mr. Jefferson seated on the floor, surrounded by half a dozen of his little grandchildren so eagerly and noisily engaged in a game of romps that for some moments his entrance was not perceived. When his presence was discovered Mr. Jefferson rose up and shaking hands with him, said, "you have found me playing the fool Baron, but I am sure to *you* I need make no appology." [1]

Another time he called of a morning and was taken into the Cabinet; as he sat by the table, among the

[1] This appears in "A Winter in Washington," Vol. II, p. 34.

newspapers that were scattered about, he perceived one, that was always filled with the most virulent abuse of Mr. Jefferson, calumnies the most offensive, personal as well as political. "Why are these libels allowed?" asked the Baron taking up the paper, "why is not this libelous journal suppressed, or its Editor at least, fined and imprisoned?"

Mr. Jefferson smiled, saying, "Put that paper in your pocket Baron, and should you hear the reality of our liberty, the freedom of our press, questioned, show this paper, and tell where you found it."[1]

Baron Humboldt was fond of repeating these and other similar anecdotes of the man he so much admired.

A French traveller of distinction, who was often with Mr. Jefferson, mentioned that having accompanied him one day to review the militia of the district, as they rode along he expressed his surprise that the President of the U. S. who was commander in chief of our military forces should on this occasion go in his citizen's dress, instead of wearing a military uniform, and enquired his reason for so doing, "To show," replied Mr. Jefferson, "that the civil is superior to the military power."[2]

When this traveller returned to France, among other enquiries made of him by the Emperor, Napoleon asked him, "what sort of government is that of the U. S.?" "One, Sire," replied he, "that is neither seen or felt."

Mr. Jefferson had no levees, but received visitors every morning at certain hours, excepting on New Year's-day and the Fourth of July. On these grand occasions not only the President's House, but the city was thronged with visitors from George Town, Alexandria and the surrounding country. They were *national festi-*

[1] See "A Winter in Washington," Vol. II, p. 37.
[2] This appears in "A Winter in Washington," Vol. I, p. 202.

vals, on which the doors of the Presidential mansion
were thrown open for persons of all classes, where
abundance of refreshments were provided for their
entertainment.   On Mr. Jefferson's accession to the
Presidency the Mayor and corporation had waited on
him, requesting to be informed, which was his birthday,
as they wished to celebrate it with proper respect.
"The only birthday I ever commemorate," replied he,
"is that of our Independence, the Fourth of July." [1]
During his administration it was in truth a gala-day in
our city.   The well uniformed and well appointed militia
of the district, the Marine-Corps and often other
military companies, paraded through the avenues and
formed on the open space in front of the President's
House, their gay appearance and martial musick, en-
livening the scene, exhilerating the spirits of the throngs
of people who poured in from the country and adjacent
towns.   At that time there were no buildings no inclosures in the vicinity of the President's house, but a
wide extended pleasant and grassy common, where the
inhabitants found pleasant walks and the herds and
flocks abundant pasture.   It exhibited really a charming and lively scene on this national festival.   Temporary tents and boothes were scattered over the surface,
for the accomodation of the gay crowds, who here
amused themselves and from whence there was a good
view of the troops as they marched in front of the President's-House; and of the President, the heads of Departments and the foreign ministers who stood around
him on the high steps of the house, receiving and returning their salutations as they passed in review.   Mr.
Jefferson's tall figure and grey locks waving in the air,
(for he always on these occasions stood with uncovered

[1] See "A Winter in Washington," Vol. I, p. 11.

head), was easily distinguished among the other official
personages who surrounded him. After this review,
the soldiers were dismissed to mingle with their fellow
citizens on the common, while the officers in a body went
to the President's-house, where the great Hall, (not then
divided, as it now is[1]) and all the reception rooms were
filled with company; displaying to advantage the collected beauty and fashion, the wealth and respectability
of the residents of the District of Columbia. Tables in
each corner of the largest-room were covered with con-
fectionary, wines, punch, lemonade, etc. where without
the intervention of servants, the company could partake
of their refreshments. There was little form or ceremony observed at these re-unions. Every one as they
entered shook hands with the President, who stood with
a cheerful kindly countenance and cordial manner, in the
centre of the Drawing-Room[2] to receive the company;
each one after the interchange of a few sentences, gave
place to others and mingled with the various groups that
promenaded the other apartments. The national airs
played by the Marine Band, which was stationed in
the Hall, awakened patriotic feelings, as well as gaiety.
No one could forget that it was the *Fourth of July!*

About three oclock the company would disperse, the
ladies to return home, the gentlemen to re-assemble at
the great public dinner, where the most respectable citizens and all persons connected with the government,
(the President, excepted,) together with the Foreign
ministers, united in celebrating the day with musick,
wine and eloquence; for the toasts given on the occasion
were always followed with a speech or a song. Such
forty *years ago*, was the manner in which the Fourth

---

[1] It was restored by Mr. McKim in 1902.
[2] Now known as the blue room.

of July was commemorated in Washington. *What a change since then!*

The first of January, the only other public reception day, the same out-of-door hilarity could not, of course, take place. The military companies after parade were dismissed, with exception of the officers, who with other citizens thronged to the President's House. Here the arrangements were the same as on the Fourth of July. Congress being in session, the company of course was more numerous and interesting, strangers of distinction from all parts of the Union at this season resorted to the seat of government; even our savage brethren from the woods and wilds of the *Far west*. On one occasion described by Sir A. Foster in his *"Notices of the U. S."* he seems to think the President failed in paying due respect to the gentlemen of the diplomatic corps. "The President took care to show his preference on New Year's day, by giving us, (the diplomatic corps) only a bow, while with them he entered into a long conversation." (Foster's Notes on U. S.).

It really may have been so, and not only the President but the whole assembled company may have participated in this neglect, so lively was the interest and the curiosity excited by the appearance of the *Osage-Chiefs* and their attendant *squaws*. And likewise of the Tunisan Minister, Meley Meley, and his splendid and numerous suite.[1] It must be confessed that in their turbaned heads, their bearded faces, their Turkish costume, rich as silk, velvet, cashmere, gold and pearls could make it, attracted more general and marked attention than the more familiar appearance of the European Ministers. These two embassies, one from

[1] See "A Winter in Washington," Vol. I, p. 23 for an account of the Indians, and the same p. 20 for the Tunisian minister.

Africa the other from the wilderness of the *Far West,*
were so unique, so extraordinary, so strangely contrasted,
that they were irresistibly attractive to the company at
large, though it seems scarcely possible that the President should have been so exclusive in his attention to
savage chieftans, as to have neglected proper civilities
to the representatives of royalty, however anxious he
might have been to court *democratic popularity,* the reason assigned by the writer for his plain dress and plain
manners.

These Osages, were noble specimens of the human-
race, and would have afforded fine studies for the painter
or sculptor. Tall, erect, finely proportioned and ma-
jectic in their appearance, dignified, graceful and lofty
in their demeanour, they seemed to be nature's own
nobility. By the President's desire they appeared in
their own national costume. In their deer-skin mocco-
sions and cloth leggings ornamented with embroidery
and fringes of coloured beads, their faces and bodies in
full paint, or as we would say in full dress and covered
with blankets, worn as Spaniards wear their cloaks,
wrapped gracefully around, leaving the right arm free.
With the exception of a tuft of hair on the crown,
the head was entirely and smoothly shaven. Ear-rings,
armlets, and a silver medal of Washington, their great
father, suspended round the neck, completed their toilette. The habiliments of their wives had been left
to the taste of the lady of the Secretary of war, and
great was her difficulty in deciding, what they should be.
Some of the ladies whom she called to the consultation,
proposed silks and satins of the gaudiest colours, others
were for showy and rich chintzes. One, rather a romantic lady, who loved the picturesque, voted for the
blankets, and other simple articles belonging to their

wildwood costume.   The middle course was adopted, and
short gowns and petticoats were provided for them of
showy, large figured chintz, without any trinkets or ornaments, these being exclusively appropriated to the lords
of creation.   A lady placed a bunch of artificial flowers
in the hair of one of these women, who instantly, in-
stinctively as it were, drew it out, carried it to her husband and stuck it behind his ear; he received it as his due
and as a matter of course.

One would have supposed in a scene so novel and
imposing as was that day exhibited to these sons of the
Forest, that some indication of curiosity or surprise might
have been discovered in words, looks or gestures, but
not the slightest emotion of any kind was visible.   Im-
perturbable as the rocks of their savage homes, they
stood in a kind of dignified and majestic stillness, calmly
looking on the gay and bustling scene around them.   But
no one that looked on their finely formed features and intelligent countenances could have mistaken their imper-
turbability for stupidity,—it was evidently the pride of the
stoic, dispising and therefore subduing the indulgence of
natural feeling.   Mr. Jefferson who had long and deeply
studied the character of our aboriginees told a friend
with whom he was conversing on this subject, that he
had on various occasions made many experiments, and
endeavours by the exhibition of the most striking and
curious objects to elicit some expression of astonishment
or surprise, but never, except in a single instance, succeeded in exacting any obvious emotion, and this was on
an occasion when he had the chiefs of a remote tribe to
dine with him.   During the progress of dinner, strange
and incomprehensible as every object around them must
have been, and distasteful as, probably the mode of
cooking was, they exhibited no emotion whatever, until

the wine, in coolers filled with ice were placed on table. On seeing the ice, one of the chiefs looked on the others with an expression of doubt and surprise, to which their looks responded. To satisfy the doubt evidently felt by all, the elder chief took hold of a piece of ice, started when he felt it, and handed it to his companions, who seemed equally startled. It must be noticed, that it was a hot day in July. The indians after being convinced it was ice, began talking to each other with eagerness and vehemence. Mr. Jefferson turned to the interpreter for an explanation. "We now believe," said the chief, "that what our brothers told us when they came back from the great cities was all true, though at the time we thought they were telling us lies, when they told us of all the strange things they saw, for they never saw anything so wonderful as this that we now see and feel. Ice in the middle of summer! We now can believe anything!" Meley-Meley expressed a most lively interest about these Osages. He examined their forms countenances and habits and was particularly struck by the mode in which their heads were shaved, leaving only a tuft of hair on the crown. He took off his turban and showed them that his head was shaven after the same fashion, and enquired if their people had always worn it so. "Who then were your fathers? where did your fathers come from? did they come from my country? for in this and other things you do, you are like my people, and our father was Ishmael." Such were some of the observations Meley-Meley made through the medium of their respective interpreters.

The Tunisan minister was the lion of the season and during the winter, he and his splendid suite were invited to all the fashionable parties, where he could not conceal his astonishment at the freedom with which he

was accosted by our ladies and the general liberty allowed them in society.   He brought most sumptuous
presents for the officers of government and likewise their
wives.   But in compliance with our laws, these presents
could not be accepted, to return them would be an offence to the government by whom they were sent, the
only course that could be devised was to have them publicly sold.   And sold they were much to the regret of the
ladies to whom they had been presented.   Rich cashmere shawls, and robes, a superb silver dressing-case,
rare essences and other splendid articles for female use,
were all disposed of.   The articles designed for the
officers of governments, such as curious and richly inlaid
sabres, muskets etc. were deposited in the State-Depart-
ment, where they are still to be seen, together with similar presents from other governments.[1]

When Mr. Jefferson's daughters were with him they
visited and received visits on exactly the same terms as
other ladies in the same society.   There had been a
great deal of difficulty about points of etiquette with
foreign ministers.   The President had decided that
our *home ministers* (viz, heads of Departments) should
take precedence of foreign ministers, and that the senators should receive the first visit from our own, as well
as foreign ministers.   Exceptions were taken to both
these regulations and a really serious matter made of
it by the English minister, Mr. Merry, who threatened
an appeal to his government.[2]   When Mrs. R. Mr. Jefferson's daughter, arived, Mrs. Merry wrote her a note
requesting to be informed, whether she wished to be
visited as the wife of a member of congress, or as the

[1] Very few are now there, the greater part having been deposited with the
National Museum.
[2] It is a well-known story.   Mrs. Merry inspired the dispute and her husband nursed it till it grew into an international incident.

daughter of the President. Mrs. R. replied, she claimed no distinction whatever, but wished only for the same consideration extended to other strangers. Even when his daughters were with him, Mr. Jefferson never had Drawing-rooms, or even private evening parties and only such as were on terms of personal intimacy ever made evening visits to the President's House. His friends and intimate acquaintance enjoyed in these evening visits all the ease and freedom of the domestic circle. Mr. Jefferson, *democrat* as he was, and accessible as he was to all classes of his fellow citizens, contrived to secure to himself the pleasure of a select and refined society, without resorting to any of the offensive and exclusive forms and ceremonies, which in European society constitute the barriers which separate the different orders of society. His personal demeanor, simple and affable as it was, had a restraining dignity which repressed undue familiarity and prevented the intrusion of promiscuous or undesired visitants. In this *home-circle,* if it may be so called, Mr. Jefferson appeared to the greatest advantage as a man. Public station and public cares were equally laid side, while the father of the family, the friend, the companion, the man of letters, the philosopher, charmed all who were thus admitted to his private society. His grand-children would steal to his side, while he was conversing with his friends, and climb his knee, or lean against his shoulder, and he without interrupting the flow of conversation would quietly caress them. Frank and communicative, (as some said even to excess,) he would talk of any thing and every thing that interested these around him. Some of his friends most delighted in hearing him talk of himself, of his residence abroad, the character and scenes that there fell under his observation, these, he delineated with such vividness and fidelity that the impressions originally made on himself were transferred to his hearers and that kind of sympathy was excited, which mingles mind with mind and heart with heart.

Those who have enjoyed his society in the *home-circle* will acknowledge that it was there they most admired and loved Mr. Jefferson, and will thus justify an assertion of one of his most violent and imbittered political opponents. "No one," said Judge P[a]tt[erso]n, (Judge of the Supreme Court), "can know Mr. Jefferson and be his *personal* enemy. Few, if any, are more oposed to him as a politician than I am, and until recently I utterly disliked him as a man as well as a politician. And how was that dislike removed? By travelling together, three day. I was on one of my southern circuits, and in a public stage found myself seated by his side. I did not know who he was, neither did he know me for the first day we travelled together, but conversed like travellers on general and common place subjects. By degrees the conversation became more specific and interesting, political as well as other topics were discussed. I was highly pleased with his remarks, for though we differed on many points he displayed an impartiality, a freedom from prejudice, that at that period were unusual. There was a mildness and amenity in his voice and manner that at once softened any of the asperities of *party*-spirit that I felt, for of course we did not converse long without the mutual discovery that he was a *democrat* and I a federalist. At the conclusion of our day's journey, when we left the carriage, the first greeting of the host, made known to me that my fellow traveller was Mr. Jefferson. He soon informed himself of my name. We travelled two other days together and at the end of our journey, parted friends, though still as politicians, diametrically opposed; I repeat that no man can be personally acquainted with Mr. Jefferson and remain his personal enemy."

The value of the testimony thus given in Mr. Jefferson's favour, will be more sensibly felt by a knowledge of Judge P[a]tt[erso]n's common opinions of his political opponents. On an occasion when he had the members of the Jersey-Bar dining at his table, along with other company, some of them ladies, as usual when the wine was circulating after dinner, toasts were given; a young lady totally ignorant of politics, having heard the eloquence of Mr. Giles, highly extolled, in the simplicity of her heart, when called upon for a toast gave "Mr. Giles."[1] Judge P. looked astounded, and almost angrily exclaimed, while he struck the table violently with his hand, "You had better give the devil next!" Yet this man did full justice to Mr. Jefferson, whose political character he looked upon in the same light as that of Mr. Giles.

Although Mr. Jefferson had been called a visionary man and certainly did love to theorize and philosophize on the perfect-ability of man, yet he was likewise an essentially practical man, and like Franklin studied the most minute circumstances that influenced the welfare, comfort and improvement of social life. Among other customs which he thought did more harm than good, was the wearing mourning for deceased relatives, and making very expensive funerals. Could these observances be confined to the rich, they would be, he said, comparatively harmless, but as such a limitation was impossible, the only way to check the evil, was by the wealthy class renouncing these expensive shows and

[1] William Branch Giles of Virginia, an exceedingly intemperate and extreme Republican.

forms of grief, which to the poorer classes were not only inconvenient, but often ruinous.

On this point, he enforced precept by example.   When he lost his almost idolized daughter Mrs. E.[ppes] keenly and deeply as he felt this bereavement, neither he nor any of his family put on mourning, neither did he make any change in his social habits, but continued his dinner parties and received company as usual, considering it as a portion of his public duty to receive and entertain members of Congress and other official characters.   In this he went too far and miscalculated the common feelings of humanity, which on such an occasion would have approved rather than condemned his secluding himself for a while from society; he had not sufficient faith in the sympathies of human nature and imputed to it an undeserved degree of selfishness, when he believed it his duty to sink the private in the public man.   At the time persons said, "What a stoic Mr. Jefferson is."   But it was not stoicism, as those who saw him watching over the declining life of this beloved child, might have told them.   During some time before her decease, he had her with him at Monticello, where he devoted himself exclusively to her.   She suffered less and breathed more easily in the open air, and was daily drawn for hours together through the grounds in a low garden-chair, he never allowed any one to draw this chair but himself.   Dearly did he prize, deeply did he grieve for his lovely and beloved child.   Mr. Jefferson was no stoic.

As the term of his official life drew towards a close, he looked brighter and happier.   Could it be otherwise, even allowing him to be an ambitious man, for had he not gained the goal and won the highest prize, the ambition of an american citizen could obtain?   He was urged by his friends to stand another election, but positively declined, "He longed," as he expressed himself in a letter to his daughter, "he longed for the privacy and tranquility of *home*." To this home he looked as a secure and peaceful haven, where he might repose after the excitements and peril of a stormy voyage. He sanguinely calculated on Mr. Madison as his successor, and consequently on a continuance of the same policy that had governed his own administration. For this excellent man, Mr. Jefferson felt not only the esteem and confidence of the most perfect friendship, but an almost paternal affection and was as ambitious for him, as he had ever been for himself. There are few if any instances of friendship so perfect, so unselfish as that which entered these two great men. In a letter to a friend, Mr. Madison gives the following account of the commencement and growth of this friendship.

"I was a stranger to Mr. Jefferson till the year 1776 when he took his seat in the first legislature under the constitution of Virginia, then newly framed; being at the time, myself, a member of that body, and for the first time a member of any public body. The acquaintance then made with him was very slight, the distance between our ages being considerable and other distances being more so. During part of the time whilst he was governor of the State, I had a seat in the council associated with him. Our acquaintance then became intimate and a friendship was formed, which was for life and which was never interrupted in the slightest degree, for a moment."

No wonder then that Mr. Jefferson looked forward with satisfaction to the close of his political life, believing as he confidently did that Mr. Madison would fill the place he vacated, and would carry out those principles and measures which he sincerely thought would best promote his country's good.

On the morning of Mr. Madison's inauguration, he asked Mr. Jefferson to ride in his carriage with him to the Capitol, but this he declined, and in answer to one who enquired of him why he had not accompanied his friend, he smiled and replied, "I wished not to divide with him the honors of the day, it pleased me better to see them all bestowed on him." A large procession of citizens, some in carriages, on horse back, and still larger on foot, followed Mr. Madison along Pennsylvania avenue to the Capitol, among those on horse-back was Mr. Jefferson; unattended by even a servant, undistinguished in any way from his fellow citizens. Arrived at the Capitol he dismounted and "Oh! shocking," as many, even democrats, as well as the British minister Mr. Foster, might have exclaimed, he hitched his own horse to a post, and followed the multitude into the Hall of Representatives.[1] Here a seat had been prepared for him near that of the new President, this he declined, and when urged by the Committee of arrangement, he replied, "This day I return to the people and my proper seat is among them." Surely this was carrying democracy too far, but it was not done, as his opponents said, from a mere desire of popularity; he must have known human nature too well, not to know that the *People* delight to honor, and to see honored their chosen favorite; besides what more popularity could he now desire, his cup was already running over and could have held no more. No, he wished by his example as well as his often expressed opinions, to establish the principle of political equality.

[1] Here is probably the origin of the apocryphal story that Jefferson hitched his horse to the fence when he was inaugurated himself.

After the ceremony of Inauguration, Mr. Madison followed by the same crowd returned home to his private house, where he and Mrs. Madison received the visits of the foreign ministers and their fellow citizens. It was the design, as generally understood, after paying their respects to the new President, that citizens should go to the President's House and pay a farewell visit to Mr. Jefferson; but to the surprise of everyone, he himself, was among the visitors at Mr. Madison's. A lady who was on terms of intimacy with the ex-President and could therefore take that liberty, after telling him that the present company and citizens generally, desired to improve this last opportunity of evincing their respects by waiting on him, added her hopes that he would yet be at home in time to receive them. "This day should be exclusively my friend's," replied he, "and I am too happy in being here, to remain at home." "But indeed Sir you must receive us, you would not let all these ladies all your friends find an empty house, for at any rate we are determined to go, and to express even on this glad occasion, the regret we feel on losing you." His countenance discovered some emotion, he made no reply, but bowed expressively. The lady had no positive information to give those who had requested her to enquire whether Mr. Jefferson would receive company, but watching his motions, found that after a little while he had silently slipped through the crowd and left the room. This she communicated to the company, who with one accord determined to follow him to the President's house. It was evident that he had not expected this attention from his friends and fellow citizens, as his whole house-hold had gone forth to witness the ceremonies of the day. He was alone; but not, therefore, the less happy, for not one of the eager crowd that followed Mr. Madison, was as anxious as himself to show every possible mark of respect to the new President.

How mournful was this last interview! Every one present semed to feel it so, and as each in turn shook hands with him, their countenances expressed more forcibly than their words the regret they felt on losing one who had been the uniform friend of the city, and of the citizens, with whom they had lived on terms of hospitality and kindness.

In the evening there was an Inauguration Ball. Mr. Jefferson was among the first that entered the Ballroom; he came before the President's arrival. "Am I too early?" said he to a friend. "You must tell me how to behave for it is more than forty years since I have been to a ball."

In the course of the evening, some one remarked to him, "You look so happy and satisfied Mr. Jefferson, and Mr. Madison looks so serious not to say sad, that a spectator might imagine that you were the one coming in, and he the one going out of office."

"There's good reason for my happy and his serious looks," replied Mr. Jefferson, "I have got the burthen off my shoulders, while he has now got it on his."

Thus closed Mr. Jefferson's eight years residence in Washington. The constant interest he had taken in the improvement of the city, the frank hospitality he had extended to the citizens, made his departure the subject of general regret.

FROM HENRY CLAY

My Dear Madam

I received your kind invitation to your party, given on the interesting occasion of your sons marriage,[1] and fully intending to attend it, I did not before reply to your friendly note. There is no house in the city to which I would go, with more pleasure, under such circumstances; but the badness of the evening, and the delicate state of my health will not allow me to venture out, and I must therefore limit myself to a cordial congratulation on the event which has happened, and the expression of a fervent wish that the young couple may realize all the happiness which they anticipate, and all that their parents desire for them.

With great esteem and regard

I am faithfully yr's

H. Clay

Mrs. M. H. Smith, *Wash'n 7 Mar. 42*

[1] Jonathan Bayard H. Smith married Henrietta E. Henley, daughter of Commodore John Dandridge Henley, U. S. N., a nephew of Mrs. George Washington, March 3, 1842.

THE END

INDEX